CW00406500

Social Identities in the New South Africa

After Apartheid –
Volume One

Edited by Abebe Zegeye

KWELA BOOKS
and
SA HISTORY ONLINE

This book forms part of the Social Identities South Africa Series and has been produced with the financial assistance of the National Research Foundation, and of the Delegation of the European Commission through the CWCI Fund

Copyright © 2001 Abebe Zegeye

All rights reserved

Published jointly by Kwela Books and South African History Online

Kwela Books
28 Wale Street, Cape Town 8001;
P.O. Box 6525, Roggebaai 8012
Kwela@kwela.com

South African History Online
P.O. Box 11420, Maroelana 0161
Info@sahistory.org.za
www.sahistory.org.za

No part of this book may be reproduced or transmitted in any form or by any means, electronic, electrostatic, magnetic tape or mechanical, including photocopying, recording, or by any information storage and retrieval system, without written permission of the publisher

Cover and book design by Liam Lynch and Omar Badsha
Cover photograph by Chris Ledochowski
Set in 10 on 13.5 pt Garamond
Printed and bound by NBD, Drukkery Street, Cape Town, South Africa
First edition, first printing 2001

ISBN 0-7957-0133-0

Social Identities South Africa
General Editor: Abebe Zegeye

The identities of South Africa and its citizens have been undergoing crucial changes since 1994, when the first democratic elections resulted in the demise of statutory apartheid. This has led to an emerging ethos of democratic rule among all citizens of South Africa. But, although changes in South African society are clearly visible in increased social mobility, migration, access to jobs, training and education and general reform in South Africa, the nature and influence of the identities being formed in response is as yet less clear. The SISA project aims to determine the nature of some of these new identities.
The project is shaped by research that indicates that South Africans, while going through flux and transformation in their personal and group identities, have a shared concern about the stability of their democracy and their economic future.

Titles in the SISA Series jointly published by
Kwela Books and South African History Online:

Social Identities in the New South Africa
After Apartheid – Volume One
Edited by Abebe Zegeye

Culture in the New South Africa
After Apartheid – Volume Two
Edited by Abebe Zegeye and Robert Kriger

Kala Pani
Caste and Colour in South Africa
Rehana Ebr.-Vally

Coloured by History, Shaped by Place
New Perspectives on Coloured Identities in Cape Town
Edited by Zimitri Erasmus

The I of the Beholder
Identity Formation in the Art and Writing of Breyten Breytenbach
Marilet Sienaert

Contents

List of contributors

- Nombuso S. Dlamini
  Education, Mount Saint Vincent University, Canada
- Rehana Ebr.-Vally
  Department of Social Anthropology, University of Witwatersrand,
  South Africa
- Janis Grobbelaar
  Department of Sociology, University of South Africa, South Africa
- Hjalte Tin
  Centre for Cultural research, University of Aarhus, Denmark
- Franco Frescura
  Development consultant, SADC region, South Africa
- Ian Liebenberg
  Department of Sociology, University of South Africa, South Africa
- Abebe Zegeye
  Department of Sociology, University of South Africa, South Africa
- Fran Buntman
  Department of Political Science, University of Akron (Ohio),
  United States of America
- John Higginson
  Department of History, University of Massachusetts, United States of America
- John Comaroff
  Department of Anthropology, University of Chicago, United States of America
- Charmaine McEachern
  Department of Anthropology, University of Adelaide, Australia
- Denis-Constant Martin
  Centre d'etudes et de recherches internationales, France

Acknowledgements

I am grateful to Prem Naidoo, formerly of the National Research Foundation (NRF) who was instrumental in getting the Social Identities South Africa (SISA) programme off the ground. Thanks are also due to Robert Kriger, also of the NRF, who patiently supported th programme right from the start. Some of the papers in this volume are updated versions of papers published in *Social Identities, Journal for the Study of Race, Nation and Culture* (Vol. 4, No. 3, 1998).

Charl Schutte, Julia Maxted and Beth le Roux are thanked for their attention to the details of content and language editing. I am also thankful to Omar Badsha and Liam Lynch for their able technical assistance.

Imposed ethnicity

Abebe Zegeye

Afrikaan deur ondertroue en die verkragting van inheems Khoisan-mense, dalk met 'n stroopseltjie swart daarby; Oosters weens die inname van ambagslui en ballinge uit Maleie en Indonesië en die Indiese kuste ...

(African [inclusive of white people/Europeans] through intermarriage and rape of indigenous Khoisan people, perhaps with a touch of black, Eastern because of the inclusion of tradesmen and exiles from Malaya and Indonesia and the Indian coasts ...)

Breyten Breytenbach 1999, p. 3

In this introduction we explore the implications of political identity, whether real or imposed, for South African society. The concept of political identities is coupled with, firstly, the notion of ethnicity imposed from above (as informed by ideology and underpinned by sectional interests) and secondly, the transition to democracy.

Fundamentally, we are interested in definitions of identity that do not openly offset 'self' against 'other'.[1]

One such definition describes identity as open-ended, fluid and constantly in a process of being constructed and reconstructed as the subject moves from one social situation to another, resulting in a self that is highly fragmented and context-dependent. The notion of fluidity and context-dependence is particularly apt. After all, conflicting racial, ethnic, gender, class, sexual, religious and national identities are a reality. Hence members of a particular group do not all have the same concerns and viewpoints.

The policies that have emerged from the 'rainbow nation' philosophy must have taken cognisance of this fluidity as they embrace the multiplicity and dynamism of groups and discard the notion of the 'natural', static and unchanging 'group' or groups as expounded by apartheid.

The relationship between political identity and ethnicity

Under apartheid legislation the South African populace was divided into various ethnic categories. Several of these categories, including Afrikaner, black, Zulu, Indian and coloured, are discussed by the contributors to this volume. Such 'ethnic' divisions were upheld as the ideological basis for "separate development" (apartheid). These identities were, in fact, often imposed or fortified by the apartheid regime and before that, the colonial rulers of South Africa (the British). Segregation was inherited from earlier colonialist rule, pragmatically maintained by colonial white political entrepreneurs and later refined by apartheid rulers.

One may, or may not, venture into referring to it as colonialism of a special type. Social identities are thus deeply embedded in the South African social structure. In 1994, the country held its first non-racial multi-party elections. The new government led by the African National Congress (ANC) came to power with the promise of eradicating apartheid divisions and enhancing the socio-economic reconstruction of South African society.

The relationship between political identity and ethnicity is a thorny issue. The commitment to democracy in South African society requires every sector of society to claim authority, rights and responsibilities. The new South African Constitution further underpins these claims. However, these claims should not be vested in ethnic antagonism, cultural supremacy or any other form of social exclusivity. Given that ethnicity, language and colour determined membership in state and society in the recently abolished apartheid system, how can formerly excluded communities be recognised without perpetuating apartheid categorisations? This chapter addresses this question by focusing on South Africa's transition to democracy.

After being on the brink of civil war for several years, South Africa has experienced relative stability in the last years of the 20th century as a consequence of almost ten years of transition-directed negotiations, founding elections, compromises and reforms on various levels. However, South Africa remains a deeply divided society.

Culture, race, historical background, language and religion have all served to reinforce this segmentation (Bekker, 1997, p. 8). Religion, for instance, played an important part in South Africa's history by providing justification for colonisation and apartheid as well as for resistance to colonial and apartheid oppression (cf. Hope and Young [1981], De Gruchy [1979], Boesak [1977], Mosala and Tlhagale [1986], Villa-Vicencio [1994] and Nel [1989 and 1997]).

Furthermore, ethnic, cultural, racial and religious differences often coincide with class differences. For instance, less than one and a half million South Africans earn more than R3 500 per month, while unemployment ranges from 48% in the Eastern Cape, to just 18% in the Western Cape, with 34% being the country's average. In addition, the largest number of those who earn less than R500 per month can be found in the poorest provinces – the Northern Cape, Northern Province, and Eastern Cape (Census in Brief, 1996, pp. 46-48). The impact of all these figures on current and future class differences is immense.

Imposed ethnicity

In addition, South African society still suffers, as do many other African societies, from the legacy of an identity-assigning colonialism and racialism imposed by successive minority governments.[2] Colonialism and racialism were powerful factors in forming the identities of Africans. Comaroff, in his contribution to this volume, details African citizens' suffering under colonialism and racialism and the long-term consequences of colonialism and racialism for them, concluding that they are still bearing a heavy burden and speaking of "the black man's burden". Comaroff contends that the final legacy of colonialism in Africa may be that it yielded two different counter-discourses of rights and images of nationhood and political order. These are, first, an image of order and nation based on a liberal ethos of universal human rights, of free, autonomous citizenship and individual entitlement. The other asserts group rights, ethnic sovereignty and primordial cultural connection.

Whether a "habitable hybrid", an acceptable mixture of group and individual identities and rights, which is the aim of the present government, can be achieved in South Africa, is the crucial question addressed in this introduction. The apartheid government, in particular, was a powerful allocator of identity (Singh, 1997). According to Pieterse (1992, p. 106), '[a]partheid is a matter of "ethnicity from above"', as the government used legislation and other sanctions to enforce acceptance of the most impoverished definitions of identity. It also attempted to suppress and distort identity by excluding and suppressing all constituents of identity except race and ethnicity. The chapters by Buntman on the social and political relations on Robben Island, where political prisoners were incarcerated; Dlamini on the social associations of Zulu youth; McEachern on the meaning of the cosmopolitan identity developed by coloured, white and black people and people of Eastern origin in District Six; Martin on the difficulty of distinguishing a "coloured identity"; Vally on the imagined *umma* of the muslim Indians in South Africa and Frescura on the residential segregation of Africans in urban South Africa, emphasise the impoverishment of identities imposed by the colonialist and apartheid governments by focusing *inter alia* on the effects of such imposed identity in different social contexts.

The struggle against apartheid – which resulted in nearly two decades of low-intensity war and mass mobilisation – served to facilitate identity formation by unifying opponents of apartheid in a common assertion of non-racialism and anti-racism. To a certain extent it also unified South Africans in anti-colonialism and perhaps a common 'Africanness'. The varied social and political movements that participated in the anti-apartheid struggle created a new identity by jointly and actively undermining apartheid notions of whiteness as representing political superiority and non-whiteness as representing political inferiority. Thus anti-apartheid organisations and movements were important agents of identity construction – and to an extent this legacy remains.

The radical inclusive definition of identity created by these movements formed the basis for many citizen-based checks on governmental authority in the new democratic dispensation. In short, anti-apartheid movements fostered links between groups in civil society and legitimised citizens' expectations to the extent that the prevailing citizen identity became quite complex. However, other anti-apartheid organisations continued to base identity on race and ethnicity. Such exclusionist notions of identity are still operative in the relative stability of the new democratic dispensation.

Parameters of identity formation in South Africa

Apartheid was based on the following principles:

- The hierarchical ordering of economic, political and social structures on the basis of race, identified by physical characteristics such as skin colour and hair texture.
- Exclusion of black people from many of the civil, political and economic rights enjoyed by white people, such as the right to vote, to move freely, to be full citizens of South Africa, and to own property and work anywhere in South Africa.
- Confining black people to inferior housing, schools, universities, hospitals, and transport and prohibiting sexual relations and inter-marriage across the colour bar. This discrimination insinuated that black cultures were inferior to those of white people.
- Institutionalising this hierarchical, discriminatory and segregated system in law, enabling the government to enforce it through various measures.

Lipton 1985, pp. 14-15

Moreover, these characteristics came to be underpinned by a *civil religion* that conferred 'Christianity' on apartheid and 'apartheid' on Christianity (Bosch, 1984; De Klerk, 1975; Du Preez, 1983).

The policy of apartheid eventually became pervasive in South Africa and came to aim at the 'separate development' of different race and ethnic groups to the extent that some were defined out of South African national politics altogether.

Each group would exercise the right to develop, in its own area, its own culture, heritage, language and concept of 'nationhood'. Thus, apartheid involved the institutionalisation of categorisations emanating from colonial anthropology. Socialisation was structured by the separation of people along racial lines, as well as, in many cases, ethnic lines.

Racial and ethnic segregation emphasised cultural 'differences', often translated into stereotypes (Malan, 1995).

We suggest that the paradigm of ethnicity has become too value-laden (even ideological) to provide an understanding of South African society that will facilitate post-apartheid tolerance, accommodation and integration on a peaceful basis.

Shared struggle, shared values, shared interests

Common interests were shaped in the struggle against white domination and, in particular, apartheid. For instance, opposition to the policies of various white governments since the last decade of the 19th century generated a sense of unity among the various (ethnic) groups in the African population. Pixley ka Isaka Seme, calling for the formation of the South African Native National Congress (SANNC – renamed the African National Congress in 1925), argued that the lack of unity among the indigenous people was the greatest obstacle to progress (Odendaal, 1984, pp. 81, 259). It is clear that a common African identity did not exist at the time, but had to be constructed to develop the unity so necessary for success. The SANNC focused on African unity and regarded fragmentation on the basis of clan and tribe as a serious danger (Greenstein, 1995).

At the same time as Afrikaner nationalists were building their nation through sentimental calls for devotion to their national cause and the *Volk* (nation), black people were also experimenting with nation building. Nationalism seemed to be the preferred political option of the time. Ethnic identification was not simply a danger in and of itself.

It was part and parcel of an imperialist tendency that seriously debilitated many African groups and contributed to the carnage of the liberation struggle. Seme praised the leaders of the many African communities in the hopes of engendering unity among them. But ethnicity did not necessarily obstruct the development of a broad African identity.

Instead, when not constructed as a force opposing African nationalism, ethnicity strengthened the African identity by promoting pride in African history. Some invoked the images of Shaka Zulu, Sobhuza of Swaziland and the Xhosa prophet Ntsikane when appealing for African national unity (Greenstein, 1995).

Proto-ethnic divisions in support of sectional interests

The most significant piece of legislation underlying apartheid policy was the Population Registration Act of 1950 that classified the South African population into four racial groups: white, black, Indian and coloured.[3] A white person was defined as someone who 'in appearance obviously is a white person and who is not generally accepted as a coloured person; or is generally accepted as a white person and is not in appearance obviously not a white person'. A black person was seen as any person who 'is, or is generally accepted as a member of any aboriginal race or tribe'. A coloured person was defined as any person 'who is not a white person or a black' sub-classified under the Malay, Griqua, Chinese and Indian groups and two residual groups, the 'other Asiatic group' and the 'other coloured group'. These categories were distinguished from one another on the basis of descent, that is, classification of the natural father, and/or social acceptance as members of a particular sub-group (Du Toit and Theron, 1988, pp. 136-137; Horrel, 1982).

Apartheid, and the material interest and prejudice which it engendered, generated privilege and status for white people while displacing and disadvantaging black people. The best evidence of this is the pattern of population movement. Black people were forced to live in 'homelands', which were generally rural areas with scant opportunities for employment. The homelands acted as labour reserves for a migratory black South African workforce, allowing the enforcement of low wages and the neglect of working conditions. Ever since the discovery of major mineral deposits in the 19th century, white entrepreneurs signed exploitative labour contracts with black people to maximise capital gains from the mineral resources of the country. Black people could only enter into such contracts if they relocated to the urbanising and industrialising regions of the country. However, they were prohibited from bringing their families to the economic cores with them.[4]

The political construction of 'communities' through residential and social segregation was perhaps the most significant factor in creating collective racialised identities. This was complemented by the homeland policy, which aimed to divide the African population by entrenching ethno-regional identities. The government proclaimed that 'South Africa was not a multi-racial society, but consisted of many "nations", each of which should have the right to control its destiny and preserve its identity' (Lipton, 1985, pp. 30). Before the colonial penetration of the region, South Africa, like many other parts of Africa, had what Ake (1993, pp. 1) termed 'ethnic polities – political societies with governmental institutions in a local space where territoriality and ethnic identity roughly coincided'. In an attempt to reinforce ethnic identity, the apartheid government, following colonial tradition, identified eight African tribes or 'nations', each of which would eventually be given 'independence' in its own homeland. All Africans were to be linked politically with their homeland, which would have as its citizens 'its *de facto* population, plus members of its tribe in "white" South Africa, its *de jure* citizens' (Lipton, 1985, pp. 23, 30). Ethnic mobilisation played a significant role in the development of apartheid and its programmes. In the process, Afrikaner social identity, the National Party (NP) and the state became inextricably intertwined (Adam and Giliomee, 1978; O'Meara, 1976; Moodie, 1975). Afrikaner nationalism went beyond culture to include a close emotional attachment with the state and national symbols and values (Giliomee and Schlemmer, 1989). Indeed, because Afrikaner leaders used their political power to underwrite Afrikaner culture, state politics became infused with Afrikaner cultural considerations, including national symbols and values (Munro, 1995).

The Afrikaner image was forged by ideologues. To be an Afrikaner entailed having a sense of belonging to that group and birth into the *Volk* (in the terms of Afrikaner ideologues an imagined community of racially similar people adhering to predominantly Afrikaner values, but which may also include markers such as language, ethnicity, religion, customs, political memory and shared experience of the 'other', according to Jary and Jary [1995, p. 433]) superseded identification with the state. Thus race, as opposed to the symbols and icons of cultural inclusiveness, remained the ultimate test of membership of the group (Adam, 1994; Bosch, 1984; Munro, 1995). The systematic repetition of certain key notions – such as that white people were superior and black people inferior; South Africa belonged to the Afrikaner; the Afrikaner had a special relationship with God; Afrikaners constituted the *(Boere)volk*;[5] the Afrikaner was threatened and the Afrikaner had a God-given task in Africa – reinforced Afrikaner identity. The Afrikaans language also became a cornerstone of Afrikaner identity (Cloete, 1992; Bosch, 1984). But there were other identities calling for space in South Africa.

The Indian population of South Africa

The first Indians arrived in Natal in the 1860s as indentured labourers, followed by traders in the 1870s. Because their village, city or caste served as the basis for identification, a common group identity did not exist at the time (Ericksen, 1993; Desai and Maharaj, 1996). However, throughout the 19th century, 'the construction of a broader collective Indian identity was fostered by the South African state', a process which became more pronounced during the apartheid era (Desai and Maharaj, 1996, p. 121). According to Minter (1986, p. 95), Afrikaner antagonism was first directed against Indian South Africans who, with their retail chains, were their closest economic competitors. But other processes also encouraged a collective Indian group identity. For the Indian community 'religion, music, customs, traditions and distinctive food tastes formed part of a womblike structure to act as a bulwark against a hostile environment' (Moodley, 1980, p. 234). The antagonism of the white minority and the hostility of the Zulu majority fostered a collective identity based on these common cultural traits. The brand of

Zulu nationalism under Inkatha and its anti-Indian sentiments consolidated this identity (Maré and Hamilton, 1987; Desai and Maharaj, 1996). A conscious effort was also made by progressive Indian organisations to draw the Indian community as a coherent bloc into the anti-apartheid struggle. Thus, the Natal Indian Congress (NIC) acknowledged the differences – heritage, culture, language, customs and traditions – between the four 'national groups' (Desai and Maharaj, 1996, p. 121). Earlier on, the Transvaal Indian Congress (TIC) moulded itself very much along the same lines.

The 'Coloured' people of South Africa

Perhaps the most significant political construction of 'community' and a collective identity is evident in the case of coloured people. As a result of the systematic separation induced by apartheid, the coloured community was forged from heterogeneous elements (or at least understood themselves to be 'coloured people' by historical coincidence). Slaves originating from Indonesia, Malaysia, India, Madagascar, East Africa and West Africa formed the early core of the coloured population in South Africa. By 1838, this heterogeneous group had one common feature – they were of mixed parentage, that is, descendants of European pioneers and Khoi-San women, settlers and slaves and former 'free black people' (i.e. political prisoners deported from the East Indies or African slaves who had bought their freedom from Cape colonial masters). They constituted all those people who could neither be considered white people nor indigenous Africans (Martin, 1998). Crudely put, they were seen to be neither 'European' nor *Abantu*, 'Native Africans'.

Despite being subject to discriminatory measures, coloured people at the beginning of the 20th century could vote, were elected into political office and formed political organisations. The coloured elite struggled to demonstrate their level of civilisation by internalising the very codes and values used by the white elite to classify them. Class differentiation in the course of the century generated differences in attitudes and political strategies and a political rift between collaborationists and anti-apartheid activists developed. Many of them were also subject to political fatalism and alienation from black South Africans as a result of National Party propaganda which instilled a fear of black South Africans (Martin, 1998, p. 533).

'Traditional and black' – the case of Inkatha

Inkatha was the most notable black organisation in South Africa to use ethnicity and regionalism as mobilising factors. Inkatha, a cultural movement with political undertones – much like the Afrikaner Broederbond – was established in 1922. It fell into inactivity during the depression years of the 1920s and 1930s along with other political organisations such as the Industrial and Commercial Union (ICU). When the organisation was re-activated in 1975, membership was determined through acceptance of the notion of a Zulu cultural solidarity, which was linked to a territory – the KwaZulu homeland (Maré, 1995). This 'national cultural movement' declared its aims to be the liberation of Africans from cultural domination by white people; eradication of socialism, neo-colonialism and imperialism; eradication of all forms of racial discrimination and segregation; and upholding the 'inalienable rights' of Zulus to self-determination and national independence (Davies *et al*, 1988). Being a black Zulu speaker and a resident of KwaZulu was no longer enough for people to 'qualify' as Zulu. People had to show allegiance to the KwaZulu 'state', the Zulu monarchy and to Inkatha. This entailed participating in Inkatha's political and cultural activities such as Shaka Day (Dlamini, 1998, p. 482).

Inkatha, while portraying itself to Africans as a political organisation following the tradition of the ANC, was thus also a Zulu nationalist movement, often displaying extreme Zulu chauvinism. The organisation solicited adherents on the basis of two themes. On the one hand, it exhibited aggressive anti-apartheid reformism, (initially) maintained a critical distance from the state and appealed to the traditions of the ANC and the liberation struggle in asserting a broad African nationalism. On the other hand, it appealed to traditionalism, ethnic loyalties, patriarchal and hierarchical values, discipline and a Zulu nationalism (McCaul, 1988). Inkatha was entrenched in the power structures of the KwaZulu homeland, with all members of the KwaZulu Legislative Assembly being Inkatha members. Thus, Inkatha wielded power in a regional appendage of the South African state as a one-party administration. It tended to portray the Zulu nation and itself as synonymous. Inkatha mobilised ethnicity by means of the proclaimed distinctiveness of the Zulu nation and their history. The extent to which this history was distorted by colonial ethnography has largely been overlooked. By virtue of its primary cultural orientation and non-boycott approach, Inkatha later became an easy target for partial co-option by the apartheid and tricameral regime (see Maré, 1992; Liebenberg and Duvenage, 1996; Liebenberg et al, 1994).

Segregation

Many theorists claim that apartheid was merely a continuation of a colonial mentality. Ben Magubane argues in his work, *The Making of a Racist State,* that apartheid was an extension of British colonialism in which British colonisers imposed territorial segregation, ostensibly to minimise inter-group conflict. The pattern of residential segregation was intensified after 1913 by the Land Act and the rule of Smuts. In 1948 the National Party came to power in a virtually 'whites only' election. Residential and social segregation came to play a significant role in the formation of collective racial identities in South Africa, becoming firmly entrenched by the 1980s. By the early 1990s very few urban dwellers lived in racially and ethnically integrated areas (Christopher, 1994; Desai and Maharaj, 1996).

This led to the development of politically constructed 'communities', where people defined as members of the same race group lived together, worshipped together and went to school together. Social segregation allowed very little social interaction between people of the different race groups. In addition, coloured people, Indian people and 'poor whites' were misrepresented as being beneficiaries of apartheid (Desai and Maharaj, 1996). The economic differentiation emerging from residential and social segregation resulted in separate schools and universities, separate newspapers, television and radio stations, and these in turn facilitated the reification of group identities (Desai and Maharaj, 1996).

In the late 1960s a new movement emerged in South Africa as a result of disenchantment among African intellectuals with liberal and multi-racial resistance against apartheid. This was to be referred to as the 'Black Consciousness Movement' (BCM). The movement can partially be traced back to dissatisfaction among students with the white-led, multi-racial National Union of South African Students (NUSAS). The students felt that the predominantly white leadership was unable to reflect the concerns of African students (Lodge, 1983).

The BCM therefore sought the psychological liberation of black people (including coloured people and Indian people) in an attempt to eradicate dependency on white leadership in the liberation struggle and shape the post-apartheid society. Underlying this was a group response to oppression and a reliance on indigenous cultural traditions. Psychological liberation would lead to solidarity among black people, thus paving the way for their mobilisation towards liberation.[6]

During the late 1970s black opposition in South Africa underwent a radical transformation. This was informed by the replacement of the exclusionist black nationalism of some members of the BCM and the Pan Africanist Congress (PAC) by a commitment to non-racialism. This was justified by the need to 'isolate the regime' and to draw the widest possible number of people into the anti-apartheid struggle, that is, *strategic populism*. All South Africans who shared a commitment to the ideals of a non-racial, democratic country were encouraged to join the 'national democratic struggle' against apartheid (A Marx, 1992, p. 126).

The United Democratic Front, a multi-class, multi-racial organisation formed in August 1983 to oppose the apartheid system included among its principles 'an adherence to the need for unity in struggle through which all democrats, regardless of race, religion or colour, shall take part together'.[7] The UDF (later to become the Mass Democratic Movement or MDM) called for the unity of all oppressed groups (Africans, Indian people and coloured people) but also for participation by individual white democrats. It argued that, to elicit immediate and long-term advantages, white people had to be included in the liberation struggle (A Marx, 1992).

The experience of political domination and economic exploitation among black people and the commitment to a non-racial democracy among white people resulted in the formation of an umbrella organisation for members from every race and ethnic group and virtually every class in the country and moved beyond religious affiliation. The UDF drew together close to 700 organisations, the most important being youth and student organisations, women's organisations, civic associations and trade unions. Many of these organisations drew their membership from various race, religious and ethnic groups in South Africa, leading to the construction of a collective identity across racial and ethnic lines.

The 1980s: reform and repression

At the same time that a shared identity was being created among anti-apartheid activists in the 1980s, Afrikanerdom became divided. The first significant break in Afrikanerdom followed the emergence of ideological differences between two camps in Afrikaner politics, the *verligte* (enlightened or liberal) and *verkrampte* (conservative) groups, in the 1970s. The two groups clashed on the question of introducing certain reforms to apartheid, including the recognition of African trade unions and the permanence of the urban African population, as well as the introduction of a new constitutional dispensation which would extend political rights to coloured people and Indian people. This led inter alia to the establishment of the Herstigte Nasionale Party (HNP – Reformed National Party) that chose to maintain Verwoerdian principles. The Broederbond, as an 'ethnic vanguard', drummed the HNP led by Dr Albert Hertzog and later Jaap Marais out of Afrikaner politics during John Vorster's rule.

A second break occurred when PW Botha mooted the idea of parliamentary representation for Indian and coloured South Africans (see Giliomee, 1982 for more detail). The ascendancy of the *verligte* camp led to the breakaway of another group in 1982 and the formation of the more right-wing Conservative Party (CP) under Andries Treurnicht. The CP based its political appeal on the language of ethnic solidarity, group identity and cultural cohesion, invoking Afrikaner 'tradition' as the wellspring of identity politics. It claimed that the NP regime had betrayed the Afrikaner culturally, politically and materially (Munro, 1995). The fragmentation of Afrikaner unity that followed led to a plethora of right-wing fringe groups.

The tricameral constitution introduced in 1984 included coloured people and Indian people in the highest decision-making organs. The contributions to this volume by McEachern and Martin leave little doubt that the identity of coloured people cannot be conceptualised apart from their identity as South Africans, while Vally's profile of the Indian community raises the question of a 'hyphenated identity' assigned to and often adhered to by the Indian people in South Africa. The decision to include coloured and Indian people at the highest level of political decision-making in South Africa created divisions within both communities. Some opted to support group politics by participating in elections for the racial assemblies. Others were strongly opposed to the tricameral parliament. Indeed, voter turnout in the 'coloured' election was just 30% and in the Indian election a mere 20% of registered voters. Coloured ethnic politics underwent another dramatic change in the late 1980s and early 1990s when the majority of MPs in the House of Representatives crossed the floor to join the NP.

This led to the ultimate dissolution of the political party which had led 'institutionalised' coloured politics for much of the preceding two decades, namely the Labour Party. Although the leading Indian political party in the tricameral parliament, Amichand Rajbansi's Minority Front, continued to exist after the 1994 elections, defections to the NP, DP and IFP (and to a lesser extent the ANC) since then have dramatically reduced its support in this community.

All these events coincided with the technocratic 'reforms' initiated by PW Botha in the early 1980s. Though the boundaries of inclusion and exclusion within the polity shifted under the tricameral parliament, continued segregation and a top-down approach marked the reforms. Selective 'co-optation' combined with repression and top-down restructuring led some critics to refer to this as an era of an imperial presidency or 'domination through reform' (Van Vuuren, 1985).

The chapter by Frescura in this volume highlights the exclusion of African people under apartheid rule at the level of local government by providing a detailed account of long-term residential segregation in two large South African cities (Johannesburg and Port Elizabeth). This directs the attention of the analyst to the still unanswered question of why coloured and Indian people received representation during this period, while Africans (by far the majority) did not. The answer to the question will probably result in a harsher judgement by historians of the apartheid regime, in spite of their eventual capitulation in the face of irresistible pressure both at home and abroad.

The Afrikaner

Afrikaner self-concepts thus moved from a 'constructed Afrikaner homogeneity' to 'pieces of broken images' (Cloete, 1992, p. 42). As Serfontein (1990, p. 19) points out:

> Afrikanerdom or the Afrikaner volk or the Afrikaners simply do not exist as a separate, identifiable group any longer. There are, however, different groups or fragments of Afrikaners, or Afrikaans-speaking whites. Some regard them-

selves as the Afrikaner volk, others simply as Boere, others as South Africans
and others again as Afrikaans-speaking Africans.

(cited in) Cloete 1992, pp. 42-43

English-speaking South Africans mostly stayed aloof from such debates. The Afrikaner-
dominated state provided enough security for other 'whites' to continue their daily
lives (especially in the economic sphere) without getting embroiled in Afrikaner politics. The state provided the needed social and economic security and stability, which
rendered political risks on any side unnecessary. The gradual militarisation of politics
was a major contributor to this security and stability. Under the State Security Council
(again dominated by Afrikaners and some carefully selected entrepreneurs) praetorian
tendencies developed, with the military becoming involved in politics. The military
however did not step in of their own accord. Rather, they were invited into politics on
a piecemeal basis, as the government became ever more vulnerable due to international
isolation and internal resistance.

Similarly to Afrikaners, however, individual self-perceptions among coloured and
Indian people indicated a variety of identities. Some regarded themselves as belonging
to a distinct 'racial group', separate from other apartheid-defined groups, while others
saw themselves as 'black people', a collective identity which included all Africans,
coloured and Indian people.

Still others embraced the non-racialism of the ANC by defining themselves as South
Africans. Indeed, broad collective practices and historical circumstances made some
members of these groups more receptive to ethnocentrism and others more receptive
to an all-inclusive and non-racial identity.

In late 1996, a survey of primary social identities carried out by Gibson and Gouws
(1998) found that nearly one-third of those interviewed identified most strongly with
the label 'African', while smaller percentages identified themselves as 'South African',
'black', or in terms of the various ethnic or religious groups. In contrast, the greatest
single proportion of white people (28%), coloured people (30%) and Indian people
(31%) thought of themselves as just 'South Africans', with only a few white people
identifying themselves as 'white'. 'Afrikaner' still formed a significant term of self-
identification among white people. Among the coloured people interviewed, nearly a
third identified themselves as 'coloured' and a small number as 'brown', while 16%
per cent of Indian people identified themselves as Indian (in addition to a number who
gave their primary social identity as Hindu or Asian). Only very few coloured people
and Indian people gave 'black' as their primary identity.

But, as Adam puts it:

Apartheid ideology had institutionalised group differences. They were imposed
and therefore rejected. Hence, the ground was laid for democratic inclusivism

rather than counter-racism. At the same time, the historical racial and ethnic perceptions of difference – partially invented, reinforced and entrenched by Apartheid, but, above all, underscored by material inequality – did not psychologically homogenise the population, the ideology of colour-blind non-racialism notwithstanding.

This legacy of Apartheid lives on in everyday racial and ethnic consciousness. Even if black people as political rulers have modified ethnic hierarchy, racism as the everyday false consciousness of socially constructed difference has not disappeared with the repeal of racial legislation.

1994, p. 25

As the Gibson and Gouws study shows, most South Africans still use racial or ethnic terms to describe themselves, with nearly 40% of the respondents selecting a general racial term and another third using a more specific sub-racial or ethnic term to indicate their primary identity. Only slightly more than one in five of the respondents claim a national identity as their primary means of describing themselves.

The study shows a strong sense of group identification in South Africa, with the overwhelming majority of respondents attaching great political significance to their primary group.[8] To deny this is to repeat the common mistake, especially on the part of the Left, to underestimate ontological commitments to racial and ethnic identities and their role in shaping historical struggles (Robinson, 1982; Maxted, 1996).

Ontological commitments or identities point to how an individual or group is structured in terms of practical historical being. Moreover, ontological consciousness is not a shadowy feature of consciousness juxtaposed with the 'real' world. In contrast, ontological commitments inform day-to-day norms and perceptions of what it is to belong to a community, nation or racialised group. Indeed, according to Hall and Held (1990, p. 175), 'from the ancient world to the present day, citizenship has entailed a discussion, and a struggle, over the meaning and scope of membership of the community in which one lives'.

South African researchers thus far have tended in most cases to investigate shifting identities without taking cognisance of identity markers such as gender, age, family, religion, economic, social and cultural position (class) and physical environment, despite the greater acknowledgement of these markers in the democratic South Africa. Therefore, ontological commitments to race or ethnicity, far from being denied, should be placed in the richer context of these identity markers. In addition, 'ethnicity cannot be divorced from other changes of the twentieth century: urbanisation, communication networks, new relationships of production ... the increase in migratory and commercial movements' (Maxted and Zegeye, 1997b, p. 66).

However, despite its apparent fixedness, ethnicity in Africa is constantly changing in response to changes in the form of the state and notions of civil society.

Accommodating identity and a deepening
of democratic processes – the civil community in Africa

The majority of states emerging from colonialism dealt with diversity by subordinating it to 'nation building'. Diversity was vilified on account of its relatedness to colonial divisions of regions, leaders, groups and communities, which divisions were aimed at delineating spheres of influence. Post-colonial leaders in order to justify the one-party state used these very divisions. These one-party states created a comprehensive apparatus of hegemony, co-opting within their structures all the important organs of civil society, including amongst others trade unions, student and youth organisations.

Even the first step towards accommodating diversity in multi-cultural constitutional democracies, we may add non-racial polities, would be the acknowledgement of the heterogeneity of society. This requirement is a tall order but, if successfully instituted, contributes significantly to the maintenance of a working democracy.

Possible impediments to democratic consolidation

Some argue that the most significant aspect of identity politics in the late 20th century is ethnic struggle. They point out that 'conflict between language, religion, physical appearance, beliefs, and customs of people from different ethnic groups has been – and probably will continue to be – a primary source of unrest in the world' (Landis and Boucher, 1987, p. 18; Ismagilova, 1997, pp. 298-299). With the exception of class struggles, and the rise of Nazism and Fascism (the latter two attempting to 'indigenise' class power bases), the majority of 20th century social conflicts have been either 'ethnic' or 'religious'. Ethnic conflicts occur when political struggles become ethnicised or when various cultural traditions become racialised and mobilised for political ends (Adam, 1994).

The essential problem in heterogeneous societies is the potential for sub-groups based on ethnic, cultural, linguistic, racial, religious, regional, class or caste identities to feel excluded. This crucial problem is discussed or at least touched upon by all the contributions to this volume. People thus excluded feel that they do not participate fully in the political system or that the government constantly acts in opposition to their preferences. Therefore many are sceptical about the prospect of creating a common democratic culture or consolidating a democracy in a heterogeneous society. Some even suggest the maintenance of separate groups within a polity through pillar-like structures, one example being the consociational theory advanced by Lijphart (1977). However, accommodating sub-groups – and especially ethnic consciousness, ethno-cultural claims and ethnic political behaviour – is widely considered to obstruct democratic consolidation as well as modernisation, industrial development, nation building, institutional and socio-economic pluralism and the promotion of individual liberties (Safran, 1991).

South Africa: back to the future

Conflicts over language in heterogeneous societies represent a fundamental threat to democracy for these theorists. They conclude that simply being multilingual, for example, makes people eschew democracy. They repeat the appalling reductiveness of the ideology of nation-statism, according to Maxted and Zegeye (1997a, p. 390), following Davidson, by asserting that 'the wealth of cultures [is] really an impoverishment'. Language policies may spark conflict because language represents culture, recognition, legitimacy and autonomy. In a like manner, ethnicity and religion, too, often give rise to enmity. Thus they should be neutralised before they become justifications for nationalism. This perspective contends that when an ethnic group struggles to achieve political power, freedom and self-determination in an autonomous region or nation-state, the group pulls apart the fabric of multi-cultural societies.

However, this argument is unhelpful in South Africa. There is a danger in understanding all conflicts engaged in by states during the 20th century as fundamentally ethnic: struggles against undemocratic regimes that fundamentally sought to undermine the 'nation-state' are equated with the struggles to build the state, even though they are not the same kind of struggle. This is because the 'nation-state' underminers did not have the kind of material, military or capital base that the nation-state builders had, which makes them categorically different. So the problem is not simply that ethnicity, in the broadest possible sense, can be mobilised by the regime, but more importantly that ethnicity can be mobilised by groups of people seeking to undo the state and its priorities. The legacy of such a cycle of 'ultimate' rule and resistance to the ruler may last for many years to come.

However, the contributions to this volume have addressed not only those factors that, if not managed correctly, may serve as continuing divisive aspects of South African society, but have also illuminated some of the more unifying elements from which a new nationhood might be built. Accordingly, the contributors have collectively manage to convey the message that the legacy of the cycle of 'ultimate' rule, although it may last for 'many years', may not last 'forever'. Some of the more encouraging aspects from the point of view of accommodating identity differences while recognising diversity, are that

- South African society has suffered the double burden of colonial and apartheid rule, both entrenching racism, but there are as yet no generally accepted signs that social relations between black and white have deteriorated in the post-apartheid era. In fact, they appear at present to be tackled in a more realistic, authentic manner and relations at a grassroots level may have improved.

– Despite continuing economic woes, unemployment, cultural and ideological differences, the exigencies of undifferentiated globalisation, an apparent loss of state power and revenue, an as yet undeveloped plan for land redistribution and a deterioration of its civil service, South Africa remains a nation committed to recognising the varied identities of its citizens. This is shown, first, by the fact that South Africa recently undertook a Truth and Reconciliation Process in which people of the most diverse political persuasions testified, although the main aim of the process was not to recognise difference. This process is detailed in the relevant chapter by Liebenberg and Zegeye. Second, the ANC and its allies earlier went out of their way to accommodate Afrikaner nationalism during the multi-party negotiations since 1994. This commitment to recognising different identities could diminish the likelihood of conflict.

– South Africa, in spite of colonialism and the apartheid struggle, has a long history of attempts at accommodating different identities, albeit sometimes in the most inadequate manner. These experiences, by exposing people to checks and balances and suffering through the struggle, cannot other than have fortified South Africa's citizens and educated them in the more peaceful ways of solving identity-related problems. The experiences referred to can in fact seed new, constructive visions of unity and nationhood amidst diversity which many analysts feel is lacking at present in South Africa. South Africa's history of conflict and diversity may indeed have placed it in an almost unique position in this respect.

– In addition, South Africa has over many decades developed a strong trade union movement which, because of the historic legacy of colonialism and apartheid, initially represented the interests largely of black people of many different ethnic origins and played a prominent role in obtaining political rights for them. This political role was transferred to the post-apartheid era when the largest trade union conglomerate, the Congress of South African Trade Unions (Cosatu), entered into a tripartite alliance with the ANC – the ruling party – and the South African Communist Party (SACP). Accordingly, Cosatu represents not only a wide variety of people with different identities at an economic level, but has a traditionally established political role to play in South Africa. This enables it to act as a political check on the government.

– In spite of some isolated differences, an unexpectedly large and powerful proportion of South Africans of vastly different identities appear to be united in their aversion to injustices such as racism and crime and in their adherence to such values as education, wealth, health and issues relating to gender relations and the environment.

However, in view of the analyses represented in this volume, it would be naive to present these aspects as unrealistically hopeful. Many daunting tasks relating to accommodating different identities remain if South Africa is to take the high road to greater political, economic and social welfare. So far we have largely discussed the ways in which the state can utilise identity. We have yet to discuss the ways in which identities formerly excluded by the state can create a different kind of state, although the authors of this volume have pointed the way.

Notes

− This chapter and the conclusion were based upon *Resisting Ethnicity from Above*, Human Sciences Research Council, Pretoria 2000, an occasional paper by A. Zegeye, I. Liebenbergand G. Houston.

1 The concept of 'identity' has become a primary medium for understanding the relationship between the personal (subjective) and the social; the individual and the group; the cultural and the political; as well as the group and the state. 'Identity' can refer to forms of (individual) personhood as well as collectivities or groups (Rousse, 1995). At the individual level, identity as a definition of personhood refers to uniqueness, that is, differentiation from other people or the whole of mankind, as well as sameness or continuity of the self across time and space (Baumeister, 1986; Erikson, 1969; Murgufa, Padilla and Pavel, 1991; Rousse, 1995). In addition, identity also incorporates the emotional attachment that individuals often have to group membership (Tajfel, 1978). Being a member of a group influences the way in which individuals see themselves, especially if certain social categories are reviled or hated. These definitions of identity are fundamental to understanding the link between the individual and personal experience and large-scale cultural, social and political processes.

2 See D.W. Kruger (1969, pp. 3ff) on the heritage of the past. See also De Klerk (1975, pp. 50ff) and Magubane (1996) on the earlier roots of a racist state in South Africa. For some insight into the impact on historiography and collective memory, see Wright (1977).

3 The other contending acts that enforced 'apartheid' from earlier times were the Land Act of 1913, the 'Native Reserves Act' and pass-carrying (a Dutch-British

invention that started in the times of Colonial Rule and became entrenched by the 1800s).

4   The impact of enforced 'internal migration' due to apartheid laws and the use of surplus black labour from rural areas (non-economic core areas) is well described by Davenport (1977), a South African historian. See also Davenport (n.d.), 'The 1913 Land Act', in *Sash Magazine*, 26(2): 13-18.

5   The *Boerevolk* were seen to be descendants of the whites who had settled in the interior of the Cape since the 17th century, relocated to areas further north in order to gain political freedom from British control, engaged in the Anglo-Boer Wars against Britain and established themselves anew after their defeat (1910 onwards).

6   The influence on the South African Black Consciousness Movement by similar intellectual streams in the United States has been under-researched. Sono (1993), Alexander (1985), Nel (1989, 1997) and Motlhabi (1985) were some of the few who dealt with this top – albeit from different angles.

7   Statement by the 'Commission on the Feasibility of a United Front against the Constitutional reform proposals', at the Transvaal Anti-SAIC Conference (cited in Barrell, 1984, p. 10). See also Houston (1999) on the national liberation struggle in South Africa with specific reference to the UDF.

8   A similar finding is reached by Roefs and Liebenberg (1999), though they are tentatively more optimistic about non-racialism.

References

Adam, H. (1994). 'Ethnic versus Civic Nationalism: South Africa's Non-racialism in Comparative Perspective', *South African Sociological Review*, 2 (2).

Adam, H. and Giliomee, H. (1978). *Ethnic Power Mobilised*, New Haven: Yale University Press.

Ake, C. (1993). 'What is the Problem of Ethnicity in Africa?', in *Transformation*, 2.

Alexander, Neville (1985). *Sow the Wind: Contemporary Speeches*, Johannesburg: Skotaville Publishers.

Barrell, H. (1984). 'The United Democratic Front and National Forum: Their Emergence, Composition and Trends', *South African Review 2*, Ravan Press, Johannesburg.

Baumeister, A. (1986). *Identity: Cultural Change and the Struggle for the Self*, New York and Oxford: Oxford University Press.

Bekker, S. (1997). Unpublished paper, 8 June.

Boesak, A.A. (1977). *Farewell to Innocence: A Socio-Ethical Study on Black Theology and Black Power.* New York: Orbis Books.

Bosch, D.J. (1984). 'The Roots and Fruits of Afrikaner Civil Religion', in W.G. Hofmeyer and W.S. Vorster (eds), *New Faces of Africa*, Pretoria: UNISA Printers.

Breytenbach, B. (1999). 'Gedagtes van 'n Kulturele Baster: Andersheid en Andersmaak – oftewel Afrikaner as Afrikaan', *Rapport (Aktueel)*, 28 November 3.

Census in Brief, (1996). Pretoria: Central Statistical Service.

Christopher, A.J. (1994). *The Atlas of Apartheid*, London: Routledge.

Cloete, E. (1992). 'Afrikaner Identity: Culture, Tradition and Gender', *Agenda*, 13.

Davenport, T.R.H. (1977). *South Africa – A Modern History* (2nd ed.), Johannesburg: Macmillan.

Davenport, T.R.H. (n.d.). 'The 1913 Land Act', *Sash Magazine*, 26 (2), pp. 13-18.

Davies, R. et al (1988). *The Struggle for South Africa: A Reference Guide to Movements, Organisations and Institutions,* London: Zed Books.

De Gruchy, John W. (1979). *The Church Struggle in South Africa*, Cape Town: David Philip.

De Klerk, W.A. (1975). *The Puritans in Africa: A Story of Afrikanerdom*, Middlesex: Penguin Books.

Desai, A. and Maharaj, B. (1996). 'Minorities in the Rainbow Nation: The Indian Vote in 1994', *Suid-Afrikaanse Tydskrif vir Sosiologie*, 27(4).

Dlamini, C. (1998). 'The Protection of Individual Rights and Minority Rights', in B. de Villiers, F. Delmartino and A. Alan (eds), *Institutional Development in Divided Societies,* Pretoria: Human Sciences Research Council.

Du Preez, J.M. (1983). *Afrikana Afrikaner: Master Symbols in South African School Text books*, Alberton: Librarius.

Du Toit, P. and Theron, F. (1988). 'Ethnic and Minority Groups, and Constitutional Change in South Africa', *Journal of Contemporary African Studies*, 7 (1 & 2), April/October.

Ericksen, T. (1993). *Ethnicity and Nationalism*, London: Pluto Press.

Erikson, E.H. (1968). *Identity: Youth and Crisis*, New York: Norton.

Gibson, J.L. and Gouws, A. (1998). 'Social Identity Theory and Political Intolerance in South Africa', paper presented at the *Meeting of the Midwest Political Science Association,* Chicago, Illinois, 23–26 April.

Giliomee, H. and Schlemmer, L. (eds) (1989). *Negotiating South Africa 's Future,* Johannesburg: Southern Books.

Giliomee, H. (1982). *The Parting of the Ways: South African Politics, 1976-1982*, Cape Town: David Philip.

Greenstein, R. (1995). 'Identity, Democracy and Political Rights: South Africa in Comparative Perspective', *Transformation*, 26.

Hall, S. and Held, D. (1990). 'Citizens and Citizenship', in S. Hall and M. Jacques (eds), *New Times: The Changing Face of Politics in the 1990s,* London: Verso.

Hope, M. and Young, J. (1981). *The South African Churches in a Revolutionary Situation*, New York: Orbis Books.

Horrel, M. (1982). *Race Regulations as Regulated by Law in South Africa, 1948–1979*, Pietermaritzburg: Natal Witness Press.

Houston, G. (1999). *The National Liberation Struggle in South Africa: A Case Study of the United Democratic Front, 1983–1987*, Aldershot: Ashgate.

Jary, D. and Jary, J. (1995). *Collins Dictionary of Sociology: Second Edition.* Glasgow: Harper-Collins.

Kruger, D.W. (1969). *The Making of a Nation: A History of the Union of South Africa, 1910-1961*, London: MacMillan Publishers.

Landis, D. and Boucher, J. (1987). 'Theories and Models of Conflict' in J. Boucher, D. Landis and K.A. Clark (eds), *Ethnic Conflict: International Perspectives*, London: Sage.

Liebenberg, I. and Duvenage, P. (1996). 'Can the Deep Political Divisions of South African Society be Healed? A Philosophical and Political Perspective', *Politeia*, 15 (1), pp. 48–61.

Liebenberg, I. et al (eds) (1994). *The Long March: The Story of the Struggle for Liberation in South Africa*, Pretoria: Kagiso-Haum Publishers.

Lijphart, A. (1977). *Democracy in Plural Societies*, New Haven: Yale University Press.

Lipton, M. (1985). *Capitalism and Apartheid: South Africa, 1910-1986*, Aldershot: Wildwood House.

Lodge, T. (1983). *Black Politics in South Africa since 1945*, Johannesburg: Ravan Press.

Magubane, B.M. (1996). *The Making of a Racist State: British Imperialism and the Union of South Africa, 1875–1910*, Asmara: Africa World Press.

Malan, L. (1995). *Cultural Identity and Needs in Bellville South and Newtown: An Ethnographic Investigation*, Pretoria: Human Sciences Research Council.

Mare, G. (1995). 'Ethnicity, Regionalism and Conflict in a Democratic South Africa', *South African Journal of International Affairs*, 3 (1), Summer.

Mare, G. (1992). *Brothers Born of Warrior Blood: Politics and Ethnicity in South Africa*, Johannesburg: Ravan Press.

Mare, G. and Hamilton, G. (1987). *An Appetite for Power: Buthelezi's Inkatha and South Africa*, Johannesburg: Ravan Press.

Martin, D-C. (1998). 'What's in the Name "Coloured"?, *Social Identities*, 4 (3).

Marx, A. (1992). *Lessons of the Struggle: South African Internal Opposition, 1960-1990*, Cape Town: Oxford University Press.

Maxted, J. (1996). 'Race and class in a transforming metropolis: Los Angeles', unpublished doctoral dissertation, University of Oxford.

Maxted, J. and Zegeye, A. (1997a). 'Regional Introduction: North, West and the Horn of Africa', in *World Directory of Minorities*, London: Minority Rights Group International.

Maxted, J. and Zegeye, A. (1997b). 'State Disintegration and Human Rights in Africa', in Pat Lauderdale and Randall Amster (ed.), *Lines in the Balance: Perspectives on Global Injustices and Inequality,* Leiden: Koninklijke Brill.

McCaul, C. (1988). 'The Wild Card: Inkatha and Contemporary Black Politics', in P. Frankel, N. Pines and M. Swilling (eds), *State, Resistance and Change in South Africa,* Kent: Croom Helm.

Minter, W. (1986). *King Solomon's Mines Revisited: Western Interests and the Burden of History of Southern Africa,* New York: Basic Books.

Moodie, T.D. (1975). *The Rise of Afrikanerdom: Power, Apartheid and the Afrikaner Civil Religion,* Berkeley: Berkeley University Press.

Moodley, K. (1986). "The legitimation Crises of the South African State", *Journal of Modern African Studies,* 24 (6), pp. 187-201.

Mosala, I.J. and Tlhagale, B. (eds) (1986). *The Unquestionable Right to be Free: Essays in Black Theology,* Johannesburg: Skotaville.

Motlhabi, M. (1985). *'The Theory and Practice of Black Resistance to Apartheid: A Socio-ethical Analysis,* Johannesburg: Skotaville.

Munro, W.A. (1995). 'Revisiting Tradition, Reconstructing Identity? Afrikaner Nationalism and Political Transition in South Africa', *Politikon,* 22 (2), December.

Murgufa, E., Padilla, R. and Pavel, M. (1991). 'Ethnicity and the Concept of Social Integration in Tinto's Model of Institutional Departure', *Journal of College Student Development,* 32.

Nel, F.B.O. (1989). *Om Mens te Wees: Die Storie van Swart Teologie in Suid-Afrika,* MA thesis, University of the Western Cape, Bellville.

Nel, F.B.O. (1997). *The Role of Christian Fundamentalism in Apartheid South Africa,* unpublished paper, London, UK.

O'Meara, D. (1983). *Volkskapitalisme. Class, Capital and Ideology in the Development of Afrikaner Nationalism, 1934-1948,* Johannesburg: Ravan Press.

Pieterse, Jan Nederveen (1992). *White on Black: Images of Africa and Blacks in Western Popular Culture,* New Haven: Yale University Press.

Robinson, C. (1982). *Black Marxism: The Making of the Black Radical Tradition,* London: Zed Press, .

Roefs, M. and Liebenberg, I. (1999). *Non-racialism in South Africa on the eve of 2000: Eyeing South African Survey Data and Notes on Policy Making,* HSRC Website: http://www.hsrc.ac.za/delivered/nonracial.html

Rousse, R. (1995). 'Questions of Identity: Personhood and Collectivity in Transnational Migration to the United States', *Critique of Anthropology,* 15, (4).

Safran, W. (1991). 'Ethnicity and Pluralism: Comparative and Theoretical Perspectives', *Canadian Review of Studies in Nationalism,* 18 (1 & 2).

Serfontein, H. (1990). 'Die Afrikaner Volk Bestaan Nie en Breyten is "A Rebel Without a Cause"', *Vrye Weekblad,* 24 August.

Singh, M. (1997). 'Identity in the Making', *Suid-Afrikaanse Tydskrif vir Wysbegeerte,* 16 (3).

Sono, T. (1993). *Reflections on the Origins of Black Consciousness in South Africa*, Pretoria: HSRC Publishers.

Tajfel, H. (1978). 'Social Categorization, Social Identity and Social Comparison', in H. Tajfel (ed.), *Differentiation between Social Groups: Studies in the Social Psychology of Intergroup Relations*, New York: Academic Press.

Van Vuuren, W. (1985). 'Domination through Reform: The Functional Adaptation of Legitimising Strategies', *Politikon*, 12 (2), pp. 47–58.

Villa-Vicencio, Charles (1994). *Civil Disobedience, Resistance and Religion in South Africa*, Cape Town: David Philip.

Wright, H.M. (1977). *The Burden of the Present: Liberal-radical Controversy over South African History*, Cape Town: David Philip.

Section One:
Social conditions and the state

The chapters by Comaroff, Higginson, Frescura, Tin and Buntman, although doing so in a widely differing manner, all point to the hardships suffered by black South Africans under colonialism and later apartheid. Together, the chapters offer a deep understanding of social conditions under colonialism and especially apartheid. They manage also to identify many crucial stumbling blocks to an overall South African identity and nationhood, even more than six years after the ground-breaking first democratic election in 1994. We now turn to each of the chapters individually.

Chapter 1:
Reflections on the colonial state in South Africa and elsewhere:
factions, fragments, facts and fictions
– John L. Comaroff

Comaroff indicates that the colonial state can create both greater equality and inequality simultaneously and can protect and serve, as well as criminalise, simultaneously. Although it can be interpreted as a fiction, a mere assertion, the colonial state is a solid force requiring attention and response and the meeting of obligations. The colonial state can be analysed in terms of modernisation theory, which implies confident liberal humanist teleologies and utopian narratives of progress on the one hand and on the other, the Marxist alternatives. These treat imperialism as a reflex of the global expansion of capitalism, the articulation of modes of production, the unequal exchange between centres and peripheries and of underdevelopment and dependency.

Comaroff calls on Marx in contending that capitalist regimes in the colonies were confronted with the resistance of producers, who as owners of their own conditions of labour employed that labour to enrich themselves rather than the capitalist colonial states. In colonial South Africa, black South Africans were integrated into the capitalist economy through the forcible destruction of their modes of production. Comaroff links this phenomenon to the pattern of colonial rule in the rest of Africa as formulated by the neo-Marxist historical canon. In Africa, there are repeated examples of African societies that were deliberately impoverished and their economies subverted in order to make them dependent on underpaid, mainly male migrant wage labour in the urban sector and underproductive, mainly female, rural agricultural labour. Consequently, capitalist development became the prime mover of the processes of underdevelopment and social transformation. The result was that the colonial state became, just before its demise, a state without a nation. The historical variability with which colonial designs were accomplished in Africa, the differences over time and space among states in this respect, remain to be documented and accounted for, according to Comaroff. However, the 'nationless state' of colonialism yielded two different counter-discourses of rights and with them, two alternative conceptions of modernity. These alternative conceptions of modernity are likely to be the final legacy of the colonial state in Africa. One of these alternative conceptions of nationhood is based on a liberal ethos of universal human rights, free and autonomous citizenship and individual entitlement. The other is supported by an assertion of group rights, ethnic solidarity and primordial cultural connection. The two alternatives are now more than ever arraigned against each other in struggles over the future of the post-colony. In South Africa they almost derailed the end of apartheid. Elsewhere they produced genocides. Almost nowhere have they yielded easily habitable hybrids, new political orders that address the problem of post-colonial empowerment. For Comaroff this is the black man's burden and the challenge that awaits Africa as a new epoch, the epoch of global capitalism, dawns and spreads new shadows over old horizons. The Comaroff chapter leaves one with little doubt that the looming global capitalism he refers to, if its demands remain amorphous and without structure, making no allowances for drastic global differences in responses to it, especially in poorer parts of the world, will deepen the black 'man's' burden in Africa. By coupling the identity of the black 'man' in colonial Africa to global capitalism, Comaroff provides a better understanding of the challenges poorer people everywhere face in meeting the essential requirements of globalisation in the present age.

Chapter 2:
Upending the century of wrong: agrarian elites, collective violence and the transformation of state power in the American South and South Africa, 1865-1914
– John Higginson

Presently, there is evidence that the most glaring features of South African apartheid and segregation in America are receding, writes Higginson. There is however a great deal of confusion regarding whether both were coincidental or the result of deliberate social engineering. Segregation resulted in both societies precipitously from the manner in which war (the Anglo-Boer War in South Africa and the American Civil War in America) and their subsequent reverberations in terrorist violence transformed state power and economic alternatives. Although segregationists concentrated on the cities, towns and industrial workplaces in both the American South and South Africa, segregation as a state sponsored practice and policy of social engineering depended primarily upon the imposition of political order in the surrounding countryside. Competing versions of social order emerged.

Violent white landowners in both societies exposed the ineffectual nature of many of both reconstruction governments' postwar administrative reforms, while compelling the reconstruction governments to reconsider the viability of their apparent postwar alliances.

In each of the two countries, collective and political violence punctuated the life histories of their leading men before, during and after the respective wars. A vigilante tradition created a perverse set of precedents for postwar reform. The action of vigilantes, insofar as they were encouraged by local elites, created an array of flashpoints that challenged the victors' conception of political order.

What turned planters and landlords into vigilantes? On occasion violence became a means for landowners to simultaneously express their grievances against the victorious central state and their reluctance to change their way of life or local social structure. Violence became for them a method and a process of expressing both their fears and aspirations. Violence was not serendipitous or spontaneous.

Moreover, landowners in both countries before the wars sought to replace work routines shaped by affection and kinship with their own putative and sovereign power in an attempt to enhance their command over black labour. The loss of the possibility of this kind of command over black labour launched both groups of landowners into campaigns of vigilante terror.

In this, some of the landowners achieved recognition and notoriety beyond their given locale. Whether they were sociopathic or not was not as important as the way in which they perceived their fortunes and circumstances. This raises for Higginson basic questions on the 'instinctual' nature of violence, particularly violence against people of another group. If collective violence of this nature can be interpreted as the result of factors that are 'caused, defensive and interpretable', it can be prevented. It is on this contention that his further findings are to be based.

A fundamental point raised in the chapter by Higginson is that violence relates to landowner control over labour, thereby fitting into the pattern of what Comaroff identified as the prime mover in underdevelopment and deliberate impoverishment in colonial Africa. In both South Africa and the South in America attempts to enhance control over labour by producers for Higginson involved the destruction of labour relations characterised by 'affection and kinship'. These were replaced by labour relations in which landlords attempted to enhance their command over their labour forces by exercising greater 'putative, sovereign power'.

The elemental change in the nature of labour relations away from those of affection and kinship appears to imply the possibility that the social and political identity of both landlord and labourer could be changed in the process. It is this possible identity change that links the Higginson chapter to the broader political identity theme of this book and provides a glimpse of the dynamics of how the political identities of those involved may have changed from their sudden origins, both in South Africa and America.

Black literature in the United States of America often refers to the generosity of 'good white folks'. Higginson's discussion makes the point that good white folks were often officials of the central state who were treating black people well for strategic political ends. These coalitions yielded suffrage, labour reform, military participation and citizenship. Ultimately, however, such coalitions rarely brought to an end the ongoing political violence by agrarian elites. Higginson's chapter in fact exposes precisely how this violence was politicised via the centralising efforts of the state.

Upon reflection, Higginson's chapter lends itself to some debate on why agrarian elites could not or would not adapt to new economic realities. This is a question raised also by Constand Viljoen's Freedom Front (FF) in South Africa. The party in effect started out by promising a return to to the Verwoerdian era of apartheid. Considering the rapidity of the present economic transformation and the way it mirrors the one of the previous century, why have not other strategies besides political violence been offered? An interesting point raised by Higginson's chapter is that political violence was deployed as a political action in the nineteenth century in response to a non-racial centralising vision of the state. It could be considered significant that local elites tend to assert their power through control of segregated or targeted minorities and that the state is obliged to exercise power through representation of itself as a neutral, egalitarian citizen-maker and rights equaliser.

Chapter 3:
The spatial geography of urban apartheid
– Franco Frescura

Frescura writes on the spatial legacy of colonialism and apartheid at a local level, especially the level of housing and their influence on the identity formation of black people in the urban areas of South Africa. Frescura's view is that in this process, an enormous backlog of deprivation for black people in South Africa arose. According to Frescura, it is true that in many respects the roots of racial segregation can be traced back to the nineteenth century and the strictures that colonial society imposed upon southern Africa's urban areas. Case studies in the region seem to indicate that, during the time of colonial influence, South Africa's suburbs were often integrated to a larger degree than is generally admitted by apartheid's historians. Although black and white were uneasy neighbours, they generally appear to have shared urban facilities with a measure of success. Disputes between the two communities usually arose over the occupation of coveted residential land, an issue which was often linked by white people to the question of public health. Occasionally matters reached a crucial point, such as in 1901 – 1903 when the British importation of fodder from Argentina brought about a nationwide outbreak of Bubonic Plague.

On this occasion the authorities unilaterally imposed draconian restrictions upon the black population, demolishing their homes, burning their belongings and displacing entire communities to sites well beyond the city boundaries. Barring such instances, however, planning decisions that created social divisions were generally made by planners on an ad hoc basis and were largely guided by considerations of economic class.

A major turning point was reached in 1923 when the Union Parliament passed the Natives (Urban Areas) Act, which laid down the principles of residential segregation and reinforced the doctrine that the African population had no permanent rights in the towns. In spite of this, the now 'white' suburbs remained racially integrated to varying degrees until 1948 when the Nationalist Party came to power. At that stage the process of separating communities was placed upon an ideological footing and was given substance by a variety of inter-linking residential, squatting, labour and security legislation. Although, over the years, the dialectic of apartheid has tended to change, its net effect upon the black community has involved the dispossession of their homes and land, often with minimal recompense. They have also been denied access to markets, infrastructure and civic amenities, leading to impoverishment and increased economic hardship.

In February 1990 the government began to dismantle the framework of laws upon which the Nationalist's dream of an apartheid society was based. Democrats throughout the world applauded this event, but almost immediately workers on the ground began to realise that whilst the legislation might have gone, the inequality generated by two generations of statutory discrimination had still to be redressed. This condition has become most evident in South Africa's urban areas where residential distributions, land uses, transport routes and statutory curbs on economic development have combined to create cities where economic inequality has become entrenched along racial lines. Planners are not unaware of this debate, but the solutions they are currently proposing vary from a liberal, market-based, long-term integration of the suburbs, through to a highly legislated interventionist policy orchestrated through a central government.

The shortcomings of either philosophy are self-evident and it seems probable that whatever solution is finally adopted, it will have to be reached within a framework that takes full cognisance of all the historical factors involved. In this chapter Frescura analyses the historical nature and physical characteristics of the Apartheid City. He examines the role played by planners in the oppression of a people and looks at the problems currently facing community-based professionals, politicians and service organisations attempting to restructure South African cities according to popularly-based democratic principles. Finally he proposes some broad guidelines for professional and ethical behaviour which planners might have to follow in order to find greater relevance in a future South African society.

For the purposes of this chapter Frescura illustrated his points using Johannesburg and Port Elizabeth as primary case studies. However, neither instance should according to Frescura be considered to be unique and surveys conducted by other researchers in this field indicate that similar patterns of growth have been experienced by urban settlements elsewhere in this country.

Frescura's view is that it is clear that although the Group Areas Act was repealed in 1991, the component elements of apartheid planning have been indelibly etched into the urban fabric of South African cities. It is probable that their effects will continue to be felt for many years to come and that their traces may never be entirely expunged from the South African urban fabric.

Changes, as Frescura sees them, are not likely to take place through a long-term, liberal, free-market exchange of land, but will probably require a series of stringent land and price controls orchestrated through a city government committed to strong democracy, community empowerment and the generation of wealth. This is not a philosophy likely to find favour with the broad white electorate, nor with white liberals or the country's neo-Democrats, all of whom have benefited extensively from the implementation of apartheid's economic measures.

However the Apartheid City was the creation of a doctrine-driven central government and was only achieved through the imposition of extreme hardships upon the black community. These families are now entitled to a form of restitution and some of the ways in which this could take place are through an improved quality of housing, life and economic opportunities.

Frescura uses an architectural metaphor to illustrate this – the edifice of apartheid was only made possible by a structure, a scaffolding, of inter-supporting laws and edicts. Once the building was completed and could stand alone and unassisted, then the scaffolding could be dismantled and removed. It is true that, since 2 February 1990, the Nationalist Government assiduously removed the legal props to apartheid, but the substantive structure of economic inequality inherited from that system is still very much in place. Its granite face will not be affected by rubber mallets, but will require a demolition tool made of sterner materials.

This also means that the planning profession will have to undergo severe structural changes if it is to meet the needs of a future democratic South Africa. It is clear that, in the past, it was the work of planners that gave the apartheid ideology its physical dimensions and permitted its implementation on the ground. The design of radial roads, limited access townships, *cordons sanitaires* and segregated facilities reveals a to-talitarian mind-set reflective of an oppressive and unjust society. It is now up to the new generation of town planners to reconcile the mistakes of the past with the realities of the future and help South Africa achieve the greatness it deserves.

Frescura's chapter appears to indicate a South Africa in which future urban residen-tial settlement will develop more on a class basis than on a racial basis, as has happened in the past. This lends added weight to the argument of many analysts who maintain after William Julius Wilson that as the influence of race in a society declines, as is happening in South Africa at present, class considerations will come to have greater significance in social stratification. Consequently, Frescura has made a considerable contribution to this volume, especially if one considers that class is also an important factor in forming identities across traditional – often racial – cleavages. Although the spectre of class divisions can create new conflicts, it can, in South Africa, also result in better human relations.

Chapter 4:
Children in violent spaces:
a reinterpretation of the 1976 Soweto Uprising
– Hjalte Tin

The chapter by Tin represents a fresh theoretical understanding, relevant to identity information, of the Soweto uprising in 1976 and subsequent events that changed the history of South Africa. It offers a spatial reading of those violent events, rather than the more usual resource mobilization, collective behaviour, conflict theory, political alienation/participation, class, race, political history and unconventional political be-haviour models. In doing this, Tin's analysis uncovers some of the contradictory and many-layered relations between children, parents and state which have, to this day, remained enigmatic. It addresses the central question of the children as attackers: how could they force the strong and seemingly well-entrenched apartheid state to defend itself against *children*?

In his conclusion Tin states that during the six months of rioting primarily by the youth in the townships of Johannesburg, Cape Town and Port Elizabeth the children developed five forms of struggle: fighting inside the townships, contesting the town-ship borders, enforcing stayaways, attacking the white city and ruling the parents. This particular violence mapped three spaces: first, the township, a space defined as different from a white town or city by apartheid ethnicity laws; second, the town or city defined by the complete variety of urban functions, including education; lastly, the private house, defined by the sway of patriarchal authority keeping it separate from all other houses in the town/city. Any matchbox house in Soweto marked a house space while simultaneously being part of the ethnic space of Soweto and the city space of metropolitan Johannesburg. In each of these spaces the children confronted adults: the father, the teacher and the policeman. With the steady disintegration of parental rule, the teacher and the policeman became more exposed.

When the educational authorities provoked the children by trying to enforce Afrikaans as the medium of instruction, the teachers' control of the schools collapsed within hours. The children suddenly confronted the state's last line of defence: police and army units deployed with firearms, armoured vehicles, helicopters, courts, prisons and draconian laws. The conflict had escalated into an all-out attack on the racist foundation of apartheid South Africa. When the children challenged the police and not only put their lives on the line, but lost them, they exposed the timidity of their parents who had been exposed to the same racial discrimination. Within weeks the parents had to acknowledge (inter alia by forming the Black Parents' Association) the children's activist leadership in the inter-generational struggle against white rule. The structure of the uprising had now come the full circle: the children returned to the house as the rulers of the parents.

Accordingly, the children's revolt posed a terrible challenge for the apartheid state, as children do for any state when they take to the street. When the patriarchal house could no longer control the children, the state had to use grossly excessive means to do so: beating small children, detaining minors in prison and killing children. By doing this the state ascribed adult status to the children and when it treated children as adults it exposed its own weakness, both morally and in terms of violence. When the children neither respected their fathers nor their teachers (and obviously not the policemen, one might add) and started burning down schools, the state had only two choices. It could talk to the children as pupils and in a flexible manner try to accommodate their demands or it could turn against the children as black adults using the full force of its repressive apparatus. The first option could possibly have affirmed the children as minors and pupils.

However, the doctrinaire and racist inflexibility of apartheid leaders such as B.J. Vorster, Jimmy Kruger and P.W. Botha left only the second option open.

The result was violence and more violence and then paradoxically the treatment of children as adults, exposing them to beatings, imprisonment and death. This gave the children enormous leverage at the *ethnic* front because here they stood on the same side as their parents: with the parents trailing behind the black children were challenging white supremacy head-on. Just how all-powerful the children became was demonstrated by their enforcement of stayaways and an anti-shebeen[1] drive to which the majority of adults complied. The ruin of the patriarchal house, the crucial input from gangs and the Black Consciousness Movement-inspired overcoming of a black inferiority complex all according to Tin contributed to shaping that formidable fighting force in South Africa, the children. This chapter surely adds to our understanding of the dynamics of the changed dispensation brought about largely through the efforts of the children of South Africa.

Chapter 5:
Categorical and strategic resistance and the making of political prisoner identity in Apartheid's Robben Island Prison
– Fran Lisa Buntman

The chapter by Buntman focuses on two kinds of resistance displayed by prisoners on Robben Island, where political prisoners were held by the apartheid regime. The first, strategic resistance, can be interpreted as a subset of a huge battery of tools, including collaboration, that were accepted and justified as successful ways to undermine apartheid. It consisted of a consideration of the long-term effects of imprisonment and torture, which were central features of apartheid. Strategic resistance always responded to apartheid from the point of view that apartheid would be overcome. Consequently, its adherents were expected to continue their lives and work regardless of whether apartheid continued to intrude into their lives or not.

The practitioners of strategic resistance were arrested in the 1950s and 1960s and had witnessed the complete destruction of the anti-apartheid movement in South Africa. They experienced sentences of many decades and spent the greater part of their adult lives as political prisoners. They had to educate themselves politically while in prison in order to be able to return to the anti-apartheid movement when they were discharged. They sometimes focused on changing the position of the warders by working with them, thereby undermining apartheid for the people who were directly responsible for applying its ideology. They also suffered on Robben Island when that prison was at its most brutal, fighting by means of hunger strikes and physical force. One of the results of their struggle was that they were able to effect considerable changes for the better in prison conditions: better food, beds, practices relating to spending money and postal service. This was brought about by means of a ranking system called classification in terms of which prisoners gained access to more 'privileges' through 'good behaviour'.

The second type of resistance is categorical resistance, in which every manifestation of apartheid was resisted at every available occasion. Both strategic and categorical resistance shape people's identity. However, categorical resistance was according to Buntman an orientation to challenging apartheid that made the core of one's resistance constant opposition to the multitude of sanctions apartheid imposed on society. It was more popular among the younger generation of political prisoners who had, since 1976, suffered the worst hardships under the apartheid regime's brutal attempts to suppress opposition to apartheid. However, by the time that the prisoners from the 1976 generation arrived at Robben Island, the basic human rights that were present in the prison were already installed, largely through the efforts of the older prisoners and their supporters outside of prison.

Buntman addresses the formation of political identity among prisoners held at Robben Island by referring to a duality of challenge and cooperation, by which is meant that prisoners were faced with the same duality as politicians in post-apartheid South Africa. This duality is exemplified by the statements of ex-President Nelson Mandela upon his release from prison. It implies that while much reconstruction work needed to be done to meet the expectations of the black majority oppressed under apartheid, there was also a need to cooperate with white people in order to make them feel "safe". In Robben Island, the prison where political leaders were incarcerated and often identified as a beacon in anti-apartheid politics, a similar duality of purpose developed that culminated in cooperation between three political organizations who later provided many political leaders in South Africa.

Robben Island was established in the early 1960s to imprison black male political prisoners. Conditions were harsh, brutal and dangerous. Many of the older prisoners, especially from the African National Congress (ANC) and the Pan Africanist Congress (PAC) had achieved a degree of unity in prison and had, with the help of supporters outside prison, wrought some changes for the better from prison authorities. Although both the ANC and the PAC were nationalist organisations opposed to apartheid's white minority rule, the ANC believed in working with a range of groups, including white people and communists, while the PAC had carved out a narrower African identity. A school-student protest that began on 16 June 1976 marked the end of a political lull, both real and apparent, in South Africa. In the intervening years a new political movement, the Black Consciousness Movement (BCM) had emerged out of a myriad of organisations that identified with its ideas, emphasising black self-liberation and psychological self-assertion under the leadership of Steve Biko. The years between 1977 and 1980 were marked by conflict among political prisoners. The conflict was based on both inter- and intra-organisational conflict and also on generation as the ANC and PAC prisoners tended to be older men while the BCM prisoners were younger and included many scholars and university students. Also, both ANC and PAC prisoners attempted to recruit the younger men.

There was in this time of conflict on Robben Island a struggle for ideological and organisational dominance. Identity as strategic resistance tended to dominate. The older men who had been imprisoned longer were more likely to engage in strategic resistance than the younger ones. They had gained improvement in prison conditions by pragmatically resisting the authorities on the island, there was some resignation to the status quo and the older prisoners. They had come to have a practical understanding of resistance, make productive use of imprisonment there and believed they could not expend their energy on constant fights with the authorities. The younger men were more likely to offer categorical resistance. They were often deeply disappointed with the behaviour of the older men they confronted in prison and were proud to define themselves as militants who would resist everywhere and always. They experienced the worst of apartheid's hardships and brutality in the repression of their revolt, with teargassing, torture, beatings, shootings, detention without trial and unjust trials being common in their time. Also, joblessness, already high, increased. Moreover, black consciousness ideology had provided an antidote to the meekness of the older generation.

There was opposition among the younger prisoners to achieving greater privileges in prison such as buying newspapers and food and opportunities for further study by exhibiting greater cooperation with the prison authorities. Buntman takes the view that political identity as strategic resistance does not replace categorical resistance, but builds upon it and requires its militant element. So, the older leadership on Robben Island eventually managed to transform BCM members. In this, ex-President Nelson Mandela's simultaneous militancy and conciliation played a crucial role in determining the abiding political identity within anti-apartheid politics on Robben Island and outside the prison, where reconciliation was often more difficult. Accordingly, much was achieved on Robben Island to bridge the generation gap. In this, political unity was attained between the two very groups of political activists and leaders who were together to lead South Africa's first democratic government (the ANC and the BCM).

Buntman's chapter has the merit of highlighting the remarkable role played by Robben Island in shaping the political identity of many people who were later to play leading roles in political and community life in post-apartheid South Africa.

Notes

1   A shebeen is an informal bar, pub or drinking place, often in the days before the demise of apartheid operating without the necessary licence.

Reflections on the colonial state, in South Africa and elsewhere: factions, fragments, facts and fictions

John L. Comaroff

What happens to people without nations...? Are they human beings if they are not citizens?

Julia Kristeva, *Nations Without Nationalism,* p. 26

Paradoxes of the colonial state

Let me begin with a truism. Whatever else it may be concerned with, the so-called 'anthropology of colonialism' exists, above all else, to interrogate the construction, objectification, and negotiation of *difference*. Difference in 3-D, so to speak. As distinction, dualism, discrimination; also as dissension, duplicity, and discord. But *not* just difference between coloniser and colonised, that manichean opposition drawn by imperial regimes – often speciously – to separate ruler from subject, light from dark (Cooper and Stoler, 1997, pp. 3, 9). Also, in a more reflexive register, differences in the way in which colonialism has been conceptualised and characterised in Western scholarship.

As we have ourselves pointed out (Comaroff and Comaroff, 1997a), a new revisionism has arisen.[1] In retreat are received forms of modernisation theory, with their confident liberal humanist teleologies, their utopian narratives of progress; similarly the Marxist (and Marxoid) alternatives, which treat imperialism as a reflex of the global expansion of capitalism, of the articulation of modes of production, of unequal exchange between centres and peripheries, of underdevelopment and dependency. Alongside them has emerged a growing concern with the contingent, constructed, cultural dimensions of colonialism (e.g. Dirks, 1992; Thomas, 1994; Cooper and Stoler, 1997, p. 4): a concern with the making of imperial subjects by means of objects, via the manufacture of desire and the commodification of need; with the reconstruction of non-European 'others', after Foucault, through dispersed disciplinary regimes (e.g.

Thomas, 1990; Mitchell, 1991); with colonies as 'laboratories of modernity' (Stoler, 1995); with the agency of the colonised and its impact on Europe and Europeans (see Trotter, 1990, p. 5). At its most extreme, the grand narrative of colonialism in the Western academy has been replaced by one which treats the phenomenon as protean, almost incoherent. Even among the less postmodern, dialectics have often given way to dialogics, political economy to poetics, class conflict to consumption, the violence of the gun to the violation of the text, world-historical material processes to local struggles over signs and styles, European domination to post-Hegelian hybridity (Comaroff and Comaroff, 1997a, p. 15).

This is something of an over-statement, obviously. There are still many who argue, influentially, for older perspectives. And some who essay a range of positions in between.[2] Indeed, I myself hold that neither image of colonialism is right or wrong; that each refers to different moments in, different perspectives on, different aspects of its workings over the long-run. I also believe that the pendulum swing across this range of positions has had a liberating effect on the anthropological study of the encounter between Europe and its significant 'others', pushing it in new, creative directions. But I do have one lingering concern with the question of the colonial state.

George Steinmetz commented three years ago, that, for all the recent attention given to colonialisms of various types and times, the colonial state itself is rarely theorised.[3] True, its functions are often spelled out:[4] for some, they lie primarily in the regulation of material processes; for others, they are to be found, more generally, in the establishment and maintenance of social order through the imposition of legal and other administrative mechanisms; for yet others, they derive from an ensemble of institutions created to open a space for, and to protect, various projects of European expansion; for a few, they inhere in violence, terror, and coercion, framed as the guarantee of physical security for the coloniser against the colonised. This inventory is not exhaustive, of course.

For one thing, postmodern notions of the workings of the colonial state, as we shall see, include a broad range of disciplinary and regulatory practices, the object of which is twofold: to recast the experienced reality, the existential world, of the colonised *and* to re-present back to Europe its own modernist sense of self, thus to naturalise its world picture and the forms of knowledge legitimated therein (see e.g. Mitchell, 1991, p. x). But, I stress, these are all functional descriptions, a mode of knowing the beast by its effects (see Corrigan and Sayer, 1985, p. 2).

What is more, their conceptual and empirical bases are far from established. Hence Steinmetz's caution. If he is correct, we have yet to answer some fairly fundamental questions.

What precisely *is* 'the colonial state?' Is it a definite or an indefinite article? One thing or many things or nothing at all? Is it a process? A series of institutional mechanisms? A specific form of governance?[5] A cultural construct? An existential state of being-in-the world? Do the various functions typically ascribed to it, from different theoretical and ideological perspectives, amount to a convincing account of its historical workings? And how does it differ from its European counterpart, the metropolitan state 'at home'?[6] Is there anything of interest to be derived from the fact that, just as the term 'state' has two connotations in its noun form – the state, that is, as political order, structure, institution; the state as a condition-of-being – so as a verb it denotes to 'give voice', to 'articulate', to 'narrate'? Does anything lie hidden in this fortuitous homonym?[7]

It is to these questions that I direct my reflections on the colonial state in 19th and 20th century South Africa. And elsewhere. I do so by exploring, in a manner deliberately eclectic and fragmentary – at times, even, frankly elementary – some of the dominant facts and fictions surrounding its social archaeology.[8] Also by interrogating the dominant theoretical approaches to its description. The point of doing a parallel, paradigmatic 'reading' of these alternative narratives is not, I stress, to tender a literature review. It is to cast radically new light on the nature of colonial governmentality, modernity, and the culture of legality at its core.

Modernist master narratives, left and right

> [T]he state is a territorial entity struggling to impose its will upon a fluid and spatially open process of capital circulation. It has to contest within its borders the factional forces and fragmenting effects ... of capital[ism] ... To do so effectively the state must construct an alternative sense of community to that based on money, as well as a definition of public interests over and above the class and sectarian interests and struggles that are contained within its borders. It must, in short, legitimise itself.
>
> David Harvey, *The Condition of Postmodernity*, p. 108

There is no need, in this context, to open up the question of why European colonisers – first Dutch, then British – found their way to southern Africa; or how 'the colonial state', in its various guises, established itself here from the late seventeenth century onwards.[9] At first, European governance covered a relatively limited, though gradually expanding, coastal territory (see Krüger, 1969, p. 325). Pragmatically speaking, it set itself a fourfold mandate, the cumulative 'responsibilities' of empire which were later to be seen and rationalised as the 'white man's burden' in Africa: (i) the 'discovery' of dark, unknown lands, which were conceptually emptied of their peoples and cultures so that their 'wilderness' might be brought properly to order – i.e., fixed and named and mapped – by an officialising white gaze;[10] (ii) the 'pacification' of native 'tribes' seen to be endemically unruly and thus requiring, even desiring, Pax Britannica or another European equivalent;[11] (iii) the facilitation of 'commerce and adventurous industry' (Barrow, 1801 – 4,1, p. 8), both metropolitan and local, thus to civilise the savages, to draw them into the virtuous beneficence of empire, and, simultaneously, to enrich the 'mother country'; and (iv) rational administration – itself taken everywhere to be a condition of possibility for the economic 'management' (read 'exploitation') of colonies (see Ajayi, 1969, p. 505) – which consisted in part of the maintenance of law and order, in part of a regime of predictable bureaucratic and fiscal practices.[12] As Weber (1968, p. 1394) would later put it, writing of states in general: 'the bureaucratic state, adjudicating and administering according to rationally established law and regulation, is ... closely related to the modern capitalist development, [which] rests primarily on *calculation* and presupposes a legal and administrative system, whose functioning can be rationally predicted ... just like the expected performance of a machine.'

'Sociologically speaking', he was wont to say, 'the modern state is an 'enterprise' just like a factory'. This, certainly, is how colonial administrations in many parts of Africa liked to represent themselves – though, as Lord Lugard (1997 [1922], p. 574) stressed, it was always deemed important to make it clear, alike 'to the educated native, the conservative Moslem, and the primitive pagan', that 'Government [was] not antagonistic but ... sympathetic to his aspirations', protective of 'his natural rights', and 'in touch with [his] thought and feeling'.[13]

The fourfold mandate taken upon themselves by colonial regimes in Africa – discovery, pacification, commerce, and rational administration – implied that the master narrative of European imperial expansion, its narrative of mastery, would place 'the state' at the centre of the story: that 'the state', in the singular, would be at once the *ur*-protagonist, the organising trope, and the *fons et origo* of an epic history; that its heroic personages would, for the most part, be public figures – *state*men – who were agents of overrule and governance, broadly conceived; also, as a result, that this history would, in its authoritative telling, be political rather than cultural, social, or even, in the first instance, economic.[14] Which, of course, has turned out to be the case.

It has been said, quite often recently, that history in its modernist form – as a chronicle of public events and heroic actions – *is* re-presentation (Comaroff and Comaroff, 1992, p. 176); the authoritative self-representation, in particular, of the nation-state (Anderson, 1983). And, since colonialism everywhere has been inextricably implicated in the making of European modernity (Stoler, 1995), in the maturation of its sovereign communities (Cooper and Stoler, 1997, p. 18), it is hardly surprising that imperial encounters should have been written as the political histories of states acting out their destinies on other peoples, other places.

In South Africa, as much if not more than anywhere else, both liberal and conservative histories place almost exclusive emphasis on the role of the colonial state in the domestication and development of the subcontinent; or did until very recently.[15]

Owusu (1975, pp. 34–35), although writing in a more general key, describes nicely the epistemic bases of the orthodox historiography of South Africa.[16] He observes that accounts in this tradition are, wittingly or otherwise, grounded in 'theories' of modernisation. These accounts take as axiomatic the *inevitability* of modernity; again, his italics, his scepticism. They emphasise its gradual, excruciatingly long-term evolution, presume the centrality of government in effecting its progress or retardation, and treat its narrative, ultimately, as political, even when focusing on material processes.

As told from this perspective, the story of the colonial state in South Africa over the *longue durée* is usually divided into four broad periods: (i) 1652–1806, the phase of Dutch mercantile rule, interrupted briefly by an English takeover; (ii) 1806–c.1870, the early British years, in which imperial governance was restricted in both geographical and administrative scope, and during which two breakaway white settler republics were established in the interior; (iii) 1870 – 1910, the age of the great mineral and industrial revolution – and 'scramble for Africa' – when the United Kingdom sought to extend its control over the subcontinent as a whole; and (iv) 1910 – 1994, the epoch of the Union of South Africa, a dominion within the British Commonwealth, which culminated in the rise and fall of apartheid.

Each of these periods is narrated around a few dominant motifs; these are the topoi that mandate the selection and interpretation of historically significant events. One is the role of the state in regulating (often bitterly agonistic, antagonistic) relations among whites; in particular, between those Europeans who later congealed into the Afrikaner 'people', an agrarian population which came to resent the liberal social attitudes of the British administration toward Africans, and English settlers, who regarded themselves as much more cosmopolitan and enlightened (see Coetzee, 1988, p. 9; Streak, 1974, p. 5).[17] Another is the centrality of the colonial state in governing 'native' populations, in overseeing their 'discipline' and 'development'. This took many forms, all clothed in a mass of legalities: among them, the introduction of so-called 'indirect rule', which ostensibly retained local government in the hands of traditional authorities (Lugard, 1922) but, in fact, made most chiefs and kings into menial civil servants of empire; the delimitation of African land into 'reserves' and 'locations'; the regulation – often by the naked manipulation of black economic viability – of flows of people, primarily as 'labour units', to centres of industrial (and, less frequently, agrarian) production; the claim to be civilising those people through enlightened rule, by such modernist means as the provision of education, the extension of public health facilities – and, more baldly, through wage work itself (see Comaroff and Comaroff, 1992, pp. 199, 204).

A third motif is the function of the state as a site for, and a mediator in, struggles between Europeans and Africans, especially over land and labour, property and rights (see Gann and Duignan, 1969, p. 5); this in spite of the fact that it was often an interested player in those very struggles, sometimes annexing territory and imposing regulatory mechanisms to further its own material interests (see Lonsdale and Berman, 1979, p. 496). Its adjudicatory role was most dramatically enacted in the innumerable official commissions of enquiry held by the British administration over the years (see Ashforth, 1990; see below). These arbitrated disputes of widely varying kinds. And, in doing so, they served also to reinforce the legitimacy of the state as a superordinate structure of governance.

The last theme, some would say the most significant, is the engagement of colonial states in the economics of empire, both at home and abroad. Liberal and conservative histories alike pay exquisitely detailed attention to the ways in which these states intervened – with greater or lesser efficacy, in the face of greater or lesser resistance – to promote European commerce; to protect the agrarian and other enterprises of expatriate settlers and frontier farmers; to facilitate the extraction of raw materials and 'native' labour power; to develop trade networks and markets of various kinds; and, from the 1870s onward, to interpolate itself into an unfolding mineral and industrial revolution.

As I have said, *all* event histories of colonialism in South Africa, written from orthodox perspectives, are ultimately distilled into sequences of actions and processes around these topoi. What is more, such histories usually treat the state as an intrinsically *benign* force, one which sought to balance the interests and welfare of the various parties under its sovereign jurisdiction.[18]

Its excesses, its tendencies toward brute domination and its descents into violence, its scandals and corruptions, its inefficiencies and incoherences, its deployment for the enrichment of some at the expense, even destitution, of others – to the degree that they are recognised at all – are typically treated as aberrations, as ruptures in an otherwise seamless narrative of progress. And they are, by and large, blamed not on the systemic contradictions of colonialism itself, or on any kind of structural consideration, but on misanthropic or misguided individuals. In this respect, Harvey (1989, p. 108) is correct: the state is portrayed here – much as it represented itself – as embodying, serving, and protecting a public good, a collective interest and sense of being-in-the-world, against the sectarian differences and struggles contained within its borders.[19]

Neo-Marxist historians of colonialism in South Africa, highly influential in the 1970s and 1980s, contest all this on a number of counts.[20] In the first place, they question the primacy of politics. For them, it was the development of industrial capitalism, its material logic, that motivated the story of empire and its aftermath; from their standpoint, the state was the administrative, bureaucratic armature of capital, a superstructure with limited autonomy, will, or agency of its own.

Its power, its physical and fiscal capacity for coercion, is held to have served one end above all others: the exploitation and regulation of labour – and, concomitantly, the construction of a homogenous black underclass – in the cause of capitalist development (see e.g. Wolpe, 1988; Magubane, 1979; Unterhalter, 1995, p. 218–19 *et passim*). Interestingly, this is a view that Weber (1968, p. 1394), typifying the modernist state in general, comes close to articulating:

> The 'separation' of the worker from the material means of production, destruction, administration, academic research, and finance in general is the common basis of the modern state, in its political, cultural and military sphere, and of the private capitalist economy ...

But it is to Marx, not Max Weber, that these historians have looked in dealing with the state in Africa. Says Harvey (1990, p. 108, after Marx), writing of 'Modernisation':

> [t]he state, constituted as a coercive authority that has a monopoly over institutionalised violence forms a[n] ... organising principle through which a ruling class can seek to impose its will not only on its opponents but upon the anarchical flux, change, and uncertainty to which capitalist modernity is always prone.[21]

Its tools of coercion vary, he adds. They include the imposition of taxes and levies; the provision or withholding of social and physical infrastructure; control over wages and salaries in the public sector; and a monopoly of the means of surveillance, of military might and police repression. For his own part, Harvey (1990, p. 109) goes on to argue that 'the relation between capitalist development and the state has to be seen ... as mutually determining rather than unidirectional'. Neo-Marxist historians in South Africa are wont to see political institutions more unidirectionally; less as a response to the anarchical flux or uncertainties of modernity – less, also, as a 'principle' through which 'ruling classes' impose their will – than as a creature of the inexorable *logic* of capital itself (see Corrigan and Sayer, 1985, p. 2).

But they would agree about the tools of coercion typically used by colonial regimes. They would also go one further step with Marx himself. In his essay on colonialism in *Capital* (1967, I, p. 765), he argues that:

> In the colonies the capitalist régime everywhere comes into collision with the resistance of the producer, who, as owner of his own conditions of labour, employs that labour to enrich himself, instead of the capitalist. The contradiction of these two diametrically opposed economic systems, manifests itself here practically in a struggle between them. Where the capitalist has at his back the [state] power of the mother-country, he tries to clear out of his way by force, the modes of production and appropriation, based on the independent labour of the producer.[22]

The integration of black South Africans into the capitalist economy of colonial South Africa – through the forcible destruction of their modes of production – is narrated in a manner reminiscent of various species of dependency and world-systems theory. Notwithstanding arguments over the details, we are told repeatedly, and with considerable persuasiveness, how African societies were deliberately impoverished and their economies subverted – 'underdeveloped' is often the verb of choice – thus to make them dependent on a mix of underpaid migrant wage labour in the urban industrial sector (done mainly done by men) and underproductive rural agriculture (done largely by women). For example, most of the contributors in the landmark volume, *The Roots of Rural Poverty* (Palmer and Parsons, 1977), show how one or other vigorous African economy became subordinated to the special conditions of *capitalist development* in Southern Africa

> by overt political controls, as well as through 'unseen' and natural factors affecting production and trade, [the mining industry and other capitalist interests] restricted local production and trade, manipulated the terms of trade to create a structure in which the black periphery invariably paid tribute to the white centre in capital funds and resources as well as labour.
>
> Parsons, 1977, p. 137

The same argument, broadly, is reiterated throughout the neo-Marxist historical canon, some of it very finely wrought (see e.g. Bundy, 1972, 1979; Marks and Rathbone, 1982; Marks and Trapido, 1987). It is capitalist development that is the prime mover of the process of underdevelopment and social transformation. The role of the state is to provide the 'overt political controls' with which to facilitate that process. No more, no less.

A qualification here. From other parts of Africa have come efforts to write a more nuanced version of the neo-Marxist narrative.[23] Lonsdale and Berman (1970, p. 487), for example, hold that government was never just 'a loyal minister to capital's needs'. Regarding colonialism, fundamentally, as an 'articulation of modes of production' (after Rey, 1971, 1973; Foster-Carter, 1978), they argue that the state was 'relatively autonomous' (see Wallerstein, 1974, p. 402).

Why? Because it had to appear as a 'factor of cohesion', an 'even-handed arbiter' presiding over the conjoining of different, often inimical, material and social worlds (p. 489); echoes here of Harvey (see above). Moreover, government could not simply oblige the political and financial interests of colonisers, as these were often contradictory and excessive.

But, if the state could 'not be the servant of capital', it certainly was 'the protector of capitalist social relations' (pp. 489–90). Here then is the nuance: it was capital*ism*, rather than capital, of which governance was a reflex. Indeed, the state is itself defined by Lonsdale and Berman as 'the historically conditioned set of institutions in any class society which ... secures the social conditions for the production of the dominant mode of production' (p.489).

Relatively autonomous? Maybe. However, far from being 'a disinterested ... arbiter', colonial administrations 'never ceased to provide the conditions for the reproduction of settler capitalism' (p. 504). Which implies that, for all the effort to refine its role, the state remains, literally, a supporting player in the political economy of colonialism. We shall return to this in due course.

Panoptics, power, and postmodern counter-narratives

> Aylesbury Prison, England, 1918. He was stripped and put in a cell with a stone floor and no glass in the window - this is January, mind ... [But] he said in his letter that it was not the cold that bothered him, it was being watched all the time. The eye in the door ... an elaborately painted eye [inside the cell]..., was deeply disturbing ... "S not so bad so long as it stays in the door. You start worrying when it gets in [your head]'.[24]
>
> Pat Barker, *The Eye in the Door*, p. 36

A new chapter has recently opened up in the historical anthropology of colonialism in South Africa. It is one which is evoking a great deal of alarm among scholars of various stripes, largely because it subverts a host of conceptual certainties and methodological mantras.[25] Born of the revisionism of which I spoke at the outset – and grounded in Michel Foucault's discourses on power, governmentality, and the modernist subject – it has not yet been fully worked out in this part of the world. Timothy Mitchell's *Colonising Egypt* (1991) is perhaps the most completely realised example in Africa, and it is written about the other end of the continent. As this suggests, the alarm is somewhat premature, anticipatory. Nonetheless, it is a harbinger of postmodern, poststructuralist, and post-Marxist perspectives that *are* beginning to make themselves felt here as never before.

It is not my intention to offer a systematic introduction to Foucault on power and governmentality. I should like, instead, to make a few summary points of typification, sketching briefly the ways in which a postmodern 'reading' of the colonial state might proceed in the South African context.

From a Foucauldian perspective, the state is *itself* a disciplinary formation. In its modernist mode, its power is less instrumental and institutional than it is 'capillary'; which is to say that it stretches, autonomically and unseen, into the very construction of its subjects, into their bodily routines and the essence of their selfhood. Indeed, it is by inculcating a deeply interiorised, individuated sense of *self*-regulation – through its various techniques of surveillance; its clinics, schools, prisons, and other sites of control; its censuses, surveys, and cognate forms of serialisation and accounting; its modes of knowing and objectifying personhood through the 'human sciences'; its 'natural' institutions like the family and fatherhood, established religion and organised recreation, competitive sports and commodified regimes of consumption – that the state imposes order on its citizenry. Order, that is, in both the sense of regularity and regulation, of convention and command, of civility and servility. This involves the fabrication of an entire space-time world – and the insinuation of its logic into the mundane practices of human beings-as-citizens. Thus are subjects subjected to modes of social control that are rendered invisible in their very enactment.

In order to analyse the workings of colonial states, then, it follows that we ought to look to their capillary techniques of regulation; to the ways in which they sought (and seek) to instil a dispositional sense of self-discipline in their subjects. But there is a caveat here. Unlike the European polities with which Foucault himself was concerned, and of which Benedict Anderson (1983) has written so influentially, colonies were never places of even tenuously-imagined homogeneity. For the most part, their administration was vested in states without hyphenation, as it were: in states without nations. Here, in a nutshell, lay the roots of the contrast between metropolitan and colonial governance, even when the second was merely an extension 'overseas' of the first: one depended, for its existence, on the ideological work of manufacturing sameness, of engendering a horizontal sense of fraternity; the other, despite its rhetoric of universalising modernity, was concerned with the practical management, often the production, of difference. Consequently, imperial regimes abroad were always caught up in a 'doubling', a contradiction: at the very same time as they spoke of transforming colonised peoples into civilised – i.e. 'modern' – free, right-bearing citizens, they dealt in heterogeneity by naturalising ethnic difference and essentialising racial inequality. The former was entailed, if nothing else, in converting 'savages' into proletarians.[26] The latter was implicit in the grammar of cultural diversity, and in the organic anthropology, on which were erected the hierarchical structures of 19th- and twentieth-century colonial rule.[27] This is the base contradiction of colonialism. Its teleology pointed one way (toward secular modern *citizen*ship and, eventually, nationhood), its reality another (toward a racinated world of ethnic *subjec*tion). In the European optic of Empire, 'natives' were always subject/citizens in the making.

But how, precisely, did colonial states set about (re)constructing the identities, the being-in- the-world, of those over whom they extended their governance? Wherein lay their applied anthropology? On the understanding that these were parallel processes – indeed, two sides of the same subject-in-formation – let us look, first, at the making of the serialised, modernist citizen, then at the fashioning of the ethnicised 'native'.

In Africa, the construction of the aboriginal as a colonial citizen, from the vantage of the state and its functionaries, had a great deal to do with the political economy and pragmatics of overrule. As long as they lived in their own communities, ruled by their own chiefs and customs, 'natives' might remain faceless and nameless. But the moment they became imbricated in colonial society – be it as workers or commodity farmers, as subalterns or servants, as sellers or buyers – they had to have individual identities, first and family names, rights and responsibilities. How, otherwise, could they enter into binding contracts or be prosecuted for wrongs? How, otherwise, could they be made to pay various monetary tariffs and levies?[28] How, otherwise, could their movements, their marriages and divorces, their persons, property, and possessions, be regulated?

In short, the making of 'savages' into 'citizens' – itself a highly variable, always incomplete process – was, typically, a corollary of (i) the mobilisation of a stable army of (often migrant) workers into the capitalist sector, which demanded that employees be tied by legal agreements and that defection from factory, farm, or mine be criminalised; of (ii) taxation, in cash, through which the cost of colonial governance could be more-or-less offset and people coerced into the labour market; of (iii) the introduction and administration of 'privately' owned assets, including land, which entailed the recognition of deeds and titles, testaments and estates; and of (iv) the oversight of domestic life, in the name of which states sanctioned the formation, location, reproduction, and dissolution of families, thus reaching deep into the everyday existence of their members.

All this was effected, over the long run, by a range of now familiar mechanisms of enumeration, serialisation, individuation, and identification. These, as Weber would have had us expect (see above), included the official registration of births (hence, also, of names) and deaths (along, in time, with the execution of wills); the certification of legal wedlock and its dissolution; population censuses (of both humans and animals),[29] the establishment of tax rolls as well, often, as the introduction of identity papers;[30] and the increasing bureaucratisation, documentation, rationalisation, and registration of all aspects of social and personal life. In many places, not least in 19th century South Africa, these processes were actively resisted. Tswana, for example, referred to them as 'the English mode of warfare': they were held to reduce 'human beings [and their relations] to pieces of paper', and were seen as instruments of violence by which indigenous peoples were dispossessed of their property and freedom of movement. Throughout the country during the 20th century, moreover, 'pass books', a notorious form of identity document which 'Bantu' had to carry on them, were periodically burned in public, leading to mass struggles with police.[31] In the late apartheid years, in fact, protesting blacks frequently targeted state offices, seeking to burn tax registers, pass records, census files, and the like.

In its effort to create colonial citizens of colour, the state was abetted, if sometimes unwittingly, by other European expatriates. The most notable were Protestant evangelists, among the earliest colonisers in South Africa. Also the most thoroughgoing: as

Bohannan (1964, p. 22) notes, they sought not just to extract labour power, raw materials, or real estate from 'heathen nations', but to recast their life-worlds *tout court*. The civilising mission was intended to effect a 'revolution in the habits' of Africans (Philip, 1828, p. 355), above all, by making them into discrete individuals (Comaroff and Comaroff, 1991, 1997a): by breaking down their 'semi-communistic ways'[32] and severing the 'promiscuous' webs of relations that bound them together; by clothing them in 'proper' garb, so that their 'private parts' would be modestly hidden, their bodies would be appropriately enclosed, and their physical secretions would not 'rub off' on each other; by persuading them to treat marriage as an ensemble of rights and duties, a contract between two consenting people – and to live, monogamously, in 'decent' nuclear family homes on neatly fenced-off squares of land; by taking their children into schools and teaching them to be self-controlled, self-motivated students, capable of advancing by dint of personal effort; by encouraging each man to work on his own behalf as wage-earner and breadwinner for his family, and to appreciate the virtues of money, the market, and private property; in short, by seeking, through every means available, to ensure that their would-be converts were self-contained beings, at once biologically and legally complete unto themselves.

If these were the techniques by which colonisers sought to recast Africans as citizens, their fabrication as ethnic, racialised subjects followed a somewhat different (dis)course. The transformation of the southern African landscape into an ethnoscape depended, first and foremost, on a colonising cartography. I noted earlier that the 'dark continent' was treated as an empty space until it fell under the European gaze, thence to be mapped, by means of conventional graphic images, onto an expansive imperial world-picture. As a much-quoted contemporary poem by Jonathan Swift had it (Curtin, 1964, p. 198; Comaroff and Comaroff, 1991, p. 324, note 6):

> ... Geographers in Afric-Maps
> With Savage Pictures fill their Gaps.

Colonial cartography replaced those pictures, and the epistemic gaps they covered, with charts based on 'scientific' observation; charts grounded in a political geography that was intended, explicitly, to facilitate imperial command.

It entailed the compilation of an atlas on which aboriginal 'tribes' and 'peoples' – invented sometimes, and ascribed a collective identity if they did not already share one[33] – were labelled, classified linguistically, and placed in bounded territories; each of the latter being designated as the realm of a legitimate political authority, be it a king, chief, headman, or potentate of some other kind.[34]

For the British, in fact, European rule without this kind of cartography did not actually amount to colonialism, *sensu stricto*, at all. As Harvey (1990, p. 255) has noted, quoting Foucault:

> If space... is always a container of social power, then the reorganisation of space
> is always a reorganisation of the framework through which social power is
> expressed. Not only a reorganisation, of course. Also a re-presentation. Espe-
> cially a representation of new ethnological fixities, of the geographies of gov-
> ernance implied in reducing the living, three dimensional worlds of indigenous
> populations to timeless, two dimensional abstractions.

Such were things that functionaries of the colonial state understood well, whether they
put them into words or not; to be sure, they underlay the imposition of 'indirect'
rule', the creation of 'tribal reserves', and the transformation of indigenous sover-
eigns into the lowest civil servants of empire, its rural tax collectors and labour recruit-
ers. Hence the obsession of imperial bureaucracies with mapping – and all that went
with it.

One thing that did go with it, with palpable regularity, were so-called 'government
commissions of enquiry' (see Ashforth, 1990). These commissions took a variety of
forms and addressed a wide range of issues. Among other matters, they investigated
existing territorial arrangements, laid down formal boundaries between political communities, and dealt with land claims and disputes; interrogated the nature of indigenous authority and defined the scope of 'native' administration, particularly in respect
of 'law and custom';[35] inquired into labour relations and contracts, and framed the
terms of wage work for blacks, including so-called master-servant provisions, which
tied employees to their employees.[36] Some had specific mandates, others were charged
with very general briefs.[37] But, whatever else they did, these government commissions
tended to see their task as *ethnological*; they documented vernacular life-ways – all the
better, ostensibly, to reduce chaos to order and to facilitate fair and just rule on the part of
the colonial state. In this regard, it is no exaggeration to say that they compiled the
first *official* ethnographic records of the peoples of the region. True, they often relied
on the earlier (and much more detailed) writings of missionaries and 'scientific' ex-
plorers. But they also did their own research, interviewing informants, predominantly
chiefs and elders, to ascertain their 'habits' and 'traditions'. Many of their descriptions
were very thin by modern anthropological standards; still, these documents became
compendia of authoritative information about local cultures. Later they gave way to (i)
annual reports, submitted by administrators of 'native' districts, which reported on
continuity and change in customary practices; and, after the formation of the Union of
South Africa, (ii) ethnological surveys written by the professionally-trained staff of the
Department of Native Affairs in Pretoria.[38]

Government commissions, in sum, gave bureaucratic currency and practical reality
to the categorical structures and cultural divisions that formed the emerging ethnoscape
of Southern Africa. What is more, by treating those categories and cultures as primor-
dially given, the state naturalised them – and, in time, elevated them into hegemonic,

taken-for-granted forms of naming-and-knowing (see Cooper and Stoler, 1997); until, that is, anticolonial struggles began to unravel them. But that was to occur later. As we have shown, the encounter between autochthonous peoples and the civilising mission in the late 18th and early 19th century was deeply implicated in the genesis of modern ethnic identities and differences here.

But the *official* inscription of such identities and differences increasingly became the business of colonial governance. In legitimising labels and authorising images of otherness – and in laying an anthropological basis for its dispersed regimes of regulation – the state tried hard to ensure both the consent and the collaboration of the colonised. Glimpses here of Gramsci, foreshadowings of Fanon.[39] Mirroring back to the colonised images of themselves as ethnic, racialised subjects occurred in many contexts, both ordinary and awesome. Such images – at once verbal, pictorial, even musical – saturated the everyday life of the public sphere and its popular media. They also found formal representation in museums, where 'traditional' cultures were marked off, their 'folkways' displayed in timeless dioramas; in scholarly treatises and manuals on language and orthography, habits, lore, and customs; in national ceremonies, monuments, and rituals, especially those evocative of the 'discovery' and forceful domination of South Africa; in the theology and practice of white settler Christianity; and in a range of other specular and spectacular events. Most potently of all, perhaps, they pervaded schooling at all levels, infused alike in formal syllabi and 'hidden' curricula; all the more so as 'native' instruction passed from the purview of Christian missions to that of the state.

There is no need here to explain why European pedagogy, with its invasive technologies of mind and body, was a crucial vector in the effort to insinuate new signs and practices among colonised peoples. For all their disagreement over the means and ends of education, liberal apologists and Marxist critics appear to agree on one thing: its efficacy in colonising the consciousness of imperial subjects. And in recasting the epistemic topography of the world they inhabited, fixing its images along new axes of knowing-and-being.[40] Those images, moreover, had a distinctive cast to them. They came from a particular, and particularly refractory, angle of vision, portraying the essential 'native' as a primitive conservative. Having had their cultures labelled, objectified, and dehistoricised[41] – and their differences primordialised – ethnic subjects found themselves all alike depicted as benighted, anachronistic antimoderns. They were said to be governed by the primal sovereignty of their customs and customary rulers (J.L. Comaroff, 1995) – under conditions that encouraged them to cling unquestioningly, and in the face of all reason, to their ancestral traditions and taboos.[42]

In response, the colonial state, practicing its own politics of unreason, criminalised some cultural practices (those, for example, surrounding 'witchcraft', polygyny, marriage payments, and 'ritual murder') and endorsed others (like so-called 'customary law') – depending, in no small measure, on the exigencies of governance. It also appealed to the primal hold of custom to prevent social change, even when (no, especially when) it was demanded by indigenous peoples; also, in some celebrated instances, to restrict or remove their rights.

Thus, to take one case, the British Bechuanaland Land Commission of 1886 (Great Britain, 1886) invoked the 'ancient tribal system' of 'communal tenure' to prevent a Tswana sovereign from introducing individual rights of property ownership in one of the provinces under his dominion; this in spite of his having had strong local support, and sound economic and political reasons, for the move (Schapera, 1983). Prior to overrule, such a legislative innovation would have been well within his jurisdiction (Comaroff and Comaroff, 1997a, pp. 399–400; Schapera, 1970). Now, however, the colonial state authorised itself to decide that his subjects were 'not ready' for the change. Similarly, and more seriously, the South African Native Affairs Commission (South Africa, 1905) argued against universal franchise by claiming that Africans preferred 'traditional' forms of collective representation. On this basis, it went on to recommend a reduction of black voting rights in national and provincial elections. The Commission also declared that economic and social arrangements based on 'individualism', to which they had long been told to aspire in the name of modernity, was not suited to aboriginal peoples; being under the primal sway of ancestral custom, they were 'unready' for this too.

In the upshot, these peoples were encouraged to see themselves as faceless Zulu or Tswana or Sotho or Xhosa or whatever, with no consideration of their class or gender or generation or personal circumstances. As Sartre (1955, p. 215; see Zahar, 1974, p. 19) once said, the distinctive experience of colonialism is being made to feel, and then to recognise one's self, as a 'native' (Comaroff and Comaroff, 1997a, p. 19). It was an experience to which the actions of the colonial state were strongly to conduce. This brings us back full circle to the doubling, the contradiction, at the core of the colonial encounter. In South Africa, the state spoke,[43] in a promissory voice, of making modern citizens – autonomous, named, right-bearing members of the body politic – out of 'natives' whom it persisted, at the same time, in treating as unmarked ethnic subjects. On one hand, 'Non-Europeans', the official term of negation by which people of colour were known, were said to be on the high road to civilisation and citizenship, prosperity and propertied individualism. On the other, they were portrayed, to themselves and the world, as anonymous antimoderns, condemned to live for the foreseeable future in the primal mire of ancient custom. The colonial state often engaged in its own internal arguments over this doubling; it was a recurring register in a broader discourse on 'The Native Problem'. The basic question in this discourse, as Cooper and Stoler (1997, p. 7) have noted, was: 'How much civilisation was appropriate' for aboriginal peoples? It was a question that was answered in many ways over the long-run. But invariably with an eye to reproducing distinction, discrimination, and dualism. Difference, once again, in three dimensions.

The colonial state in critical perspective: absence, absurdity, incoherence

> The actual history of states has been one of continuous growth, both in their
> claim to regulate the lives and property of their subjects, and in their physical
> capacity to enforce such claims ... Yet, paradoxically, the increase in the state's
> range and power has produced countervailing decreases in effectiveness.
>
> Kenneth Minogue, *State*, pp. 239–40

How persuasive, then, are these paradigmatic perspectives on the colonial state, in
South Africa and elsewhere? The differences between them are fairly stark, of course.
Which is why the weaknesses of one appear to be the strengths of the other. For
example, modernist approaches, both orthodox and Marxist, would seem to be on
secure, uncontentious ground in interrogating political economy – in its formal and
institutional dimensions – to get at the workings of the colonial state; the absence of
these very dimensions, it is often said (see Comaroff and Comaroff, 1997a, p. 15), is
the most serious deficiency in postmarxist, postmodern accounts of the same thing.
On the other hand, Foucauldians have been quick to point out that the very construction of something called 'political economy', hardly a category given by nature, itself
occurred as a function of the history of modernity. And of its endemic forms of
power. From this perspective, the reciprocal inattention of pre-Foucauldian sociolo-
gies of the colonial state to its technologies of discipline and representation – to the
ways in which it made its subjects by means of commodities, embodied routines, and
other capillary processes at once cultural and material – is an even more egregious
absence.

These complementary allegations carry considerable weight; each has some right on
its side. But the matter is more complex than it may first look. For one thing, the
obvious corollary does *not* follow: it is not possible simply to add a measure of political economy to postmodern approaches – or more concern with the mechanics of
capillary power to older orthodoxies – and expect a prescription for better understanding the colonial state. As I have already intimated, 'political economy' is an analytic
term with its own archaeology, not a species of empirical phenomena. What it describes, how it is to be understood, is highly contested, both within and across theoretical paradigms - not to mention ideological positions; hence the subtitle of *Capital:
A Critique of Political Economy* (Marx, 1967).

Conversely, capillary processes of governmentality, while obviously important to
take fully into account, pose a paradox of their own: the more comprehensive they
were, the more persuasive in explaining colonial domination, the less colonial states
ought ever to have encountered any resistance, any antagonistic forces at all. They did,
everywhere. And their historical epoch came to a crashing end. Of which more in a
moment. But, even taken purely on their own terms, both modernist and Marxist

perspectives, in all their variants, suffer from critical flaws, fallacies, failures. Let us mention just a few and allow the matter to rest; this on the understanding that paradigmatic critique – by contrast to more specific forms of theoretical exegesis – occurs at a level of generality to which there will always be exceptions and qualifications.

Modernist approaches, left and right alike, may be taken to task on four basic counts. First, in dealing with imperial governance, they seldom distinguish sufficiently between its various spheres and levels; most notably, but not only, between the metropolitan and the colonial state. I have already remarked the ontological difference between them. Its political outworkings are equally crucial. Often cadres and functionaries 'at home' and 'abroad', and in different ministries and departments, fell into bitter conflict with one another over questions of policy, the material and moral economics of colonisation, and the proper means of extending European dominion. It is here, in fact, that some of the most acute 'tensions of empire', to use Cooper and Stoler's (1989, 1997) felicitous phrase, manifested themselves.

These tensions were in part structural, in part perspectival: the imperatives of colonialism, like the fiscal commitment necessary for effective governance, did not appear the same, or equally compelling, to everyone engaged in the business of overrule; such things varied a great deal according to the changing exigencies of time, place, and position. To take one Southern African instance, Sir Charles Rey (1988), self-styled 'monarch' of Bechuanaland, spent years in an acrimonious tussle with Westminster and Pretoria over the appropriate investment of the British exchequer – and, concomitantly, the most suitable form of administration – in the unprofitable Protectorate. Conflicts of this kind, at their most extreme, determined the historical destinies of particular colonies and their indigenous populations. But even when they did not, they affected the ways in which the state exercised its authority, extracted labour and taxes, related to the industrial and/or agrarian economy, and mobilised different technologies of control over both settlers and aborigines.

Second, in treating the colonial state as a generic entity, a monothetic class of phenomenon, modernist discourses have tended to elide an enormously wide spectrum of political, ideological, and imaginative forms. The point is almost too obvious to warrant remark: to speak of the Raj, at the height of its elaboration, in the same breath as the administrations of, say, Lesotho or Zanzibar is not unlike treating an elephant, an emu and an egret as the same kind of creature because they are all part of the animal kingdom. The implication that follows is also self-evident: that 'the colonial state' describes not a thing but a genus of forms and processes, and of historically fluid, evanescent ones at that; that 'it' cannot be typified or theorised in the singular, in the indicative mood, or in the continuous past or present tense; and that generalisations or abstract statements about its workings, especially those derived from paradigmatic cases, are inherently open to deconstruction. For example, Mitchell's (1991) account of imperial governance in Egypt, cogent as it may be, can simply not be replicated for

Swaziland or Uganda. Similarly, when Kaviraj (1995, p. 25) argues that the state was the 'controlling structure' at the epicentre of the colonial world, he seems to take South Asia as his unspoken point of reference; writing from much of Africa in the 19th century, this claim would be flatly wrong.

Third, modernist discourses – again, conservative, liberal, and Marxist alike – have failed adequately even to note, let alone to explain, what we may call 'the Minogue Paradox'. Recall Kenneth Minogue's (1987, p. 239) observation: while states in general have had a history of cumulative growth – in their institutional complexity and the range of their formal authority over the lives and property of citizens – their elaboration has been accompanied by a contrapuntal decrease in the efficacy of their control. This has had many manifestations, from the dramatic collapse of once potent regimes, most recently in Central and Eastern Europe, to the creeping inability of others to exercise a monopoly over the means of violence, to contain the workings of the market or the flow of money, to guarantee the commonwealth or ward off moral panics, to meet the costs of reproducing infrastructure or to turn back the expansion of the 'private' sector; these things being widely, if somewhat crudely, taken as signs of the coming 'crisis' of the nation-state (J.L. Comaroff, 1996). Colonial administrations, likewise, appear to have evinced the Minogue Paradox. The more powerful they became, the more they monitored and managed the life-worlds of those over whom they ruled, the less effective they seem to have been, over the long run, in realising their own objectives: in making 'natives' into compliant subjects, in yielding up a profit to the metropole, in stifling resistance, sometimes even in sustaining the coherence of their own modes of governance (Bissell, 1998) – and, in the finality of history, in surviving the onslaught of anticolonial forces. The Minogue Paradox, in other words, raises a fundamental challenge: how to explain the exquisite counterpoint of legitimacy and limitation, of regulation and resistance, of power and paralysis that animated the history of the colonial state. It is a challenge as yet unmet, a dialectic as yet insufficiently interrogated in modernist narratives of the encounter between Africa and Europe.

The fourth has to do with the relationship between the colonial state and capital. As we saw earlier, both Marxist and liberal traditions have emphasised the close connection between them. From the perspective of the first, recall, the state was a reflex of capital(ism), its ensemble of political, legal, and coercive mechanisms for regulating the labour market; in particular, for overseeing the formation, reproduction, and exploitation of a black proletariat. For the second, grounded in so-called 'modernisation' discourses of one kind or another (see above), it was an essentially benevolent institution that existed to administer the economy for the common good; to mint, manage, and monitor the supply of money, guarantee the banking system, and levy taxes to finance public spending; to ensure law and order, especially among labourers; to facilitate the development of commerce and industry. While this view has been taken to task, repeatedly and effectively, for its ingenuous, roseate view of colonial governance –

and for ignoring the role of the imperial state in creating, racinating, and naturalising inequality – the Marxist alternatives also underplay the complexity of its relationship to the workings of political economy.

Indeed, the state *was* never just a reflex of capital. It often did serve capitalist interests, of course. Even more, there were periods in which government and business appeared indistinguishable. But there were also times when the private sector found itself locked in struggle with the administration – and when the latter took direct action against the former (Lonsdale and Berman, 1979, p. 489). Thus, for instance, in the late 19th century, British officialdom demanded, on more than one occasion, that gold mining companies improve the occupational and living environments of their employees. It also stepped in, on occasion, to legislate minimal conditions in other spheres of the economy. Furthermore, for all the idea that the primary function of colonial authorities was to oversee the recruitment and regulation of labour, a function discharged with variable success, the reality was a lot less straightforward (Comaroff and Comaroff, 1997a). All else aside, many 'natives' migrated in search of work voluntarily, sometimes under the impact of missionary teaching, long before an imperial bureaucracy intervened. In this respect, it is worth noting that the state, as a forcible presence, was a relative late-comer on the scene in much of the South African interior.[44] All of which points to a rather obvious conclusion: that, for all their interconnections, affinities, and articulations, the history of governance is irreducible to a history of political economy or *vice versa*.[45]

Some of the same critical points apply as well to postmodern, poststructuralist, postmarxist analyses of colonial governance. There is no need to expatiate here on the oft-made allegation, noted above, that these analyses short-circuit the manifest materialities of colonial capitalism, not to mention the imbrication of the state in them. More interesting, for present purposes, are three other lines of critique, each of which takes seriously the achievement – *never* to be trivialised – of Foucauldian histories in illuminating the relationship between power, governmentality, and the making of the modern subject. One is that the disciplinary processes associated with the capillary power of colonial regimes – the inculcation of a self-regulating, self-controlled, self-motivated, self-conscious sense of human *be*-ing, of being at once biologically discrete, legally constituted, and socially individuated – were not a function of the state alone. Or even primarily. In most places, they were the provenance of the civilising mission undertaken by Christian evangelists, social reformers, and other 'noncommissioned' agents of empire.[46] In part, this had to do with the unspoken division of imperial labour, in part, with the pragmatics of overrule. Even when, in South Africa and elsewhere, European overseas administrations were at their most elaborate, their instrumental mastery over the everyday lives of indigenous peoples was always incomplete; at times, notably limited. This is not to say that colonial governance was never intrusive, coercive, or violent. It certainly could be. But, in many places, it quickly ran up against the limits of its own possibility; which, in turn, led its functionaries to rely on other expatriates – including those who took pains to distance themselves from political authority – to achieve the end of constraining, chastising, regimenting, and refining '*the* native'. In sum, to see states as the primary vector in the making of racialised subjects, in colonising consciousness, in remapping space, time, and personhood, in exercising capillary power, is to misplace the *deus ex machina* of empire and the export of capitalist modernity.

But there is another, yet more obvious problem with the poststructuralist, postmarxist stress on the capillary character of colonial governance. Put plainly, it is this. Colonial states, like states everywhere, depend(ed) *at once* (i) on instrumental, institutional, tangible forms of coercion, (ii) on means of violence either immanent or manifest, physical or symbolic, (iii) on diffuse, invisible modes of surveillance and discipline, and, in some measure, (iv) on the positive production of consent. As this implies, the instrumental and the capillary are dimensions of all state power; conditions, in fact, of its very existence. True, their proportions vary, with concrete consequences. But, insofar as power, in its modernist guise, is the relative capacity to construct realities – to fashion human subjects and social forms, material value and truth-value, perceptions and intentions, and appropriate modes of action in the world – it always has latent and patent, interiorised and exteriorised, spoken and unspoken, private and public, productive and repressive coordinates. It makes no historical sense, therefore, to reduce colonial rule, *sui generis,* to the insinuation of a singular kind of subjection; all the more so in light of its often unsystematic, murky, even incoherent executive practices. And its simultaneously civilising, criminalising, promissory, exploitative, humanitarian and punitive tendencies. One thing that Foucauldian approaches have not done, significantly, is to explain the *limits* of the capillary. Until they do, the term remains a suggestive adjective, a partial description of colonial governance, not a theory of its workings. Nor is it a description that has elicited unanimous consent. Cooper (1994, p. 1533), for one, makes the case for a competing metaphor:

> power in colonial societies was more arterial than capillary – concentrated spatially and socially, not very nourishing beyond such domains, and in need of a pump to push it from moment to moment and place to place.

Which leads to the third line of critique. It is often said that Foucauldian analyses of governmentality leave no room for resistance; indeed, this is now a rather tired reproach. There is, however, a related point to be made, a point both more telling and more troubling. To put it in the interrogative voice, if the capillary techniques of the colonial state *were* effective, if they *did* inculcate disciplined subjection, why did imperial regimes abroad differ so widely in deploying them? Even more mysterious, why, ask Cooper and Stoler (1997, p. 8), did colonisers spend so much time defining and defending categories and representations which were untenable – and which interfered with their mastery over indigenous populations? Why did they sometimes go to absurd lengths to display their firepower, especially when it was fairly flimsy?[47] Why, in short, were colonial states so prone to failure, to drawing disruptive attention to their own administrative practices and procedures? And why, when they did rely on those very capillary techniques – ostensibly silent, invisible, innocent means of imposing control – did they frequently incur angry reactions? Colonial subjects, it seems, were not easily hoodwinked. Among Tswana, for instance, the figure of the government agent was despised precisely because of his role in counting, taxing, and otherwise regulating the minutiae of their everyday lives. A few of these men were actually put to death.[48] But still more instructive, as a counter-narrative of noncapitulation, is something I alluded to above: that these same people spoke of the colonial culture of legality – the reduction of everything to official documents, contracts, and titles – as 'the English mode of warfare' (J.L. Comaroff, 1997, p. 256). Tswana, clearly, knew violence when they saw it. Or, more accurately, when they could not see it. There is every reason to believe that their heightened awareness of invisible forms of coercion, of silent technologies of surveillance and control, arose out of the contradiction at the core of overrule; out of the fact that 'natives' were promised full, right-bearing citizenship in an enlightened new world, but found themselves delivered into ethnic and racial subjection. This 'doubling' could not but draw their attention, at times ruthlessly, to the means of colonial governance – rendering even the most subtle of those means at once starkly visible and resonantly audible.

As a result, far from instilling self-discipline, the capillary techniques of colonial states played a great part in sparking the dialectics of challenge and riposte, of action and counter-action, of transgression, transformation, and hybridisation; greater than did the brute exercise of imperial instrumentalities. All of which amounts to the exact opposite of what a Foucauldian narrative, at least in unedited, vulgar form, might lead us to expect. That narrative does not, cannot, account for the essential paradox of colonial governance: its capacity to be ordered yet incoherent, rational yet absurd, violent yet impotent; to elicit compliance and contestation, discipline and defiance, subjection and insurrection. Sometimes all at once. And, disconcertingly, in ways that blurred the boundaries between these, apparently antithetical, species of action.

Re-stating the problem, problematising the state(s)

> States, if the pun be forgiven, state ... They define, in great detail, acceptable forms and images of social activity and individual and collective identity ... Indeed, in this sense 'the State' never stops talking.[49]
>
> Corrigan and Sayer, *The Great Arch*, p. 3

It is this paradox, among other things, that makes it impossible to arrive at a point of closure by (re)formulating a neat ideal-typification of '*the* colonial state'. Or of its historical physics. To wit, the very object of composing my reflection as a series of contrapuntal critiques has been to show that the beast *resists* two-dimensional representation; that its variabilities, fluidities, hybridities, limits, and disarticulations over time and space were an overdetermined expression of its inner workings and its dealings with significant 'others'; that it was an immanent structure of diverse possibilities whose concrete political, material, and cultural forms were made, remade, and sometimes unmade in historical practice. As this suggests, the intent behind this somewhat didactic excursion is not to prove received accounts wrong. It is to demonstrate that, while each describes an important aspect of the dynamics of colonial states, all of them are partial, perspectival, incomplete. This, I would submit, flows from paying disproportionate attention to their generic properties rather than to their generative processes; to their existence as an abstract noun rather than as an active verb.

Which takes us back to the conundrums, the Big Questions, I posed at the outset. Recall them. What precisely *is* 'the colonial state?' A definite or an indefinite article? One thing or many or nothing at all? A process? A series of mechanisms? A specific form of governance? A cultural construct? A condition of being-in-the-world? Do the various functions typically ascribed to it amount to a convincing account of its historical workings? How does it differ from its European counterpart, the metropolitan state 'at home'? And, finally, is there anything to be made of the fact that the word itself also connotes to 'articulate', to 'give voice', to 'narrate'? We are now in a position to engage these questions – those that remain unanswered – and, in doing so, to direct the discussion toward its conclusion, re-stating the problem of the state as a discourse in the interconnections of governmentality, materiality, modernity, and legality.

Let us begin with the first. The colonial state, in South Africa as elsewhere, was always an aspiration, a work-in-progress, an intention, a phantasm-to-be-made-real.[50] Rarely was it ever a fully actualised accomplishment. An 'ideological project', Philip Abrams (1988, p. 76) called it - adding, provocatively, that, being 'essentially [an] imaginative construction', a 'triumph of concealment' (p. 77) even, it was 'the distinctive collective *mis*representation of capitalist societies' (p. 75). Shades, here, of things written long ago. Corrigan and Sayer (1985, p. 7) remind us, in paraphrase, that Marx (1967) believed 'the State' to be in an important sense an illusion. Of course, institutions of government are real enough. But 'the' state is in large part an ideological construct, a fiction: [it] is at most a message of domination – an ideological artifact attributing unity, structure and independence to the disunited, structureless and dependent workings of the practice of government.

Not just Marx either. Weber (1948, p. 78) too. For him, it was a *claim* to legitimacy, a means by which politically organised subjection is simultaneously accomplished and concealed, and it is constituted in large part by the activities of institutions of government themselves. A truly curious force of history, this, at least if we agree with Marx and Weber: simultaneously an illusion,[51] a claim to authority, a cultural artifact, a present absence/absent presence, a principle of unity masking institutional disarticulation, and a potent construct which manifests itself, with tangible effects, in the quotidian activities of government and politics.[52] But *ought* we to concur with Marx and Weber, whose perspectives, as we all know well, derived from a very particular place in the modernist political history of Europe?

In 19th and 20th century Africa, the colonial state *was* often an elusive entity, even when agencies of governmen asserted their presence most vociferously. Typically, too, it was many things at once, even when imagined as one: less a singular, definite article than an indefinite, *variably integrated* ensemble of sites, institutions, narratives, and material processes, it was the political frame (i) in which power, *qua* human agency, sought to authorise itself, against resistance sometimes, thus to speak and act for a political *community*, for its past and its future; (ii) in which executive and bureaucratic cadres ruled with differing degrees of autonomy, entering into common cause at times with various social fractions, usually defined by (if not named in the language) class, race, and/or gender; (iii) in which taken-for-granted cultural conventions, their coercive aspect camouflaged in the habits of everyday life, were posited as a precondition of collective being-in-the-world.

Colonial regimes in Africa varied widely in the extent to which they managed to condense legitimate power in themselves, to suppress a politics of difference, to manufacture consent, and to ritualise the subjection of citizens to the state. Such things, patently, depended on a range of historical contingencies too broad to list here. (Not least, the [re]actions of colonised peoples to overrule, and relations, especially over their dealings with 'natives', among settlers, missionaries, and political cadres at home and abroad (Cooper and Stoler, 1997, Comaroff and Comaroff, 1997a.)

So, too, did the degree to which partisan blocs – often, but not always, colonial capitalists of one kind or another – succeeded in insinuating themselves into, and in appropriating, the mechanisms of government, including the use of force. Which is why some overseas administrations were weak, others strong; some highly intrusive, others scarcely visible; some energetically protective of expatriate business, industrial, and agrarian enterprises, others less so; some brutally violent, others barely coercive at all; some frequently contested, others at least acquiesced in; some prone to ostentatious ceremony, others very matter-of-fact in their regulatory routines; some institutionally integrated, well-ordered, and fairly efficient in their technologies of rule, others in more-or-less constant disarray, their component agencies so independent of one another as hardly to be parts of a single order of governance at all.

Indeed, the explanation of these patterns of variance, of their historical formation and transformation, is *the* task awaiting the anthropology of colonialism once its conceptual groundwork is done.

According to modernist political sensibilities, as every foundational college course in Political Science teaches, there can only ever be one state in a territory. Hence the difficulty, in scholarly discourses as well as in populist ones, of contemplating imperial governance without speaking of '*the* colonial state'. Even when, as in some historical contexts, the term describes a largely unconnected set of administrative practices and institutions. Or, in extreme situations, almost none at all. Insofar as the state – the singular, definite *imagined* article – is the *sine qua non* of modernist politics, it exists, alike at the metropole and the colonial margin, as a narrated and enacted description of order: order, again, in the double sense of regularity and regulation, of convention and control, of civility and sovereign command over a land mass and all who dwell within. In other words, whatever its organisational lineaments, the state is a *state*ment, an ongoing assertion: it gives voice to an authoritative orldview, sometimes backed by (open or concealed) displays of might. To return to an intimation made earlier, there in the interrogative mood, the homonym – the state (n), to state (v) – *does* have a more than fortuitous connection. The noun is the abstract entity enunciated, realised, made manifest by the verb. And by the power that it takes to speak, persuasively, in the active voice.

But, and here is my point, the argot spoken by colonial regimes was not arbitrary. Their vernacular, the language of modernity, was the language of the law. Modern state-formation, Corrigan and Sayer (1985, p. 1) note, was a 'cultural revolution'. At its heart lay the spirit of legality. Many have tied industrial capitalism, modernity, the nation-state, governmentality, the rights-bearing citizen, and the rise of *lex naturae* into a single historical equation; the equation on which is founded the logos of the present epoch, beginning with the Age of Revolution, 1789–1848. What I seek to add here, modestly, is the proposition that it was the deployment of this language of the law, its ascent to hegemonic authority, that held colonial states together, even at their most disarticulated, least coherent, most impotent; that afforded them a means to make fact appear out of phantasm, illocutionary force out of illusion, concrete realities out of often fragile fictions, one thing out of many; that allowed them to represent themselves, and to act, as guarantors of civility against savagery and barbarism; that legitimised *all* aspects of their power, capillary and coercive, volitional and violent, arterial and instrumental; that mandated their right to manage and mediate diverse identities and interests.

This *lexi*con – if another pun may be forgiven – constituted two interrelated public spheres. On one hand, it laid down both the terms and the terrain of cooperation, commerce, competition, and contention among settlers and expatriates, thus establishing the state as the *axis mundi* of European colonial society. On the other, it provided an ostensibly neutral medium for people of different cultural worlds, different social endowments, different material circumstances to enter into contractual relations, to transact commodities, and to deal with their conflicts. In so doing, it created an impression of consonance amidst contrast; of the negotiatibility of incommensurables; of the existence of universal normative standards which, like money in the domain of the market, facilitated exchanges across otherwise intransitive boundaries. But the language of legality was also mobilised to delineate the moral frontiers of civil society, criminalising 'native' cultural practices deemed uncivilised, politics deemed primitive, counter-modernities deemed dangerous (see Stoler, 1985: *passim*). To be sure, law was the hydra-headed, blunt instrument by which colonial states sought, in the name of modernity and progress, to assert control over the space and time of their subjects: over the continuity and change – the duration and disjuncture, if you will – of 'traditional' habits and habitats, ways and means.

As Charles Taylor (1989) has said, there are good reasons for the primacy of the law, and the discourse of rights, at the heart of European cultures of modernity. Its special significance here, however, lies in the convergence of two features of African colonial states, both of which we encountered earlier.

The *first* is that most of these states were states *sans* nations; as I said above, states without hyphenation. This was the case virtually everywhere until the late years of the Age of Empire. True, white expatriates, many of whom persisted in talking of Britain or France or Germany as 'home', always liked to think of the colony as a proto-Euronation. It was an affectation in which colonial regimes participated by creating many of the figurative trappings, the signs and symbols, of nationhood; indeed, given that the imperial gesture represented itself as a civilising mission, and as political modernity incarnate, they had no alternative.

Lord Lugard might have had it that British administrations abroad were protective of the 'natural rights' of 'natives', in touch, even, 'with [their] thought and feeling'. But the colonial state, precisely because it was *not* constitutive of a nation, was founded largely on the legalities of *ex*clusion and the politics of difference. It barred the vast majority of the autochthonous peoples – those over whose territory it asserted sovereign jurisdiction – from full membership in the polity, rationalising racial restriction in the righteous language of statutory 'protections'; in the claim that, if they were allowed to by law, Africans would alienate their land, sell their birthright, and lapse back into savagery. It will be remembered that colonial commissions, discussed above, regularly (de)limited and/or removed the rights of ethnic subjects; this, along with a panoply of executive orders, prevented all but few blacks from becoming right-bearing citizens, equal before the law and unmarked by colour, in a secular modern political community.

Under these conditions there was little prospect of the emergence of a sense of nationhood based, imaginatively and affectively, on horizontal connection (Anderson, 1983) – even if colonial regimes had wanted it otherwise. Most colonies were, in any case, carved out with careless inattention to their cultural integrity or sociological viability, and were subjected to long periods of divide-and-rule. What is more, the very act of narrating, representing, and ritualising a nation that did not exist – a practice often carried to symbolic excess – merely drew the attention of indigenous elites to their legal disempowerment. Even more, to the impossibility of their incorporation, as anything but demeaned persons, into colonial society; 'pariah' was the word used, in 1913, by Sol Plaatje (n.d., p. 17), one of South Africa's first black polemicists. This, in turn, is often taken to explain the rise of mass political resistance across Africa, particularly after World War II.[53] Whether true or not, many decolonisation movements at the time *did* congeal into (often uneasy) nationalisms: that early counter-claims for an independent African modernity should have appropriated the terms of European politics, with its deep roots in the culture of constitutionalism and the language of the law, seems overdetermined.[54]

So too, in this light, was the Minogue Paradox, also referred to earlier: namely, that the more elaborate colonial states became – the wider the reach of their formal author-ity, the greater the extent to which they monitored and managed the life worlds of those over whom they ruled – the less effective they appear to have been in making 'natives' into acquiescent subjects, in stifling dissensus and defiance, sometimes even in sustaining the coherence of their own modes of governance. At least, not without a heavy measure of force, much of it self-defeating over the long run. This, to round out the circle, tended to drive imperial administrations abroad to ever further binges of legalistic regulation, especially in dealing with insubordination and counter-violence. The latter were usually treated not as politics but as crime (see above); *in extremis*, they elicited forms of repression intended, in good proportion, to instil into settler populations and 'respectable natives' a faith in law and order. And in the rights and responsibilities attaching to citizenship. Which leads to the *second* feature of the culture of legality at the core of the unhyphenated colonial state. Julia Kristeva (1993, p. 26) hinted at it in asking, pointedly, 'what happens to people without nations ...? Are they human beings ...?' The answer, in the African context, is clear: their humanity was rendered incomplete, ambiguous. This, after all, was entailed in the effort of colonial regimes to convert 'natives', simultaneously and contradictorily, into *both* right-bearing citizens and culture-bearing ethnic subjects. The former – in the guise of autonomous, free individuals – epitomised the European bourgeois sense of refinement. The latter, by contrast, were specimens of a primordial, imperfect *homo sapiens*, barely above beasts in their 'natural' proclivities and their promiscuous, 'primitive communism'. (In colo-nial South Africa, blacks were regularly referred to by terms connoting animality, among them *skepsels*, Dutch for 'creatures'; Comaroff and Comaroff, 1992, p. 52.)

There is no need to reiterate the implications of this bipolar construction of the colonial subject/citizen – of its promises, its paradoxes, its unfulfilled telos – save to say that it had the widespread effect of inculcating in Africans a 'double consciousness' of their place in the world (see DuBois, 1968). And to note that, in the mass anticolonial struggles of the twentieth century, it expressed itself in the uneasy coexistence of two counter-discourses of constitutional entitlement. Many of those who contested European domination in the name of nationhood and self-determination spoke articulately of jural equality and universal human rights; rights, that is, for *individuals*. Especially to the new African middle classes, and to members of the orthodox Christian churches, this liberal discourse of rights was always appealing; hence the tendency for popular political movements – among them the African National Congress in South Africa, whose leaders were predominantly mission alumnae – to frame their aspirations and objectives in the language of legality, equity, and due process. But there was another discourse of rights as well. This one made political claims, and pursued the ways and means of empowerment, in the name of ethnic *groups*, many of them formed during the colonial epoch. It subordinated individual entitlements to those of collective, culturally-defined identities, asserting – also in the language of the law – the liberty of indigenous peoples to sustain their sovereign self-determination within a federated national polity. And it made a case for a plural legal system cognisant of 'customary law', for allowing a great deal of autonomy to 'traditional' authorities, and for a moral order based on 'ancestral' conventions. This, in South Africa again, is the kind of political community to which the Zulu-centric Inkatha Freedom Party gestured; along, interestingly, with other racially and ethnically based political organisations, black and white. In sum, these two discourses of rights arose, dialectically and in complementary opposition, out of the contradictory manner in which the colonial state sought to construct its subject/citizens. Each fashioned its own vision of the present and future. Each essayed its own idea of modernity. Each spoke its own version of legalese. And each aspired to its own political culture, its own form of postcolonial governance.

Coda

The problem of the colonial state begins with its very (mis)conception. With the fact that, much of the time, we speak of it loosely, *sans* any sense of specification. Even worse, we take its presence so for granted that it is virtually absent from our theoretical discourses. By juxtaposing orthodox approaches of the left and the right against Foucauldian revisionism – and by subjecting both to the kind of critique intended to cast the nature of the beast itself in a fresh light – I have sought to problematise it anew. And in such a manner as to make sense, at least in broad lines, of the alternative African modernities fashioned in the late colonial epoch and transported into the postcolony.

It will be clear now why I have insisted on treating colonial governance as a process of becoming: as both a verb and a noun, as a state and a statement, as an aspiration made real in varying proportions through historical practice. Why it is, too, that '*the* colonial state', notwithstanding its singular imagining in modernist politics, was always both one thing and many; always at once an ideological project and a (more or less articulated) institutional order; always both a fantasy and a reality – indeed, a reality with the capacity to affect the everyday lives, and deaths, of those human beings who fell within its purview.

As I said earlier, the historical variability with which colonial designs were accomplished in Africa, the contrasts over time and space among states, remains to be documented and accounted for. In the meantime, I suggest that, beneath all the diversity – indeed motivating the multivocal, polyvalent, disparate character of imperial governance abroad – lay a number of contradictions. These arose, in large part, from the most fundamental constitutive feature of the colonial state: from the fact that it was, until just before its demise, a state *sans* nation. It was this that expressed itself in, even impelled, the construction of an oxymoronic subject/citizen, that embodiment of 'double consciousness'; which set in motion the Minogue Paradox, the inverse correlation between the elaboration of the colonial state, its institutional and capillary technologies of rule, and its efficacy in regulating 'native' life without resistance; which threw even more than usual emphasis on the language of legality in constructing an ordered world; which yielded two different counter-discourses of rights, and, with it, two alternative conceptions of modernity.

It is this last phenomenon, the production of alternative modernities, that is likely to be the final legacy of the colonial state in Africa; of the way in which it condensed a particular order of governmentality, legality, materiality, and civility. Perhaps also its most bloody and terrible. The two images of nationhood and of political order – one based on a liberal ethos of universal human rights, of free, autonomous citizenship, of individual entitlement; the other assertive of group rights, of ethnic sovereignty, of primordial cultural connection – are, more than ever before, arraigned against each other in struggles for the determination of the continuing present and millennial future of many postcolonies. In South Africa they almost derailed the end of *apartheid*. Elsewhere they have produced genocides. Almost nowhere yet have they yielded easily habitable hybrids, new political orders that address the problem of postcolonial empowerment. This is the heritage of the colonial state and its imperious civilising mission, the 'black man's burden' of which Basil Davidson wrote (see p. 63). It is also the challenge that awaits Africa as a new epoch, the epoch of global capitalism, dawns. And spreads new shadows over old horizons.

Notes

– This paper grew out of a lecture delivered first at the Institute of Ethnology, Academia Sinica, in June, 1997; an earlier version is to be published in its Bulletin and an abbreviated and amended one in *Perspectives on African Modernities*, (eds) J-G. Deutsch, P. Probst, and H. Schmidt, London: James Currey. Nadia Abu El-Haj and Kathleen Hall read a penultimate draft of the present version and offered constructive, insightful criticism; I owe to both my warm thanks. As always, I must also acknowledge a deep debt of gratitude to my wife, colleague, and co-author, Jean Comaroff.

1 The content of this and the next two paragraphs is a paraphrase of a statement made in the Introduction to Comaroff and Comaroff (1997a).

2 Dirks (1992), Thomas (1994), Stoler (1995), and Cooper and Stoler (1997). These scholars have explored the cultural dimensions of colonialism - to great effect - without eschewing its material and political dimensions.

3 Steinmetz made this comment in a research proposal to the National Science Foundation; he was kind enough to allow us to read a draft in 1995.

4 It is striking that a recent review essay on the anthropology of colonialism (Pels, 1997, p. 163–83) barely mentions the state, even though its subtitle includes the term 'governmentality'. This is not just an oversight on the part of the author; it is a reflection of work done in the discipline over the past decade or so. There are, of course, exceptions to Steinmetz's general observation. See, for just one example from African history, Lonsdale and Berman (1979); I shall return to this essay below.

5 Note here Morton Fried's (1968, p. 145) comment that '[i]t is impossible to offer a *unitary* definition of the state' (italics added). Also Philip Abrams's (1988, pp. 60–61) complaint that, for all its concern with the state, the social sciences have yielded very little by way of knowledge or understanding; 'the sociology of the state', he says, 'is still best represented by the fragmentary observations of Max Weber'. Abrams does add, however, that 'the state ... has proved a remarkably elusive object of analysis'.

6 See Cooper and Stoler (1997), who distinguish between the 'metropolitan' and the 'colonial' state.

7 Note that the English verb ('to state') does *not* share an etymology with the noun ('state'). These are purely homonyms. As Fried (1968, p. 144) explains, 'the state', in its political instantiation, derives from Machiavelli; it has its origins in the Italian words *stare* and *stato*. Among its significant cognate referents were 'status' and 'estate'.

8 Because Britain was the dominant power in South Africa from the turn of the 19th century onwards, I do not specifically address the differences between various European styles of colonial rule in Africa, a topic on which there is now a large literature. For a brief overview, written from an orthodox liberal perspective, see Gann and Duignan (1969).

9 A station was first established at the southern tip of Africa by the Dutch East India

Company in 1652, primarily to provision its long-haul vessels. The founder of this settlement, Jan van Riebeeck, is spoken of as a Columbus-like figure in conventional apartheid histories of South Africa; he is its heroic *fons et origo*. The Dutch administered what grew into the Cape Colony (also known as the Cape of Good Hope) until 1795, when it was taken over by Britain; this as a consequence of her war with France, which had invaded Holland and was thought likely to seize the Dutch outpost en route to 'the East'. In 1803 the colony was returned to the Batavian Republic under the Treaty of Amiens. But it was taken back in 1806 by the British, in whose hands it remained until the Union of South Africa was created (1910).

10   Ealy British visitors to the interior often made explicit comments to this effect. For an important example, see Barrow (1801–4), whose *Account of Travels* was especially influential as its author was founder of the Royal Geographical Society. Sent to investigate the state of the frontier in South Africa by His Majesty's Government, he spoke of the country as 'naked' (p. 57), morally empty. (Allegedly, earlier Dutch colonisers had not mapped much of the terrain which, for Barrow and his compatriots, was tantamount to not having made their presence felt at all; even more, it was proof of their own degeneration under the 'soporific' influence of Africa, which had robbed them of the spirit of discovery, experiment, and improvement necessary for proper colonisation (p. 67; see Comaroff and Comaroff, 1991, p. 95; Streak, 1974, p. 5; Pratt, 1985; Coetzee, 1988, p. 29).) The frontispiece of Barrow's own volume is a detailed map of the colony, full of virgin spaces. Note, too, that other Europeans, not representatives of the colonial government, made similar observations. Until the establishment of a mission station in what was to become Bechuanaland, declared the London Missionary Society's *Evangelical Magazine* (1840, p. 142), this was a 'vacant' land where 'the moral wilds presented a scene more sterile than the neighbouring desert'; this despite the fact that it contained towns much larger than the white colonial centres of the time. Carter (1989, pp. 9, 17, 27–28, 32), writing of Cook's voyages along the Australian coast, makes a parallel point in stressing that it was the European act of naming that made space into place.

11   The apparent irony that 'natives' might actually desire Pax Britannica is a theme of George Orwell's novel, *Burmese Days* (1934, p. 40); see Comaroff and Comaroff (1992, p. 181).

12   As Ajayi (1969, p. 508) goes on to point out, this also involved the creation of 'rational units of local government'. See Afigbo (1971, pp. 6–8) on the constitution of such units in French West Africa; also Lugard (1997 [1922], p. 578–79), who links the 'recognition' of these units to systems of colonial taxation. More generally, Gutkind (1975, p. 109), among many others, stresses the connection between 'law and order' and 'economic development', the former being seen - in postcolonial contexts as well as colonial ones - as an indispensable condition of the latter.

13 Lugard (1997 [1922], p. 583) wrote at length on the importance of not offending
    native feeling. He called for the careful study of local 'etiquette and ceremonial', and
    for the treatment of chiefs with respect. 'Native races alike in India and Africa are
    quick to discriminate between natural dignity and assumed superiority'; hence nei-
    ther 'vulgar familiarity' nor 'an assumption of self-importance' on the part of
    colonisers was appropriate. But, he added, remarkably, 'The English gentleman
    needs no prompting in such a matter - his instinct is never wrong'.

14 In this kind of liberal political history, individuals emerge as marked historical
    figures by virtue (i) of assuming, playing out, and (often, if not always) transform-
    ing public roles; or (ii) of their part in events and actions subsequently re-presented
    as significant to the teleology of the nation-state. Their heroic history-making is
    rather different from the kind of heroic history of which Sahlins (1985) writes. In
    the latter, culturally constituted personages – as metonymic actors and embodiments
    of collective categories and projects – come to stand for social being; their deeds,
    therefore, reproduce and transform the political community as an autonomic reflex
    of their very existence.

15 There are, of course, significant differences between liberal and conservative histo-
    ries. Typically, the former are written by British or by English-speaking South African
    scholars - and, sometimes, by blacks, usually alumni of mission schools. These
    accounts often glorify the British presence in South Africa, and stress its humani-
    tarian heritage; conversely, they vilify the actions of Afrikaans-speaking white set-
    tlers. Conservative histories, by and large, are written by Afrikaans scholars. (There
    are a few exceptional cases.) Here I treat the two like as a single epistemic tendency
    in South African historiography, and refer to them, purely for convenience, as 'or-
    thodox histories'. This is because - despite the different constructions they put on
    particular incidents and the different value they give to specific actions - both are
    positivist in their methods and their modes of interpretation; both are 'liberal' in
    their stress on the primacy of individual agency, especially heroic agency, in the
    making of history; both are emphatically empiricist in orientation; and so on. In
    this respect, they differ from the neo-Marxist approaches to be discussed below,
    and from others which, although important in their own right, fall outside my
    present scope.

16 This was true of scholarly writings (alike by English, Afrikaner, and black scholars)
    until the rise of a neo-Marxist history in the 1970s – and, later, of a culturally-
    oriented historical anthropology; see below. (It remains so of school books, which
    have not yet been replaced by post-apartheid texts.) Nor is it restricted to South
    Africa. In introducing a collection of essays on colonialisms across the world, Cooper
    and Stoler (1997, p. 18) note that, twenty years ago, 'the colonial state would have
    been the point of departure' for almost any such volume; for affirmation of their
    point, see e.g. Gann and Duignan (1969).

17 Anyone who has even a passing familiarity with South African history knows that this resentment came to a head in the 1830s with the abolition of slavery by the British administration in the Cape Colony. The antecedents of modern Afrikaners were, in the main, farmers who relied on a bonded workforce for their livelihood; having developed a biblical rationale for racial difference, they saw neither moral nor material virtue in free labour. In response to abolition, they left the Colony in a mass migration toward the interior, a migration known as the 'Great Trek', which resembled the (roughly contemporaneous) westward movement in North America. This ended in the establishment of two Afrikaner settler republics in the hinterland, with which the British colonial administration - not to mention indigenous chiefdoms - had strained relations; these gave way, every now and again, to open hostilities over land, sovereignty, and dealings with 'native' peoples (see below).

18 For an especially clear summary statement to this effect, in respect of Africa at large, see Gann and Duignan (1969, p. 22); also, from the opposite perspective, and in a highly critical vein, Rodney (1997 [1972], p. 585).

19 Echoes here of Engels who, in *The Origin of the Family, Private Property and the State* (1968, p. 586) argues that the state is a product of society at a certain stage of development; 'it is the admission that this society has become entangled in an insoluble contradiction with itself, that it has split into irreconcilable antagonisms which it is power less to dispel ... [I]n order that these antagonisms and classes with conflicting economic interests might not consume themselves and society in fruitless struggle, it became necessary to have a power seemingly standing above society that would alleviate the conflict, and keep it within the bounds of "order" ... this power ... is the state'.

20 These historians came to be known as 'revisionists'. For the sake of clarity, however, I refer to them here as 'neo-Marxist', since I use the term 'revisionist' in another connection above. This, in any case, is a more specific description of their theoretical orientation.

21 There is, here, an implicit reference back to Owusu's point about the entailment of more orthodox, non-Marxist historiographies of colonialism in the epistemic murk of theories of 'modernisation'. (My use of Michael Taussig's 1987 term – with its playful, parodic gesture toward the postmodern in dealing with forms of terror of deadly, all-too-modern seriousness - is itself intended ironically, of course.)

22 Marx did not have 'native' peoples in mind in writing this; he was concerned with European settlers in colonies abroad. Nonetheless, the statement applies nicely to the way in which neo-Marxist historians have seen the resistance of African producers to engagement with the development of capitalism in South Africa – and the processes to which it gave rise.

23 In some celebrated cases - themselves much discussed in South African history – capital and the colonial state converged in one personage. For example, Cecil John

Rhodes, capitalist *extraordinaire*, became the Prime Minister of the Cape of Good Hope in the late 19th century. In circumstances such as these, the political careers of prominent men of business are held, by neo-Marxist historians, to be a reflex of their material interests rather than the other way around (see e.g. Maylam, 1980).

24 The eye in the door is the core metaphor in Barker's novel of World War I, the second of her trilogy on the subject. The large eye was painted on the inside of the cell of William Roper, a conscientious objector, who was jailed for his refusal to be drafted and for his opposition to the war - as were other members of his family and circle of friends. The eye reappears as an icon of state surveillance and its internalisation on pp. 58, 68, and 75.

25 Vaughan (1994; and, for a response, Bunn, 1994); also recent discussion of our own work - in, among other places, the *South African Historical Journal,* Volume 31, 1994 - which, despite our repeated statements to the contrary, is seen in some South African circles, as 'postmodern'.

26 Hence Ann Stoler's (1995) recent, and controversial, effort to interrogate Foucault on race and colonialism.

27 'Labour units' was the term to be used for them under *apartheid.*

28 Says Charles Taylor (1989, pp. 11–12), in this respect: 'What is peculiar to the modern West' is that the respect accorded to human beings, as citizens, came 'to be [formulated] in terms of rights' - specifically, of *universal* 'subjective right[s]', a form of 'legal privilege' enjoyed by 'disengaged subjects'.

29 A fair amount has been written recently on the significance of enumeration, and of population censuses in particular, in colonial overrule. For two notable examples, see Cohn (1990) and Appadurai (1993); also, more generally, on the growing salience of statistical rationality for modern governance, Hacking (1990).

30 But seldom electoral (voter) rolls. Typically, colonial citizenship did *not* extend to universal franchise for 'natives' until the final years of the imperial epoch.

31 Blacks - referred to officially as 'Bantu', a pejorative ethnological designation, in the apartheid years - were regularly made by police to show their 'passes'. These contained information about their birth places, ethnic identities, permission to travel and work away from home, and so on. Failure to present a pass on demand was punishable by a fine or imprisonment, as a result of which, South Africa had the highest incarceration rate in the world after World War II. Details of their substance and implications of pass laws are documented in the annual handbook of the South African Institute of Race Relations.

32 This phrase was used by Roger Price, a London Missionary Society [LMS] evangelist, in a report written from the Kuruman station on 12 December 1896. (See Council of World Mission, LMS South Africa Reports, 2-4; housed at the School of Oriental and African Studies, University of London.) Terms like 'socialistic' and

'communistic' (usually preceded by 'simple' or 'primitive' appear frequently in the writings of contemporary missionaries.

33 On the processes by which ethnic identities were constructed in colonial southern Africa, see e.g. Harries (1983), J.L. Comaroff (1987, 1995), Vail (1989), and Comaroff and Comaroff (1997a, Chapter 8).

34 For example, Modjaji, the rain queen of the Lovedu (see Krige and Krige, 1943).

35 There is now a large literature on the creation of 'customary law' under colonialism; for just four notable examples, see Chanock (1985), Moore (1986), Starr and Collier (1989), and Mann and Roberts (1991).

36 See e.g. Union of South Africa (1925).

37 Great Britain (1886) was the report of a land commission charged with the limited task of investigating land claims and disputes in British Bechuanaland, where a crown colony had just been established. (British Bechuanaland was absorbed into the Cape of Good Hope in 1895, whence it became part of the Union of South Africa in 1910.) In South Africa (1905), the South African Native Affairs Commission 1903-1905 was charged 'to enquire into and report on' the 'status and conditions of the Natives' (p. 1).

38 The Department of Native Affairs underwent a series of name changes overtime, but its ethnological publication series continued to flourish. The volumes became more and more detailed over the years, being based on fairly extensive empirical research, if not field work in the conventional anthropological sense of the term. Some of the publications treated the peoples of a district (e.g. Breutz, 1953, 1956; van Warmelo, 1944c), others a single 'tribe' (van Warmelo, 1944a and b) or two 'tribes' (van Warmelo, 1953), and yet others an ethnographic theme (Breutz, 1969; van Warmelo, 1931) or survey (van Warmelo, 1935).

39 See Gramsci's (1971) much discussed comments on the consent and collaboration of the ruled as a defining feature of hegemony; see, e.g., Femia (1971, 1985). And, of course, Fanon's (1963, 1967) writings on the colonisation of the minds and consciousness of imperial subjects.

40 See Kallaway (1984) for a general overview of the part played by education in the black South African past. The most unreconstructedly liberal, positive view of its modernising effects under colonialism is to be found, perhaps, in Inkeles and Levinson (1974). For the opposite perspective, see, among many others, Livingstone *et al.* (1987); and, for a sophisticated, well-known study of education and the reproduction of inequality, Willis (1977). I should add that our own view of the role of schooling in the colonisation of Southern Africa (Comaroff and Comaroff, n.d.) is somewhat more complicated than any of these writings might suggest.

41 This was foreshadowed in the accounts of early British missionaries in South Africa. John Philip (1828, 2, p. 118), for one, had commented on how Tswana followed their traditions of old 'without question'; tribal councils, added Robert

Moffat (1842, pp. 249–50), 'inveighed against any aggression' upon ancient ways, 'threatening confiscation and death to any who would arraign the wisdom of their forefathers'. In the late 19th and early twentieth centuries, it is true, indigenes were commonly categorised into 'savages' (or the uncivilised'), the 'semi-civilised', and the 'civilised'; this classification saturating government reports (see e.g. South Africa, 1905), the contemporary prose of black literati (see e.g. Molema, 1920, p. 307), and white travel and adventure writings (see e.g. Chilvers, 1929). But such differences were ignored or explained away in stereotypic representations of '*the* native'. Thus, for example, Rev. John Mackenzie - self-styled liberal, 'friend of the natives' and humanitarian imperialist - explained that, even when they took on the trappings of civilisation, Africans 'still preferred their own customs'.

42 The same stereotype also saturated the contemporary writings of whites, liberal and conservative alike. Thus, for example, Sarah Gertrude Millin (1933, p. 237), in her famous book on Cecil John Rhodes, wrote:

The native plants as his forefathers planted, he practices the animal husbandry of his forefathers, he believes religiously in the plenitude of cattle ... Since the native believes in the agricultural methods of his ancestors, he suspects of witchcraft, and thus discourages, any exceptional native who successfully follows the methods of the Europeans.

43 We reify 'the state' here purely for rhetorical effect. There is, in contemporary Foucauldian scholarship, a strong tendency to treat the state as if it were a historical agent in its own right, rather than an institutional site within which human agency is exercised.

44 In what was to become Bechuanaland, formal overrule occurred in the wake of the discovery of diamonds (c. 1867). This was some eight decades after the presence of Europeans - primarily missionaries, settlers, and traders - was first felt by indigenous peoples. Even then, the grip of the colonial state was tenuous and uneven, and remained so for a long while (see Turrell, 1982, p. 52). Not only did prisons remain in private hands, but much migrant labour came from beyond colonial borders - at its own volition in the early years. Even when it intervened in the recruitment of workers, the state often ran into difficulties; see Comaroff and Comaroff (1997a, Chapter 4).

45 This resonates, oddly, with Gallagher and Robinson's (1953, repr. 1982) once controversial claim that, beyond the visible purview of the 'formal' British empire, lay a huge 'informal empire'. The limited horizons of the first, they argued, were attributable to the reluctance of politicians to expand it further. While not ruled by governors or other personnel of state, this second empire fell under invisible forms of economic, cultural, and social influence emanating from London. For a brief but informative discussion of the argument, and its intellectual genealogy, see Cain and Hopkins (1993, p. 7).

46 As is well-known among anthropologists, Gluckman *et al.* (1949, *passim*) used the

term 'non-commissioned officers' to refer to the role of 'native' headmen in the colonial administrations of Central Africa.

47 The documentary record is replete with excessive displays of firepower on the part of relatively impotent colonial regimes. Perhaps the most comic was the despatch, in 1933, of the British Navy into the heart of land-locked Bechuanaland to discipline Chief Khama of the Ngwato, largest of the Tswana polities. This was occasioned by the flogging at his court of one Phinehas McIntosh for repeated violence against his (Ngwato) wife. McIntosh, who regarded himself as Tswana and as a subject of Khama but who was seen as a white man by the colonial authorities, did not protest his treatment. But the idea of a black ruler sentencing a 'European' to corporal punishment was too much for the British government to bear. And so the heavily armed sailors left their ships and travelled *by train* to the fringes of the Kalahari Desert, there to show off their capacity for brute force to the assembled 'natives'; see Crowder (1988).

48 See, for example, Shillington (1985, p. 75) on the infamous Burness murders in the South African interior.

49 Thanks to Terry Woronov, a graduate student in anthropology at the University of Chicago. Her excellent essay on the New Life Movement in China in the 1930s alerted me to this passage.

50 At the start of their thoughtful essay on the topic, Lonsdale and Berman (1979, p. 487) promise to treat the colonial state 'as a complex historical process' rather than as an ensemble of governmental institutions. In their analysis of the Kenyan case, however, as in their general statements, they tend toward a more conventional characterisation.

51 Miliband (1969, p. 49) goes further in arguing that 'the 'state' is not a thing ... [I]t does not, as such, exist'.

52 Hegel, of course, had a very different notion of the state; one in which its concrete existence, as an actualised Idea (1952, p. 279), was taken for granted - as were its phenomenological coherence and its basis in mind and reason: 'The state must be treated as a great architectonic structure, as a hieroglyph of the reason which reveals itself in actuality' (p.288). As a 'living mind', he added elsewhere (1971, p. 265), it 'is as an organised whole, differentiated into particular agencies'. Marx (1978), famously, excoriated Hegel for his position on the state and civil society; especially for his generic, ahistorical, indeed purely philosophical, treatment of the former.

53 For discussion, see e.g. Isaacman (1990); Ranger (1967, 1977).

54 According to Davidson (1992), the encounter of nationalisms in the post-war period - during the years leading up to (formal) decolonisation - left Africans with a modernist political order utterly unsuited to their present and future. For him, the legacy of the nation-state was the 'black man's burden' (see Comaroff and Comaroff, 1997b).

References

Abrams, P. (1988). 'Notes on the Difficulty of Studying the State (1977)', *Journal of Historical Sociology,* 1 (1), pp. 58–89.

Anderson, B. (1983). *Imagined Communities: Reflections on the Origin and Spread of Nationalism,* London: Verso.

Afigbo, A.E. (1971). 'European Administration and the Growth of Nationalism in West Africa (c. 1900–39)', in A.E. Afigbo, E.A. Ayandele, R.J. Gavin and J.D. Omer-Cooper (eds) *The Making of Modern Africa, Volume II, The Twentieth Century,* London: Longman.

Ajayi, J.F.A. (1969). 'Colonialism: An Episode in African History', in L.H. Gann and P. Duignan (eds) *Colonialism in Africa 1870–1960, Volume I, The History and Politics of Colonialism 1870–1914,* Cambridge: Cambridge University Press.

Appadurai, A. (1993). 'Number in the Colonial Imagination', in C.A. Breckenridge and P. van der Veer (eds) *Orientalism and the Postcolonial Predicament: Perspectives on South Asia,* Philadelphia: University of Pennsylvania Press.

Ashforth, A. (1990). *The Politics of Official Discourse in Twentieth-Century South Africa,* Oxford: Clarendon Press.

Barker, P. (1995). *The Eye in the Door,* New York: Plume (Penguin Books).

Barrow, J. (1801–4). *An Account of Travels into the Interior of Southern Africa in the Years 1797 and 1798,* Volume I, London: T. Cadell & W. Davies.

Bissell, W. (1998). 'Conservation and the Colonial Past: Urban Planning, Space, and Power on Zanzibar', D. Anderson and R. Rathbone (eds) *Africa's Urban Past,* London: James Currey.

Bohannan, P. (1964). *Africa and Africans,* New York: The Natural History Press.

Breutz, P.-L. (1953). 'The Tribes of Marico District', Union of South Africa, Department of Native Affairs, Ethnological Publication No. 30, Pretoria: Department of Native Affairs.

– (1956). 'The Tribes of Mafeking District', Union of South Africa, Department of Native Affairs, Ethnological Publication No. 32, Pretoria: Department of Native Affairs.

– (1969). 'Sotho-Tswana Celestial Concepts', in *Ethnological and Linguistic Studies in Honour of N.J. van Warmelo,* Union of South Africa, Department of Bantu Affairs, Ethnological Publication No. 52, Pretoria: Department of Bantu Affairs.

Bundy, C. (1972). 'The Emergence and Decline of a South African Peasantry', *African Affairs,* 71 (285), pp. 369–88.

– (1979). *The Rise and Fall of the South African Peasantry,* London: Heinemann.

Bunn, D. (1994). 'The Insistence of Theory: Three Questions for Megan Vaughan', *Social Dynamics,* 20, pp. 24–34.

Cain, P.J. and A.J. Hopkins (1993). *British Imperialism: Innovation and Expansion 1688– 1914,* London: Longman.

Carter, P. (1989). *The Road to Botany Bay: An Exploration of Landscape and History,* Chicago: University of Chicago Press.

Chanock, M. (1985). *Law, Custom, and Social Order: The Colonial Experience in Malawi and Zambia,* Cambridge: Cambridge University Press.

Chilvers, H.A. (1929). *The Seven Wonders of Southern Africa* Johannesburg: Government Printer, by Authority of the Administration of the South African Railways and Harbours.

Coetzee, J.M. (1988). *White Writing: On the Culture of Letters in South Africa,* New Haven: Yale University Press.

Cohn, B.S. (1990). 'The Census, Social Structure and Objectification in South Asia', in B. Cohn (ed.) *An Anthropologist among the Historians and Other Essays,* Delhi: Oxford University Press.

– (1996). *Colonialism and Its Forms of Knowledge: The British in India,* Princeton: Princeton University Press.

Comaroff, J. and J.L. Comaroff (1991). *Of Revelation and Revolution, Volume I, Christianity, Colonialism, and Consciousness in South Africa,* Chicago: University of Chicago Press.

– (n.d.). *Of Revelation and Revolution, Volume III, Reading, Rioting, and Arithmetic,* in preparation.

Comaroff, J.L. (1987). 'Of Totemism and Ethnicity: Consciousness, Practice, and the Signs of Inequality', *Ethnos,* 52, pp. 301–23.

– (1989). 'Images of Empire, Contests of Conscience: Models of Colonial Domination in South Africa', *American Ethnologist,* 16, pp. 661–85.

– (1995). 'The Discourse of Rights in Colonial South Africa: Subjectivity, Sovereignty, Modernity', in A. Sarat and T.R. Kearns (eds) *Identities, Politics, and Rights,* Ann Arbor: University of Michigan Press.

– (1996). 'Ethnicity, Nationalism, and the Politics of Difference in an Age of Revolution', in E. Wilmsen and P. MacAllister (eds) *The Politics of Difference: Ethnic Premises in a World of Power,* Chicago: University of Chicago Press.

– (1997). 'Legality, Modernity, and Ethnicity in Colonial South Africa: An Excursion in the Historical Anthropology of Law', in R. Rawlings (ed.) *Law, Society and Economy: Centenary Essays for the London School of Economics and Political Science 1895–1995,* Oxford: Clarendon Press.

Comaroff, J.L. and J. Comaroff (1992). *Ethnography and the Historical Imagination* Boulder: Westview Press.

– (1997a). *Of Revelation and Revolution, Volume II, The Dialectics of Modernity on a South African Frontier,* Chicago: University of Chicago Press.

– (1997b). 'Postcolonial Politics and Discourses of Democracy in Southern Africa: An

Anthropological Reflection on African Political Modernities', *Journal of Anthropological Research,* 53 (2), pp. 123–46.

Cooper, F. (1994). 'Conflict and Connection: Rethinking Colonial African History', *American Historical Review,* 99 (5), pp. 1516–45.

Cooper, F. and A.L. Stoler (1997). 'Between Colony and Metropole: Rethinking a Research Agenda', in *Tensions of Empire: Colonial Cultures in a Bourgeois World,* Berkeley: University of California Press.

– (eds) (1989). *Tensions of Empire,* special section in the *American Ethnologist,* 16 (4).

Corrigan, P. and D. Sayer (1985). *The Great Arch: English State Formation as Cultural Revolution,* Oxford: Basil Blackwell.

Crowder, M. (1988). *The Flogging of Phinehas McIntosh: A Tale of Colonial Folly and Injustice, Bechuanaland 1933,* New Haven: Yale University Press.

Curtin, P.D. (1964). *The Image of Africa: British Ideas and Action, 1780–1850,* Madison: University of Wisconsin Press.

Davidson, B. (1992). *The Black Man's Burden: Africa and the Curse of the Nation-State,* New York: Times Books.

Dirks, N.B. (1992). 'Introduction: Colonialism and Culture', in N. Dirks (ed.) *Colonialism and Culture,* Ann Arbor: The University of Michigan Press.

DuBois, W.E.B. (1968). *The Souls of Black Folk,* New York: Fawcett.

Engels, F. (1968). *The Origin of the Family, Private Property and the State,* reprinted from the 1942 edition (New York: International Publishers), in *Karl Marx and Frederick Engels: Selected Works,* Volume I, New York: International Publishers.

Fanon, F. (1963). *The Wretched of the Earth,* translated by C. Farrington, New York: Grove Press.

– (1967). *Black Skin, White Masks,* translated by C.L. Markmann, New York: Grove Press.

Femia, J.V. (1975). 'Hegemony and Consciousness in the Thought of Antonio Gramsci', *Political Studies,* 23, pp. 29–48.

– (1981). *Gramsci's Political Thought: Hegemony, Consciousness, and the Revolutionary Process,* Oxford: Clarendon Press.

Foster-Carter, A. (1978). 'The Modes of Production Controversy', *New Left Review,* 107, pp. 47–77.

Fried, M. (1968). 'State', in D.L. Sills (ed.) *International Encyclopedia of the Social Sciences,* New York: Macmillan and the Free Press.

Gallagher, J. and R.E. Robinson (1953). 'The Imperialism of Free Trade', *Economic History Review,* 2nd Series, 6, pp. 1–15, reprinted in J. Gallagher (1982) *The Decline, Revival and Fall of the British Empire,* edited by A. Seal, Cambridge: Cambridge University Press.

Gann, L.H. and P. Duignan (1969). 'Introduction', in L.H. Gann and P. Duignan (eds)

Colonialism in Africa 1870-1960, Volume I, The History and Politics of Colonialism 1870–1914, Cambridge: Cambridge University Press.

Gluckman, M., J.C. Mitchell and J.A. Barnes (1949). 'The Village Headman in British Central Africa', *Africa,* 19, pp. 89–106.

Gramsci, A. (1971). *Selections from the Prison Notebooks,* edited and translated by Q. Hoare and G. Nowell Smith, New York: International Publishers.

Great Britain, Colonial Office (1886) .*Report of the Commissioners Appointed to Determine Land Claims ... in British Bechuanaland,* London: HMSO, C4889.

Gutkind, P.C.W. (1975). 'Are the Poor Politically Dangerous? Some Thoughts on Urbanism, Urbanites, and Political Consciousness', in M. Owusu (ed.) *Colonialism and Change: Essays Presented to Lucy Mair,* The Hague: Mouton.

Hacking, I. (1990). *The Taming of Chance,* Cambridge: Cambridge University Press.

Harries, P. (1988). 'The Roots of Ethnicity: Discourse and the Politics of Language Construction in South-East Africa', *African Affairs,* 87 (346), pp. 25–52.

Harvey, D. (1990). *The Conditions of Postmodernity: An Enquiry into the Origins of Cultural Change,* Oxford: Blackwell.

Hegel, G.W.F. (1952). *Hegel's Philosophy of Right,* translated by T.M. Knox, Oxford: Clarendon Press.

– (1971). *Hegel's Philosophy of Mind. [Being Part Three of the Encyclopaedia of the Philosophical Sciences (1830)]* translated by W. Wallace, Oxford: Clarendon Press.

Inkeles, A. and D.H. Smith (1974). *Becoming Modern: Individual Change in Six Developing Countries,* Cambridge: Harvard University Press.

Kallaway, P. (1984). 'Introduction', in P. Kallaway (ed.) *Apartheid and Education: The Education of Black South Africans,* Johannesburg: Ravan Press.

Kaviraj, S. (1994). 'On the Construction of Colonial Power: Structure, Discourse, Hegemony', in D. Engels and S. Marks (eds) *Contesting Colonial Hegemony: State and Society in Africa and India,* London: British Academic Press.

Krige, E.J. and J.D. Krige (1943). *The Realm of a Rain-Queen: A Study of the Pattern of Lovedu Society,* London: Oxford University Press for the International African Institute.

Kristeva, J. (1993). *Nations Without Nationalism,* translated by L.S. Roudiez. New York: Columbia University Press.

Krüger, D.W. (1969). 'The British Imperial Factor in South Africa from 1870 to 1910', in L.H. Gann and P. Duignan (eds) *Colonialism in Africa 1870-1960, Volume I, The History and Politics of Colonialism 1870–1914,* Cambridge: Cambridge University Press.

Livingstone, D.W. and Contributors (1987). *Critical Pedagogy and Cultural Power,* South Hadley: Bergin & Garvey.

London Missionary Society (1840). 'South Africa – Lattakoo Mission', *The Evangelical Magazine and Missionary Chronicle,* 18, pp. 142–43.

Lonsdale, J. and B. Berman (1979). 'Coping with the Contradictions: The Development of the Colonial State in Kenya, 1895–1914', *Journal of African History,* 20, pp. 487–505.

Lugard, F.D. (1922). *The Dual Mandate in British Tropical Africa* ['Methods of Ruling Native Races', pp. 193–213] excerpted and reprinted, 1997, in R.R. Grinker and C.B. Steiner (eds) *Perspectives on Africa: A Reader in Culture, History, and Representation,* Oxford: Blackwell.

Mackenzie, J. (1871). *Ten Years North of the Orange River: A Story of Everyday Life and Work among the South African Tribes,* Edinburgh: Edmonston & Douglas.

Magubane, B. (1979). *The Political Economy of Race and Class in South Africa,* New York: Monthly Review Press.

Mann, K. and R. Roberts (eds) (1991). *Law in Colonial Africa,* London: James Currey.

Marks, S. and R. Rathbone (eds) (1982). *Industrialization and Social Change in South Africa: African Class Formation, Culture, and Consciousness, 1870–1930,* London: Longman.

Marks, S. and S. Trapido (eds) (1987). *The Politics of Race, Class and Nationalism in Twentieth-Century South Africa,* London: Longman.

Marx, K. (1967). *Capital: A Critique of Political Economy,* 3 volumes, New York: International Publishers.

– (1978). 'Contribution to the Critique of Hegel's *Philosophy of Right [The State and Civil Society],* in R.C. Tucker (ed.) *The Marx-Engels Reader,* 2nd edn, New York: W.W. Norton.

Marx, K. and F. Engels (1965). *The German Ideology,* London: Lawrence and Wishart.

Maylam, P.R. (1980). *Rhodes, the Tswana, and the British: Colonialism, Collaboration, and Conflict in the Bechuanaland Protectorate, 1885–1899,* Westport and London: Greenwood Press.

Miliband, R. (1969). *The State in Capitalist Society,* London: Weidenfeld and Nicholson.

Millin, S.G. (1933). *Rhodes,* South Africa: Central News Agency; Rhodesia: Kingstons.

Minogue, K. (1987). 'State', in J. Kuper (ed.) *Political Science and Political Theory,* London: Routledge & Kegan Paul.

Mitchell, T. (1991). *Colonising Egypt,* Berkeley: University of California Press.

Moffat, R. (1842). *Missionary Labours and Scenes in Southern Africa,* London: John Snow, New York: Johnson Reprint Corporation.

Molema, S.M. (1920). *The Bantu, Past and Present,* Edinburgh: W. Green & Son.

Moore, S.F. (1986). *Social Facts and Fabrications: 'Customary' Law on Kilimanjaro,* Cambridge: Cambridge University Press.

Orwell, G. (1934). *Burmese Days,* New York and London: Harcourt Brace Jovanovich.

Owusu, M. (1975). 'Comparative Politics, History, and Political Anthropology', in M. Owusu (ed.) *Colonialism and Change: Essays Presented to Lucy Mair,* The Hague: Mouton.

Palmer, R.H. and N.Q. Parsons (eds) (1977). *The Roots of Rural Poverty in Central and Southern Africa,* Berkeley: University of California Press.

Parsons, N.Q. (1977). 'The Economic History of Khama's Country in Botswana, 1844–1930', in R. Palmer and N.Q. Parsons (eds) *The Roots of Rural Poverty in Central and Southern Africa,* London: Heinemann.

Parsons, N.Q. and M. Crowder (eds) (1988). *Monarch of all I Survey: Bechuanaland Diaries 1929–1937 by Sir Charles Rey,* Gaborone: The Botswana Society; London: James Currey.

Pels, P. (1997). 'The Anthropology of Colonialism: Culture, History, and the Emergence of Western Governmentality', *Annual Review of Anthropology,* 26, pp. 163–83.

Philip, J. (1828). *Researches in South Africa; Illustrating the Civil, Moral, and Religious Condition of the Native Tribes,* London: James Duncan.

Plaatje, S.T. (n.d.) *Native Life in South Africa,* New York: The Crisis.

Pratt, M.L. (1985). 'Scratches on the Face of the Country; or, What Mr Barrow Saw in the Land of the Bushmen', *Critical Inquiry,* 12, pp. 119–43.

Ranger, T.O. (1967). *Revolt in Southern Rhodesia,* London: Heinemann Educational Books.

– (1977). 'The People in African Resistance: A Review', *Journal of Southern African Studies,* 4 (1), pp. 125–46.

Rey, P.-P. (1971). *Colonialisme, Néo-Colonialisme et Transition au capitalisme,* Paris: Maspero.

– (1973). *Les Alliances de classes: 'sur l'articulation des modes de production', suivi de 'Materialisme historique et luttes de classes',* Paris: Maspero.

Rodney, W. (1972). *How Europe Underdeveloped Africa,* excerpted and reprinted in R.R. Grinker and C.B. Steiner (eds) (1997) *Perspectives on Africa: A Reader in Culture, History, and Representation,* Oxford: Blackwell.

Sahlins, M.D. (1985). *Islands of History,* Chicago: University of Chicago Press.

Sartre, J.-P. (1955). *Literary and Philosophical Essays,* translated by A. Michelson, New York: Criterion Books.

Schapera, I. (1970). *Tribal Innovators: Tswana Chiefs and Social Change, 1795–1940,* London: Athlone Press.

– (1983). 'Report on the System of Land-Tenure on the Barolong Farms in the Bechuanaland Protectorate', abridged, *Botswana Notes and Records,* 15, pp. 15–38, first published, 1943.

Shillington, K. (1985). *The Colonisation of the Southern Tswana, 1870–1900,* Johannesburg: Ravan Press.

Sillery, A. (1952). *The Bechuanaland Protectorate,* Cape Town and New York: Oxford University Press.

South Africa, Native Affairs Commission (1905). *Report of the South African Native Affairs Commission, 1903–5,* Cape Town: Cape Times Ltd.

South Africa, Union of (1925). *Report of the Select Committee on Subject-Matter of Masters and Servants Law (Transvaal) Amendment Bill,* Cape Town: Cape Times Limited, Government Printers [S.C.12–25; printed by Order of the House of Assembly].

Starr, J. and J.F. Collier (eds) (1989). *History and Power in the Study of Law: New Directions in Legal Anthropology,* Ithaca: Cornell University Press.

Stoler, A.L. (1985). 'Perceptions of Protest: Defining the Dangerous in Colonial Sumatra', *American Ethnologist,* 12 (4), pp. 642–58.

– (1995). *Race and the Education of Desire: Foucault's History of Sexuality and the Colonial Order of Things,* Durham: Duke University Press.

Streak, M. (1974). *The Afrikaner as Viewed by the English, 1795–1854,* Cape Town: Struik.

Taussig, M. (1987). *Shamanism, Colonialism, and the Wild Man: A Study in Terror and Healing,* Chicago: University of Chicago Press.

Taylor, C. (1989). *Sources of the Self: The Making of Modern Identity,* Cambridge: Harvard University Press.

Thomas, N.J. (1990). 'Sanitation and Seeing: The Creation of State Power in Early Colonial Fiji', *Comparative Studies in Society and History,* 32, pp. 149–70.

– (1994). *Colonialism's Culture: Anthropology, Travel and Government,* Cambridge: Polity Press in association with Blackwell.

Trotter, D. (1990). 'Colonial Subjects', *Critical Quarterly,* 32 (3), pp. 3–20.

Turrell, R. (1982). 'Kimberley: Labour and Compounds, 1871–1888', in S. Marks and R. Rathbone (eds) *Industrialization and Social Change in South Africa: African Class Formation, Culture, and Consciousness, 1870–1930,* London: Longman.

Unterhalter, E. (1995). 'Constructing Race, Class, Gender and Ethnicity: State and Opposition Strategies in South Africa', in *Unsettling Settler Societies Articulations of Gender, Race, Ethnicity and Class,* London: Sage.

van Warmelo, N.J. (1931). *Kinship terminology of the South African Bantu,* Pretoria: Government Printer (Ethnological publications, no. 2).

– (1935). *A Preliminary Survey of the Bantu Tribes of South Africa,* Pretoria: Government Printer (Ethnological publications, no. 5).

– (1944a). *The Bakgatla ba ga Mosêtlha,* Pretoria: Government Printer (Ethnological publications, nos 17–22, pp. 3–11).

– (1944b). *The Bahwaduba,* Pretoria: Government Printer (Ethnological publications, nos 17–22, pp. 23–32).

– (1944c). *The Tribes of the Vryburg District,* Pretoria: Government Printer. (Ethnological publications, nos 17–22, pp. 33–43).

– (1953). *Die Tlokwa en Birwa van Noord Transvaal,* Pretoria: Government Printer. (Ethnological publications, no. 29).

Vail, L. (ed.) (1989). *The Creation of Tribalism in Southern Africa,* Berkeley: University of California Press.

Vaughan, M. (1994). 'Colonial Discourse Theory and African History, Or Has Postmodernism Passed Us By?, *Social Dynamics,* 20, pp. 1–23.

Wallerstein, I. (1974). 'The Rise and Future Demise of the World Capitalist System: Concepts for Comparative Analysis', *Comparative Studies in Society and History,* 16 (4), pp. 387–415.

Weber, M. (1948). *From Max Weber,* edited by H. Gerth and C. Wright Mills, New York: Routledge and Kegan Paul.

– (1968) *Economy and Society: An Outline of Interpretive Sociology,* Volume II, edited by G. Roth and C. Wittich. Berkeley: University of California Press.

Willis, P.E. (1977). *Learning to Labour: How Working Class Kids Get Working Class Jobs,* New York: Columbia University Press.

Wolpe, H. (1988). *Race, Class and the Apartheid State,* London: James Currey.

Zahar, R. (1974). *Frantz Fanon: Colonialism and Alienation. Concerning Frantz Fanon's Political Theory,* translated by W.F. Feuser, New York: Monthly Review Press, first German edition, 1969.

Upending the century of wrong: agrarian elites, collective violence, and the transformation of state power in the American south and South Africa, 1865–1914

John Higginson

The setting

Power and violence have played an integral part in shaping the lives and expectations of people in the American South and South Africa for at least two centuries. After protracted periods of terror and mass civil disobedience, both societies are struggling to make popular elections and the drafting of new laws and constitutions the only legitimate means of political contest. But as the recent bombings in the northern Cape and Rustenburg in South Africa and more than a decade of arson against churches used primarily by African-Americans in the South suggest, violent forms of contest can, on occasion, assume renewed vigour.[1] Presently, there is evidence that the most glaring features of South African *apartheid* and American segregation are receding. But a great deal of confusion remains about whether both were coincidental misfortunes or deliberate instances of social engineering.[2] This confusion turns largely on a mis-understanding of how violence assisted in maintaining the two social systems.[3] The refusal of former president PW Botha and the Afrikaner National Party (NP) to con-tinue to co-operate with the Truth and Reconciliation Commission in South Africa provides us with an excellent example of the kind of selective amnesia that feeds confusion about past events.[4]

In 1899 Jan Smuts, the Attorney General of the South African Republic, who later became a general in the Republic's guerilla army, wrote a scathing polemic entitled *The Century of Wrong*.[5] Smuts's polemic sought to indict the British Empire for war crimes and the excessive use of atrocious violence against Afrikaner civilians during its pros-ecution of the Anglo-Boer or South African War of 1899–1902.[6] My present research retreats from Smuts's narrowly focused charges, however, focusing instead on an ex-amination of interwar violence during the South African War and American Civil War and the postwar reverberations of this violence in the countryside. Despite military defeat, violence had a direct and forceful impact on the expectations of white landown-

ers in both societies during the generation that followed the two wars.[7] On occasion it
became a means for landowners to express simultaneously their grievances against the
victorious central state and their reluctance to change their way of life or the local social
structure.[8] White landowners in both settings perceived violence as both a method
and a process that could express their aspirations as well as their fears.[9]

I have chosen to focus on white landowners in the Marico and Rustenburg districts
of South Africa's Transvaal and those of Edgefield County, South Carolina and Caddo
Parish, Louisiana in the southern United States. I chose these areas because they were
notorious for long and deep traditions of regulator or vigilante violence.[10] As late as
the 1980s and 1990s representative segments of the white population in these areas
resorted to violence in order to combat what they perceived as unnecessary and super-
imposed efforts to change the local political and racial order.

The campaigns of terror foisted on these areas after the American Civil War and the
Anglo-Boer or South African War of 1899–1902 were neither serendipitous nor
spontaneous.[11] These atrocious forms of interwar violence had notable local precedents and socialised the next generation of white landowners.[12] Assassinations, torture, and more general forms of terror served as the catalysts for an undeclared civil
war between rural blacks and rural whites.[13] Important differences marked the details,
taxonomy, and outcomes of terror and collective violence, but in the sharp contests
for land and labour between black and white people in the countryside of both societies,
white landowners in two differently constituted agrarian societies shared a common
'grammar of motives'.[14]

In 1867 Reconstruction in the United States had become a radical attempt to establish political equality between blacks and whites in the South. The Reconstruction
administration of Alfred Lord Milner in the Transvaal had no such brief, even though
British officials did speculate on the likely impact of increasing the number of politically enfranchised Africans as a means to underscore a British military victory between
October 1899 and April 1901. Black participation in the prosecution of the two respective national wars forced the issues of black equality and black autonomy in the rural
areas to the surface in ways that aggravated the specific grievances of the defeated landowners.[15]

Former slaveholders and Boer landlords met the initiatives of the central governments and aspiring blacks with wave upon wave of protracted violence because they
had lost power, not simply because of the frustration and anxiety engendered by
postwar disruption.[16] While much of the violence appeared irrational or 'desperate' to
the casual observer, it had an inner logic, and the white landowners' decision to use
violence came only after a careful assessment of the two governments' firepower and
organisation.[17] The suppression of black autonomy was not a foregone conclusion.
The successful intervention of the two central governments vitally depended upon a
bold restatement of the commercially alienable nature of private property and the right

of the state to establish political order in the most war ravaged areas of the country-side. Meanwhile white supremacy in its prewar forms had become more or less dys-functional in the initial attempts to reorganise economic life in the countryside after the wars.[18] 'Farm burnings', the expropriation of cattle and moveable property, and the forcible eviction of landowners from their holdings smashed the moorings of defer-ence that had bound African-American slaves and African peasants to their masters and landlords and to their conceptions of ownership and justice.[19] At the close of the two national wars the most militant members of the local elite – many of whom had served the cause of the Confederacy and Boer republics in elite regiments and death squads – wanted it understood that they would continue to fight well beyond the formal surrender. In their view it was not possible for white men of property and substance to abandon their expectations and claims on power in countries in which one's standard of living continued to be closely identified with the colour of one's skin.[20] The re-elaboration of the state's power in the two countries assumed a most urgent character in those areas of the countryside where people of African descent were a preponderant majority or where their subjugation as dependent labourers appeared to be the only means of placating white landowners.[21]

During the two respective postwar periods the circumstances of agriculture also came to be more securely tied to burgeoning markets for food and commercial staples such as cotton. But the hands that drove the wagons and pulled the plows had to know which seasons of the year were likely to produce the greatest yield of corn, sorghum, wheat or cotton. They had to insure that draft animals could keep to a straight row and not trample on previously planted crops, smaller livestock, fences, or themselves; and they had to know readily when more labour and material were needed to get in the crops. These monotonous tasks had to be carried out and arcane informa-tion about seasons and crops committed to memory whether the hands and heads that actually performed them were black or white. Hence our examination of the vio-lent actions of white landowners at the close of the nineteenth century tells how a place was made for segregation, white supremacy in its most mature and strident form.[22]

Segregation in both societies precipitously resulted from the manner in which war and its subsequent reverberations in terrorist violence transformed state power and economic alternatives. Segregationists concentrated on the cities, towns, and industrial workplaces of the American South and South Africa, but segregation as a state spon-sored administrative practice and policy of social engineering depended primarily upon the imposition of political order on the surrounding countryside. Competing ver-sions of political order emerged.

Violent white landowners in both countries exposed the ineffectual nature of many of the postwar administrative reforms of the two reconstruction governments, while compelling these same governments to reconsider the viability of their apparent post-war political alliances.[23]

In the long run these two national upheavals profoundly affected the political and social exigencies of the four areas under study. In each, collective and political violence punctuated the life histories of their leading men before, during, and after the respective civil wars. A regulator or vigilante tradition created a perverse set of precedents for postwar reforms. Insofar as the actions of vigilantes were initiated and encouraged by local elites, they made for an array of flashpoints that challenged the victors' conception of political order.[24]

The principal actors

What turned planters and landlords into vigilantes? Was it the sudden clash of expectations and outcomes that came with the war and its immediate aftermath? Did larger if largely hidden concerns drive the aggrieved parties to violence? Violence and aggression in any society automatically embrace related problems of social and political costs, morality, social cohesion, and authority – in short, who, through the agency of the state, can legitimately do violence to another person? Secondly, because there is no known human society where violence and aggression do not occur and because the range of expression of aggression can also vary – from a hostile glance to the extermination of entire segments of a population – it is more useful to think of violence as capacity rather than instinct.[25] Actual acts of terror and their perpetrators only amount to the most obvious aspect of the problem. To assess the wellsprings of an act of violence we need to put the details into a relation consistent with the aims of the perpetrators and the amount of force and constraint that a given society would impose upon them before, during and after the act was completed. Assuming that violent acts are gratuitous is almost always a serious error of judgement.

Two examples serve to illustrate the caveat. On the Monday before 15 October 1865, exactly seven months after the surrender of the Confederate military forces and just before a particularly eager Freedmen's Bureau official, one Captain Gates, was to distribute yearly contracts among black labourers , a freedman known as 'Frank' was fired upon by a band of white 'regulators' on a plantation in the Barnwell section of the old Edgefield district of South Carolina.[26] Frank was wounded in the arm by a bullet while trying to escape his tormentors. He and another freedman named 'Cato' were captured by a band led by William Patrick, a notorious vigilante and former Confederate cavalryman.

Both men were taken to the farm of William Patrick's brother George that evening but managed to escape early the next morning. Frank made it safely to the Union military post in nearby Ridgeville, but Cato, who had been shot through the knee, fell behind. Late Tuesday afternoon his body was found astride the main road riddled with bullets and horribly mutilated – his ears, tongue, and eyes had been cut from his face.[27]

What do we make of these events? Does it help us to know that the regulators watched the twenty or so black labourers work for more than an hour before they rode through the rows to take Frank and Cato; or that the youngest and more notorious of the Patrick brothers, William, had been sent to an elite cavalry company from infantry once the Hampton Legion, arguably one of the most ideologically motivated of Confederate brigades, was reorganised in 1863?[28] How seriously should we take the public renunciation of this violent act by local planters; or the assertion by local Freedmen's Bureau officials that the planters were 'bitter troublesome and that frequent threats are made that when Gates was gone they would have it out with the niggers'? How ideologically motivated were all the principal actors – white vigilantes, freedpeople, Freedmen's Bureau officials, and Union soldiers? What kind of reasoning did each employ in determining a connection between a hostile gaze or threat and a violent act?

Over thirty years later in South Africa another violent act took place. In late October or early November 1900, six months after Pretoria, the Transvaal Republic's capital, had fallen to Lord Roberts's forces, a squadron of British troops discovered the bodies of nine African men near the summit of the Magaliesberg mountains. The bodies were lying in a heap. A number had been mutilated. Ears, tongues and genitals had been cut off. Five were identified as Africans who had been in the service of British military intelligence. The other four had been tenants or labourers on Boer farms in the portions of Rustenburg and Marico occupied by the British and had apparently offered information about the wartime activities of their landlords to British authorities, or so officials of the occupying force surmised.[29]

The nine men had been tried by an informal tribunal. The tribunal had been convened by the former president of the Transvaal parliament or *Volksraad*, B.A. Klopper, who also served as its presiding magistrate.[30] All nine were condemned to death and summary execution followed. Hendrik Schoeman, the son of a Boer general, and Piet Joubert, the son of the recently deceased General Commander of the republican army, as well as others acted as an escort for the nine.[31]

Who performed the summary executions? Did the mutilations occur before or after summary execution? Why did the sons of the generals most associated with the republican army's most recent losses have to be present? Was the site of the executions, among the solitary and rugged mountains that allegedly mirrored the qualities of Boer men, coincidental – particularly at a time when the formal republican army was retreating and virtually nonexistent in the west?[32] Would such experiences become normative ones for younger soldiers?[33] To what extent did such experiences suggest a model for postwar relationships between returning Boer soldiers, particularly those who were sent to distant prison camps in Bermuda, Ceylon and India, and their wives, children, and African tenants and labourers?[34] American slaveholders and Boer landlords in the upland regions of their two respective countries sought to enhance their command over black labour and to neuter the relationship between black people and their families before the outbreak of the two national wars. The details of this process in these two distinct societies were often quite different, but landowners in both countries sought to replace work routines shaped by affection and kinship with their own putative sovereign power. While the more insightful and intelligent landowners realised that this kind of control was more of an aspiration than a reality, it served nevertheless as an ideal measure of actual circumstances.[35]

It was the loss of the possibility of this kind of command over black labour that launched both groups onto campaigns of vigilante terror. These two violent odysseys appeared to culminate with the end of Reconstruction in the United States and the outbreak of the Generals' Rebellion of 1914 in South Africa. Violence aimed at blacks and, on occasion, the state achieved new mass forms of expression in both countries during succeeding generations but for radically different reasons in some instances. Landowners remained at the centre of subsequent violence, which was partly sustained by the changing agrarian economy, but the white landowners' sense of honour and self-sufficiency proved poor remedies for the ills brought by rapid economic transformation.[36] A wide range of circumstances that were inimical to the imposition of political order obtained in both areas of the two countries in question during the immediate postwar periods. Some of the most salient were:

1 habits of independence and independent economic activity on the part of a potential class of dependent labourers;

2 a regulator or vigilante tradition among the conquered white population that could not be absorbed or defanged by the new methods of administration;

3 entailed legal conceptions of private property that militated against the commercial sale of land and increased the risk of potential investors;

4 the absence of infrastructural features such as rail lines, regular postal services, telegraph and telephone lines, and other features that would speed the commercialisation of agriculture;

5 the absence of schools to socialise the children of the vanquished and habituate them to the new political order; and

6 the absence of a critical number of active collaborators who would be willing to be the eyes and ears of the state until a regular local judiciary and police constabulary were established.[39]

In the face of opposition from landowning whites, the re-elaboration of state power in the two countries gained expression through stopgap, as opposed to long term, measures to reorganise the local police constabularies and magistracies, state sponsored land enclosures, and settlement of white loyalists in communities known to be hostile to the state's objectives. In these struggles race, labour, and land blended into one another.[38] But the central governments in both countries did not always take the lead in achieving broad systemic outcomes to such struggles. Consequently, the new administration sometimes ceded the initiative to the old elites.

A dangerous paradox arose therefore between segregation as a comprehensive state policy of social engineering and its likely executors in the local setting.[39] As a result, the coming of segregation in both countries was accompanied by more bloodletting than many historians have cared to admit. In fact, segregation's most sanguinary moments came when the central state was simultaneously attempting to absorb the most talented members of local elites and also determine the outcome of local situations during periods of rapid economic change.[40] The difficulties arose when the national state did not exert its full force in either endeavour. Consequently, my examination of the violent quickening of local white elites in portions of the American South and South Africa's Transvaal amounts to a means of discussing how segregation in South Africa and the United States could be predicated upon the broad acceptance of locally derived *Herrenvolk* conceptions of democracy and yet act as a fulcrum for the intervention of the central state in local situations.[41] Despite deep and persisting economic divisions within the white population, those who participated in the violence believed that they could minimise the moral and political impasse created by these divisions by resurrecting the military formations of vanquished armies in the guise of 'sabre and musket clubs' and 'commandos', while they masked this activity with the innocuous proceedings of farmers' associations. These men sought to create a political climate in which violence committed on behalf of private property and white supremacy – the two being readily conflated when convenient – were not only viewed as normal but indispensable.

Vigilante activity was not a sustained fact of life throughout the two periods and countries in question. Rather it tended to coalesce with other statements of grievance and, in turn, expand and contract in relation to the general political climate at a given moment. For example, in January 1905, with the formation of the Boer political movement *Het Volk,* under the leadership of Louis Botha and Jan Smuts, its subsequent victory at the polls in 1906, and the disbanding of the South African Constabulary (SAC) in 1907, there was a marked increase in the incidents of vigilante activity and the violent self-presentation of white farmers in everyday life.[42] 'Progressive' English speaking white farmers in Marico and Rustenburg had a hand in such violence and often benefited from its short-term consequences.

Methods and data

People often grasp complex realities best when they are presented as a series of anecdotes.[43] I do not mean to imply, as Napoleon did, that the past is merely a set of lies that the powerful conspire to foist upon a gullible public. Nor do I agree with the postmodern conclusion that all tales are equally valid. If my proposed research project proves anything, it is that all anecdotes are not equally valid or true, even when they appear to conform to the received wisdom.

Who works? Who owns? – these are the questions that lay at the heart of the violent circumstances that my project will examine. But such questions come wrapped up in a series of 'hows'. How malleable was the culture of the producing classes? How could the need for labour in town and countryside be met without engendering 'labour shortages'? How could the pursuit of a specific version of law and order advance or retard the number of labourers willing to come forth? And it was in relation to the 'hows' that the central state faltered – at least from the vantage point of local agrarian elites. Hence the elites viewed the disbanding of the agencies through which the power of the central state expressed its will such as the South African Constabulary (SAC) in the Transvaal and the Freedmen's Bureau and the Provost Marshal's Courts in Louisiana and South Carolina with a mixture of relief and trepidation. It was during the course of the dismantling of these institutions that the most volatile protests of white landowners took place. The dismantling of the SAC and the Freedmen's Bureau were important illustrations of the net effect of such protests.[44]

The common features of the politics of ex-slaveholders and landlords in the upland regions of the South and South Africa turned on three negative aspirations: 1) retaining the prewar form of command over black labour; 2) prohibiting or , at least, impeding the number of blacks who owned or rented land and who, by virtue of their direct access to productive land, would expect to take an active role in the political affairs of a given community; 3) limiting the number of blacks who possessed and exercised the political franchise. The three were not mutually exclusive; nor did they possess a fixed rank among the concerns of white landowners. Instead white landowners perceived the immediacy of any one of these goals in relation to their own capacities and power at a given moment.[45] They could not capture the habits and traditions of the past in their pristine form.

These two agrarian elites possessed important differences as well. Many were a consequence of sheer numbers: demographic change in the upland back country of both countries was quite dramatic in some cases during the respective postwar periods. Ex-slaveholders and Boer landlords also had different expectations from the relationship between the law, the judicial process, and the state's institutions – even when terror was the mutually resorted to catalyst to get the relationship going.

By cross referencing archival materials on Boer and Confederate prisoners of war with regimental histories, estate, death and marriage records, pension records, land conveyances, civil suits, and government and newspaper accounts of violent flashpoints, I have derived a provisional sample of 3 200 men and their families. Most of these 3 200 men were at least on the fringes of one kind of violent activity or another during the course of their active life. Out of this 3 200 I have identified a hard core of about 1 200 whose names appeared on a more or less regular basis in narrative descriptions of collective violence and outrages in newspapers and in testimony given at government commissions. By the standards of our time and perhaps their own, some, but not most, would have been reckoned as sociopaths of one sort or another. Some, in fact, achieved recognition and notoriety beyond their given locale; but of course, honour and prestige are not sufficient insurance that the recipients of such are not sociopaths.

Whether such men were sociopaths or not was not as important as how they perceived their fortunes and circumstances, or that apparently normal people saw their circumstances similarly. Either their organisations were fairly complacent about risks or all the members of such groups – normal and abnormal – believed that no risk was too great in the attempt to overthrow the two respective governments.

There were levels of commitment among the 3 200. All were not willing to kill or die. But most were quite willing to be silent – or to conceal or destroy evidence, give temporary shelter to a man on the run, repair or purchase weapons, and engage in low level but consistent hectoring of government officials they perceived as inimical to their interests. The various levels of commitment to violence among the people composing my evidentiary base also raise important questions and second my earlier concerns about the 'instinctual' nature of violence – particularly violence against people of another group. If collective violence of this nature is the result of factors that are 'caused, defensive, and interpretable', it is also preventable.[46] The latter contention will be the principal one that my findings will engage.

Notes

– I would like to thank Joye Bowman, Eugene Genovese, Thavolia Glymph, Michael Hanchard, Bruce Laurie, Julie Saville, Keith Shear, Ronald Story, Gloria Waite, Michael West, Nan Woodruff , Charles Tilly, Roderick Aya and Abebe Zegeye for their patient and sympathetic reading of earlier forms of this essay and related work. I also wish to thank the Catherine T. and John D. MacArthur Foundation for the fellowship that made lengthy sojourns in archives in South Africa and the United States possible. The flaws in this provisional product are all mine, however.

1 See for example, *Weekly Mail and Guardian*, 1997; see also 'South Africans rally in sympathy after Rustenburg Bomb Blast', (http://www.786.co.za/alqalam/dec96/rutnbrgbomb.htm); Henry Eichel (1998); Kevin Sack (1996).

2 See van Onselen (1996, pp. 19–26); see also K. Mbenga (1997).

3 In the American instance John Cell presents us with a masterly account of one such instance of bloodletting – the 1898 'Revolt of the Red Shirts' in North Carolina. Cell claimed, 'If that law [an 1896 statute that abolished county control of voter

registration] were to remain on the books, eastern North Carolina Democrats contended with some justification, white supremacy would not just be threatened in their region. It would be dead'. What is so striking about Cell's description here is that it flatly contradicts his argument that segregationists were inclined toward more moderate means: see Cell (1982, pp. 184–85 and 3–4); for a countervailing view see Fredrickson (1988, pp. 254–55); see also Dubow (1989).

4   See 'Ex Police Minister Fingers P.W. Botha in Bombing', 21 July 1998, Reuters web site: http://dailynews.yahoo.com/headlines/top_...euters/980721/news/stories/ safrica_3htm).

5   Smuts framed the problem in the following manner: 'Brother Africanders ... The hour has come when it will be decided whether, by vindicating her liberty, South Africa shall enter upon a new and grander period of her history, or whether our people shall cease to exist... and South Africa shall in future be governed by soulless goldkings acting in the name of and under the protection of an unjust and hated government 7 000 miles away...', see Jan Smuts (1900).

6   Smuts was not alone in speculating on the consequences of the war. Lionel Curtis, a future member of Lord Milner's staff and mayor of Johannesburg, wrote to his mother in this vein five months after the outbreak of the war: 'I don't think that I should say that this war has made men cruel but I do think that 200 000 odd Englishmen will come out of it with a hazier sense of *meum* and *tuum,* and that will not help them to govern justly': see Lionel Curtis (1951).

7   See Thomas Pakenham (1979); Jeremy Krikler (1993). See also Vernon Burton (1978); Gilles Vandal (1991).

8   For a glimpse of the anxieties of white farmers over the question of the political franchise and land redistribution see: *South African Native Affairs Commission* (henceforth SANAC)1903–1905, see also 'Testimony of A.H. Malan'; for the official gloss on these deep-seated anxieties see 'Testimony of W. Windham', *SANAC,* IV; see also *Report of the Joint Committee in Reconstruction* (1865).

9   See the entire file of personal correspondence in folder Ab in *Donald Rolfe Hunt Papers* (Historical Papers of the William Cullen Library, University of the Witwatersrand, Johannesburg, South Africa: henceforth DRHP) 1655; see also 23 August 1865 report of Brigadier General E.A. Wild to Major General R. Saxton at Beaufort, South Carolina and the 23 October 1865 report of Lieutenant Colonel C.S. Brown to the Chief of Staff for Brevet Brigadier General C.H. Howard from Anderson, South Carolina in the *Bureau of Refugees, Freedmen, and Abandoned Lands, Record Group 105 of the National Archives of the United States* (henceforth: NAFB).

10 Former Confederate Lieutenant-General Mart Gary remarks about a blueprint for terror in South Carolina, the 'Edgefield Plan', gave resonance to this tradition, 'Never threaten a man individually if he deserves to be threatened, the necessities of the times require that he should die': see Vernon Burton (1978); for Rustenburg

and Marico see *Kemball-Cooke Papers* (Historical Collections: University of the Witwatersrand, Johannesburg, South Africa: henceforth KCP) A62 Ab 2f, testimonial in the *Volkstem* of Rustenburg by the Reverend D. Postma; see also *KCP* A62 f, Statements of J.W. Meyer, Floris P. Coetzee, Nicolaas van der Walt and petitions of farmers from the Ceylon Estate in Rustenburg.

11 At the close of the South African War a vigorous and, occasionally, vituperative debate broke out among the Boer generals about whether the British block houses had, in fact, snapped resistance in the countryside. Beneath the apparent terms of the debate was the more volatile issue of whether the defeat of the republican army had been caused by a greater use of African irregulars and Boer collaborators in the closing months of the war: see Christaan De Wet (1902); see also Jeremy Krikler (1993); Peter Warwick (1982); for the origins of vigilante and terrorist activity in the post Civil War South see particularly the observations of Brigadier General Edward A. Wild to Brevet Major General R. Saxton and those of Lieutenant Colonel John Devereux to Major H.W. Smith on the cases coming before the Provost Courts and the activities of the Provost Marshals in Edgefield, South Carolina in *NAFB* RG 105, 869, reel 34.

12 See Bernard Mbenga (1997, pp. 129–37); Charles van Onselen (1990); see also Richard Maxwell Brown (1969); Orville Vernon Burton (1985).

13 See F.J. Newnham's 1905 force report; see also the markedly similar accounts of violence and contestation at Braaklagte and Leuuwfontein in Marico in 1903, 1907, 1942 and 1990 in Central Archives Depot/Bantu Affairs Office: Pretoria 2895 (Marico District) and *South African Truth and Reconciliation Hearings,* 'The Case of Diali and Mokgatle', Phokeng, 20 May 1996, pp. 7–9; for the massacre of thousands of freedpeople and white Republicans that accompanied the seminal elections of November 1868 in Louisiana and South Carolina see *Senate Report,* 42 Congress, 2nd session, report no. 41, pt 1, 20–22; see also Table 1 in Gilles Vandal (1991, p. 374); Vernon Burton (1978: p. 37); Allen Trelease (1971).

14 See George Fredrickson (1981); Jeremy Krikler (1993, pp. 31–37); see also C. Wright Mills (1959).

15 See Eric Foner (1989); Ira Berlin *et al.* (1990); see also S.E. Katzenellenbogen (1980); Shula Marks and Stanley Trapido (1979); for the usefulness of the comparison, see Charles Francis Adams (1902).

16 For an account that privileges relative deprivation theory as an explanation for the actions of former slaveholders see George C. Rable (1984); for an opposing view, see Eugene Genovese (1996); for an analogous explanation of the actions of Boer farmers, but one which is open to the prospect of tracing specific grievances as the catalyst for violence see Donald Denoon (1973).

17 For an insightful critique of explanatory models based on various theories, see Roderick Aya (1990).

18 See Eric Foner (1983); see also Charles van Onselen (1992).

19 See Jeremy Krikler (1993, pp. 39–41); Peter Warwick (1982, p. 45); see also Eric Foner (1884).

20 See, for example, the statements taken from Boer prisoners by R.A. Brownlea, General Dixon's intelligence officer, after 500 of them were captured on various farms between Rustenburg and Krugersdorp in February–March 1901: *Family History Archives of the Church of Latter Day Saints of Jesus Christ* (henceforth FHACLDS) microfilm J-47878136782, 'List of Farms and Inhabitants West of Pretoria: R.A. Brownlea for 'Daag' Intelligence, General Dixon's Force 10/4/01'; see also Lou Falkner Williams (undated).

21 Various state officials were painfully aware of the potentially explosive consequences. In 1903, for example, the former sub native commissioner of Piet Retief, L.E.N. Tyrrell, penned a revealing letter to the government sponsored agricultural journal under the *nom de guerre* 'gentleman farmer': see Tyrrell (1903); Tim Keegan summed up the dilemma nicely, 'It would probably be true to that black resources, skills, and enterprise kept a whole generation of Afrikaners afloat on the land': see Tim Keegan (1988); *Testimony taken by The Joint Selection Committee to inquire into The Condition of Affairs in the Late Insurrectionary States,* part 1 volume 3, 'testimony of David T. Corbin' (Washington DC: Government Printing Office, 1872), 68–88; Ted Tunnell (1989); Allen Trelease (1971).

22 In 1903 a 'gentleman farmer' assessed the Transvaal's agriculture in the following manner, 'I am speaking of production by our primitive South African methods, where the farmer sits on the verandah and sends three boys to plough with six or ten oxen, and an ordinary single furrow. Of course, with improved farming the cost would be much less'. See 'Notes, Queries and Replies', *Transvaal Agricultural Journal,* 3 (1, April): 72–73; see also Timothy J. Keegan (1987); see also *Report on Cotton Production,* vol. I (1884): 68-77; Gerald Jaynes (1986).

23 Upon his removal as resident magistrate of Rustenburg, H. Kemball-Cooke bestowed his papers and notes on his successor, but with a bit of a warning, 'I have not destroyed these documents because after I have 'shuffled off this mental coil', I have asked you to use your discretion as to the preservation or destruction of any papers I may have left behind me ... I fancy that you may gather from some of them that I tried to do my duty to 'brother Boer', in the sense that an Englishman looks upon his duty to those under him': see *KCP* A62f; see also Shula Marks and Stanley Trapido (1979, pp. 56–57); David Yudelman (1983); see *NAFB* microfilm M869 Reel 34, 'Reports of Murders and Outrages, Oct. 1865–Nov. 1868' and 'Report of Conditions and Operations, July 1865–Dec. 1866'; Roger Shugg (1939); Howard White (1970).

24 See Donald Denoon (1973), pp. 63–68 and 108; 'testimony of A.H. Malan', *SANAC,* 570; *DRHP* A1655, File Ac6, 'Confidential Memo to Native Commissioners in

Conference at Johannesburg (Lagden), 18 June 1902'; see also Anon (1867); Ted Tunnell (ed.) (1989); Allen Trelease, *White Terror,* 130.

25　See James Gilligan (1996); see also C. Wright Mills (1959), pp. 40–45.

26　See *NAFB* microfilm M869 Reel 34, 'Reports of Murders and Outrages, Oct. 1865–Nov. 1868' and 'Report of Conditions and Operations, July 1865–Dec. 1866'.

27　See *NAFB* microfilm M869 Reel 34.

28　See the February–March 1863 correspondence of Confederate Brigadier Generals H.Q. Jenkins and John Bratton, and Captain J.S. Austin in *FHACLDS* microfilm 1447437 (correspondence and muster rolls of the Hampton Legion for 1862 and 1863).

29　*British Parliamentary Papers* (henceforth: BPP) CD 821 LXIX, 15 November, 1901, Kitchener to Under Secretary of State, War Office, London, 'Case at Magaliesberg'; see also *FHACLDS,* 'List of Farms and Inhabitants West of Pretoria: R.A. Brownlea for 'Daag' Intelligence, General Dixon's Force 10/4/01.

30　Toward the end of February 1901, B.A. Kloppers Sr surrendered to Colonel Airey at Hartbeestfontein 118. His son, and five other relatives were also captured. One of the seven, or possibly F.G. Wolmarans, one of the first Afrikaners in the Rustenburg-Krugersdorp area to break the oath of neutrality and take up arms again, recounted the details of the tribunal to British intelligence officers: see *FHACLDS,* 'List of Farms and Inhabitants West of Pretoria...'

31　*BPP* CD 821 LXIX, 'Case at Magaliesberg'.

32　Many fleeing Boer soldiers did not think of themselves as 'deserters', but rather as engaged in *vlucht volmoed* – flight in full courage: see Christiaan De Wet, *The Three Years War,* 191–92 and 345; see also the observations of British staff and parole officers *FHACLDS* K-23892 1367078, 'Cape Town: Staff Officer, Prisoners of War 1-226; Paroles nos. 390–469, 1900–1902 volume no. 117 (old no. 114).

33　As late as August 1903 British commandants in the camps for Boer prisoners in Bermuda worried that the rigours of war had 'hardened' some of the younger prisoners and made them indifferent to exercising cruelty. Jan Smuts and J.H. de la Rey had expressed similar concerns earlier in the war: see *Bermuda Archives* (henceforth: BA) CS 6/1/20, Governor's Despatches, no. 96, 13 August 1903, 'Lt Governor-General and Commander-in-Chief to Rt. Hon. Joseph Chamberlain'; see also W. Hancock and J. van der Poel(1966) pp. 472–74 and 561.

34　See Anon (1905).5.

35　See *DRHP* A1655, File Ac24, 'Memo to the Native Commissioner, Lydenburg, from Hunt concerning land tenure, occupation, rights in the area under his jurisdiction, 19 March 1913'; see also the insightful description of the range of peasant-landlord relations in Rustenburg in Belinda Bozzoli with Mmantho Nkotsoe (1991); for the American South see C. Vann Woodward (1990); Nell Irvin Painter (1976); See *First Session of the Forty-Fourth Congress, 1877-76,* Document No. 85, 'Message from the President of the United States, communicating, in answer to a Senate resolution of 20 July 1876, information in relation to the slaughter of American citizens at Hamburgh, S.C. (Washington: Goverment Printing Office, 1876); see also Julie Saville (1994); Ted Tunnell (1989, pp. 87–93); for the Generals' Rebellion see A.M. Grundlingh, 'Die Rebellie van 1914: historiografiese verkenning', *KLEIO* (1979) vol. II, 18–30; G.D. Scholtz (1942); T.R.H. Davenport (1963).

36 See W. Fitzhugh Brundage (1993); Stewart E. Tolnay and E.M. Beck (1995); see also Helen Bradford (1987); Tim Keegan (1988, pp. 134–37).

37 In 1917 for instance the prospects for a widespread rebellion of rural Afrikaners resurfaced in Rustenburg. Louis Botha, the President of the Union Government, sent for Linchwe, the paramount chief of the Kgatla Tswana, to warn him that if his people continued to 'provoke' white farmers, he would send Imperial troops into the western Transvaal. Local police, however, thought it more prudent to supply each white farmer with at least 50 rounds of ammunition: see *South African Police* documents microfilmed by Robert Edgar and housed at the Center for Research Libraries in Chicago, Illinois. The materials in question are 'Confidential: South African Police, Office of the Commissioner to Secretary of Justice, 3rd September 1917 (3/527/17)', Pretoria; Kafferskraal (Rustenburg), Bus 99, 1 October, 1917, 'Unie Verdedigingsmacht, Hoofdkwartier no. 9 Miltair Distrikt'. Pretoria 3/527/17; see also Barbara Fields (1983); Eric Foner (1989, pp. 406–20).

38 See Donald Denoon (1973), pp. 63–68; Barbara Fields (1983, p. 2124); Michael R. Hyman (1989).

39 See *BPP* CD 1897, 'Reports of the Transvaal Labour Commission, 1904: testimony of J.L. Hulett'; see also Shula Marks and Stanley Trapido (1979, pp. 61–68); see also *Report on the Condition in the South,* 'Congressional Report on the 1866 New Orleans Riot', House Report number 261, Forty-Third congress, Second session, 1875, part 2, 11.

40 See C.L. Andersson (1907); see also Frank Tannenbaum, (1924).

41 See N.G. Garson (1962); see also Joel Williamson (1984).

42 In 1906 *Het Volk* attempted to foster greater solidarity among Afrikaners across class lines by urging the poorer strata of the rural population to memorialise posthumously family members who had died during the war with detailed death notices. These attempts took the form of Sarel Johannes van der Merwe's. Sarel's notice stated that he 'fell in action' at Zeerust on 11 May 1902, less than three weeks before the formal surrender, at the age of 15. Hundreds of such notices were filed between October 1905 and February 1906: see *FHACLDS* R-51583 0991008, 'Transvaal: New Estates'.

43 See Eric Hobsbawm (1972).

44 See R.S. Godley (1935); see also observations of General Edward A. Wild to Brevet Major General R. Saxton (Edgefield, South Carolina) in *NAFB* RG 105 M869 Reel 34.

45 See James Gilligan, *Violence,* 211–15; Barrington Moore (1978).

46 James Gilligan, *Violence,* 211.

References

Adams, C.F. (1902). *Lee at Appomattox and Other Papers,* New York: Houghton, Mifflin and Company.

Andersson (1907). 'A Paper on the Defence of South Africa', 26 September in *Fortnightly Club Papers* A241 (Historical Collections, University of the Witwatersrand, Johannesburg, South Africa).

Anon (1905). 'Bad Gun Accident, Kafir Killed', *Pretoria News,* 12 August.

Anon (1867) 'The Future of the Freedman', *New Orleans Times-Picayune,* 3 February.

Aya, R. (1990). *Rethinking Revolutions and Collective Violence,* Amsterdam: Het Spinhuis.

Berlin, I., T. Glymph, S.F. Miller, J. Reidy, L.S. Rowland, J. Saville (eds) (1990). *Freedom: A Documentary History of Emancipation,* vol. 3, New York: Cambridge University Press.

Bozzoli, B. with M. Nkotsoe (1991). *Women of Phokeng,* Johannesburg: Ravan Press.

Bradford, H. (1987). *A Taste of Freedom: The ICU in Rural South Africa, 1924-1930,* Johannesburg: Ravan Press.

Burton, V. (1978). 'Race and Reconstruction: Edgefield County, South Carolina', *Journal of Social History,* 12 (1), Fall, p. 37.

– (1985). *In My Father's House Are Many Mansions: Family and Community in Edgefield, South Carolina,* Chapel Hill, NC: University of North Carolina Press.

Cell, J. (1982). *The Highest Stage of White Supremacy,* New York: Cambridge University Press.

Curtis, L. (1951). *With Milner in South Africa,* Oxford: Basil Blackwell.

Davenport, T.R.H. (1963). 'The South African Rebellion, 1914', *English Historical Review,* 127 (306), p. 78.

De Wet, C. (1902). *The Three Years War,* New York: Charles Scribner and Sons.

Denoon, D. (1973). *A Grand Illusion,* London: Longman.

Dubow, S. (1989). *Segregation and the Origins of Apartheid in South Africa,* London: Macmillan.

Eichel, H. (1998). 'In Church Suit against Klan, Dees Goes after Top Officials', *Boston Sunday Globe,* 19 July.

Falkner Williams, L. (undated). *The Great South Carolina Ku Klux Klan Trials, 1871–1872,* Athens, Georgia: University of Georgia Press.

Fields, B. (1983). 'The Nineteenth Century American South: History and Theory', *Plantation Society,* 2 (4), pp. 7–27.

Fitzhugh Brundage, W. (1993). *Lynching in the New South: Georgia and Virginia, 1880–1930*, Urbana: University of Illinois Press.

Foner, E. (1983). *Nothing But Freedom: Emancipation and Its Legacy*, Baton Rouge: Louisiana State University Press.

– (1884). *Nothing But Freedom*, 35–39; *Report on Cotton Production in the United States: Supplement to the Tenth Census*, vol. 1, Washington DC: Government Printing Office.

Foner, C. (1989). *Reconstruction: America's Unfinished Revolution*, New York: Hill and Wang.

Fredrickson, G. (1988). 'The South and South Africa: Political Foundations of Segregation', in *The Arrogance of Race*, Middletown: Wesleyan University Press.

– (1981). *White Supremacy: A Comparative Study In American and South African History*, New York: Oxford University Press.

Garson, N.G. (1962). 'The Boer Rebellion of 1914', *History Today*, 12 (2), pp. 132–38.

Genovese, E. (1996). *The Slaveholders' Dilemma*, Columbia, South Carolina: University of South Carolina Press.

Gilligan, J. (1996). *Violence: Our Deadly Epidemic and its Causes*, New York: G.P. Putnam's Sons.

Godley, R.S. (1935). *Khaki and Blue: Thirty Five Years' Service in South Africa*, London: Lovat Dickson and Thompson Limited.

Grundlingh, A.M. (1979). 'Die Rebellie van 1914: historiografiese verkenning', *KLEIO*, 2, pp. 18–30.

Hancock, W. and J. van der Poel (eds) (1966). *Selections from the Smuts Papers*, vol. I, London: Cambridge University Press, pp. 472–74 and 561.

Hobsbawm, E. (1972). 'From Social History to the History of Society', in F. Gilbert and S.R. Graubard (eds) *Historical Studies Today*, New York: Norton.

Hyman, M.R. (1989). 'Taxation, Public Policy, and Political Dissent: Yeoman Dissatisfaction the Post-Reconstruction South', *Journal of Southern History*, LV (1), February), p. 1.

Irvin Painter, N. (1976). *Exodusters*, New York: Norton.

Jaynes, G. (1986). *Branches Without Roots: Genesis of the Black Working Class in the American South, 1862–1882*, New York: Oxford University Press.

Katzenellenbogen, S.E. (1980). 'Reconstruction in the Transvaal', in Peter Warwick (ed.) *The South African: The Anglo-Boer War, 1899–1902*, London: Longman.

Keegan, T. (1988). *Facing the Storm*, London; Zed Press.

– (1987). *Rural Transformations in Industrialising South Africa*, London: Macmillan.

Krikler (1993). *Revolution From Above, Rebellion From Below*, Oxford: Clarendon Press.

Marks, S and S. Trapido (1979). 'Lord Milner and the South African State', *History Workshop*, 8, Autumn, pp. 50–81.

Maxwell Brown, R. (1969). 'Historical Patterns of Violence in America', in Hugh Davis and Ted Gurr (eds) *Violence in America*, Washington DC: US Government Printing Office.

Mbenga, B.K. (1997). 'Flogging of Chief Kgamanyane by Commandant Paul Kruger, Saulspoort, April 1870', *Journal of Southern African Studies*, 23 (1), pp. 127–40.

Moore, B. (1978). *Injustice: The Social Bases of Obedience and Revolt*, White Plains, New York: M.E. Sharpe.

Newnham F.J. (1905). 'The Native Locations in the Transvaal', in *Newnham Collection, Historical Collections*, University of the Witwatersrand, Johannesburg, South Africa.

Pakenham, T. (1979). *The Boer War*, New York: Random House.

Rable, G.C (1984). *But There Was No Peace*, Athens, Georgia: University of Georgia Press.

Report of the Joint Committee in Reconstruction (1865). 39th Congress, 1st session, House Reports, 2 (30), p. xvii.

Sack, K. (1996). 'Burnings of Black Churches Investigated', *New York Times*, 21 May.

Saville, J. (1994). *The Work of Reconstruction: From Slave to Wage Laborer in South Carolina*, New York: Cambridge University Press, pp. 114–17.

Scholtz, G.D. (1942). *Die Rebellie 1914–1915*, Johannesburg: Voortrekkerpers Beperk.

Shugg, R. (1939). *Origins of the Class Struggle in Louisiana*, Baton Rouge: Louisiana State University Press.

Smuts, J. (1900). *A Century of Wrong*, Dordrecht: Eerste uitgawe.

South African Native Affairs Commission (1904) 'Testimony of G.G. Munnik', 1903–1905, IV, Cape Town: Cape Times Limited: Government Printers, pp. 477–78.

– 'Testimony of A.H. Malan', Farmers' Association: Rustenburg, p. 570.

– 'Testimony of W. Windham', 4, pp. 431–36.

Tannenbaum, F. (1924). *Darker Phases of the South*, New York: C.P. Putnams and Sons.

Tolnay, S.E. and E.M. Beck (1995) *Festival of Violence: An Analysis of Southern Lynchings, 1882–1930*, Urbana: University of Illinois Press.

Trelease, A. (1971). *White Terror*, New York: Harper and Row.

Tunnell, T. (1989). *The Crucible of Reconstruction*, Baton Rouge: Louisiana State University Press.

– (ed.) (1989). *Carpetbagger From Vermont: The Autobiography of Marshall Harvey Twitchell*, Baton Rouge: Louisiana State University Press.

Tyrrell, L.E.N. (1903). 'Notes, Queries and Replies', *Transvaal Agricultural Journal*, 3 (1), April, pp. 72–73.

Van Onselen, C. (1990). 'Race and Class in the South African Countryside: Cultural Osmosis and Social Relations in the Sharecropping Economy of the South-Western Transvaal, 1900–1950', *American Historical Review*, 95, April, pp. 99–123.

– (1992). 'The Social and Economic Underpinning of Paternalism and Violence on the Maize Farms of the South-Western Transvaal', *Journal of Historical Sociology*, 5 (2), June, pp. 134–36.

– (1996). *The Seed is Mine,* New York: Hill and Wang.

Vandal, G. (1991). 'Bloody Caddo: White Violence Against Blacks in a Louisiana Parish, 1875–1876', *Journal of Social History,* 25 (2), Winter, p. 374.

Vann Woodward, C. (1990). *Origins of the New South, 1877–1913,* Baton Rouge: Louisiana State University Press, pp. 185–86.

Warwick, P. (1982). *Black People and the South African War,* London: Cambridge University Press.

Weekly Mail and Guardian (1997). 'New bomb blast links to AWB', 10 (http://wn.apc.org/wmail/issues/NEWS36.htm).

– (1997). 'South Africans rally in sympathy after Rustenburg Bomb Blast', (http://www.786.co.za/al-qalam/dec96/rutnbrgbomb.htm).

White, H. (1970). *The Freedmen's Bureau In Louisiana,* Baton Rouge: Louisiana State University Press.

Williamson, J. (1984). *The Crucible of Race: Black-White Relations in the American South Since Emancipation,* New York: Oxford University Press.

Wright Mills, C. (1959). *The Sociological Imagination,* New York: Grove Press.

Yudelman, D. (1983). *The Emergence of Modern South Africa,* Westport: Greenwood Press.

CHAPTER THREE

The spatial geography of urban apartheid

Franco Frescura

Introduction

It is true that, in many respects, the roots of racial segregation can be traced back to the nineteenth century and the strictures that colonial society imposed upon southern Africa's urban areas. Case studies in the region seem to indicate that our suburbs were often integrated to a larger degree than is generally admitted by Apartheid's historians, and although black and white were uneasy neighbours, they generally appear to have shared urban facilities with a measure of success. Disputes between the two communities usually arose over the occupation of coveted residential land, an issue which was often linked by whites to the question of public health.

Occasionally matters reached a critical point, such as in 1901–1903 when the British importation of fodder from Argentina brought about a nation-wide outbreak of Bubonic Plague. Upon this occasion the authorities unilaterally imposed draconian restrictions upon the Black population, demolished their homes, burned their belongings, and displaced entire communities to sites well beyond the city boundaries. Barring such instances, however, planning decisions which created social divisions were generally made by planners on an ad hoc basis, and were largely guided by considerations of economic class.

A major turning point was reached in 1923 when the Union Parliament passed the Natives (Urban Areas) Act, which laid down the principles of residential segregation and reinforced the doctrine that the African population had no permanent rights in the towns. In spite of this, the now "white" suburbs remained racially integrated to varying degrees until 1948 when the Nationalist Party came to power. At that stage the process of separating communities was placed upon an ideological footing, and was given substance by a variety of inter-linking residential, squatting, labour and security legislation. Although, over the years, the dialectic of Apartheid has tended to change, its net effect upon the black community has involved the dispossession of their homes and land, often with minimal recompense. They have also been denied access to markets, infrastructure and civic amenities, leading to impoverishment and increased economic hardship.

In February 1990 the government began to dismantle the framework of laws upon which the Nationalist's dream of an Apartheid society was based. Democrats throughout the world applauded this event, but almost immediately workers on the ground began to realise that whilst the legislation might have gone, the inequality generated by two generations of statutory discrimination had still to be redressed.

This condition has become most evident in South Africa's urban areas where residential distributions, land uses, transport routes and statutory curbs on economic development have combined to create cities where economic inequality has become entrenched along racial lines. Planners are not unaware of this debate, but the solutions they are currently proposing vary from a liberal, market-based, long-term integration of the suburbs, through to a highly legislated interventionist policy orchestrated through a central government.

The shortcomings of either philosophy are self-evident, and it seems probable that whatever solution is finally adopted, it will have to be reached within a framework which takes full cognisance of all the historical factors involved.

In this paper I analyse the historical nature and physical characteristics of the Apartheid city. I examine the role played by planners in the oppression of a people, and look at the problems currently facing community-based professionals, politicians and service organisations attempting to restructure South African cities according to popularly-based democratic principles. Finally I propose some broad guidelines for professional and ethical behaviour which planners might have to follow in order to find greater relevance in a future South African society.

For the purposes of this paper I illustrate my points using Johannesburg and Port Elizabeth as primary case studies. However, neither instance should be considered to be unique, and surveys conducted by other researchers in this field indicate that similar patterns of growth have been experienced by urban settlements elsewhere in this country. Also, where reference is made to such terms as black, white, Indian and coloured, this is in the context of former apartheid and Group Areas classifications.

1   The Johannesburg case study

Following the discovery of gold on the farm Langlaagte in April 1886, the Witwatersrand saw an almost immediate influx of people. This was not limited to those directly involved in mining activity, but included a large number of other men and women offering a variety of skills and services of the kind necessary to the establishment of human settlement. By August 1886 Johannesburg could already boast of some 3 000 inhabitants, most of whom were white, and on 4 October 1886 the site of present-day central Johannesburg was declared a township. The first building plots were subdivided on a grid-iron pattern and sold by public auction two months later, in December of that year.

The sub-division of what became the new town's central district was a typical product of 19th century mining camp planning, and was made with impermanence of settlement in mind. Even after it was realised that the gold reef ran both deep and wide, and the introduction of the cyanide process made deep level mining economically feasible, the general consensus of the time was that Johannesburg's life span would not exceed 25 years. Thus, initially at any rate, life in the new town was one of uncertainty and, for a number of years, many of its buildings retained their prefabricated iron-and-timber character.

It is interesting to note that the residential townships which comprised early Johannesburg, such as Jeppestown, Fordsburg, Turffontein, Mayfair and Newlands, were also laid out on a similar grid-iron system. Not surprisingly these suburbs were also sited close to the Main Reef diggings. Seeing that the mines spread in an east-west direction, it would appear that the Reef acted as one of the earliest factors determining the growth patterns of the young town's residential sector.

1.a)   Residential expansion to the north

For the first 70 years of its life, Johannesburg's residential development occurred predominantly north of the Main Reef. This trend was based upon geographical and early historical factors which, until relatively recent times, have acted as strong deterrents to settlement south of the city. Almost from the onset the rapid development of an industrial belt, spanning from east to west, created an effective barrier between the town's northern and southern areas.

The nature of the mine's surface workings, their mine-head establishments, workers' compounds and the lack of road infrastructure made it difficult to transverse this area. As a result few traffic and transport routes were driven through it. These problems were compounded during the rainy season when this land became an impassable muddy quagmire.

Thus whilst the residential suburbs north of the Reef were able to spread east and west with relatively little constraint while remaining in close proximity to the town centre, suburbs to the south found themselves located at a considerable distance from the business hub. Another factor which soon came into play was the presence of the sand dumps whose growing bulk around the gold mines began to impinge more and more upon the civic consciousness of the town. Eventually these became associated with Johannesburg's skyline to the extent of being considered one of its more picturesque land marks. In the interim however, under windy conditions, they gave rise to an unpleasant pollution problem which particularly affected its southern areas. It should also be borne in mind that Johannesburg's southern suburbs are low lying and generally unprotected by the topography. This means that unlike the northern areas, which are shielded by a series of ridges, they are exposed to bitterly cold winter winds; that temperature extremes throughout the year are generally greater south of the Braamfontein ridge than to its north; and that the discomfort of sand raised by strong winds was aggravated in the southern areas, and tended to be perennial rather than seasonal.

It is not surprising therefore that, as many of early Johannesburg's citizens began to gain in financial substance, they chose to make their homes in the northern areas. Initially this trend to the north was relatively modest, the better homes being located in Doornfontein and Belgravia, below the Braamfontein ridge, and in Berea above it. These developments were probably facilitated by the fact that Johannesburg's major road links to other population centres in the Transvaal were mostly to the north: Rustenburg, the Barberton goldfields, and most important, Pretoria, capital of the Zuid Afrikanse Republiek. Significantly however, the earliest working class suburbs, both black and white, were also located north of the diggings.

After the Anglo-Boer conflict, the population's drift to the town's northern residential areas gathered in momentum. Not unnaturally, property developers began to take note of this trend and by 1909 many of Johannesburg's northern suburbs had already been proclaimed. This is not, of course, a reliable indicator of growth, for many of these areas did not reach full development until nearly 40 years later. However some residential building activity did take place, enough it seems to determine the town's main residential and infrastructural thrust for the next half century.

The majority of these suburbs were aimed at a middle and upper-middle income clientele, families who would seek land out of reach of the environmental ravages and pollution of mining activity; who would want to live under more favourable climatic conditions, specifically in the cold winter months; and who, most importantly, would also be prepared to pay substantial rates and taxes which would subsidise the development of a physical infrastructure in this area. This, in its turn, allowed the northern suburbs to be laid out in stands much larger than their average southern counterparts.

Plots in the older townships had seldom been larger than 500 m², a size probably based on European standards prevailing at that time. However, later suburb development was characterised by land parcels of up to 4 000 m², and in some cases even more. An interesting factor which has survived to the present day is the elitist image attached to some of the northern suburbs, obviously obtained from the mining magnates who bought into these areas.

This, in its turn, attracted the town's white collar workers who were encouraged to settle in the surrounding suburbs. Thus a difference which was originally based upon physical and climatic factors, ultimately became entrenched as one of social class.

The development of apartment buildings, or flats, was only initiated in Johannesburg during the 1920s, beginning in the town centre, spreading into Hillbrow and Braamfontein, and later into Berea and Yeoville.

1.b)   Developments to the east and west

One of the major factors influencing the physical development of Johannesburg, and of the Witwatersrand as a whole, has been the role played by the railway. When the Cape line reached Johannesburg in 1892, it joined the existing east-west railway linking the various mining villages on the Reef. At the onset, trains from the south entered the town from Elandsfontein in the east, making use of an existing natural embankment running from Jeppestown to what was then Park Station, near the old Wanderers. In about 1905 an additional line was laid, linking Johannesburg to Vereeniging via Roodepoort, and a decade later Cape-bound trains were able to travel the more direct westerly route via Potchefstroom and Kimberley.

The introduction of a railroad into Johannesburg's urban fabric had the effect of strengthening what had already become a distinct separation between the residential areas to the north, and the mining, commercial and industrial sectors to the south. However, while it proved to be an effective barrier which promoted these residential trends, it also proved an equally effective curb to the northward expansion of the Central Business District (CBD). It therefore became a powerful structural component of the town's form. It was not until the early 1960s that land pressures in the CBD reached a crisis point. Faced with an inability to expand into undermined land to its south, it was forced to move into Braamfontein, a suburb which had, in the intervening years, become socially and economically depressed.

The town's initial east-west development was encouraged by the growth of working-class residential areas in close proximity to the gold mines. This move was reinforced by the establishment of transport infrastructures, including the railway and, later, a suburban tram network which linked the town centre to the suburbs and permitted rapid expansion to follow in those directions. Growth to the east took place at a relatively faster pace as this area provided added employment opportunities on the Elandsfontein railway yards, renamed Germiston in 1904, and the Boksburg and Brakpan gold and coal mines.

Because the residential suburbs to the east and, more specifically, to the west of the CBD have remained in close physical proximity to areas of blue-collar employment, these areas have retained their working-class character to the present day. One of the reasons for this has been the inherited residential textures of these areas, determined to a great degree by their small stand sizes, generally between 500 and 1 000 m^2 and, in the case of Laurentzville, as little as 250 m^2. This encouraged the construction of modest, affordable cottages rather than large and more expensive houses.

1.c)   Early population growth

Prior to the discovery of the Main Reef in 1886, the Transvaal Republic is estimated to have been the home of some 40 000 white immigrant and 300 000 indigenous residents. Of these about 600 whites inhabited the Witwatersrand which, by the standards of that time, was considered to be a fairly well populated area. Within a year of the discovery of gold in Johannesburg, the whole Reef was estimated to have some 7 000 people, with 3 000 residing in Johannesburg itself. The rise of population numbers thereafter can only be described as phenomenal, following an exponential growth pattern for virtually all sectors of the population. By 1890, a scant four years after the discovery of gold, it had multiplied ten-fold on both the Rand and in Johannesburg. Five years later, in 1895, Johannesburg was known to hold 102 000 people, this number being equally divided between white and black residents.

After suffering from a temporary setback during the Anglo-Boer conflict of 1899-1902, population patterns resumed their previous trends of rapid growth, assisted in part by the influx, in 1904, of some 50 000 Chinese indentured labourers. Following their repatriation in 1909, they were replaced on the mines by the introduction of a migrant black labour system. Initially these men came from Mozambique, but later on they were also drawn from British colonies further afield in southern and central Africa.

1.d)   The development of the segregated city

Before 1822 the indigenous population of the southern Transvaal is estimated to have numbered some 150 000, many of whom lived in large settlements of up to 7 000 persons. However, the ravages of the Difaqane, from 1822 to 1837, and the invasion of the region by land-hungry Dutch farmers in 1836 forced many families to leave their ancestral lands. By the time gold was discovered on the Witwatersrand in 1886, their nearest homesteads were located 110km away, near Rustenburg. The ZAR's subsequent imposition of a 'hut tax' forced rural residents to enter into white employment. Johannesburg offered both work and higher wages and within a few years the town had become the home of a large, unskilled and predominantly male labour force. Some found jobs as domestic workers in the suburbs, most laboured on the mines.

Early Johannesburg did not offer its black citizens much in the way of housing. While the mines generally looked after their own, and most domestics could expect to have sleep-in quarters, the remainder had to fend for themselves. Almost from the onset, when the town was first laid out, separate suburbs, or 'locations' as they were known, were allocated for black, Malay and Asian occupation. Not only did this conform with existing ZAR policies, but the idea of separate residential areas for black and white also suited the mining companies who had recently adopted the 'compound' as a means of housing their black labourers.

The concept derived its name from the Malay word 'kampong', meaning an enclosure. Originally it was implemented for security reasons and was used to confine employees to their quarters for the duration of their labour contracts. This system had previously been used on the Kimberley diamond fields to prevent the pilfering of gems. However, its application on the Witwatersrand was not as harsh. Compounds consisted of single-sex hostels housing between eight and sixteen men per room. Early buildings were set about a central square accessed through a single gateway. The planning of later complexes, which could house up to 5 000 workers each, was amended to a fan-shaped pattern, with buildings radiating out from a central access point.

This refinement was claimed by mine management to facilitate 'riot control', a euphemism used to denote labour disputes which arose from time to time, and which mining companies had little compunction in settling through the use of force. It is evident that, almost from the beginning, this programme gave rise to a number of social problems. Alcohol abuse, venereal disease and prostitution were common occurrences among mine labourers of that time. Matters were not assisted by the general male-female ratio which remained high right up to the late 1930s. In 1902, for example, the total black population on the Rand was 64 664, of which only 7 615 were women.

Early maps of Johannesburg show its 'locations' to have been sited on the outskirts of white-designated suburbs, on land commonly known as Brickfields. It included Burgersdorp, a low income area where many indigent Afrikaners had also made their homes. This was a poorly drained piece of ground which had originally served as a brickyard, providing the materials for many of Johannesburg's first brick buildings.

Considering the rudimentary methods of waste disposal available there, and the clay nature of the soil, it did not take long for a serious health hazard to develop. Before 1899 Johannesburg's white community had made repeated complaints about this area to the ZAR government. However 'Uitlander' grievances fell upon deaf ears in Pretoria and little could be done during the hostilities. In 1902 the matter was reopened and a Sanitary Commission was appointed to investigate the Brickfields.

In November 1903 its report was tabled, recommending that the site be expropriated and redeveloped. These findings were overtaken by events on 19 March 1904 when an outbreak of bubonic plague is reported to have taken place in Burgersdorp. Virtually overnight the inhabitants of Brickfields were evacuated, the area was fenced off with corrugated iron sheeting and everything within fired to the ground by the Fire Brigade. It was subsequently renamed Newtown and redeveloped as a suburb for light industrial use.

Following these events, the residents of Brickfields were moved to a 'health camp' near the Klipspruit Sewage Farm, or present-day Kliptown, some 20km from the town centre. Some were accommodated in corrugated iron dwellings, but most were simply provided with materials to build their own homes. Although this settlement was intended to be of a temporary nature, it remained in existence until the mid 1970s, when it was cleared to make way for new housing developments. Despite having been dispossessed of their homes in the Brickfields, the residents of the resettlement camp near Klipspruit were given no compensation for their properties, nor were they provided with a sanitary infrastructure. The services available to this community remained rudimentary for many years, affecting its quality of life. It must be assumed that, because they had now been removed from the town centre, their welfare had ceased to be of direct concern to its citizens.

The people of Klipspruit were not alone in this plight and generally very little was done by the authorities of early Johannesburg to improve the housing conditions of black workers. A small measure of relief was afforded in 1917 when a disused compound on the Salisbury Jubilee Mine was rented by the Town Council and converted to a single-sex hostel to house one thousand men. Two years later, between 1919 and 1922, a housing scheme to provide homes for 5 000 people was completed in Western Native Township, but this was a small concession made following the influenza epidemic of 1918. By this stage the black urban population of Johannesburg had risen to 116 120 people and these projects made little difference to the living conditions enjoyed by the majority of the town's black citizens.

There is no doubt that the question of land ownership was a major issue in the housing of black workers. The 'Gold Laws', inherited from the ZAR, precluded 'persons of colour' from owning land in virtually the whole of Johannesburg. This included citizens from a wide range of backgrounds, including black, Indian, Malay, Chinese and mixed race. Thus the reservation of prime business and residential land for the exclusive use of whites became a political issue at an early stage of the town's history. Western Native, for example, had not been claimed for white use as its land had previously been used as a brickfield, which was subsequently levelled and used as a refuse tip.

By the 1920s other townships, also suffering from poor infrastructural conditions, had arisen in such places as Newclare, Sophiatown, Prospect and the Malay Location. A number of other areas were also considered to be slums by public officials. However officers from the Medical Officer of Health's department refused repeatedly to condemn them or to have them cleared, knowing full well that the vast majority of their inhabitants were black and that no other facilities existed for their rehousing.

In 1925 a single men's hostel was built at Wemmer. At this stage the ratio between men and women had dropped only minimally to 6:1. Therefore official emphasis was still upon the provision of single sex compounds, rather than in the construction of family homes. However it is probable that official figures failed to reflect the true state of affairs. A form of 'influx control' and the carrying of passes for blacks had been introduced by the ZAR as early as 1890. Thus although the 1925 figures showed the presence of 117 700 men as against 19 000 women, it is probable that there were far more black women in Johannesburg than was officially indicated. It is credible that, in time, many workers began to bring their families to the town. Being illegal residents their presence could not be declared, and their numbers thus increased the pressure upon an already overloaded informal infrastructure.

Much of the blame for these conditions must lie with the Johannesburg Town Council. By this stage many smaller towns in South Africa had already established their own separate departments to handle what they called 'Native Affairs'. Johannesburg, on the other hand, waited until 1927 before taking any action, and only set up a Committee of Native Affairs in 1928. Before then the affairs of 'native administration' had been handled by the Department of Parks and Recreation.

1.e)   The first black suburbs

By 1930 large extensions had been made to Western Native Township, and the new suburb of Eastern Native had also been established. The latter was never permitted to grow to any significant size and today survives only as a Municipal single men's hostel. In the same year 2 500 acres were purchased near Klipspruit, and in 1931 a start was made on the suburb of Orlando, named after Councillor Edwin Orlando Leake. However progress was slow, and by 1939, Johannesburg could only boast a total of 8 900 houses, and hostel accommodation for 6 700 single men. By then the black population was 244 000 with a male to female ratio slightly below 3:1.

The next five years were an important period in the history of Johannesburg's black residential sector. With most of the white labour force engaged in overseas war duties, increasing demands were made upon local skilled and unskilled labour. The war effort not only boosted the industrial and manufacturing sector, but its demands for material production broke down many old prohibitions upon the use of black labour. As a result more black workers were brought into urban centres, effectively sensitising them to labour and other economic issues, and forging them into a well-politicised industrial proletariat. The effects of this were only felt fully during the 1950s, once the ANC and PAC began organising campaigns of resistance against continued white political, cultural and economic domination. By the end of the War, Johannesburg's black population had increased to 395 231, with a male to female ratio of nearly 2:1. Over 20% of this population consisted of young children, a clear indication that many families had cut their rural links and were forging a new urban society. It also meant that the needs of education would henceforth also have to be taken into account when planning for the infrastructural needs of the black community.

1.f)   The squatter movement

Between 1936 and 1946 Johannesburg's black population grew by 59% to a total of nearly 400 000. During the same period the comparative growth of the white sector

was 29%. However, up to 1945 the Municipality had only erected a total of 9 573 low
income housing units and made available 7 270 beds in male, single sex, hostels. This
means that officially, only some 55 000 persons were being housed in municipal resi-
dences. The remainder had to make do as best they might, and although some people
worked and slept over in the white suburbs, few could claim a home of their own. The
majority were forced to move illegally into vacant tracts of land in such areas as Orlando,
Pimville, Dube, Newclare and Alexandra where squatter suburbs sprang up virtually
overnight. When the largest of these camps was eventually cleared in 1955, it was
found to have housed an estimated 60 000 persons. The lack of sanitation and the
overcrowding of housing in these areas caused the overload of an already meagre
infrastructure. In time these communities also began to demand other facilities, such
as schooling, which was either rudimentary or non-existent, or was being withheld by
the authorities as a matter of policy.

Over the years the quality of life available to residents in these areas has become a
matter of some debate. Liberal commentators have pointed, with some reason, to the
richness and variety of sub-cultures which existed in places such as Sophiatown. It is
true that these squatter areas gave rise to some of this country's most notable black
poets, writers, artists, singers, musicians and political leaders. It is also true, however,
that they suffered from a high crime rate, and that residents were generally at the
mercy of profiteers, slum-lords, farmers of shacks and any carpetbagger unscrupulous
enough to exploit the despair and plight of others. Richard Rive has pointed out that,
contrary to the romantic image that white liberals have painted about District Six, in
Cape Town, the residents themselves considered it to have been a slum and often 'could
not wait to get out'. The same sentiments were also expressed by the people of Pageview,
or 'Vietas', in Johannesburg prior to the demolition of this area.

Not unnaturally, such conditions also gave rise to a generation of political leaders
and socially involved persons who voiced the grievances of black workers. Patrick
Lewis has called them 'leaders outside the law' and, in view of subsequent events, it is
significant that the City Council of that time found itself powerless to act against
them. It was only the coming to power of the Nationalist Party in 1948 which temporarily stilled the voices of legitimate black protest and forced many of its leaders into
exile or jail.

Predictably a riot did eventually occur in August 1947 when municipal offices
were attacked and three white policemen were killed. The Council's attitude at the
time may be best summed up by a memo they submitted to the Governmental
Commission of Enquiry into this event. Under the heading of 'Fundamental Causes',
they claimed that :

> In the submission of the Council, the fundamental cause of the riot is the
> attitude of mind produced in the urban native population by the series of

squatter movements which have occurred in Johannesburg since 1944 and which may best be summarised as one of contempt for authority and for constitutional methods in favour of direct action, however illegal and violent, coupled with growing political and national consciousness of the urban Native population.

Writing some 19 years later, Patrick Lewis, a self-professed liberal and a former Johannesburg City Councillor during that period, also attempted to dismiss the social and political realities of the squatter movements. He claimed that their leaders were acting as the agents of financially motivated profiteers and slum lords, a naive assertion which indicates, if nothing else, an ignorance of local housing conditions, and of the needs and aspirations of urban black residents.

The period between 1939 and 1945 is also significant for it marks a time when the economic and residential make-up of Johannesburg's urban black population underwent final and irrevocable change. Before the War this community was marked by a sizeable component which retained seasonal links to the rural areas. This was owed to the rotational nature of the migrant labour system, which brought rural workers to the city on eleven month contracts and then expected them to return home until the cycle was repeated the following year. After 1945 the make-up of urban black society changed to include a greater proportion of children. This indicated a tendency on the part of black families to sever their rural roots and to establish permanent homes in urban areas. In 1948 the Nationalist Government attempted to reverse this trend by introducing a policy of forced 'repatriation' to 'independent states' having a predominantly agrarian economic base. This promoted a myth of 'rural ethnicity' which sought to deny the existence of an industrial proletariat, a position which the Government only abandoned relatively recently.

Thus the planning and implementation of urban housing programs in Johannesburg after 1945 had to take into account the existence of an expanding and permanent urban black population. However a realisation that demographic changes had taken place was slow in percolating through to the civic decision-making process, and of the 10 730 house contracts placed between 1940 and 1947, only 1 538 were built. Instead it was thought that relief for squatters could be found in a policy of temporary housing. Although some units were built on a short-term basis, they were experimental in nature and suffered from some notable technical and planning flaws. Further housing activity took place between 1947 and 1951, when a total of 6 788 units were built. It was not until 1951 when two acts, designed to ease the nation-wide housing crisis, were promulgated. The 'Prevention of Illegal Squatting Act' was the first of over one hundred pieces of similar legislation designed to give local authorities the means of removing squatters from land; the 'Native Building Workers Act' authorised the utilisation of skilled black labour on low-income housing schemes. The combination of the two, together with a large infusion of State funds, allowed municipal housing agencies to initiate new and large-scale housing programs in Johannesburg's black residential areas.

1.g)   Low-cost housing developments in the post-war era

The immediate effect of the 'Native Building Workers Act' was the formation of a Housing Division within the City Council. With the assistance of Governmental sub- sidies, and a series of loans raised from Johannesburg's mining companies, most specifically Sir Ernest Oppenheimer of Anglo-American, the Housing Division was able to implement a number of site-and-service schemes which eased the crisis to a small degree. By the time building operations reached their peak in Johannesburg in 1958, 40 houses per day were being handed over for occupation by the Housing Divi- sion, and by 1969 a total of 65 564 houses had been built in Soweto alone.

The houses were built as the result of research conducted by the National Building Research Institute (NBRI) between 1948 and 1951. Although this project is generally considered to have been the result of group effort, much of it revolved around the ideas of Douglas Calderwood, a young architect working at the NBRI at the time. He subsequently incorporated his work into two academic dissertations for which he was awarded an MArch and, later, a PhD, by the Department of Architecture at the Univer- sity of the Witwatersrand. The dwellings were probably designed by another young architect employed by the NBRI, Barrie Biermann, who has since become better known for his research in Cape Dutch architecture. Biermann's knowledge of the Cape ver- nacular is evident from the plan of the average Soweto house, a four-roomed unit which resembled a double-pile 'lang huis'. It became generally known as the NE 51/6, where 'NE' stood for 'Non-European', '51' was 1951, the year of Calderwood's doctoral thesis, and 11611 was the drawing's number in the thesis. Other designs included the NE 51/7, consisting of a pair of semi-detached NE 51/6s, and the NE 51/9, a slightly larger version of the NE 51/6 with an internal bathroom. In later years Johannesburg's Housing Division also evolved their own versions of the NE 51/9, which they called the 'Type L' and the 'Type M' respectively. Few of these, however, are known to have ever been built.

These designs, however, should not be read in isolation of white opinions prevail- ing at that time. In April 1950, the Minister of Native Affairs, Dr E.G. Jansen stated in Parliament that it was a:

> wrong notion that the Native who has barely left his primitive conditions should be provided with a house which to him resembles a palace and with conven- iences which he cannot appreciate and which he will not require for many years to come.

Jansen, who went on to become Governor-General of the Union of South Africa, was, in many ways, echoing the sentiments of previous colonial governments. In 1894, during the planning stages of Vrededorp and the nearby Malay Location, for example, President Kruger is reputed to have slashed the size of plots down to 250 sq. ft, claiming that:

> *Ek sal hulle nie plase gee nie, maar net sitplekke.* (I will not give them farms, but only places to squat.)

Calderwood's work for the NBRI in the early 1950s was therefore designed to meet such governmental standards and, ironically, forms the basis for Nationalist housing policy right up to the mid-1980s.

The planning of Soweto incorporated a number of important features. There is no doubt that its town planners were inspired by 'garden city' theories current in Europe at that time. Its streets broke with the grid-iron pattern common in other parts of Johannesburg, and were designed to promote a hierarchy of traffic routes. Suburbs were laid out to create neighbourhoods, and green areas and civic spaces were integrated into the overall plan. Houses were detached and each was set on its own plot of land.

The idealism of the planners however, was offset by the unavoidable fact that Soweto was the brainchild of racist and segregationist thinking. This manifested itself in a number of ways, summarised in a later section of this paper.

Many of Soweto's suburbs also owe their birth to the destruction of other black residential areas, such as Western Native, Eastern Native, Sophiatown and the Moroka squatter camp. Each of these, in its own time, represented a pocket of political resistance against white racism and segregationist ideology. Each was destroyed in its turn, wilfully and systematically, by a governmental bureaucracy bent upon breaking down existing social structures and democratic political movements. Resettlement was therefore used as a political weapon, deliberately dispersing neighbourhood units and support groups, separating families and neighbours, as a means of maximising the shocks of removal and dispossession. Soweto is the spawn of apartheid, and its location, planning and architecture serve as constant reminders of this fact to its residents.

The growth and development of Soweto may be summed up by the tabulation below. The year refers to the date of the suburb's declaration; the population and housing figures reflect the numbers as they stood on 30 June 1964.

Township	Year	Population	No. Houses
Pimville	1906	29 088	1 232
Eastern Native Township	1926	3 968	627
Orlando	1930	65 593	11 314

Jabavu	1948	25 468	5 100
Dube	1948	12 727	1 957
Mofolo	1954	28 284	4 543
Central Western Jabavu	1954	25 468	1 432
Moroka North	1955	15 207	2 693
Molapo	1956	8 188	1 466
Moletsane	1956	10 360	1 962
Tladi	1956	10 000	1 860
Dhlamini	1956	9 015	1 422
Tshiawelo (Chiawelo)	1956	20 152	3 989
Zondi	1956	8 861	1 548
Phiri	1956	11 332	2 190
Mapetla	1956	11 476	2 105
Jabulani	1956	11 721	2 039
Naledi	1956	19 923	4 043
Senaoane	1958	8 732	1 511
Zola	1958	30 630	5 572
Emdeni	1958	11 680	2 298
Total		**360 994**	**60 902**

After 1963 Municipal housing activities in Soweto began to wind down and after 1969 these came to a virtual standstill. In 1973 the West Rand Administration Board (WRAB) took over the control and day-to-day administration of Soweto from the Johannesburg's NEAD. However, by the 1970s housing had, once again, become a major political issue in Johannesburg's black community, and although the 1976 Soweto student uprising was sparked off primarily by dissatisfaction with current standards of black education, popular grievances with local housing conditions were important lateral issues in the conflict that ensued.

2   The Port Elizabeth case study

The first immigrant structure in Port Elizabeth was erected by the British in August 1799. Named Fort Frederick, after Frederick, Duke of York, its main function was to guard the landing place and water supplies at Algoa Bay. It is also probable that the British intended to establish a military presence in the region to deter potential Dutch uprisings in the district of Graaff-Reinet, and to protect Cape Town, and hence the India sea route, from possible French attack. The township of Port Elizabeth was laid out in 1815, but was not developed until 1820 when some 5 000 British settlers arrived in the Eastern Cape. Initial settlement focused upon the harbour as the town's major area of economic activity. However as the bay's microclimatic factors began to exert themselves, so then white residential areas began to move to the cooler and less humid higher ground overlooking the bay, and into areas which provided a measure of shelter from its persistent, year-round winds.

The economic development of the village was initially slow. James Backhouse (1844), who visited the place in December 1838, described it as follows:

> Port Elizabeth is situated on the foot of a steep hill, at the margin of Algoa Bay; it is much like a small, English sea-port town, and contains about 100 houses, exclusive of huts; the houses are of stone or brick, red-tiled, and of English structure. The town is said to have been chiefly raised by the sale of strong drink.

Thus at its onset Port Elizabeth served predominantly as a service centre for the agricultural hinterland of the Eastern Cape. Its basic function was to handle, and later process, goods and materials passing through its harbour. However developments elsewhere in the southern African interior provided economic stimulus to the new town, and by the 1860s it had overtaken Cape Town as the Colony's premier port. The growth of an ostrich feather industry in Graaff-Reinet, Oudtshoorn and the Albany, the discovery of diamonds in the northern Cape and of gold in the Transvaal, and the outbreak of successive wars against the Basotho, the Griqua, the Bapedi, the Batswana and the Boer Republics, were all to benefit Port Elizabeth. As a result numerous manufacturing industries began to be established locally, and during the early years of the 20th century the town became a focal point for food processing, motor vehicle assembly, and a variety of associated industries, which created extensive employment opportunities. This, as well as increasing rural poverty in the region, attracted many workers to the town to the point that, until the 1960s, it maintained its place as South Africa's third largest urban centre.

2.a)   Colonial segregation

Port Elizabeth, as it stands today, owes its form to a number of physical and historical constraints. However, since the early 1900s, colonial segregation planning and a policy of statutory racial separation implemented after 1950, has resulted in what has become a prototypical model of the 'apartheid city'.

The early population of Port Elizabeth consisted, in the main, of Europeans, as well as persons of mixed race which the apartheid system subsequently labelled as 'Coloureds' and 'Cape Malays'. Initially few members of the indigenous population were attracted to the town and, almost from the onset, economic status was related to skin colour. Whites held a virtual monopoly over higher paid jobs and consequently could afford better housing in areas which were usually physically removed from 'other' groups. Thus segregation was an integral part of early Port Elizabeth, with the industrial areas of South End and North End being predominantly Coloured, while the Central and Western suburbs were mainly white. However, while white attitudes to Coloured and Malay citizens remained relatively tolerant, official policies toward indigenous residents were markedly different.

Thus, as a rising number of black workers began to enter Port Elizabeth seeking employment, so then a number of so-called 'locations' began to be established on the outskirts of the white suburbs. Rosenthal (1970) has defined locations as being 'Large Native Reserves as well as small areas in municipalities earmarked for residence by Africans'.

The pattern was first established in 1834 when the Colonial Government made a grant of land to the London Missionary Society (LMS) to provide a burial ground and residential area for 'Hottentots and other coloured people who were members of the Church' (Baines, 1989). This was located at the crest of Hyman's Kloof, better known today as Russel Road. Other workers however chose to erect their homes closer to their places of employment, or where a supply of potable water was available. The major Black suburbs of that time were:

Bethelsdorp	1803
Fingo and Hottentot Location	1830
LMS outstation	1834
Dassiekraal	c1850
Korsten	1853
Stranger's Location	1855
Gubbs Location	1860
Cooper's Kloof Location	1877
Reservoir Location	1883

With few exceptions these Black suburbs were informal in nature, and residents there were forced to endure living conditions which contemporary observers described as being squalid and open to exploitation by capitalist landlords. Many whites considered them to be unhealthy and petitions were repeatedly organised demanding that they be removed to the outskirts of the town. These requests were in direct opposition to the needs of the growing commercial and industrial sectors which preferred to locate their labour sources close to the harbour and the inner city area. These conflicting vested interests created political tension within the Port Elizabeth Council which were only resolved in 1885 when the Municipality adopted its first set of markedly segregationist regulations. As a result suburbs for the exclusive use of black residents who were not housed by employers, and who could not afford to purchase property, were established on the outskirts of Port Elizabeth. Most prominent amongst them were:

Racecourse	1896
Walmer	1896
New Brighton	1902

In 1901 an outbreak of Bubonic plague struck the town. This was the direct result of Argentinean fodder and horses being imported into South Africa by the British military during the Anglo-Boer conflict. These cargoes also carried plague-infected rats, and although many members of the White and Coloured communities were also affected, the black population bore the brunt of the Plague Health Regulations. In 1902 most of Port Elizabeth's old locations were demolished (with the exception of Walmer), their resident's personal belongings were arbitrarily destroyed, and restrictions were imposed upon intertown travel. Although these curbs might initially have been necessary, they were only loosely applied to whites, and were maintained upon the lives of black residents well after they were eased elsewhere, this in spite of repeated complaints by the community's leaders.

Because New Brighton was located relatively far from the centre, many families preferred to settle in Korsten which, at the time, was beyond the Port Elizabeth municipal boundary, but was still substantially closer to town. The suburb also did not enforce stringent bye-laws upon the domestic brewing of beer, an activity which, at that time, was an important source of revenue for the black community.

During the colonial period therefore, the location system created a pattern of residential segregation based upon perceived racial and economic differences. However such divisions proved to be only partial, and it was only the implementation of Group Areas legislation after 1950 which brought about a structural separation of Port Elizabeth's residential areas. None-the-less it was during this time that the seeds of the Apartheid City were sown.

2.b)   Post-colonial segregation : 1910-1950

By 1950 the population of New Brighton had grown from 3 650 in 1911 to 35 000. Almost all of it was black. This polarisation was reinforced by the Native Urban Areas Act of 1923 which required municipalities to establish separate locations for their black citizens, and made black residents in 'white' areas subject to a permit system which Apartheid legislation subsequently extended into the now-infamous 'dompas'. The Native Land and Trust Act of 1936 also precluded blacks from purchasing land outside designated areas.

Existing suburbs, as well as new housing projects for whites, began to include racially restrictive clauses in their title deeds. In this way most of Port Elizabeth's western suburbs were reserved for exclusive white residence.

2.c) Apartheid ideology and implementation from 1950 to date

When the Nationalist Party came to power in 1948, the City of Port Elizabeth underwent a number of extensive changes in its land use patterns through the implementation of racially motivated segregationist legislation. This included the separation of citizens into so-called 'White', 'Bantu', 'Coloured' and 'Asian' suburbs. Apartheid legislation laid down that such areas should be set apart by buffer strips at least 100m wide.

These often coincided with existing physical barriers. As a result, industrial areas such as Struandale, and natural features such as the Swartkops River and its escarpment, and pieces of empty land such as Parsonsvlei, were used to define the parameters of the city's suburbs.

It is important to note that apartheid ideology did not view black workers as a permanent component of urban life, but held that, at some stage, they would return of their own initiative and free will, to some mythical rural 'homeland'. This is an attitude which had important political repercussions in later years. Not only did it relate directly to the quality of 'Bantu' education, which in turn sparked off the Soweto student uprising of 1976, but it also created residential conditions which will take many years, and a substantial proportion of the national budget, to eradicate. Because of this, black access to land tenure, quality housing, infrastructure, social amenities and economic opportunities was severely curtailed.

Black suburbs were developed on the remote outskirts of the city making daily travel to the workplace expensive. Also, little retail and business development was permitted within the townships (as they began to be called), forcing residents to conduct the bulk of their shopping in the central city area. The Apartheid City thus did not merely seek to beggar its Black citizens, it also entrenched in its fabric the 'company store' relationship existing between its black suburbs and the white-controlled CBD.

Matters did not change substantially after 1981 when the Government acknowledged the permanent status of urban Black communities and put in place an Ibhayi Town Council which would administer Port Elizabeth's Black suburbs as a separate municipality. At this stage, the zoning of all industrial, retail and business development within the boundaries of a neighbouring white Port Elizabeth ensured that the two Municipalities did not share equally in the city's tax base. This is one of the ways in which Port Elizabeth's black citizens have been subsidising the white community in its expensive segregated lifestyle.

The process of apartheid expropriation, relocation and residential control had the effect of increasing New Brighton's population from 35 000 persons in 1951 to 97 000 in 1960. As a result KwaZakele was established in 1956, and following the demolitions of Salisbury Park, Fairview and South End in the late 1960s, Zwide was declared in 1968. After the Government brought its programme of intensive subsidised housing, which it initiated in 1952, to an end in the mid-1970s, increasing pressures of urbanisation brought about the establishment of Motherwell in 1982 as yet another independent municipality.

It also needs to be borne in mind that although the Nationalist Government single-mindedly pursued a policy of racial segregation in the case of white areas, it tended to ignore racial mixing and even intermarriage in other communities.

Thus even though new segregated suburbs such as Gelvandale, Bethelsdorp and Bloemendal were established for exclusive coloured occupation, with Malabar being set aside for Indians, some areas such as Korsten which, historically, had enjoyed a mixed population, retained much of their integrated character well into the 1980s. Other communities, however, such as Fairview and South End, saw their homes literally bulldozed to the ground and their lands given over for exclusive white settlement.

It is also important to note that, throughout the colonial, segregationist and apartheid eras the original mission settlement at Bethelsdorp remained a major focus of Khoikhoi and, later, black residential activity.

3   Identification of the apartheid city

Apartheid city planning is marked by a number of features which, read in a historical context, could be interpreted as part of a segregationist residential policy. Taken as a whole, however, they fall into a pattern which reveals a wider ideological intent. These characteristics may be summarised as follows:

3.a)   Segregation of residential areas

Selected residential suburbs were set aside for the exclusive use of specific communities. This segregation did not only take place along racial lines but, in some cases, was extended to perceived 'ethnic' groupings in the black community itself.

As a result certain areas of Soweto, near Johannesburg, were set aside for Nguni, Sotho, Tswana and Venda language groups, and even the Nguni suburbs made allowance for Zulu, Xhosa, Ndebele and Tsonga sub-divisions. In the case of black/white segregation, this was regulated by legislation which controlled so-called 'Group Areas', miscegenation and intermarriage between the races.

On the other hand, the separation of 'ethnic groups' was entrusted to white bureaucrats with little knowledge of anthropology, or empathy for indigenous value systems. Separation between white and not-white citizens was strictly enforced, often by brutal police action, whilst little attention appears to have been paid to residential mixing and integration within the not-white group.

3.b)   Use of buffer zones

Group areas were separated by means of buffer zones, which were 100m minimum width, but in some cases, could be as much as 250m. In the case of some smaller municipalities the mandatory existence of buffer zones had a negative effect upon the growth of white residential and business areas, leading these to openly ignore regulations promulgated under an ideology they officially espoused.

3.c)   Use of natural features

In many instances planners were allowed to incorporate natural features, or areas where construction was difficult, into their buffer zones. In Port Elizabeth the Swartkops estuary and its escarpment have been used, and although a future democratic local government may well seek to bridge the gap between black and white residential areas, the existence of these buffers could well prove insurmountable obstacles.

3.d)   Industrial belts as buffer zones

Although buffer zones were used to create and reinforce racial segregation, this land was invariably retained under white municipal control and in many cases was developed as industrial townships.

Thus although businesses in these areas employed workers from the nearby black suburbs, their rates and taxes were paid to the white municipality under whose control they fell. The factories were therefore contributing to the tax base of the white municipality, and subsidising its white infrastructure.

3.e)   Extended city planning

Black residential suburbs were invariably removed from the CBD, an obvious link with the colonial Segregated City. The distance from the city centre varies from instance to instance. New Brighton, for example, was established during colonial times on land immediately beyond the city boundaries.

Soweto, on the other hand, was the product of apartheid planners who originally wished to locate it in the vicinity of Newcastle, in Natal. It was their intention to link it to the Witwatersrand by a high-speed railway system (as yet not invented) which would have covered the distance in under two hours. Although this proposal was successfully blocked by the Johannesburg Council, the location of Soweto was ultimately guided by the establishment of Kliptown and Nancefield in 1904 to the southeast of Johannesburg.

3.f)   Extended road links

One of the most noticeable features of the Apartheid City is the wide spread of its residential suburbs linked by relatively long travel links. An integrated city on the other hand, would probably have developed along more compact lines.

3.g)   Military control

Many black residential suburbs established during and after the 1950s are also marked by their proximity to military bases and airfields. It is not an accident that the Lenz Military Camp and the Baragwanath Military Airfield are located in close proximity to Soweto.

3.h)   Radial street planning

Similarly many black towns were planned to facilitate military operations within their streets. This is not a recent paranoia, but dates back to the time when Verwoerd was Minister of Native Affairs. The results are etched in the road plan of Soweto, whose radial streets connect a series of vacant hubs. The theory was that, in times of civil unrest, nests of sub-machine guns could be located on this land, covering the radial roads and enabling troops to isolate trouble spots in a series of pincer movements. Although the student uprising of 1976 exposed the weakness of such thinking, military interference in urban planning has not ceased and up to comparatively recent times plans for new black residential suburbs had to be scrutinised, and vetted, by the local military. A military and totalitarian mindset is also revealed by the limited number of access points provided to black suburbs, to facilitate sealing off an area during times of civil unrest. A major urban centre such as Soweto, with a population of 1.5 million people, can only be accessed by motor vehicles at four points; New Brighton has three.

The planning of radial roadways and the provision of limited access to an area was not the invention of the architects of apartheid, but is a salient feature of mine compound planning.

3.i)   Social infrastructure

The development of separate residential areas must also be read in the context of prevailing white political philosophy. Nationalist thinking perceived South Africa's black citizens to be perpetually rural, and any access they might have to an urban area was only temporary. Their homes were therefore a reflection of such impermanent status, and their suburbs were not permitted to develop features of any permanence. For this reason social amenities were usually neither plentiful nor well equipped.

3.j)   Housing

Stands were kept deliberately small, usually at less than 300 m², whilst the white equivalent was kept at 700 m². Black housing was small, poorly built, devoid of internal doors, ceilings and internal services. Most housing stock consisted of the state-built NE 51/6, which were less than 50m in area. These were not sold, but were retained in government ownership and rented out. The state also refused to conduct any maintenance upon their properties, and would not allow residents to extend or improve these, even at their own expense. Services were kept to a minimum, with rudimentary roads, water and sewage reticulation, and no provision was made for electricity or telephone.

Despite the fact that houses were built using a conventional technology, the textures of the townships remained consistent with those of a squatter camp. The housing process included no consultation with client communities, and plans were often designed at a ministerial level by politicians, farmers and lawyers.

4   The apartheid tax base

Its is probable that, in addition to the above, a number of other characteristics could be assigned to the Apartheid City which do not find direct physical manifestation. Perhaps the most contentious of these centres upon the allegation that apartheid's planners set out, coldly and deliberately, to beggar their black co-citizens. This was done in a number of ways :

- Since 1913 Parliament has promulgated a succession of legislative measures which have limited land ownership by the black community, curtailed the extent of its settlement, and removed its existing rights to tenure. This has effectively excluded them from the landed bourgeoisie, and prevented them from accumulating wealth through property investment. In rural areas also, black farmers were denied access to markets by the development of a transport infrastructure which deliberately avoided those regions better known today as 'homelands'.
- In the urban areas, no major manufacturing or retail developments were permitted to set roots in the black suburbs. This created a 'company store'

relationship between white business and its black workers, where the latter
were expected to earn their wages in the white city, and spend this money
in white-owned shops. This created a cash monopoly which decreased levels
of community wealth and reduced its potential for generating savings, and
therefore investments.

— When separate local government structures were established in the black
suburbs during the 1970s, white municipalities were allowed to retain control of the industry and commerce - within their boundaries. Thus, despite
the fact that their profits were earned from citizens of ail races, their rates
and taxes were paid into the coffers of white municipalities. In this way the
black community has, for many years, been made to subsidise the infrastructure and living standards of its white neighbours.

— Because of its extended plan, unnecessarily long transport routes, and duplication of amenities, the Apartheid City has been enormously expensive
to service. This financial burden has not been carried by the white taxpayer
alone, but it has been the lot of all of this country's citizens.

5　Some future projections

Hendrik Verwoerd has been described by a number of historians as the 'Architect of
Grand Apartheid', and is credited by his followers to have been a man of great intel-
lect. His successor, Balthazar J. Vorster, was an advocate and, reputedly, an astute and
capable leader. It must be assumed, therefore, that both men were intelligent enough
to project their vision forward to a time when bigotry could no longer form the ideological basis for national government. Grounding their social engineering in theories
of crude 'baasskap', they used the legislative process to make 'class' synonymous with
'race'. Their measures were sweeping and breathtaking in their intent, covering the full
range of social concerns from sex through to labour, from field through to house.
Thus apartheid did not become merely the means of plundering the wealth of the
country, and of placing it in white, predominantly Afrikaner, hands. It was also a
social system which ensured that, once racism had abated, class would replace race as
the primary means of social differentiation. Apartheid therefore set out to create in
perpetuity a proletariat which, through no coincidence, was also black.

This has become increasingly obvious since the repeal of the Group Areas Act in
1991, when many workers in the field of planning began to realise that the effects of
Apartheid will be with us for many generations to come. This does not refer only to
the idiosyncratic road plans, or the physical barriers it placed between communities,
but also includes the ghetto textures of black residential areas. It is not enough to
believe that, given enough time and sensible land use deregulation, these effects will be

minimised and even wiped out. Life in a black suburb differs radically from that enjoyed in a white area, and few of our black citizens are currently prepared to enter into exile in their own city.

Current experience has also indicated that, despite the removal of Group Areas limitations, most middle and upper income Black families are trapped in their old suburbs through an inability to dispose of their properties without suffering massive financial losses. The plight of lower income Black families is obviously worse.

Therefore, if we are to overcome the after-effects of the incubus we have been labouring under these past 54 years, it will be necessary for our city planners to initiate action of a deliberate and proactive nature to begin the breakdown of its major features. This will undoubtedly require a great deal of courage, as some of the following measures might indicate:

- The integration of middle and upper income suburbs, perhaps through a subsidised equalisation of land. This will not only give black families access to existing white suburbs, but also make existing black suburbs more attractive to white residents.
- The establishment of new low and middle income housing estates in such a manner as to undermine and break down the existing geography of spatial segregation. Notable areas of action in Port Elizabeth might include developments at Driftsands, Fairview and Parsons Vlei.
- The alteration of existing land textures in black residential areas, through a gradual process of erf consolidation.
- Improving working class access to inner city land. This may be done in a number of ways:
  - Improving public transport links between outlying areas and inner cities, possibly through a heavily subsidised light rail system.
  - Creating areas of medium rise living within the inner city, giving a selection of rentable as well as purchasable residential space. In Port Elizabeth this could take place in North and South End, the east end of Walmer and the lower Baakens Valley.
  - Changing the nature of some existing inner city areas, from light industrial and manufacturing to a mixed residential/light industrial use. This will permit shop keepers and crafters to live above their work premises, subsidising their living standards and encouraging light industrial and manufacturing entrepreneurship.
  - Redeveloping and changing the nature of some areas of existing mixed land usage which are currently suffering from low development and urban blight.
  - The decentralisation of retail and business functions to the black sub-

urbs. In some instances this might extend to developing new decentralised urban nodes.

–   The energetic revitalisation of historical CBD areas. In the case of Port Elizabeth, this includes the demolition of the existing motorway between Russell Road and South End and its replacement with a four lane parkway. This would allow the CBD to extend into the Harbour area and encourage the rationalisation of the present ore-dump and tank farm facility. The northern face of the Donkin Reserve should also be developed to revitalise Chapel Street.

–   Like most other major urban centres in South Africa, Port Elizabeth has run out of industrial land, and new industrial estates will need to be planned and woven into the city fabric. The fact that Port Elizabeth came within a shade of losing its present cement manufacturing facility in New Brighton stands as evidence to this fact.

It is also obvious that the patterns of autocratic, top-down planning which local authorities had formerly adopted will have to undergo dramatic revision if all communities are to be given a voice in determining the kind of city they wish to live in. Planning decisions in the future will need to be made in the context of a united, democratically elected, local city administration.

As those already engaged in such processes know, this can be a cumbersome exercise, fraught with problems. Matters may be facilitated, however, if city administrators were to adopt the following principles and incorporate them in their modus operandi:

–   that city planning must be undertaken as part of a consultative process between all affected communities, and must involve their civic representatives as well as all other interested parties. The idea that elected officials and paid bureaucrats can be allowed to make decisions first, and then inform their constituencies, must be relegated to the past.

–   that all urban development will need take place within the context of a wider national policy of land rationalisation and appropriate use.

–   that building work will also need to involve the creation of labour models which will maximise current labour resources and create opportunities for new skills and new entrepreneurial participation.

–   and that they will take place in the context of a wider planning process which takes due regard of a regions' historical and natural heritage.

Conclusions

It is clear that although the Group Areas Act was repealed in 1991, the component elements of Apartheid planning have been indelibly etched into the urban fabric of our cities. It is probable that their effects will continue to be felt for many years to come, and that their traces may never be entirely expunged from the South African urban fabric.

Changes are not likely to take place through a long-term, liberal, free-market exchange of land, but will probably require a series of stringent land and price controls orchestrated through a city government committed to strong democracy, community empowerment and the generation of wealth. This is not a philosophy likely to find favour with the broad white electorate, nor with white Liberals or the country's neo-Democrats, all of whom have benefited extensively from the implementation of Apartheid's economic measures.

However the Apartheid City was the creation of a doctrine-driven central government, and was only achieved through the imposition of extreme hardships upon the black community. These families are now entitled to a form of restitution, and one of the ways in which this could take place is through an improved quality of housing, of life and of economic opportunities.

To use an architectural metaphor, the edifice of apartheid was only made possible by a structure, a scaffolding, of inter-supporting laws and edicts. Once the building was completed and could stand alone and unassisted, then the scaffolding could be dismantled and removed. It is true that, since 2 February 1990, the Nationalist Government has assiduously been removing the legal props to apartheid, but the substantive structure of economic inequality inherited from that system is still very much in place. Its granite face will not be affected by rubber mallets, but will require a demolition tool made of a sterner materials.

This also means that the planning profession will have to undergo severe structural changes if it is to meet the needs of a future democratic South Africa. It is clear that, in the past, it was the work of planners that gave Apartheid ideology its physical dimensions, and permitted its implementation on the ground.

The design of radial roads, limited access townships, *cordons sanitaires* and segregated facilities reveals a totalitarian mind-set reflective of an oppressive and unjust society. It is now up to the new generation of town planners to reconcile the mistakes of the past with the realities of the future, and help our people achieve the greatness they deserve.

I wish them well in their endeavours.

References

Aron, Helen. (1972). 'Parktown, 1892–1972', Johannesburg: Studio Thirty Five.

Baines, G. (1989). 'The Control and Administration of Port Elizabeth's African Population, 1834–1923', *Contree*, 26, pp. 12–21.

Baker, Jonathan. (1990). 'Small Town Africa - Studies in Rural-Urban Interaction'. Sweden: Nordiska Afrikainstitutet.

Backhouse, James. (1844). *A Narrative of a Visit to Mauritius and South Africa*, London: Hamilton, Adams.

Caldwell, Sharon Edna. (1987). 'The Course and Results of the Plague Outbreaks in King William's Town, 1900–1907', BA Hons treatise, Rhodes University, Grahamstown.

Cartwright, A.P. (1965). *The Corner House*, Purnell: Cape Town.

Cartwright, A.P. (1968). *Golden Age*, Purnell: Cape Town.

CED, Johannesburg City Council, *Metropolitan Johannesburg*.

CED, Johannesburg City Council. *Greater Johannesburg Area Population Report*.

Christopher, A.J. (1991). *Port Elizabeth Guide*, University of Port Elizabeth.

Clayton, A.J. (1986). *Facts and Figures*, Port Elizabeth City Engineer's Department.

Del Monte, Lance. (1991). *One City Concept: Land Use*, Port Elizabeth: Metroplan.

Frescura, Franco and Radford, Dennis. (1982). 'The Physical Growth of Johannesburg'. Johannesburg: University of the Witwatersrand. Infraplan. 1988. *Port Elizabeth Metropolitan Study*, East London: INFRA-PLAN.

Lemon, Anthony. (1991). *Homes Apart*, Cape Town: David Philip.

Lewis, Patrick R.B. (1966). *A City Within a City: The Creation of Soweto*, University of the Witwatersrand, Johannesburg.

Leyds, G.A. n.d. *A History of Johannesburg*.

Nead, (1965). *Memorandum on the History of the Non-European Affairs Department*, Johannesburg City Council.

Neame, L.E. (n.d.). *City Built on Gold*.

Oberholster, J.J. (1972). *The Historical Monuments of South Africa*, Cape Town: NMC.

Rosenthal, Eric. (1970). *Encyclopaedia of Southern Africa*, London : Frederick Warne.

Strategic Facilitation Group. (1991). *Development Facilitation*, Port Elizabeth: SFG.

Taylor, Beverley. (1991). 'Controlling the Burgeoning Masses : Removals and Residential Development in Port Elizabeth's Black Areas 1800–1900'. Working Paper No 51. Grahamstown: Institute for Social and Economic Research.

Transvaal Chamber of Mines. (1887–1973). Reports.

Wilson, Francis. *Labour in the South African Gold Mines, 1911-1969*, Johannesburg: Ravan Press.

CHAPTER FOUR

Children in violent spaces: a reinterpretation of the 1976 Soweto Uprising

Hjalte Tin

An entire generation of South Africans sacrificed their youth in June 1976 ... As the government, we have declared June the month of the youth ... By so doing, we shall have paid a fitting tribute to the June 16 martyrs.

Tokyo Sexwale in *The Sunday Independent*, Johannesburg; June 16, 1996

Speaking on the 20th anniversary of the Soweto uprising, Tokyo Sexwale, then Premier of Gauteng, himself a few years older than the children of 1976 and in exile a year before the uprising, remembered the children as the sacrificed youth and martyrs and not as actors, creative subjects of historical change. In the many anniversaries that have followed 1976 an idealised picture of the uprising has emerged hiding the children under layer after layer of adult patronising shame and political expediency. Yet, the fact remains, that the children, *as children*, somehow found a weak spot in the rule of apartheid and were able to attack the state so successfully that 1976 became the turning point of Apartheid. The Nationalists would soldier on for almost two decades, but the polished surface of post-Rivonia apartheid was irrevocably shattered.

This article offers a reinterpretation of the Soweto uprising based on a spatial reading of the well-known facts of violence. What has to be explained is the children as attackers: what stuff was their power made of? How could they force the strong and seemingly well-entrenched apartheid state into defending itself against *children*? I suggest an answer may be located in the interlocking confrontations of the children with the state, as *minors* in house space, *pupils* in town space, and *black* people in ethnic space.

1 The agency of the children of Soweto

The children are indeed emblematic in all accounts of the uprising. Tom Lodge, for example, headlines his chapter on the Soweto uprising 'Children of Soweto' (Lodge,

1983, pp. 321–361). At the same time, however, one can perhaps detect, below the moral outrage over police killings of children, a certain bewilderment on the role of the children. After all, how could children be so dangerous to the state, how could they ignite this fire when adult protest, like the widespread strikes a few years previously, had failed to do so? Conventional explanations, such as class and race, do not really capture *the children's* uprising, because how do you account for a generational conflict in terms of class or race?

In the many works documenting the Soweto uprising I have come across no studies on the children of Soweto in their own right. Writers on the uprising have speculated about the children's *adult* leaders: it has been argued that they were inspired and led by workers and trade union groups (Hirson, 1979), ANC sympathisers (Brickhill and Brooks, 1980), or (older) Black Consciousness Movement students (Pityana and Ramphele, 1991). But in fact very little planning and leadership at all seemed to have propelled the uprising. Of course there is some truth to all these accounts, but as interpretations they are nevertheless basically inadequate, I think, because they silence the agency of the children and turn them into victims of an acting state. However, the power of the children was certainly much more than the moral power of the victim. The children of Soweto actually pushed back the armed state by violence and only because of that did they gain power - and were killed.

Already on day one the events exploded in a way no-one controlled, neither the children, the political opposition groups, nor the government. Yet, if a pattern of the uprising cannot by plotted by a 'BCM', 'ANC' or workerist (or any other) master narrative, it does not mean that violence took place everywhere in a random, chaotic fashion. The uprising was a violent contest over structured space. Thus by reading the structure of that space we may gain new insight into the South African uprising of 1976. Let me by way of introduction summarise the argument of the chapter.

2   The argument of the three spaces:
   children as minors, pupils and black people

The children of Soweto met the state in three clearly defined but overlapping spaces:

2.a)   Minors

First, the children met the state as *minors* when the state ruled the house through the fathers. Family life defined by decent, conjugality and patriarchal authority (sometimes vested in a female) had carved out and preserved a private space different from public space; I term this space 'house space'. By its laws and practices the South African state recognized house space to be beyond its direct reach: as *minors* the children were the responsibility of the father and not directly of the state. The state possessed no instruments to rule children as children: if parental rule broke down the state could in an emergency only treat the children as adults.

2.b) Pupils

Secondly, the children met the state as *pupils* in the schools, that is in the functionally defined town space. In school the children were confronted with state rule implemented by the teacher. Here they were no longer ruled as daughters or sons of the father but as 'pupils', that is determined by their function in the educational-occupational system. The work of the pupils had a clear functional rationality as they learned whatever the state thought necessary for fulfilling future functions, but also to themselves as a move towards jobs and exactly this function was threatened by the imposition of Afrikaans as medium of instruction: it made it impossible to pass exams and harder to get jobs.

2.c) Black people

Finally, the children met the South African state as *blacks* at the frontiers of the ethnic-racial space. On the streets the state confronted the children in the figure of the policeman (and even the soldier) enforcing ethnic segregation.

Now, common to all three fronts was a generational conflict. In all three instances the structure of rule pitted children against adults; but not the same adults. My argument is that the three children-adult structures of rule relied upon and supported each other - and when one collapsed the others would become extremely vulnerable. The intricate interlocking of the generational conflict of patriarchs versus minors with the functional conflict of pupils versus teachers and the racist (ethnic) conflict of blacks versus policemen produced the explosion of June 16.

Before investigating the three conflictual spaces more closely let me briefly recount what happened during the uprising.

3 What happened?

The initial spark to six months of almost non-stop nation-wide insurrection was provided by police over-reaction to a street procession of secondary school pupils. They were marching to Orlando stadium in central Soweto to protest against the recent insistence by the educational authorities that arithmetic and social studies be taught in Afrikaans. Police shot into a crowd of 15 000, killed two and injured many; one of the children killed was 13-year old Hector Petersen (Lodge, 1983, p. 328). The image of the schoolboy being carried away by a crying friend quickly became the famous icon of Soweto. Twenty years later it was reproduced in giant-size on the stone walls of the Castle in Cape Town, the cradle of white rule in South Africa, now with a new flag flying over the ramparts and June 16 inaugurated as a national holiday.

The official, conservative estimate was at least 575 dead (including only 2 whites) and 2 389 wounded (ibid, p. 330). Brickhill and Brooks estimate that more than a thousand may have been killed and five thousand wounded. (Brickhill and Brooks, 1980, p. 256). It is doubtful whether more accurate figures can be collected today. Some of the police data from 1976 are in Pretoria, but most are scattered in the 'archives' of more than 1 400 local police stations, in varying states of completeness both as to the original reporting and the subsequent filing. Death registers are highly incomplete in part because of secret burials and clandestine emigration.

The weapons used by the attackers in 1976 were household weapons only, a fact repeated again and again in the newspaper reports:

> Stoning, looting, and burning ... Marauding bands of stone-throwers ... Stone and brick-throwing Africans ... Gangs had set up road blocks and were demanding money from motorists ... Gangs of youth were demanding petrol from motorists and paraffin from shops to set fire to buildings ... A hysterical mob burnt public buildings and set fire to six buses ... Rioters stoned passing cars.
>
> *Cape Times,* June 19, 1976

Not a single firearm was reported used by the state-attackers while the state used all available forces to suppress the uprising. Police and other armed units fired teargas and 16 433 rounds of ammunition in Soweto, 17 000 rounds in East Rand, 2 815 in Mamelodi (Pretoria) and 4 522 rounds in Western Cape. (Cilliers commission, cited in Brickhill and Brooks, 1980, p. 255).

The sheer volume of violent events is overwhelming; schools were burned down, state offices gutted, people shot and funerals held almost continuously for six months across the country. However, what is central to my argument is not so much the sequence of events as their spatiality. Rioting almost exclusively took place in *townships*, with Soweto and the other Witwatersrand townships ahead of Cape Town and Port Elizabeth far behind Cape Town. Durban was quiet, a strange fact which may, para-doxically, help us later in interpreting the violence of Johannesburg and Cape Town. In order to map the attack on the state the spatiality of violence within each township is more important than the national distribution of flash points because the battle in one township in many ways resembled battles in other townships without being seg-ments of a coherent front. Children in each township rioted with hardly any co-ordi-nation except for the encouragement in knowing that fellow children were on the streets all over the country.

4   The township terrain

All South African townships were racially segregated municipal housing established if at all possible at some distance from 'white' cities. To defend the white town against the threat of huge concentrations of poor, oppressed, black people the state went to great lengths to segregate the townships spatially from the rest of the city, walling them in using physical barriers like highways, railroads, and industrial areas. Often the township would get an African name hiding discursively their true functional integration into the 'white' town.

Driving into Johannesburg in 1976 from the west along the R41 you would follow the mountainous slag-heap of *eGoli*, the town of gold: Durban Roodeport Deep Gold Mine, Rand Leases Goudmyn, Main Reef Gold Mine and Crown Mines separating the white town inside the enormous ramparts from the black township outside the ramparts. Soweto (South Western Townships) was established in the 1930s by the white municipality on the highveld ten kilometres outside Johannesburg and quickly grew to be the largest cluster of townships in South Africa, a sprawling area of more than a hundred square kilometres, some fifteen kilometres long and ten kilometres wide and home to one and a half million black people in 1976. This vast area was separated to the west and South from rural Transvaal and the Coloured townships of Eldorado Park and the Indian township of Lenasia by the railroad and the Kliprivier swamps. Soweto was cut off completely from white Johannesburg to the north and east by the barrier of slag heaps and vast slimes dams of the gold mines.

The whole twenty kilometre-long zone separating the white and black parts of metropolitan Johannesburg was only traversed by one railroad, one expressway and two highways. There was no urban built-up connection whatsoever between Soweto and Johannesburg. This extreme town planning forced all interaction with the city to go through a few easy-to-control entry-points (bus terminals and train stations; in 1976 taxi ranks were not yet important). To go to town the people of Soweto had to exit via one of these gates. As very few blacks owned cars the roads were mainly used by the police and commercial deliveries; indeed not a single road-sign on the highways from Johannesburg read 'Soweto'. The South Western Townships was a non-place for whites, where their black labourers would disappear in the evening on overcrowded trains.

Apartheid laws forced black people to live in Soweto. Every town in South Africa was segregated by the infamous Group Areas Act into areas for the four official races, black, white, coloured and Indian. The Urban (Bantu Areas) law forbade black people to own property; they were forced to lease sites from the municipality and build one of the ubiquitous twenty-five square-metre matchbox houses after a standard municipal blueprint. Row after row of identical houses most lacking electricity and piped water along unpaved streets (stones everywhere and wide enough for armoured personnel carriers to operate) with the smoke of coal braziers hanging in the cold morning air was a picture often given of Soweto. State proclamations divided township space into four portions: demarcated and beaconed sites for dwellings; public space such as sports fields and graveyards; streets, roads and other public thoroughfares and commonage; unused open land; in no way did a township constitute an urban area in its own right.

There was no industry and few shops in the township, but many municipal beerhalls and bottleshops. White tax-payers did not contribute financially to the upkeep of the townships as a system was invented long ago in Durban (the Native Beer Law of 1908) whereby Native Townships had to be funded solely by income from the municipal sale of beer and liquor to the township population. Except for schools, police stations and small offices for the local white administration of the township (in 1972 removed from local municipal control to central state administration by BAAB, Bantu Affairs Administration Boards) and the despised black councils set up by the apartheid state (UBC, Urban Black Councils, nicknamed, for example, Useless Boys' Club, United Black Crooks), all other urban functions were in the 'white' town: department stores, industry, offices, and public institutions from universities to jails. The township lacked focal public space, such as town squares, parks, main avenues or a city centre.

As I will attempt to show below, the peculiar terrain of the township generated a highly specific mixture of violence. Five forms of violence, all created by the children in response to the different terrains and adversaries they encountered may be distinguished: fighting inside the township; contesting the township border; enforcing stayaways from the white town; attacking the white town; and ruling the parents.

4.a)   Fighting inside the township

Like Pallas Athena the uprising sprang to life on the very first day in the fully formed shape of street battles. Children marched non-violently with placards; they threw stones, bricks and bottles at the police. They stoned and burned all cars and commercial vehicles encountered in the township. Police and border troops batoncharged, teargassed, shot and killed; they deployed armoured personnel carriers (Hippos) to contest control over Soweto streets and helicopters to ship in weapons and throw tear-gas at rioters. In the evening of June 16 they had already reached the maximum level of force sustained during the next months. This was a testimony both to the simplicity of this battle-form and to the universality of explosive discontent. By spontaneous repetition of the children's battles in Soweto, children across the nation set alight townships and locations in Cape Town, Pretoria, East Rand, The Free State, Bophuthatswana and Natal within a week. Yet, after countless battles throughout this six month period a more advanced form of street battle never emerged. Like Pallas Athena the street-battle did not grow older. But as we shall see, more elaborate forms of struggle were developed meeting the challenges of other sites of contest.

Also kick-started on the long day of June 16 was the first form of countering white control of schools: burning down of schools. During the following ten days, fifty Transvaal schools were damaged by fire. Street fights between youths and police demanded a certain minimum town-size, while arson attacks on schools could and did spread to very small towns. School-burning became the primary transmitter of the uprising from metropolitan to rural areas, including the homelands, as in Ndwedwe, north of Durban, where 280 girls burned down a mission school on July 27. When the schools re-opened after the winter holiday on July 22 the other principal form of resistance to Bantu education was launched with widespread boycotts of classes. The school boycott became massive when police began raiding the schools to capture the leaders of the Soweto Students Representative Council and the schools remained empty for the rest of the year (and the following year). An almost 100% boycott of exams was observed in Soweto by the end of term in November 1976.

Only a few hours into the uprising arson spread from schools to all other buildings associated with white rule in Soweto (Bantu Affairs Administration Boards and Urban Black Councils, post offices, beerhalls and bottlestores). Very quickly state presence at township level began to break down: water supplies were attacked, BAAB officials stoned; shops and houses belonging to black people collaborating with the white state were looted and burnt down. During the first three months the following damage was reported in Soweto alone: 24 schools, 3 clinics, 9 post offices, 18 bottle stores, 18 beer halls, 14 private business premises, 3 libraries, 1 court building, 19 shops, 2 community halls, 19 houses, 42 West Rand Administration Board buildings and at least 114 vehicles. (*SAIRR 1977*, p.85)

4.b) Contesting the township border

As the street-battles pushed the armed and bureaucratic forces of the state out of the townships, the contest spread immediately from the public space inside the township to the border between the black and the white town. Within 24 hours of igniting the uprising youths had erected barricades in order to keep out the police and prevent commercial vehicles from entering Soweto; the state retaliated by stopping trains and busses going from Johannesburg to Soweto. The next day the police claimed to have sealed off Soweto. From July onwards buses going to town were firebombed by children. On August 5, pupils and adults demonstrating for the release of pupils detained in Johannesburg tried to walk on the city but were turned back at New Canada Station at the border of Soweto by police using automatic rifles. The next day residents of Soweto erected roadblocks and confronted the police; trains and busses were withdrawn and commercial deliveries to Soweto stopped. Violence escalated into running battles between demonstrators and police at the entry-points to Soweto on August 9. Meanwhile, the epicentre of violence shifted for some time to the Cape where police used helicopters to reach barricaded state personnel violently defending themselves in the three black townships of Langa, Guguletu and Nyanga on August 12. As the uprising petered out in December the police pushed back across the township border; for instance nearly 1 000 police officers sealed off Guguletu in Cape Town on December 2–3 and searched house to house in the township. More than 300 were arrested.

4.c)   Enforcing stayaways from the white town

Stayaways were the first major step beyond the street battle and introduced the first direct children-patriarch confrontation. On August 4, the pupils called for the first stay-away; they picketed stations and bus terminals, attempting to persuade adults to stay at home, 'by a greater degree of coercion than was used by the inciters of any of its successors' (Lodge, 1983, p. 329). Children sabotaged railroad lines and signals; buses carrying workers to the city were stopped and burned; 60% of Johannesburg's black work-force stayed away from work that day (*SAIRR 1977*, p. 66). On August 15, T.J. Makhaya from the Soweto Urban Black Council said at a meeting that children who stopped workers from going to work 'should be killed' and during the following week workers wanting to go to work despite student blockades were allowed by the police to carry knobkerries and sticks (ibid, p. 66).

The second stayaway came on August 23. Brickhill and Brooks claim the second stayaway was a greater success than the first (Brickhill and Brooks, 1983, p.321), while Lodge claims fewer stayed away than on August 4th (Lodge, 1983, p.329). The stayaways resulted in the flare-up of hostel-pupil antagonism. On August 24, a Zulu *impi* from Mzimhlope hostel went on a rampage in Soweto, police complicity was alleged and in an ominous overture of violence to explode a decade later Mangosuthu Buthelezi flew up to Soweto on August 26 and held a speech urging 'unity' between hostel and township.

The third stayaway occurred on September 13; up to 70% absenteeism was reported in some areas; police made a swoop in Alexandria 'to protect those who wished to go to work' arresting hundreds of people. A stayaway followed on September 15 in Cape Town with up to 50% absenteeism (*SAIRR 1977*, p. 69). The fourth and final stayaway on November 1 faltered both in Transvaal and the Cape. The Christmas boycott of department stores in the white town in December was a weak sequel to the stayaways.

4.d)   Attacking the white town

The first attack on whites outside the township seems to be a stoning incident on July 20 where at least 20 whites were injured on the Pretoria-Witbank highway. The first major attack reported on a target in a white area was the Brakpan post office completely destroyed by fire on August 14. Drivers were stoned at highways outside the coloured township of Bonteheuwel, Cape Town and the first coloureds shot dead by police on August 25. Shops in Rondebosch East, Cape Town, were firebombed on September 1. But the dramatic symbolic escalation of the struggle came on September 2 and 3, when two days in a row black and coloured pupils entered central Cape Town by train and successfully staged large demonstrations on Adderley Street; for the first time police used teargas in a white area. Factories were stoned and forced to close in Parow, Cape Town on September 8. Later in September these attacks were repeated in Johannesburg when two factories were gutted and black children demonstrated on the central Eloff and Jeppe Streets with fierce clashes, several shootings and stabbings; police arrested 400 in a 'giant mopping-up' operation.

For some hours, in fact, the children symbolically conquered the very heart of metropolitan South Africa by their violent presence and this reversal of the attacker-defender polarity across the township border sent shock-waves through the white town. In a desperate move the Minister of Justice said on September 8 that white industrial and other areas had to protect themselves as police were busy in the townships. White vigilante groups sprang up, patrolling factories, white schools, universities (including Stellenbosch) and residential areas. Parents guarded white middle-class suburban schools in Claremont and Wynberg; hundreds of white vigilantes patrolled Cape Town white residential areas; several vigilante incidents were reported in Cape Town and Johannesburg; 3 blacks were killed by white vigilantes on September 12 in the Cape (*SAIRR 1977*, p. 75). A week later police warned vigilantes not to kill blacks, but still people were organising themselves into a permanent 'Home Guard' (ibid, p. 77). On November 27, for the last time during the uprising pupils demonstrated in the white city centre of Cape Town; police dispersed the crowd with batons.

While discussing attacks on the white town it is important to note that the uprising *never* moved into the white residential areas; only two whites were killed during the entire six months of violence and only because they were unfortunate to be caught in Soweto on the day the uprising started.

4.e)　Ruling the parents

Finally, the children challenged the parents head-on in the heart of the townships. In a desperate bid to re-arm patriarchal rule of the children the Minister of Justice, Jimmy Kruger held a meeting with *makgotlas* (black vigilante groups of older males) in September giving them legal recognition by the police. This battle was to become ever more deadly during the next decade, however, in 1976 the children proved much stronger than the parents. On October 8, all *shebeens* in Cape Town (small informal black-owned bars and a central source of income) were ordered by the pupils to close within a week. On Octber 11, 3 000 youths (Brickhill and Brooks, 1980; SAIRR says only 300) closed at least 100 *shebeens* in Cape Town and the liquor was destroyed. On October 18, roadblocks were set up in Cape Town to enforce the anti-alcohol drive, adults were searched and bottles smashed and several *shebeens* destroyed. By the end of October several more attacks on shebeens took place in Soweto by students and people carrying bottles on the street were attacked. Extending their custody of the parents the Soweto Students Representative Council on October 16 called for mourning over the victims of the uprising to last until New Year and the abolition of Christmas celebrations including purchasing of gifts in white shops.

In an ultimate move of defiance towards the parents and their perceived submission to apartheid children fled from South Africa and joined the small armed groups in exile. By December there were in Botswana at least 8 homes housing 150 youths each that had fled from South Africa.

To sum up, the violence of 1976 was almost exclusively urban and confined to townships. First the children contested the patriarchal authority over the house. Secondly the children contested apartheid state control of township space and succeeded for some time to do so. Finally they managed to launch violent attacks outside the township on the 'white' city. Who were these children?

5   Frontline children

We know little about the children. Photographs document pupils marching, exuberant teenagers, surging forward, school-girls in uniforms and polished shoes, shouting with clenched fists or doing the v-sign, boys running, smiling, shouting, waving placards and a few sticks. Some of the placards read: 'To hell with Afrikaans', 'Afrikaans is not a good subject for us' 'The black nation is not a place for impurities, Afrikaans stinks'. No adults were in sight, no adults were leading, following or present at all. Then, some days into the uprising everybody seemed to be on the streets, huge men with rifles ran after children, smoke belched from car-wrecks and gutted houses and this strange coexistence of dynamism and passivity was peculiar to all pictures of uprisings. Crowds standing still watching, some running, some throwing stones, some shooting, all within the same frame. This 'dynamic heterogeneity' is typical of spontaneous, uncoordinated, and un-led violence. Weeks later parents and some political leaders showed up at the funerals. And still the pupils were marching with placards like, 'How long must we be kicked, choked, bitten, raped and killed?' 'Kruger release detainees in prison or else ...!'

Court records bear witness to the central importance of the children. It was mostly youths that were arrested and brought to trial. Of 229 post mortems done on riot victims in Johannesburg and reported on October 13, the largest category of victims was the 10–20 years old; 224 were black, 3 coloured, 2 white and 9 out of 10 were male. By 30 October 1976, the following number of cases of persons convicted for 'public violence' had been reported in the press: 526 children under 18 years of age had been sentenced to corporal punishment and whipped and lashed, and only 139 adults; in September a sentence of five lashes was imposed on an eight-year-old African child for attending an illegal gathering in Port Elizabeth. No children, but 111 adults had been imprisoned, 393 children had received a suspended sentence or fine, as opposed to 30 adults.

The children were variously called children, youths, pupils, or students. They were certainly not university students but pupils up to around twenty years of age from schools and high schools. I call them children because they still lived at home. This is important for the dynamic of the uprising because it constantly fuelled the children-parent conflict, but also because it gave the street fighters unsurpassed access to safehouses, well established protective networks and logistical support, much better than any guerrilla army could hope for.

The children lived at home, but not in any home and particularly not in the shacks at the bottom of the African society. The children were presumably mostly 'legal' townspeople with parents having permanent urban residence permits and employment, many of them office-work and able to support kids through high-school. As such many of the children belonged to the urban black elite with roots to Sophiatown and the pre-apartheid mixed urban life. High-school children did not come from the illegal shacks, they were not the children of the rural squatters but of the black urban insiders. The uprising was not a class-revolt. Tom Lodge therefore, correctly I think, argued against a workerist interpretation of the uprising (*inter alia* Brickhill & Brooks, 1980; Hirson, 1979).

It is also relevant to point out that Soweto was not a predominantly industrial working class community; it had a disproportionately large white collar/petty bourgeois group – numbering 50 000 – and the township's population had been virtually untouched by the revival of working-class consciousness and trade unionism that had begun elsewhere. It is likely that the bewildered and self-accusatory response of the middle-class oriented *World* newspaper was a much more generalised perception among Soweto adults than the advocates of a township-based syndicalism would have us believe. (Lodge, 1983, p. 333).

Five months into the uprising Aggrey Claaste wrote in the *World*:

> It may be that we have become so shell-shocked that nothing seems to touch us the raw ... So many parents these days are taking very calm the horrid fact that their sons and daughters have fled the country. If parents do not shrug their shoulders with indifference when their sons and daughters are arrested, they do something very similar ... They sigh wearily, they shake their heads – and they trudge off to that miserable job, travelling in those miserable trains, as if the whole world was a bed of roses.

I am able to trace this attitude back some months in Soweto. Early this year when the clouds of discontent were building ominously in our schoolyards, we shook our heads and clicked our collective tongue. Then the kids boycotted classes. Still we shook our collective head lethargically and hummed our collective disquiet. Then the boycotts began to spread. The reaction was the same from the whole world of adulthood. The scenario began to hot up. We were frightened. We were shocked. But all we did was despair. The lens moves to the graveyards and this time the adults are in the line of fire. What a moan there was in Soweto! What a tearing out of hair and collective gnashing of teeth there was! And that was all.

This time they were picking up our babies right in our own homes. Oh what a clicking of tongues there was this time! So many frightened mothers and fathers dashing out in their cars to hide their children. My language spells it out very clearly – 'Singa, magwala' (we are cowards).

Lodge, 1983

Aggrey Klaaste confronted 'we, parents, adults, mothers, fathers' to 'children, sons, daughters, kids, babies'. It is revealing to compare this view of the polarity of the uprising with the children's own, different, version. As an example I quote two extracts from some of their pamphlets probably distributed in August and September:

The Black Students' Message to their Beloved Parents.
Dear Parents,
The Black students throughout Azania have shown their extreme dissatisfaction with the education that is handed out to them, an education which shackles the mind and which is only intended to create a mere efficient black labour force to be exploited by those in power, more than this, the Black students have demanded a radical change from the entire oppressive apartheid system which dehumanizes and belittles one, a system that not allow the full development of man, what we have seen in Soweto and in other areas throughout the country appears to be the first stirrings of a monster and we may be standing in the tip of a powder keg which could shake the whole of South Africa ...

Peaceful demonstrations by the students have been met with force by those in power a call on workers who are also our parents by students to join them have been met with the escalation of police brutality and increase in the number of legalised murders.

To Town!!! To Eloff!!! To That Exclusive White Paradise!!
... Johannesburg or Soweto, the Capital and supposed centre of this national drive, has already lagged behind the countryside. Where the heart of Cape Town – Adderley Street – was rocked by revolutionary demonstrators. Are we made

of a different metal from them? Surely not, they are mortals like ourselves. But their discontent about the present oppressive structure has made them bold. They burnt buildings, they took possession of what was forcefully raped from them a few centuries ago. They did not plead for work anymore. They brought so much panic to the already frightened whites, that all guns obtained in public market were sold out ... surely, a retreat is impossible when our brothers studying in other parts of the country have raised [sic] their schools to the ground and brought educational machinery to a halt. These people also value their education, but have abandoned it for a better cause, namely the elimination of oppression. We cannot retreat to classrooms unless we reverse the whole course of events this year ... Let us not betray the nation by pursuing selfish ends like writing exams ... do we also want Vorster's certificate? To hell with a paper! Certificate! The certificate we want now is our land, and for that we shall fight till the racists are defeated.

The pupils did not repeat Klaaste's duality. The first pamphlet confronted 'Black students' with two parties, 'beloved parents, workers' and 'those in power, the system'. The second pamphlet had a different polarity again with 'brothers, revolutionary demonstrators' opposing 'whites, racists'. We can observe three very different oppositions, (i) children vs. parents is the patriarchal conflict embedded in the house; (ii) students and workers vs. the system (of exploitation) is the functional opposition localised to town space, and finally (iii) blacks vs. white racists is the ethnic-racial antagonism constituting ethnic space. Now my point is that they exactly articulate the three spatial fronts where the children met the state; in a chain-reaction oppositions on all fronts came to fuel the violence. In the Soweto uprising we can pinpoint, I will argue, the first link to snap and the source of strength of the children and the fatal weakness of the state to the house space.

6   Children in house space: Minors

Works of literature may allow us a glimpse of the intimate structures of patriarchal rule. Three South African autobiographies, set in different times and both urban and rural settings, capture the child ruled by the father. Rolihlala, a Xhosa boy, grew up in the Transkei in the 1920s and remembers his father as:

> [a] tall, dark-skinned man with a straight and stately posture, which I like to think I inherited ... [he] had a stern manner and did not spare the rod when disciplining his children. He could be exceedingly stubborn ...
>
> Mandela, 1994, p. 5

Bloke Modisane, ten years Nelson Mandela's junior, writer on *Drum* magazine, actor, and playwright, spent his childhood in Sophiatown, Johannesburg. In his moving autobiography *Blame Me on History* he gives an intimate picture of life back in the 1930s in Sophiatown, the most vibrant black urban neighbourhood of South Africa. His childhood experiences are not all that different from Nelson Mandela's rural upbringing a decade earlier in terms of patriarchal dominance:

> My father, Joseph, was always a signal of authority, unapproachable, the judge symbol; the only time he came close to me was to administer the cane or lay down the law of Moses, and this six-foot-two giant towered above my world, the only force I ever feared, the authority I respected; perhaps I should have loved him too ...
>
> Modisane, 1963, p. 20

In the 1950s a girl grew up in the deep rural north of South Africa. Today called one of South Africa's most powerful women by a leading newspaper, Mamphela Ramphele has a keen eye for the patriarchal dominance over women and children in the house:

> Like most of his contemporaries, my grandfather was an authoritarian patriarch. He ruled his family with a firm hand. To underline his control over his descendants, he issued an edict that all his grandchildren were to refer to him as Papa and his wife as Mama, whereas their own parents were to be called Brother and Sister. This was a major symbolic statement about the lines of authority within the family ... Children were regarded as part of the family estate – property to be handled as one pleased.
>
> Ramphele, 1963, p. 13

It is important not to forget that the strict patriarchal family was shared by all races in South Africa. Annette Seegers characterises the Afrikaner family of the 1960s as:

> [a] strong, ordered unit and within it, men are patriarchal figures ...
>
> Deference is the rule. Children indeed live with rule-making parents. Even children well into their teens are not, for example, encouraged to be present in adult company or to interrupt adults' conversion. Punishment for transgression at home range from admonitions ... to corporal punishment, the latter still a common method of dealing with males in Afrikaner households and schools ... Under pressure, women support men, not children ...
>
> Since relative age determines adult rank, childhood ends only with the death of the parent.
>
> Seegers, 1993, p. 479

The four autobiographical glimpses show the house as the kingdom of the patriarch where he may rule as he pleases, repress his women and children, subject to little more than laws against murder and the rules of tradition. But at the same time he has a deal with the state that he cannot escape, he is both an agent of state rule over his dependants and he himself subject to rule by the state.

A landmark event in the Apartheid State's encroachment upon Black patriarchal sovereignty was the forced removal of the black population from 'white' towns of South Africa. The so-called Natives Resettlement Act of 1954 tore away the protection of ownership and provided for the removal of owners and tenants nullifying their legal rights to urban freehold in White designated areas. Inner suburban property owned by blacks was expropriated and the population forcibly resettled on the urban periphery where they could no longer own property and were under total white municipal control; a total of 750 000 people were moved to newly established townships outside the white towns of South Africa. After the forced removal of Sophiatown's black population, described poignantly by Bloke Modisane in his autobiography and its development as a white area it was infamously renamed 'Triomf'. Grand apartheid was a crushing blow for the black adult generation of the 50s and it was up to the next generation to strike back, the children of the 70s. In the 1960s and until the eve of the Soweto uprising the patriarchal family was under strain from modernity promising greater opportunities for women and children in all industrialising societies, and from apartheid's twisted version of modernity restricting these opportunities for the black population.

By 1976 the rule of the black patriarch had become highly ambiguous, which was one of the key triggers of the uprising. Black people fought a desperate struggle for an urban foothold and the influx of distant relatives and sub-tenants resulted in the Soweto matchbox houses bursting at the seams; the municipal authorities calculated an average of 13 people per twenty-five square-metre house. Black Jacks, the black council police, would drive around at night waking up people controling their permits and tax-receipts and 'deporting' those without 'exemption' from the rules against black people in the 'white' town. Females often dominated the extended families and in many houses the real head of the house was a woman, blurring the lines of patriarchal authority. Often the husband would be controlled by his wife's mother. To survive, the patriarchs had adjusted to the white demands, 'to support their family', but the children did not buy this excuse, to them the fathers had become spineless. He was split between demands made on him by his radical children and by the repressive state and many children lost respect for what they saw as the pitiful survival-strategies of their fathers, avoiding the hassle of the overcrowded house, drinking beer in some shebeen after work and leaving the family to its own devices.

The parents had a way of behaving and talking suited to survival around the white workplace and in the white town. Conversely, the language of the children was aimed at confrontation with white authority. 'Tsotsi' is Sotho for rebel, one that is different, non conforming, an urban rebel. The opposite word was 'mogoe', country bumpkin, a dull conformist, and it was often levelled at the Zulus, new in town. The *tsotsi* would not just have his own lingo, his clothes would also mark him. He would be a sharp dresser wearing ironed trousers and clothes proclaiming that he did not work manually. The worst he could think of was wearing blankets.

Many youngsters lived totally beyond the norms of their parents. Nobody could tell these children when to be at home or how to behave. They could return with a stolen car and the father would be too intimidated to ask what was going on. Young boys got stolen taxi-vans from white areas, suddenly they learned to drive, became mobile and could organise their oppositional activities across the vast distances of Johannesburg. Coloured parents were afraid their children might have contact with blacks, but the children did as they pleased. Coloured girls would stop straigthening their hair and come home with black boys; they would stop attending church. It was outrageous, but the parents had lost their grip on the children. Clearly the patriarchal house was under heavy fire from within.

It is probably uncontroversial to state that inspiration and mental power to want and to dare demonstrate came from the Black Consciousness Movement (BCM) and initial leadership of the pupils came from the Soweto Students Representative Council (SSRC). As early as 1972–73, children 12–13–14 years old would discuss armed struggle against the state. From 1973 onwards children collected military magazines with recipes for bombs. These small BCM-groups included both coloured and black youth. The priest Dale White organised picnics where banned literature on civil war and petrol bombs and so forth was studied. By 1974–75, maps had been produced detailing escape routes out of South Africa. These small groups would seek confrontation with the whites, demonstrating their lack of fear of the police and their readiness to name stool pigeons.

In early 1973, the Apartheid State struck against some of the BCM leaders. In an ironic full-circle the state tried to enlist support from the house it had already ruined. Steve Biko, Barney Pityana and Harry Nengwekhulu, three BCM leaders:

> were detained for a while by security police before being transported individually to their various places of birth... Banning orders subtly employed traditional controls to discipline errant black political activists by sending them back to their natal homes. Symbolically they can be said to have invoked parental control over political transgressors.
>
> Ramphele, 1993, p. 83

Of course it did not work in this case, but ten years later the state was to turn fathers against sons on a frightening scale of 'parental control' with older male vigilantes trashing adolescent 'comrades'. Less recognized than the BCM inspiration is, perhaps, the role played by gangs in building up the fighting force of the children. In the early 1970s gangsters were the first to supply weapons, stolen cars and money to BCM-groups, all very young boys. Two important persons were the famous Don Matera and Jimmy Mathews. Historically criminal gangs had played an ambiguous role in challenging the police and setting up models for resistance and admiration among youths. Discussing the gangs operating in Sophiatown, Johannesburg, during the 1950s, Tom Lodge wrote:

> These gangs were frequently very large, often had a quasi-military structure and ... were to be found in the vanguard of any communal confrontation with the police. ... [t]he gangsters must have been a source of considerable anxiety to the authorities. They represented an anarchic, violent and elusive current of resistance which lay beyond the capacity of the state to control, co-opt, or suppress.
>
> Lodge, 1983, p. 102

One controversial aspect of the gangs was their Coloured background growing originally out of the Cape slave society and becoming a prominent feature in the organisation of Coloureds in the Cape and in Johannesburg. The gangs in Sophiatown were either Coloureds or Sothos setting the fashionable urban standard to be dreamt of by rural blacks coming to town. The *comtsotsi* (comrade-tsotsi, i.e. rebel-gangster) was the norm which children aspired to, amongst other things by mastering the *tsotsitaal*, the tsotsi-lingo. The gangsters would talk about the township as '*die kas*' a box where you could hide from the police. The *tsotsitaal* was a crucial means of survival, when you had to develop ways to tell friend from enemy. Sotho '*dla*' was hip talk amongst youth and gangsters, making it possible to navigate in a violent ethnic space. It was mock-military and contained a silent hand-language as well, securing survival. Gangster culture and ways of organising attacks on the state (not political violence in the narrow sense) was something from which the parents were totally excluded, yet, most boys in high school had brothers or other relatives who had contact with gangsters.

Outside the confines of the Soweto house was a real wilderness, full of dangers for children. Parents had every reason to fear for the life of their children once they darted out to join their comrades in the streets or in the far-away camps of the nebulous freedom fighters. But instead of the parents forbidding their children to roam the streets the children forced their fathers (and mothers) back into the house, forbade them to drink and prevented them from celebrating Christmas. The children ruled their parents and reversed in a most spectacular way the patriarchal rule of the house during the uprising. Granted, adolescents per se question parental rule everywhere. If anybody were to revolt against generational rule in the house it would be them. Only in South Africa was the rule of the elders so violent and linked so intimately to the other vectors of rule that generational stirrings started to rock the whole structure of apartheid. The link between state and patriarchal repression, the 'farming out' of repression from the state to the house-patriarch was inherent in the rule of the house. To function, apartheid needed the deeply ambivalent co-operation of black patriarchs in order to rule black children.

7   Children in town space: Pupils

The Nationalist government itself created the pupils. To meet the growing need for an educated black work force to undertake ever more complex town functions 'Bantu Education' exploded in the 1960s and 1970s. Education transformed ever more children into pupils and it collected them in schools, thus creating a whole new front where children *en masse* confronted apartheid.

> Between 1950 and 1975, the number of African children at school rose from around one million to over 3,5 million ... Secondary expansion was especially dramatic between 1965 and 1975, when it increased nearly fivefold. Class sizes averaged over 60 in Soweto and reached 100. Under-trained teaching staff in acutely under-resourced schools found it difficult to cope and corporal punishment was commonplace. Schools became sites of expansion, of expectation, of deprivation and of explosive political potential. (Beinart, p. 219)

Yet, no matter how poor the education was it retained a core functional rationale both for the white society needing an ever better trained work-force and for the individual Black pupil striving for an improved life-chance. It is important to note the absence of rural-urban influx-issues which came to fuel the violence of South African cities a decade later. Then, in June 1976, the imposition of Afrikaans as the language of instruction condemned the pupils to do badly at the examinations. Critique was not initially centred on the content or ideology of the curriculum. Majakathata Mokoena, one of the student leaders of '76, visited his old higher primary school in 1996 and his comment is an example of this non-ideological, functional critique:

> The curriculum was exactly the same as before. I asked the principal, why is it that we still have nine hours per week of vernacular and you have about five hours of mathematics and science? It makes no sense. Science and mathematics are critical. We should actually be having more science hours in schools. The best-performing countries do that.
>
> *Sunday Independent,* June 16, 1996

The Bantu Education schools were petrol waiting for a match; then the state decided to ignite the Afrikaans-language issue. In Parliament the Deputy Minister of Bantu Education, Dr. Andries Treurnicht, denied any knowledge of well documented protests against the imposition of Afrikaans. As late as June 14, Councillor Leonard Mosala from the Soweto Urban Bantu Council warned that enforcing Afrikaans in schools could result in another Sharpeville. Speaking of the children, he said:

> They won't take anything we say because they think we have neglected them. We have failed to help them in their struggle for change in schools. They are now angry and prepared to fight and we are afraid the situation may become chaotic at any time.
>
> SAIRR 1977, p. 57

The Afrikaans daily *Beeld* tracked down Andries Treurnicht in Windhoek for an urgent comment on the crisis. His answer betrayed a stupefying narrow-mindedness.

> In the white areas of South Africa [i.e. outside the homelands] the Government should have the right to decide the medium of instruction in African schools, as the Government supplied the buildings and subsidised the schools.
>
> (ibid. p. 59)

When the explosion came on June 16, the pupils did not shrink back into the house as minors, they attacked the state on the terrain where the state ruled them as pupils, i.e. in the schools.

The attack was successful, they actually reversed state rule in the schools. When the children burned down schools they effectively negated state rule of them as pupils. Boycotts worked almost as well once patriarchal rule in the house had broken down and no one could force the children to attend school.

As the SAIRR remarked somewhat at a loss, 'Parents, teachers and police appeared to be helpless in the face of the continued refusal of children to go to school' (SAIRR, 1977, p. 64).

The school-burning and boycott of examinations were efficient in turning pupils into street-fighters, but it carried the obvious dilemma between collective struggle and individual improvement. The avant-garde injunction 'Let us not betray the nation by pursuing selfish ends like writing exams,' in the document cited above and later the slogan 'Liberation before education' became bitterly contested within the struggle. In the end the children paid a heavy price for their boycotts. Nobody rewarded the street-fighters of 1976 without education in 1996 with good positions on the labour-market.

It took the Minister of Bantu Affairs almost two weeks to back-track on the original Afrikaans question. It was in vain, of course, as the language issue had ignited

violent protest which immediately expanded to include the fundamental racial contradictions of apartheid.

8   Children in ethnic space: Black people

The June 18 editorial headline in a leading Afrikaans daily, *Die Burger,* 'Now it has
happened' gives a measure of the racial fear of the whites for their repressed 'other':

> The most alarming aspect of the event is probably the demonstration it gave
> once again of the unthinking, excessive, almost lustful fierceness of which a
> mass is capable ...We know how a black mass at the slightest provocation can be
> whipped up into irrational frenzy.

The fear was echoed in most headlines in white newspapers on the morning of June 17.
Die Transvaler: 'Shock violence – whites chopped to death', *Rand Daily Mail:* 'Bands of
marauding blacks rampaged through Soweto last night', *The Star:* 'Mobs take over',
'Drunken Tsotsis on prowl', *Beeld:* 'Hell in Soweto', with a photo across the breadth
of the page of the dead body of Dr Melville Edelstein (the white township-employee
killed on the first day and one of the only two whites killed during the entire uprising).
Frantz Fanon knew the talk of the white racists very well.

> The colonial world is a Manichean world ... At times this Manicheism goes to its
> logical conclusion and dehumanizes the native, or to speak plainly, it turns him
> into an animal ... The native knows all this, and laughs to himself every time he
> spots an allusion to the animal world in the other's words. For he knows that
> he is not an animal; and it is precisely at the moment he realizes his humanity
> that he begins to sharpen the weapons with which he will secure his victory.
>
> Fanon, 1963, p. 43

After a helicopter swoop over the riot-torn areas on June 18, Minister of Justice Jimmy
Kruger declared that '[T]he situation would return to normal this weekend. The police
are capable of handling the trouble and *the public has no reason to fear*' (*Cape Times,* 19
June, 1976; italics added). He blamed the unrest on Black Power ideology imported
from America and promised that, 'The White man will overcome it.' Of course 'the
public' and 'the white man', which were one and the same to Mr. Kruger, had reason
for fear, because the 'trouble' was that violence was starting to move back across the
ethnic border. Minister John Vorster declared, 'I can unfortunately come to no other
conclusion than that we do not have to do with a spontaneous outburst but with a
deliberate attempt to encourage polarisation between Black and White' (*Cape Times,*
June 19, 1976). Such as the policy of the National Party Government, perhaps? Children looking from inside a little Soweto matchbox house out at a police station behind
razor-wire and sandbags and a street made wide enough for a Hippo to operate, would

see the beachhead of an oppressive state on their own territory. There was a very real and violent ethnic front between the township and the white city. In the street-battles the children did not move the front very much; their dramatic achievement was turning around the *meaning* of township space for a short, fateful moment.

Townships were invented as a solution to an unsolvable contradiction in the racist project:

> The Native should only be allowed to enter urban areas which are essentially the white man's creation when he is willing to enter and minister to the needs of the white man and should depart therefrom when he ceases so to minister.
>
> (1922)

As early as 1922, the argument was not only racist; it was also, of course, built on a false assumption - that black people did not live in towns, because while 'ministering' to the white man's need the native obviously had to live somewhere in the town. In 1922 every sixth South African city-dweller was black and by 1976 the black urban population outnumbered the white urban population two to one. Now, two fundamentally different meanings were implied in the 'entering and departing of the native from the white man's town': a move across the town-countryside border, i.e. the migrant worker solution; or a move across the white town-black town border, i.e. the township solution. The first was the grand racist ideal, built on the utterly false and cynical notion of men staying temporarily in single-sex hostels while working in town and keeping a home in a black homeland where women and children tilled the soil happily. The migrant solution to the racist vision of white towns reached its extreme form with the 'independence' of the Transkei in 1976. South Africa would meet all the violence inherent in this ideal in the 'civil war' of 1986. But this was not the antagonism fuelling the uprising of 1976. In 1976 the contradictions of the second model were the ones to explode, the township model with urban blacks living in a 'white' town.

To live in a township was a personal limbo position for black people no longer slaves, but still racially discriminated against and expelled from the 'white' town: you could work in town but not live there. Slaves had lived in the white man's house (cf. Shell, 1994), in the racist intimacy of Senzala (the slave huts) and Casa-Grande (the slave-owners estate including slave huts and manor) to use the designations introduced by the Brazilian sociologist Gilberto Freyre in his landmark investigation of patriarchal-racist rule in colonial Brazil. In 1976, many urban blacks still lived in servants quarters (cf. Cock, 1989) and in particular in hostels (cf. Ramphele, *A Bed Called Home*). The hostels bore the closest resemblance to the Senzala: a naked dormitory, intimately and harshly integrated into the Casa-Grande. All kinds of exploitation, whether latifundista or capitalist, demand this functional integration of the slave/worker with the overseers/owners of the production-process. In the functional domain the township was pure dormitory housing annexed to a 'white' town. All the personal decisions associated with ownership like where to build, how to build and who should live in the house were appropriated by the white municipality and state. The owner of a Soweto matchbox house enjoyed no full patriarchal sovereignty. Thus the township added up to a Senzala dependent upon and dominated by the Casa-Grande of the white town. Because the township house was not a fully sovereign patriarchal space, the township did not constitute a fully-fledged urban space.

But in the ethnic domain the township was much more than a Senzala; it was also a ghetto. Separation of the races, laid down in the Group Areas Act, created the township as a ghetto, an ethnic space where a kind of separate and autonomous identity, however suppressed, would manifest itself in contrast to the apartheid-declared identity of the 'white' town. Each scrap of urban life added to the endless rows of matchbox houses potentially built up a fateful ethnic counterpoint to the white town, the black ghetto confronted the white town. The township always had this 'doubleness': Senzala ambiguously counterpoised ghetto.

The township could not solve the dilemma of urban apartheid between functional integration and ethnic separation. In order to keep the township a barren dormitory, racist exploitation had to contradict ethnic separation. We see this contradiction played out in the riot-space. The police could not isolate Soweto from Johannesburg because the black workers were needed in the 'white' town to continue racist exploitation; on the other hand they desperately tried to keep the black children out of Johannesburg, to uphold the ethnic border. This was the contradiction of apartheid: by functional necessity it created an ever growing black urban population, while fervently believing in the racist ideal of White towns. Only in a collective act of make-believe were reality and ideal reconciled and the townships and their millions obliterated from the horizon of the daily life of most whites. On August 20, after two days of terrible violence in the local townships where 33 people had been killed, the Minister of Bantu Affairs M.C. Botha said in a speech in Port Elizabeth that the basis on which blacks were present in White areas was 'to sell their labour and for nothing else' (SAIRR, 1977, p. 67).

But the children shredded this indulgent dream. Their violence reversed the meaning of ethnic space: suddenly when the children surged into central Cape Town and Johannesburg the township no longer was the ethnic Other of the dominant white town, it became dominant for a moment and the white town had to defend itself. The funerals became central political manifestations and the police tried to silence the children and their growing number of adult supporters; for example on October 24 when 5000 mourners attending a funeral for riot-victims in Soweto were attacked and people giving black power salutes were shot by the police; seven were killed and 51 injured. For a short while the children were able to seal off Soweto from Johannesburg (with the help of the police) and standing at the grave declared the ghetto a liberated space. In the discursive battle between children and state, the liability of the state, the unsolvable contradiction between Senzala and Ghetto became the strength of the children. Distinguishing a black worker travelling between Senzala and Casa-Grande from a black pupil transgressing the ethnic border of the ghetto demanded the one thing which apartheid had destroyed: patriarchal control of the black house.

Conclusion

During six months of rioting primarily in the townships of Johannesburg, Cape Town and Port Elizabeth the children developed five forms of struggle: fights inside the township, contesting the township border, enforcing stayaways, attacking the white town and ruling the parents. This particular violence mapped three spaces: first of all the township, a space defined as different from a 'white' town by apartheid laws of ethnicity; secondly the town defined by the total variety of urban functions including education and finally the private house, defined by the sway of patriarchal authority keeping it separate from all other houses and places in the town. Any matchbox house in Soweto marked a house space while simultaneously being part of the ethnic space of Soweto and the town space of metropolitan Johannesburg. Now, in each of these spaces children confronted adults: the father, the teacher and the policeman. With the steady disintegration of parental rule the teacher and the policeman became more exposed and when the educational authorities provoked the children with the Afrikaans issue the teachers' control of schools collapsed within a few hours. The children then suddenly confronted the state's last line of defence: police and army units deploying firearms, armoured vehicles and helicopters and courts, prisons and draconian laws; the conflict had escalated into an all-out attack on the racist foundation of apartheid South Africa. When the children challenged the police and put their lives on the line – and lost their lives – they exposed the timidity of their parents subjected to the same racial discrimination. Within weeks the parents had to acknowledge (*inter alia* by forming the Black Parents' Association) the children's activist leadership in the intergenerational struggle against white rule. The structure of the uprising had made a full circle: the children returned to the house as rulers of the parents.

It is a strange fact that Durban saw almost no rioting in 1976. One possible explanation, which may support my general argument about the house, is the peculiar development of the townships in Durban. Unlike Johannesburg and Cape Town, Durban was located very close to a homeland and traditionally African urbanisation was low and migrancy high. Neither fathers nor mothers migrating to the city, living in male hostels or (female) servants quarters had their children with them. Typically the children stayed behind in the periurban or rural areas with other, older, family-members. Most African squatters were removed from municipal land during the 1960s and the state provided low cost housing for these people far out of Durban in KwaMashu and Umlazi, areas included in the homeland of KwaZulu (Haarhoff, 1984, p. 130). In

1976 Mangosuthu Buthelezi became chief minister of the KwaZulu homeland government and increasingly the conservative cultural values propagated through Inkatha
came to dominate the homeland. One central effect was to strengthen patriarchal control of children both at home and in the schools and being a homeland the Afrikaans
issue did not apply. In 1976 the only Black townships under municipal control were
the small townships of Lamontville and Chesterville. The low degree of African municipal urbanisation caused a relative absence of Black children anywhere near the city
centre in 1976 and nothing like the concentration of angry high school children Soweto
had. Tougher patriarchal control, virtual absence of the Afrikaans issue and almost no
townships twinned with 'white' Durban precluded a children's revolt beyond a few
instances of copying events in Johannesburg. In any case, Durban remained a side-
show.

The children's revolt posed a terrible challenge for the apartheid state – as children
do for all states whenever they turn to the street. When the patriarchal house could no
longer control the children the state had to use grossly excessive means, such as beating
small kids, detaining minors in prison and killing children. By doing this the state
acknowledged adult status to the children and when it treated the children as adults it
exposed its own weakness both morally and in terms of violence. When the children
neither respected their fathers nor their teachers and started burning down schools the
state had only two choices: it could talk with the children as pupils and in a flexible way try
to accommodate their demands, or it could turn against the children as blacks with
the full force of its repressive apparatus. The first option could possibly have
reconfirmed the children as minors and pupils, but the doctrinaire and racist inflexibility of apartheid leaders like Vorster, Kruger and Botha left only the second option
open. Violence and more violence and then paradoxically the treatment of the children
as adults: beaten, imprisoned and killed. This gave the children enormous leverage at
the *ethnic* front because here they stood on the *same* side as their parents: with the
parents trailing behind the black children were challenging white supremacy head on.
Just how all-powerful the children became was demonstrated when they enforced
stayaways and later declared an anti-shebeen drive and the majority of adults complied. The ruin of the patriarchal house, the crucial input from gangs, and the BCM
inspired overcoming of a black inferiority complex all contributed to the shaping of
that formidable fighting force, the children.

References

Brickhill, Jeremy and Alan Brooks. (1980). *Whirlwind before the storm*, London: Inter-
    national Defence and Aid Fund for Southern Africa.
Christopher, A. J. (1994). *The Atlas of Apartheid*, London and New York: Routledge;

Johannesburg: Witwatersrand University Press.

Cock, Jacklyn. (1989). *Maids and Madams: A Study in the Politics of Exploitation*, Johannesburg: Ravan Press.

Fanon, Frantz. (1963). *The Wretched of the Earth*, New York: Grove Press.

Frederikse, Julie. (1986). *South Africa: a Different Kind of War – From Soweto to Pretoria*, London: James Currey.

Haarhoff, Errol John. (1984). *A Spatial analysis of African Urbanisation and Informal Settlement in Natal/KwaZulu*, unpublished PhD dissertation, Durban: University of Natal.

Hirson, Baruch. (1979). *Year of Fire, Year of Ash*, London: Zed Books.

Kane-Berman, John. (1993). *Political Violence in South Africa*, Johannesburg: South African Institute of Race Relations.

Lodge, Tom. (1983). *Black Politics in South Africa since 1945*, Johannesburg: Ravan Press.

Magubane, Peter. (1986). *June 16. The Fruit of Fear*, Johannesburg: Skotaville Publishers.

Mandela, Nelson. (1994). *Long Walk to Freedom. The Autobiography of Nelson Mandela*, Randburg: SA, Macdonald Purnell.

Marx, Anthony W. (1992). *Lessons of Struggle. South African Internal Opposition, 1960–1990*, Cape Town: Oxford University Press.

Mbeki, Govan. (1996). *Sunset at Midday. Latshon'ilang'emini!*, Braamfontein: Nolwazi Educational Publishers.

Modisane, Bloke. (1963). *Blame me on History*, Johannesburg: A.D. Donker/Jonathan Ball Publishers.

Mostert, W.P. & J.M. Lötter (eds). (1990). *South Africa's Demographic Future*, Pretoria: Human Sciences Research Council.

Mzamane, Mbulelo Vizikhungo. (1982). *The Children of Soweto*, Harlow: Longman.

Ndlovu, Sifiso. (1999). *The Soweto Uprising: Counter Memoires of June 1976*, Randburg: Ravan Press.

No Sizwe [Neville Alexander] .(1979). *One Azania, One Nation. The National Question in South Africa*, London: Zed Books.

Pityana, B., M. Ramphele, M. Mpumlwana & L. Wilson (eds). (1991). *Bounds of Possibility. The Legacy of Steve Biko & Black Consciousness*, Cape Town: David Philip; London: Zed Books.

Ramphele, Mamphela. (1993). *A Bed Called Home. Life in the Migrant Labour Hostels of Cape Town*, Cape Town: David Philip; Athens: Ohio University Press; Edinburgh: Edinburgh University Press.

Ramphele, Mamphela (1995). *A Life*, Cape Town: David Philip.

Seegers, Annette. (1993). 'Towards an Understanding of the Afrikanerisation of the South African State', *Africa*, 63 (4).

Seekings, Jeremy. (July 1995). *Social ordering and control in South Africa's black townships: an historical overview of extra-state initiatives from the 1940s to the 1990s*, unpublished paper presented to the South Afrtican History Society biennial conference, Rhodes University, Grahamstown.

Shell, Robert C.-H. (1994). *Children of Bondage. A Social History of the Slave Society at the Cape of Good Hope, 1652–1838*, Johannesburg, Witwatersrand University Press. Hanover, NH: University Press of New England.

South Africa (1962). 'Regulation for the administration and control of townships in Bantu areas', Proclamation No. R 293, Pretoria: Government Gazette.

South African Institute of Race Relations. (1977). *Yearbook 1976*, Johannesburg.

Tin, Hjalte. (1996). *Winnie Mandela's Banning Order, The Territoriality of Power and Political Violence*. Working Paper 34–96, Centre for Cultural Research, University of Arhus.

Tin, Hjalte. (1998). *The Spaces of Civil War. From a Global Typology of Civil War to a Topography of Violence in South Africa, 1976, 1986, 1996*, unpublished PhD thesis, University of Aarhus.

Categorical and strategic resistance and the making of political prisoner identity in Apartheid's Robben Island Prison

Fran Lisa Buntman

In his first public pronouncements after being released from prison, Nelson Mandela's message was seen as 'radical, uncompromising ... a speech from hell ... a speech for the warpath' (Waldmeir, 1997, p. 157). In contrast, the day after his release, Mandela offered a different image of himself. Now he was a gracious conciliator who praised apartheid president, F.W. de Klerk, the man who had released him, as a 'man of integrity'. Mandela further assured whites that his African National Congress (ANC) wanted them to 'feel safe'.

This duality of challenge and cooperation was not Mandela's alone. Indeed, it hinted at two different understandings of resistance that shaped anti-apartheid politics over decades. This article will focus on the ways these often contrasting ideas of resistance shaped political prison politics and prisoner identity in Robben Island prison when, after 1976, revitalised protest brought together at least two generations of activists and three political organisations in apartheid's cells.[1]

Conflict among the three groups arose primarily because the more established organisations attempted to recruit the new inmates. These tensions were underscored by generational conflict which tended to revolve around questions of how to execute the struggle in prison (as well as upon release). At the heart of the dissension over appropriate prison conduct lay a debate about resistance: what actions constitute resistance, what criteria are used to assess the effectiveness of resistance, and what are the most effective means of resistance?

Prisoners tended to emphasise either pragmatic or principled approaches to resistance, and the choice of approach was shaped by the history of prisoner struggles, the political context outside the prison, and state strategy – especially the practice of classifying prisoners as entitled to different levels of prison 'privileges'.

In turn, attitudes to and practices of resistance informed and indeed constructed political identity: the identity of Robben Islanders became identities of resistance. The identity of Robben Islanders who resisted as a point of political principle became one of what I call 'categorical resistance', while I label as 'strategic resistance' opposition and challenge as a means towards the end of *Realpolitik*.

Categorical resisters define their political identity in direct relation to the enemy; opposition calls for negating the enemy's attempt to affect or influence political prisoner behaviour. Strategic resisters choose rather to attempt to shape or influence the structure and system being challenged. While identity as strategic resistance tended to be the predominant political identity on Robben Island, categorical resistance continued to play a vital role in informing debates about, and options for, individual and collective resistance. Both categorical and strategic resistance shaped not only prisoner identity and politics, but the national anti-apartheid struggle as well as the subsequent negotiated transition and now, the first years of democratic rule.

Robben Island Prison and its Community

Robben Island prison was established in the early 1960s to incarcerate black male political prisoners. Conditions were harsh, brutal, and dangerous. Only the sustained resistance of political prisoners, with the assistance of outside supporters, gradually and unevenly led the prison authorities to improve the circumstances of incarceration. A mark of the success of protest action was not simply that conditions were ameliorated, but that a large degree of prisoner unity had been forged among different political organisations, most importantly the ANC and the Pan-Africanist Congress (PAC).

Both were nationalist organisations opposed to apartheid's white minority rule, but the ANC believed in working with a range of groups, including whites and communists, whereas the PAC broke away from the ANC to carve out what was, for the most part, a more narrow African identity. The apartheid government banned both groups in 1960, and over the next few years the police and security apparatus crushed, killed, exiled, and in Robben Island and elsewhere, jailed leaders, members, and supporters of these once dominant political movements, leading to a sharp decline in resistance politics. A school-student protest that began on 16 June 1976 marked the end of this political lull, both real and apparent. In the intervening years a new political tendency, Black Consciousness, which emphasised black psychological and self liberation, had emerged. The myriad organisations that identified with its ideas came to be identified as the Black Consciousness Movement (BCM).

Members of all three organisations (as well as two other smaller groups, not considered here) met in Robben Island from the mid-1970s. The years between 1977 and 1980 were marked by considerable conflict among political prisoners. While there were disagreements over ideology and strategy – both inter- and intra-organisational – the fact that the ANC and PAC prisoners tended to be older men imprisoned in the 1960s and the BCM men were younger and included school and university students, conflict was also based on generation. In political terms, when the 1976 uprising occurred, Robben Island was a fairly stable community divided between the two liberation movements, the ANC and the PAC, with the former in the majority. (There were also a few members of the BCM and APDUSA, the African People's Democratic Union of South Africa.) It was, for the most part, an aging population; a prisoner assessment of Island soccer clubs, 'Age distribution and youthfulness of [soccer] clubs', indicated that soccer players faced a 'decline of fitness and the increasing chronicity of injuries' (Mayibuye Centre Archives 17.1, Memo of 14 April 1974). While in contemporary interviews most former prisoners recall an optimism and vitality about their prison struggle, the political quiet was often discouraging. There was also a certain degree of resignation and depression among prisoners as long sentences took their toll. Certainly, this was the impression of the youth who began arriving from the mid-1970s. It is also born out in the assessment of the state of soccer which noted a 'general saturation level' because the soccer clubs had played each other so often that 'it can be predicted to a high level of accuracy which clubs will win and which tactics will be used or attempted'. Furthermore, the memo noted:

> the effects of imprisonment are becoming noticeable ... [In addition, a] more mature outlook towards sport has been attained. We do not now feel the need to prove ourselves narcissistically in our sport any more.

Although the prisoners on Robben Island were not to know about the 16 June uprising until August (Mandela, 1994, p. 420), the arrival of the 'children of '76' made an impact that shook the prison to its core. These new prisoners were, for the most part, different from the existing population in at least two respects: they were usually younger, and tended to identify with or be members of Black Consciousness groupings. Both these differences were to cause conflict, and much of the 1977 to 1980 period was characterised by intense disagreements, at times to the point of physical fights, over questions of ideology, recruitment, leadership, and appropriate strategies to deal with the authorities. While elements of conflict, disagreement, and dissension continued after 1980, for the most part, the conflict did end with a high level of convergence over the new or renewed rules governing the prisoner society.

Organisational Conflict and Recruitment

Robben Island is often, and correctly, identified as a beacon in anti-apartheid politics. Its positive image, including a 'university', arose in large part because the prisoners developed a community that encouraged a high degree of political tolerance among the divergent groups, significant solidarity in developing sporting, cultural, and educational activities, and challenged the harsh conditions the prisoners faced at times, especially from about 1962 to 1972 (see Buntman, 1997). It is, however, indisputable that there was significant conflict among prisoners, especially in the early and mid-1960s and in the period under review.

The primary organisational conflict resulted because the ANC and PAC wished to recruit the new arrivals to the prison who had been imprisoned in the wake of the uprising. Although most of the youth identified with the BCM, they were not necessarily members of BCM organisations, nor did they necessarily have much political understanding of the movement's ideology. Therefore their political identification as Black Consciousness was often weak and they tended to lack sophisticated political understanding. Tenuous links to political organisations and ideologies were further undermined in prison by a competition for membership by other political groupings which had long histories and significant political experience.

Recruitment on Robben Island was not a new phenomenon. Politically uncommitted or wavering inmates would be potential draftees for competitive political organisations who would seek to enlist them in their movement and ideology. But with the political community largely stable in the years before 1976, there was little need to recruit. Mature political leaders recognised that recruitment would have a destabilising effect on the political community, and would only want to risk that for good reason. But the waves of new Black Consciousness prisoners did provide 'good reason'. First, the Soweto uprisings were the most significant political event in resistance politics in over a decade. An organisation that ignored them did so at the risk of its continued existence. Second, the older men who had spent so many long years in prison did not want to see the establishment of the BCM as a third rival on the ANC-PAC stage. Third, when affiliations were unclear, recruitment was seen as necessary to ensure every inmate was under a political discipline. Any prisoner not subject to organisational discipline was susceptible to co-option by 'the system', both in the prison and on release (Macozoma interview). Fourth, and probably of most importance, the inmates on Robben Island had always regarded it as their duty to produce capable activists who would eventually go back into their communities. The youth of '76 represented the future of the movements and the liberation struggle. These were the future activists, leaders, and soldiers, and so their recruitment was a necessity. Recruitment was, of course, a starting point for the critical process of training activists, teaching them organisational histories, ideologies and strategies, and preparing them for their political obligations and mandates upon release. The new arrivals from the Soweto uprisings made older prisoners aware 'that you had a political force that could fall either way' (Macozoma interview).

In the perspective of most former Islanders, the PAC assumed a natural alliance existed between themselves and the new Black Consciousness supporters, because of the similarity of their political philosophies. In the accounts of some, this meant that the PAC's approach to recruitment was more low key, an attitude that the natural affinities would inevitably bring the BCM into the PAC (Macozoma and Molala interviews). Others argue that the PAC and BCM entered into a formal alliance (Masuku interview).

The ANC, on the other hand, wanted to recruit or at least actively engage the new prisoners from the outset. The ANC claimed that, 'as an organisation, we had decided, especially in our [the single cell or leadership] section, not to go out of our way to recruit' (Kathrada interview). Prisoners, however, widely perceived, in the words of Black Consciousness leader Nkosi Molala, that 'the ANC ma[de] no bones about its position *vis-à-vis* the Black Consciousness Movement', that is, its desire to recruit the new inmates (Molala interview). The ANC had long made it a practice to write to new arrivals, welcoming them, and usually engaging in political interchange. BCM leader Mosibudi Mangena (1989, p. 86) recalls that:

> Like many other prisoners, I had a pen pal in another section. This was one of the ways in which we kept in touch as prisoners in different sections who were not supposed to communicate with one another. The clandestine 'postal system' would deliver the letters we wrote to each other every now and then. More often than not, the notes we exchanged involved comments and debates on political and ideological issues. Because many of us in the BCM were generally younger, most older people in the older compartments of the liberation movement imagined we ought to be targets of their political education exercises. Thus, when one or the other of them had an opportunity to correspond with one or another of us, he would almost invariably launch himself into ideological questions.

More direct or personal ideological engagement recruitment was often difficult, as most of the '76 arrivals were, at least initially, separated from the rest of the prisoners, who were themselves in different sections of the prison. Over time, however, ANC leaders and members came to be placed with BCM supporters, and most used the opportunity to recruit or at least influence their fellow inmates. Moreover, some Black Consciousness affiliates came to question the Movement on their own. Such reconsideration was especially important in the case of Terror Lekota, a nationally recognised leader of the BCM who publically joined the ANC and then recruited others to his new organisation, consequently enraging many of his former comrades.

Prison is always a tense environment, and overt and subtle recruitment efforts provoked great stress on Robben Island. Some interpersonal violence, both spontaneous outbursts and planned attacks, was a consequence. High levels of conflict and especially physical confrontation were always dangerous to the political prisoner community, as prisoner unity was one of the political community's most significant weapons against the state. Both the arrival of new prisoners, especially prisoners who had previously worked across partisan lines, and existing inmate recognition of the danger of division and confrontation, led to negotiations to re-establish a norm of coopera-tion and mutual respect. By 1980 new agreements had been established between the organisations, agreeing to mutually acceptable protocols regarding recruitment, and the prevention of new conflict. But by then the ANC was the largest organisation on the Island; in part due to the arrival of captured Umkhonto we Sizwe guerrillas, and in part due to the success of its recruitment campaigns. They, and to a lesser extent the PAC, as organisations and as the older generation, had also managed to persuade the younger men that there was much to merit their strategies for coping with prison life.

The Relationship between Generational and Organisational Conflict

Generational and organisational conflict are each specific phenomena. Although former Islanders tend to explain their prison conflict in terms of ideology and movements, age grouping and generational consciousness are also important explanations for events and processes on Robben Island (especially after 1976). There was, however, also a significant intersection between the organisational and generational factors. First, the BCM was largely an expression of a younger generation. Black Consciousness was developed by university students at a time when the older liberation movements ap-peared dormant, if not dead. It represented the perspectives of a new, young genera-tion, as well as a political philosophy of liberation. Second, on Robben Island the BCM was often not taken seriously as a political organisation by the older men in the older movements precisely because it was an organisation composed of youth. This is to some extent captured by Mangena's description of the letter writing process with older, non-Black Consciousness inmates, cited above. Cindi (interview) similarly com-ments that:

> they would treat us as youth. We would always correct them and say look, we may be young in age, but our organisation is on a par with your organisation. It's not a youth organisation. It's a political organisation. So it must be ac-corded the same status. There's no youth political organisation as it were. It's just one political organisation. But there would be resistance. And naturally, people always wanted us to be submerged under them.

Third, and to anticipate the argument concerning political identity discussed below, there was a significant overlap between the political identity of the youth and the BCM on the one hand, and the older men and the ANC and PAC on the other hand. The youth, as a grouping with a generational consciousness, and the BCM, as a grouping with an ideological consciousness, shared a political identity which demanded militant defiance as a matter of course. Indeed, they identified such defiance as core to their political identity, which demanded publicly challenging the regime's authority at all times.

The generational consciousness of the older men was intertwined with their experiential base of being long-term political prisoners, and developing a curiously and ironically intimate understanding of the behaviour of their enemy in the prison. The older men's perspective tended to cut across ideological and factional lines, so that a consensus existed that one's resistance – critical to the prisoner's political identity – demanded a careful strategic approach. When political identity assumes strategic resistance, resistance may be less visible, but not necessarily less effective.

Understanding Generational Conflict and Convergence

The struggle for ideological and organisational dominance was then a key to explaining the tensions and conflicts on Robben Island between 1977 and 1980 or 1981. They were also, however, and perhaps more importantly, a struggle over the appropriate understanding and methods of resistance by political prisoners in (and beyond) an apartheid jail. As such, these competing logics tended to be the divergent understandings of two generations of political activists.

By the mid-1970s, the older men, mostly imprisoned since the 1960s, had their attitude to resistance within prison shaped by three predominant factors. First, having experienced deprivation and brutality at the hands of an uninhibited state, they measured their current conditions and attitudes against their past experiences. The enormous improvements in prison conditions had been won by their struggles, perhaps leading progress to be measured more from what was than from what standards ought to prevail. Second, there was probably at least some sense of resignation to the status quo, especially as the struggle appeared near a standstill from the mid-1960s to the mid-1970s. Political resignation was no doubt exacerbated by aging, as the men began their second decade of imprisonment from 1972 onwards. Third, and of particular importance, these Robben Islanders had come to have a very pragmatic understanding of resistance. They had come to believe that if one is to withstand, and more importantly, make productive use of imprisonment, one could not expend one's energies on constant fights with the authorities (or indeed, among prisoners). One had continuously to strive for basic rights and privileges, and beyond that, one had to continue the anti-apartheid struggle in prison through developing organisations and the members that composed them.

This attitude of pragmatic resistance is exemplified in the following comment by Nelson Mandela (cited in Schadeberg, 1994, pp. 18–19):

> We soon became aware that in terms of our daily lives ... an ordinary warder, not a sergeant, could be more important to us than the Commissioner of Prisons or even the Minister of Justice. If you went to the Commissioner of Prisons or the Minister and said, 'Sir, it's very cold, I want four blankets', he would look at the regulations and say, 'You can only have three blankets ... more would be a violation of the regulations'. If you went to a warder in your section and said 'Look, I want an extra blanket', and if you treated him with respect, he'd just go to the storeroom, give you an extra blanket, and that's the end of it.

There were times, in this reading, to make a public or principled stand or launch a protest on an issue or demand, but that was not all the time. To achieve results often required a pragmatic route, which could and did include being polite to the enemy. Indeed, Mandela acknowledges the efficacy of this approach when he recounts a lesson he learned by having prisoner grievances ignored by publicly challenging the authority of a prison official. He argued:

> The best way to effect change on Robben Island was to attempt to influence officials privately rather than publicly. I was sometimes condemned for appearing to be too accommodating to prison officials, but I was willing to accept the criticism in exchange for the improvement.
>
> Mandela, 1994, pp. 364–65[4]

While Mandela is the best-known exemplar of this perspective, and was perhaps the most extreme, he was certainly not alone. When Harry Gwala (interview), usually considered one of the ANC's most hardline and uncompromising representatives, was asked whether the youth were right in their criticism of the older leadership as too conciliatory, he replied that the new young prisoners were very inexperienced

> ... Those people in prison were very militant by all means. Otherwise they would never be inside [prison] for militant actions. But ... [we] always distinguished between when to embark on mass action and when to talk. Whereas at times young people's actions bordered on anarchy.

Indeed, the young men and often boys of the 1976 generation were proud of their tendency to define themselves as militants who would resist everywhere and always. This militancy and deliberate defiance was a result of at least three factors. First, they were products of apartheid's hardships. They had come of age in the overcrowded homes, schools and townships that racism and apartheid created, at a time when the already poor standard of living showed signs of decline, with rising inflation and declining employment. On top of this, they experienced the brutal repression of their 1976 and 1977 rebellion: tear-gassing, beatings, shootings, detention without trial, torture in jail, and unjust trials. They tended to feel that little could be lost and much might be won with a persistent expression of anger and pain. Second, the youth of the 1970s were often appalled at the silence and acquiescence of their parents, teachers, and the older generation, who had been subdued into silent submission. Aggrey Klaaste, editor of the black newspaper *Weekend World*, berated his generation as cowards (Lodge, 1985, p. 334). Third, Black Consciousness ideology had provided an antidote to the older generation's meekness. Steve Biko and other BC leaders encouraged, especially among students, 'a sense of rebellion and self-assertion – the beginnings of a generational consciousness' (Johnson, 1989, p. 100). If the white apartheid regime wanted the compliance and resignation of mutes, they would be the opposite: militant, vocal, and angry. 'At least among urban youth', Anthony Marx (1992, p. 61) notes, 'the days of bowing and scraping were long gone, with the positive self-identity consistent with BC [Black Consciousness] expressed as an angry desire to tear down rather than build up'. These were the boys and men who were to arrive on Robben Island and violently clash with the authorities, and in turn, come into conflict with the older generation, who often had very different notions of appropriate strategies and tactics.

The younger men were often deeply disappointed with the behaviour of the older men they confronted in prison. Many of those sent to prison were, in part, being punished for 'eulogising' those of Robben Island, 'for calling them our leaders' (Cindi interview). Zithulele Cindi (interview, emphasis added) was a member of one of the first and most senior BCM leadership groups to come to the Island. He recalled that when he met the older ANC and PAC leaders, they didn't match expectations:

> ... We came with our vibrant militancy and our outright defiance ... We got there and we found these people who we look up to as our leaders ... sheepishly [cringing] ... So we then had to embark on a defiance now of the warders [prison guards].

Their challenge to the authorities was often successful:

> We would say 'hey', black style [clenched fist up] and they'd say 'keep quiet'. And we'd say, 'there's nothing wrong in greeting ... this is our form of greeting'... .So they accepted that. We scored a victory. Then we moved it a step further ... [The point was t]o restore their [the older prisoners'] dignity.

In turn, the older men tended to feel that the new activists and prisoners did not understand the enormous improvements in conditions they had achieved, and the tremendous costs associated with those changes. Nor did they believe that defiance for defiance's sake was always the wisest strategy. Johnson Mlambo (interview) of the PAC recalls that:

> by and large all the people that came in after '76 felt that the old organisations [the PAC and ANC] were more or less dead and that they are everything. Even when we advised them how to handle the prison authorities etc., they felt that, well, some of our advice was uncalled for. And some of the things we predicted actually happened ... Here is the group of people now coming in, and they ... mix with other people of the Black Consciousness Movement but there is no-one ... enlightening them because of their, you know, over-assertiveness ... They were a younger generation who perhaps felt that 'why is this like this, why is this like that', and who did not want to give credit to what had gone on before. What we were, where we were, [was] because of so many struggles ... They were to some extent also a little reckless as far as the militancy [was concerned] ... [But that is] always to be expected from young people.

Disagreements over classification in many ways epitomised the generational conflict, but it also had implications for the conflict over recruitment. South African prisons classified prisoners into four categories – A being the highest, and D the lowest – to reward good behaviour with certain privileges and punish bad behaviour with the retraction of those privileges. Thus, A group prisoners, for example, were allowed to buy food and, when legalised in 1980, buy and read newspapers. This was denied to prisoners of lower classifications.

Classification also determined one's right to study, the number of letters that could be sent and received, and the number and length of visits (and later whether these would be contact visits or not). Political prisoners had always challenged classification, arguing that political prisoners should not be classified: 'We are all prisoners. Why should there be differentiation? If there's to be a privilege we [should] all get it' (Cindi interview).

They furthermore opposed the fact that political prisoners would initially be classified at the lowest D rung, although criminals would be classified initially at the B rung (Alexander, 1994, pp. 76–80; Mandela, 1994, pp. 347–48; Macozoma interview). Although the older Robben Islanders had opposed classification, they accepted it as a necessary evil. Ahmed Kathrada (interview) comments:

> We never took a decision that we are going to refuse classification. Our demand was always that all political prisoners should be treated as A groups. There should be no discrimination among political prisoners, because the rationale for promotion was your so-called behaviour, and we said it's an insulting thing to tell us how to behave ... So we never used to ... ask ... to be classified ... but we said we won't refuse if we appear before the [classification] board. PAC was

the same, you see, PAC never refused classification ... Neville Alexander ... [of the Unity Movement] resisted for a while, but he eventually became A group.

In contrast, however, the Black Consciousness leadership rejected classification.[3] In part they rejected it for the same reason the older generation of political prisoners had opposed it; that it was 'prison apartheid' that assumed the state had the right to judge political prisoners, and manipulate their behaviour by using the carrot and stick of classification to reward and punish prisoners. In addition, the Black Consciousness adherents saw classification as creating a hierarchy among prisoners that would lend itself to divide and rule tactics, as well as other negative behaviour. In particular, once the ANC (and to a lesser extent, the PAC) began recruiting, or at least discussing politics with, the new young prisoners, BCM members argued that it became a means of bribery. In effect, Black Consciousness opponents of both classification and recruitment by the other organisations accused the older men with their A privileges of buying food, of seducing vulnerable young activists into their organisations, or at least perspectives, with food. For this younger generation, this was a complete violation of the behaviour appropriate to political prisoners. Black Consciousness leader Pandelani Nefolovhodwe (interview) elaborates:

> All cadres belonging to our organisation went in being classified D and went out being D. We saw in the classification process of the South African prison authorities ... bribery and that which will destroy the spirit of comrades. So we formulated a policy, as the Black Consciousness Movement ... that we are not going to be classified. That as I get in, I'll go out as I am ... We were many and you could have imagined that one of us become A, enjoy certain privileges, and the rest of the people are not A. It causes a lot of friction. [The authorities] sometimes used to offer [classification]: 'we think you are behaving very well and we would want you to be a B'. We say 'No, keep it. I'm alright where I am. I eat your food free, I don't need to buy biscuits'.

Nefolovhodwe argued that even if organisational abuses were excluded, accepting what in prison were luxuries opened up the potential for coming to depend on these, which could then be used against one. This pragmatic asceticism was not unique to the Black Consciousness; another member of the younger generation who embraced militancy as key to his political identity was the ANC's James Mange (interview), who constantly fought the seductive lures of the state and his organisation. With a D classification for nine years, from 1981 to 1990, 'there would be pressure from friends and families and so on, because I couldn't get contact visits and they tried talking me around to changing'. But Mange resisted such pressures with the certainty that material comforts were ideologically and strategically inappropriate for a political prisoner or prisoner of war:

> In the first place I shouldn't have been here [in prison] – [the] circumstances that brought me here are war ... As far as I'm concerned I'm still on enemy territory. And in order to preserve my sanity, my strengths, I'll have to learn to do without. Prison can become very frustrating if you learn not to do without. That stick that always lands above your head, you can write five letters, you can have seven visits or whatever, contact visits, that sort of straight-jackets you.

Mange's personal symbol of defiance was to retain long dreadlocks, which were forbidden by the prison rules:

> I had dreadlocks this long, you know [indicates]. And prison regulations doesn't have room for that. But that was one of my weapons. *Because that said to me victory all the time ... I can't exchange my will-power for the small nothings that you are offering* [Mange interview, emphasis added].

There is certainly sound political sense in the argument that classification is not only offensive, but a clever divide and rule strategy the state could manipulate to the detriment of anti-apartheid struggles. Furthermore, the privileges of higher classification could potentially lead to the prison being a little less harsh and even more 'liberal', but liberalisation of the prison was also often recognised as something that could lead to problems for organisational coherence.

Petros Mashigo (interview), an ANC member, noted that often support for hunger strikes (intended to improve conditions or challenge the state in some way) would be divided along the lines of classification, where those with higher classifications and therefore more privileges would oppose embarking on hunger strikes, and those with lower classifications and a harsher existence would support the strike strategy. This differentiation in attitude based on material well-being lends significant support to Mange's (interview) contention that 'in a resistance movement it is only rebelling that keeps you brave', and validates a concern that access to privileges in prison might blunt the resistant and defiant edge of prisoners.

The absence of an all-powerful enemy can further lead to apathy or (greater) divisions in the ranks, and political organisations may have less to offer members when there is the competition of movies, television, and a relatively undisciplined life. Saki Macozoma (interview) reminds one that there is another pole to prison life, where people spend all day talking about movies they have seen and women they have known – and manufacture the stories in any case. The counter attractions increased with the liberalisation of the prison, when there were more movies, sport, and so on.[4]

Robben Island life presented, however, a number of problems with the principled anti-classification argument. First, while it was difficult for all to renounce privileges that might slightly mitigate the hardships of prison life, those who had very long and life sentences would be hurt the most by the strategy. Most of the BCM leadership were given five and six year sentences, and most of the '76 militants were given similar sentence lengths.[5]

In contrast, however, many of the older generation, the incoming guerrillas, as well as some of the 1976 generation, had much longer sentences. Arguably, for men dealing with long-term imprisonment, the relative gains made by strategic asceticism would or could be lost by the greater losses of the renunciation.[6] For example, the more prisoners were able to have support from families via letters or visits, the more they were likely to cope with their sentences.[7]

Second, practical problems began to emerge with the ban on improved levels of classification. For example, the ANC's Ahmed Kathrada (interview) was critical of the Black Consciousness hypocrisy of denouncing classification but accepting its benefits:

> A number of Black Consciousness chaps came ... with the idea ... they shouldn't accept classification. So what these Black Consciousness chaps did is they used to work with this PAC chap who was in the Tuck Shop, and he used to wangle his books, so they used to order food. [And when the authorities allowed newspapers but said] newspapers are only for A groups, so they used to read all our newspapers ... So it was all a sham this thing of boycotting classification.

Finding ways around classification is not necessarily denied by those who opposed it. Saths Cooper (interview), a BCM leader, did not accept classification, he said, but 'I got classified unknown to me, and then discovered I was B group, so I said why should I deny myself writing all these letters ... and I wrote the letters'. That did not, he continued, lead to tension, because:

> the thing that was most problematic was the A group status, because that allowed you food stuffs and you see it was also an elitist thing because most prisoners came from very humble backgrounds, no money whatsoever, so it caused all those types of tensions ... There was a time when I benefited from getting bought food stuff without being classified [chuckle] because the guy who was in charge of the shop would just write it as, you see I think he had a stock ... to account for the amount rather than the items, so he would give me the stuff.

What for Cooper was a clever manipulation of the system was for Kathrada a lack of honesty in the way one carried out the strategies of struggle. The point is not to judge the perspective of either man, who in any case represents many others who shared the same opinions, but rather to illustrate that the strategy of avoiding classification could be as vulnerable to problems of principle and practice as using classification directly.

Certainly, in the rumour mill that is prison (Motlanthe interview), and the very tense environment between and among generations, organisations and factions, that defined Robben Island in the late 1970s and early 1980s, these competing approaches to dealing with the state (in this case in the form of classification), did not resolve the conflict.[8]

Third, and of great importance, rejecting classification ignored an achievement and fundamental insight of the older generation, namely that prisoner struggles to create improvements not only provided material benefits that helped people survive their incarceration with the least possible harm to an individual, but they also promoted political organisations' well-being and were further used by the prisoners to create new gaps and contradictions within which to continue the struggle.

In other words, improving conditions was not only an end in itself; improved conditions and increased privileges and rights were used to further the anti-apartheid politics. One significant example of this phenomenon concerns academic studies. The constant struggle for academic studies fulfilled several critical goals. On an individual level within the prison, it helped keep people mentally alert, and increased the worth of their day-to-day lives. In addition, it could provide people with a means to make a living upon release.

For the collective, political ends of the various organisations, not only did academic study allow people the intellectual sophistication to master complex ideological arguments, but it provided a steady stream of books that were critical to political education in the prison. (Because this use of books was outlawed, prisoners would transcribe whole books so that the handwritten copies would provide a library after the student had to return them.) The utility of privileges for political ends was not only seen in study rights. A second example is that prisoners used the contact visits allowed in the 1980s to smuggle in contraband, in one case money to bribe a warder to buy a short-wave radio, critical for communication (Banda interview). A third instance was that of the use of a photograph to smuggle codes from the ANC on Robben Island to the ANC in exile, to facilitate communication.

That secret message and hundreds like it were smuggled between prisoners and their officials in exile over the 30 years that the ANC was banned. They formed a fabric of interwoven instructions and information that would help determine the shape of South Africa's democracy ... [ANC political prisoner from 1964 to 1976, Mac Maharaj explained that aside from the importance of being informed about events beyond the prison for psychological well-being], we could debrief prisoners about problems they had encountered infiltrating the country or trying to carry on the struggle in South Africa. That information would be passed on to the leadership in Lusaka.

[Prisoners' letters] had to deal strictly with family business. Consequently, the codes were built around words like children and parents.

Wilkinson and Waugh, *The Sunday Independent*, 25 June 1995, p. 5

In these examples, the uses of privileges provide critical examples of resistance to incarceration, and the political conditions that sustained that imprisonment. In this context, then, strategic resistance is seen as a constructive political act that aims to challenge the status quo not only by opposition, but by creation and imaginative use of material conditions.

As well as classification, another compelling example of the appropriate means to resist apartheid within the prison concerns the warders. Once again, the older generation, usually irrespective of their organisational affiliation, claimed the advantages of 'taming' the warders. Mandela's (1994, p. 365) view that '[t]he most important person in any prisoner's life is ... the warder in one's section' is based on the understanding that a non-conflictual and even cordial relationship with the warders could have an enormous impact on the prisoners' day to day existence. Mlambo (interview) recounts that the humanity of prisoners could change the perspective of the warders who 'had been conditioned to treat you as animals, but, by and large, with the march of time, some of them start to see the human being in you'. Alexander (1992, pp. 77–78) too recalls this lesson learned on the Island:

> Perhaps the greatest irony of all was that eventually we became the teachers, literally, of some of these warders ... The authorities quickly realised that they couldn't keep any set of warders for too long because of the danger of fraternisation was obviously very great... . I want to underline the role of people like Nelson Mandela and Walter Sisulu in particular [in teaching us how to deal with the authorities] ... While we were terribly impetuous and would have run ourselves suicidally against the prison walls ... [t]hey realised that if we adopted a particularly humane, dignified, friendly attitude (short, of course, in collaborating in our own indignity) that eventually we would break through.

The older generation sought to persuade the younger men that the best interests of anti-apartheid resistance within and without the prison demanded a strategic approach. In Mandela's elaboration of the value of working with or at least neutralising the warders, the one achievement could be to open these state functionaries to the wisdom of the ANC's position. But, arguably more important in the bigger picture, Mandela (1994, p. 366, emphasis added) also points out that:

> Having sympathetic warders facilitated one of our most vital tasks on Robben Island: communication. We regarded it as our duty to stay in touch with our

men in [the] F and G [sections of the prison], which is where the general prisoners were kept. *As politicians, we were just as intent on fortifying our organisation in prison as we had been outside.*

One of the highest forms of resistance is to continue (and even to further) one's political organisation and political struggle within or as a result of prison. Therefore, strategic resistance to facilitate this end was crucial. Gradually, the younger generation came to embrace the perspective of the older men. For some, this change was achieved through joining the older liberation movements, most notably the ANC, though the PAC also had new recruits from the Island. Organisational identity and affiliation was not, however, the only or even necessarily most important means to embrace a more far-reaching vision of resistance. Saths Cooper (interview, emphasis added), a one-time BCM leader who later became nonpartisan, believed the BCM's '*heavy idealist militant youth orientation*' had much to learn from the ANC. Mike Xego (interview) came into Robben Island as a Black Consciousness adherent, but joined the ANC on Robben Island. He recalls:

> Our perception of the old comrades [was] that they were too compromising with the warders. We would punch the warders. If warders touched us, we would quickly punch back. There were daily skirmishes ... Gradually Madiba [Mandela] and the others were told to tame us. It was not the regime but the ANC that cracked us. One by one, the ANC underground on Robben Island worked on us – on individuals – talking with us and smuggling notes to us.

The learning process was by no means all one way, and the older generation benefited and learned from the younger men too. First, the '76 generation further pushed back the boundaries the state had imposed on political prisoner life. It is probably no coincidence that hard labour in the quarries, and the beginning of the availability of somewhat more constructive occupations such as carpentry and sewing began in the late 1970s at the time the state was under greater pressure to give into these demands from the militant prisoners, as well as from heightened external monitoring.

Second, at least in the ANC, the youth, including the increasing numbers of captured guerrillas, developed a more sophisticated underground organisational structure for their prison organisation. This new structure put a heightened emphasis on secrecy from the authorities as well as communication among the ANC's constituent parts in different sections of the prison. Both ANC members and members of other organisations argue that the younger men brought a new intensity to political education and debate.

Third, the younger generation played a critical role in revitalising prison life; they were a reminder that the struggle had continued, and one's imprisonment was not in vain. (Such reminders that the struggle continued were often tragically bittersweet. In

1963 Johnson Mlambo [interview] had himself been a young man when he went to prison for a twenty-year term. He recalls being 'particularly shocked' when he met a new prisoner, 'and the young man was born after I had been on Robben Island for more than a year. And here is this young man coming to serve his sentence ... I realised that the intervening period has been long enough to have someone born, grow up and to come and serve his own sentence on Robben Island'.) They also were an invaluable source of news and contemporary culture, on an island that had been deliberately, if not entirely successfully, cut off from the world for over a decade. With the arrival of the '76 youth, sport again flourished, not least because there were now some professional soccer players (Mlambo interview).

Fourth, the youth exposed the older men to new thinking, and forced them to rethink their attitudes on many crucial points, from the idea that black people encompassed all the oppressed, African, Indian and Coloured (Cindi interview), an enduring legacy of the Black Consciousness philosophy, to the sense of alienation and anger that young, disenfranchised South Africans experienced. The importance of the alienation of black South Africa youth is most poignantly captured in Nelson Mandela's (1994, p. 437) account of the lesson he learned from BCM prisoner Strini Moodley after watching a documentary about the Hell's Angels, which 'depicted the Hell's Angels as reckless, violent, and antisocial, and the police as decent, upstanding, and trustworthy'. In the ensuing discussion, almost all the prisoners criticised the bikers for their lawlessness, until Moodley pointed out the similarities between the rebellion against authority of the Soweto youth of 1976 and the Hell's Angels.

> [Strini] reproached us for being elderly middle-class intellectuals who identified with the movie's right wing authorities instead of with the bikers ... [T]he larger question that concerned me was whether we had, as Strini suggested, become stuck in a mind-set that was no longer revolutionary. We had been in prison for more than fifteen years; I had been in prison for nearly eighteen. The world that we left was long gone ... Prison is a still point in a turning world, and it is very easy to stay in the same place in prison while the world moves on.

The younger men did bring their older counterparts into a newer world. But the mutual benefit of the generational mix was mutual, as illustrated by two comments made by Kgalema Motlanthe (interview).

> One particularly 'enriching lesson that I picked up throughout my [ten year] stay on the Island' was to learn to accept that although an enthusiastic young activist might make time for five political discussions or classes a day, many 'elderly people would want to take part in political education classes ... twice [or] a maximum of three times a week, and not more than that'.

An older person's inability to absorb the same material did not, however, make him any less competent. Motlanthe also taught others not to label someone as falling within a political tendency because they could not 'quote any of the works' that 'young, literate, enthusiastic people' could quote. On the other hand, the older men could see the positive influence they had on the young men, and be inspired by that:

> I think that one of the things that sustains the older comrades ... was the fact that there was always an intake of new people and they could see their efforts, those of political education, transforming people, and those people actually leaving prison to go out and actually contribute in the struggle.
>
> Motlanthe interview

One of the achievements of the men on Robben Island, young and old, was that most of them did not 'stay in the same place in prison as the world move[d] on'. Among the reasons for this was the process of conflict and convergence between organisations and, perhaps more importantly, generations, described here. Underlying this process is a debate over the appropriate understanding of resistance within Robben Island. In turn, this raises the question of the nature of political identity that was being forged by these resistant subjects.

Generational Conflict: Implications for Resistance and Identity

The two generations who met and interacted on Robben Island had conflicts of understanding as to the nature of the anti-apartheid struggle and the response it demanded within the prison walls. The arrival of the '76 generation was not the first time there were debates over how to fight apartheid in the prison, but their arrival initiated a new level and stage within those debates. This heightened awareness was exacerbated and complicated by inter-organisational differences, particularly with the emergence of the BCM as a significant force in liberation politics. The resolution of the inter-generational conflict (and, to a lesser extent, the organisational conflict) involved identifying appropriate forms of, and goals for, resistance. In turn, the different conceptualisations of resistance held by the two groups reflected two different political identities.[9] The defining feature of categorical resisters' identity is defiant resistance, where agents actively resist, or believe the need to resist, overtly, always, and everywhere. The key element of strategic resisters' identity employs resistance with tactical and long-term goals in mind, usually in covert form, and often including apparent compliance with an oppressor or opponent.

Against an apartheid state that wanted pliant and servile black people who knew their place, and against parents who seemed to be accepting of that role, in 1976 the black (urban) youth of South Africa rose up as a generation to rebel and assert themselves. Their frustration and activism, coupled with the state's violence, created a political identity that largely defined itself in opposition to anything that suggested the authority of the apartheid state. Going to apartheid prisons, Robben Island included, was a journey into the very heart of the regime which would now be confronted in a far more intimate, far more controlling, far more total way than anything apartheid represented on the 'outside'. The white regime was personified by the warders and the militarised prison hierarchy and therefore, in the logic of this political identity, had to be confronted at every turn; resistance was required, insistent, and categorical.

The anger and militancy of the youth – 'our vibrant militancy and our outright defiance' (Cindi interview) – made all the more sense in the face of provocative warders and other prison authorities. The prisoners were determined to match every action of their enemy, and their enemy's very existence, with militant resistance. Resistance was their *raison d'etre*; resistance *was* their political identity, as young, angry, black, and proud political prisoners. The conviction that underlay political identity as categorical resistance was not exclusive to youth or Black Consciousness adherents. Thami Mkhwanazi, who was convicted of recruiting youths for military training, while not publicly questioning his organisation, the ANC, presents himself as having a political identity of categorical resistance (and indeed others corroborate his ongoing defiance). He writes that he and PAC lifer Jeoff Masemola 'were bound by the principle of telling the prison authorities where to get off' (Mkhwanazi, *Weekly Mail,* August 21 to August 27, 1987, p. 19). Similarly, he describes Toivo Ya Toivo, the South West African People's Organisation leader as militant and hostile to members of the Prisons Service. He refused to appear before the institutional board for classification, thereby denying himself any chance of upgrading so he could buy food or subscribe to newspapers. (Mkhwanazi, *Weekly Mail,* August 21 to August 27, 1987, p. 18)

James Mange rejected both the PAC and the BCM as viable movements or philosophies for him to embrace, and despite his fraught relationship with the ANC on the Island, was for a long time a high profile figure of that organisation. For Mange, his own political identity, and indeed those of other revolutionaries and militants, demanded confrontations with the authorities as a matter of principle. Moreover, the sense of purpose needed to live as a prisoner of war on enemy terrain demanded no compromises to personal or organisational indulgences. In that sense, his dreadlocks performed some of the function of an ascetic's hairshirt. His long hair would be a constant reinforcement of the vocal and ever-present resistance his political identity demanded.

Ironically, the state was not the only source of opposition to the definitionally defiant prisoners. (Indeed, state opposition would largely reinforce the resistant identity, because that identity was defined in terms of, and against, the state and its representatives.) The other source of challenge to the younger men was their fellow political prisoners, albeit mostly from a different generation. The dissonance between the groups was originally put down to generational (and organisational) differences. A generational difference implies that individuals and groups occupy different historical spaces with an associated set of perceptions and experiences. Different generations have different collective experiences and world views that shape their identities. The youth who rebelled in 1976 were born into an environment virtually devoid of any (at least open) political resistance, to parents who apparently silently acquiesced in their subordination. Their response to that was to do and be the opposite, that is, to be militant and defiant and overt in their resistance.

This insistent rebellion was strengthened in their personal experience of the suppression of their protests. In contrast, the older generation had both seen their protests, both vocal and violent, of the 1950s and early 1960s, crushed, and gone on to experience the limits to automatic protests in the prison in the 1960s and early 1970s. In this context, resistance had to be very strategic; it had to guarantee the conditions of physical and mental survival, and moreover to use the prison to achieve far-reaching political change and influence political events outside the prison. The younger men did not immediately see that the resistant political identity of the older generation involved a different understanding of how to challenge the status quo in (and beyond) the prison.

For the youth, resistance was their moral and practical core as political prisoners; it was categorical resistance. For the older generation, resistance was a tactic or manoeuvre, not necessarily a principle, and a means and not necessarily an end; it was strategic resistance. Their resistance included oppositional acts to protect and preserve physical, moral, and political integrity, but was defined more broadly; resistance was also the beginning of the process and continuum that aimed at more far-reaching resignification and emancipation in the polity. This distinction does not imply that the militant youth did not aspire to fundamental social change. The point is that the categorical resistance approach requires a person or organisation to engage in perpetual defiance which may, ironically, deflect from the broader goal of remaking a socio-political order.

As it was elaborated on Robben Island, strategic resistance resonates with the philosophy of pragmatism which, rather than evoke, in David Goldberg's (1993, p. 215) words, 'unprincipled instrumentalism', directs one towards establishing in theory and in practice the contingent social circumstances and relations of cooperative power that would at specific space-times best facilitate human flourishing and self-development.

In this understanding of political identity as strategic resistance, prisoners needed to expend time and energy developing themselves and their organisations to affect and impact upon the political terrain both within and beyond the prison. This certainly did not imply ignoring the jailing state – aside from anything, this was impossible, as the very conditions of prisoner defined political organisation and education on the Island violated rules and were by definition acts of resistance against the prison rules.

What it did demand, or at least this was the interpretation of its practitioners, was that prisoner's attempt to create a truce-like situation with the authorities in order to create the space for organisational development within and beyond the prison. The creation and protection of such organising space demanded knowledgeable and disciplined members of organisations who further could – and did – rejuvenate, support or redirect external anti-apartheid struggles upon release. Indeed, many a graduate of Robben Island went on to shape political history based on his prison training.

Political identity as strategic resistance existed in a continuum and as a process of resistance where actors, in this case the Robben Island prisoners, resignify the meaning of their circumstances in order to make emancipation (Pieterse, 1992) and self-governance (Buntman, 1997) the object of prisoner life. Categorical resisters emphasise the conventional understanding of resistance as a negative baseline refusal. On the other hand, by employing strategic acquiescence, limited compliance, and other tactics of apparent cooperation with – or at least a limited confrontation against – the prison authorities, the strategic resisters employed resistance as a means to resignify, remake, and reconstruct the dominant world. In this way, winning concessions for greater correspondence elevated morale and provided a mechanism for illegal communication or the right to formal education uplifted the training of activists.

Nevertheless, strategic resistance does not displace the necessity for categorical resistance; strategic resistance often builds upon or otherwise requires the militant and overt opposition of categorical resistance. In the 1960s and early 1970s the older prisoners had challenged the state overtly through such confrontational means as hunger strikes and legal action in order to improve conditions and demand expanded rights and privileges. The arrival of a new generation of prisoners was inspiring for the older prisoners who were, for example, 'encouraged by [the] ... radicalism' of captured guerillas who were sent to Robben Island in the early 1970s (Mandela, 1994, p. 404).

The youth of '76 had a similar rejuvenating effect on the prison, both psychologically and in terms of achieving material and substantive improvements in jail life. Furthermore, categorical resisters are correct to point out the real risks to sustaining resistance when prisoners come to rely on privileges. The privileged place of categorical resistance in their political identity allowed them to see, for example, that prisoners with higher classifications were less likely to support hunger strikes than those with lower classifications. The imperatives of categorical and strategic resistance could, and often did, coexist, mutually reinforcing or anticipating each other.

Often, however, the different requirements of categorical resistance and strategic resistance were incompatible. For example, a state tactic in a hunger strike would sometimes be to raid cells and seize contraband political material. In this case, the need for immediate improvements or the satisfaction of an urgent demand expressed in the hunger strike may put the broader goals of political education or communication in danger.

This contradiction may have been unavoidable, and it may have been necessary to stress an immediate and militant public protest even if a longer term goal of resistance was undermined. Similarly, the reverse is true. The recognition of these inevitable and difficult choices, neither 'right' nor 'wrong', and the attempt to try and balance them, in many respects captures the generational convergence achieved by political prisoners on Robben Island. It also suggests the specificity of the conditions shaping political identity and understandings of resistance, in this case, the conditions and history of Robben Island.

Conclusion: Generational Convergence and the Broader South African Political Context

Prior to his murder, Steve Biko (1978, p. 146) saw the 1976 uprising and the state repression as 'a very useful weapon in merging the young and old. Before then there was a difference in the outlooks of the old generation and the younger generation'. His observation involved astute analysis and excellent foresight, both for much of South Africa's recent political history and the narrower context of Robben Island. The importance of generational differences and convergence on Robben Island continued beyond the early 1980s, as the following three examples illustrate. In about 1985, Motlanthe (interview), recalls Islanders being able to 'stabilise' a group of youth who had been brutalised by the political violence engulfing the country at that time. Another, especially poignant, instance involved ANC member Lassie Chiwayo. He was sent to Robben Island at age 22, after harrowing experiences at the hands of the state, including torture and the attempt to blackmail him after his father's death, itself a result of his son's detention. In Witbank and Bethal prisons, prison officials attempted 'to break us; they did not think that being in prison was enough of a punishment' (Chiwayo interview). Consequently he and his fellow prisoners adopted seriously 'antagonistic attitudes against whites ... All that we knew was that any person that is white, especially prison warders, deserved assault'. Such an approach was to be fundamentally challenged on Robben Island:

> But with the sort of leaders we found on Robben Island we were, to a very large extent, transformed. I would say we were completely transformed, but completely different, new attitudes.

The third example suggests the continued legacy of negotiating with the authorities in the name of the smooth running of the prison, but to the advantage of the prisoners. To facilitate communication between two different sections of the prison, inmates in one section used their Recreation Committee to attempt to persuade the authorities that the sections should be allowed to mix for recreational and sporting purposes. They used pragmatic arguments, including issues from which the authorities would benefit. Thus they noted that new prisoners have a difficult time adjusting which causes problems for warders who need to deal with the resulting tensions, and that the existing prisoners can play an orientation function:

> A [section] consists of new arrivals to this Island. Problems of adjustment in warder-prisoner relationships which normally occur due to tensions are likely to be avoided as B-sec[tion]. Old inmates can have a positive influence on [the new inmates in] A-sec[tion].
> Mayibuye 41.1, 'Book of Occurrences, Recreation Committee', B-Section Recreation Committee Meeting with W/O van der Mescht, 30 August 1988

Mandela's simultaneous militance and conciliation upon release reflected abiding political identities within anti-apartheid politics: identity as categorical resistance and identity as strategic resistance. Both Mandela and the movement he represents have, and continue to employ, harsh challenge and amenable engagement. The convergence that was achieved in prison and among the ANC more generally, was often more difficult to achieve outside prison and political movements. Chiwayo (interview), who was elected to the then Senate in the 1994 democratic elections, said that the transformation of his and other young people's political attitudes on Robben Island was so dramatic that:

> upon release we found it very difficult to relate to our peers. I still find it difficult to relate to my peers now. Most of them do not understand because the manner that one behaves in is the same manner [as] ... Madiba [Mandela] and any of the elder leaders of the ANC ... Young people in general ... have this tendency that they are impatient and they don't give serious and deep thought [to] what they do.

But Robben Island facilitated a bridging of a generation gap that in turn allowed a unity between the two very groups of political activists and leaders who would together lead South Africa's first democratic government, synthesising armed struggle and revolutionary slogans, on the one hand, and organisation-building and pragmatic negotiation on the other.

Notes

1   I consulted two sources of primary research material were used for this article. First, the Robben Island archives at the Mayibuye Centre archives at the University

of the Western Cape. These archives contain two main sources of information: first, the prisoners' records of their sporting and cultural activities within the Island prison, and the political education or 'mrabulo' materials used by African National Congress (ANC) prisoners, especially in the mid-to-late 1980s and early 1990s. Second, I conducted interviews with ninety people, mostly former Robben Island prisoners, as well as a more limited selection of interviews with members of the then government and Prisons Service and various supporters of the political prisoners, including human rights activists. In addition, relevant interviews conducted by others, in particular Gail Gerhart and Tom Karis, were made available to me. Respondents I interviewed were chosen to cover as broad a range of former prisoners as possible, in terms of organisational affiliation (before, during, and after imprisonment), age, region, economic position, and former and current political role. Interviewees were chosen by a number of methods, both random and targeted. Interviewees were chosen by 'snowballing'; following their public comments or writings, including public references by others; through social and academic engagement; because they fulfilled certain demographic and political categories; and through identification by a government office providing financial assistance to former prisoners. Throughout the interviewing process I sought to interview the broadest range of respondents in terms of a wide range of demographic and political criteria and affiliation.

2 In many ways, this comment is a metaphor for both Mandela's initiation of negotiations with the South African government and the advantage the state took of engaging prisoners in private conversation when they could not speak to the banned ANC itself, in terms of the public rules the then governing National Party had established.

3 This statement is true for the few years following the 1976 uprising. Earlier and later, however, when there was, respectively, only one or a few BCM members, they accepted classification (see, for example, Mangena, 1989, p. 97).

4 Denis Goldberg (interview), who served his sentence in Pretoria Central Prison, similarly comments: 'I will say that as the conditions began to improve, so the tensions would arise in our community. There was less a need to face a common enemy every minute of the day. The community also changed because we were of a particular generation initially'.

5 A former Robben Islander who was incarcerated for five years for recruiting soldiers for Umkhonto we Sizwe said the older men would so emphasise that five years was a short sentence (one could barely receive all the necessary political education in that time, they said), that he only realised well after his release what a significantly long sentence five years in prison really is, perhaps all the more so for a young person, barely out of his teens (Anonymous interview). Similarly, Sibusiso Ndebele (interview), who too was on Robben Island, said that a seven year sentence was not considered a long sentence for South Africa.

6   James Mange (interview), a member of the ANC who often differed with the leadership, and who was sentenced to twenty years, was however probably the most insistent on rejecting classification as inimical to the demands of being a political prisoner. He ultimately accepted A classification when it was offered with no strings attached.

7   Former prisoners do not necessarily explicitly make the argument that those with longer sentences will be hurt most by the loss of privileges. It does, however, seem clear, that the losses of benefits would be greatest for them. Michael Dingake (1987, pp. 159–60), who had a fifteen year sentence and who only had three visits during that time wrote: 'Letters are a prisoner's lifeline, not only letters, visits and other channels of communication, photos'. Nelson Mandela (1994, p. 370) explains that he asked his wife Winnie Mandela to forgo her protest against carrying a pass, so that she would be allowed to visit him. He writes that 'I thought it more important that we see each other than to resist the petty machinations of the authorities, and Winnie consented to carry a pass. I missed her enormously and needed the reassurance of seeing her, and we also had vital family matters to discuss'. One might well imagine that Mandela, or others in a similar position, may have taken a different approach if they were faced with a 'short' sentence, rather than a life sentence.

8   The question of money was a key controversy in the history of recruitment. Some ex-Islanders accuse the ANC of selectively supplying funds (through external funders) to some of its prison members but not others, as well as using the promise of financial support as a weapon in recruitment (Mange interview, Cindi interview). The accusations of abuse of finances could and did go in more than one direction. Kgalema Motlanthe (interview) argues that: 'In [the] Black Consciousness Movement the SASO [South African Student Organisation] group came with funds, and had access to funds because they had Shun Chetty, one lawyer, who was working for them almost full time'. Motlanthe (interview) further asserted that the contradictions between Black Consciousness leaders denouncing classification and then reaping the benefits of classification was one reason for one-time BCM supporters to leave that organisation.

9   Neither generations nor political identity are of course reducible in reality to neat, two-dimensional boxes, and I am not trying to suggest that age, generational consciousness, or attitude to resistance are the only components of political identity. My reading of this period of Robben Island's history does, however, suggest there is a value to highlighting the role of generations in informing understandings of resistance, and in turn, political identity.

References

Archive

Mayibuye Centre Archive, Robben Island Collection, University of the Western Cape, Bellville, South Africa.

Interviews

Interview with Vronda Banda by Fran Buntman, 5 September 1994, Johannesburg.
Interview with Lassie Chiwayo by Fran Buntman, 4 November 1994, Cape Town.
Interview with Zithulele Cindi in Karis-Gerhart Collection, 5 July 1989, Johannesburg.
Interview with Dr Saths Cooper by Fran Buntman, 25 November 1994, Johannesburg.
Interview with Harry Gwala by Fran Buntman, 20 June 1994, Pietermaritzburg.
Interview with Denis Goldberg by Fran Buntman for Liberty Life Foundation, 3 March 1995, London.
Interviews with Ahmed Kathrada by Fran Buntman, 18 July and 31 October 1994, Johannesburg and Cape Town.
Interviews with Saki Macozoma by Fran Buntman, between December 1987 and February 1988, Johannesburg.
Interview with James Mange by Fran Buntman, 2 August 1994, Sharonlee.
Interview with Thomas Velaphi Masuku by Fran Buntman, between December 1987 and February 1988, Johannesburg.
Interviews with Johnson Mlambo by Fran Buntman, 8 and 18 July 1994, Johannesburg.
Interview with Nkosi Patrick Molala by Fran Buntman, between December 1987 and February 1988, Johannesburg.
Interviews with Kgalema Motlanthe by Fran Buntman, 5 and 7 December 1994, Johannesburg.
Interview with Sibusiso Ndebele by Tom Karis, Decmber 15, 1989, Durban, South Africa in Karis-Gerhart Collection.
Interview with Pandelani Nefolovhodwe by Fran Buntman, 13 September 1994, Johannesburg.
Interview with Joe Shithlibane by Fran Buntman, November 20, 1994, Dawn Park, South Africa.
Interview with Mike Xego by Tom Karis in Karis-Gerhart Collection, 8 October 1993, Port Elizabeth.

Published Materials

Alexander, N. (1992). 'Robben Island: A Site of Struggle', in N. Penn, H. Deacon, and N. Alexander (eds) *Robben Island: The Politics of Rock and Sand*, Cape Town: University of Cape Town, Department of Adult Education and Extra-Mural Studies.
– (1994). *Robben Island Dossier 1964–1974*, Cape Town: University of Cape Town Press.
Biko, S. (1978). *I Write What I Like*, London: Heinemann.
Buntman, F. (1997). *The Politics of Conviction: Political Prisoner Resistance on Robben Island, 1962–1991, and its Implications for South African Politics and Resistance Theory*, unpublished PhD dissertation, University of Texas at Austin.
Dingake, M. (1987). *My Fight Against Apartheid*, London: IDAF/Kliptown.
Goldberg, D.T. (1993). *Racist Culture: Philosophy and the Politics of Meaning*, Cambridge: Blackwell Publishers.
Johnson, S. (1989). 'The Soldiers of Luthuli': Youth in the Politics of Resistance in South Africa', in S. Johnson (ed.) *South Africa: No Turning Back*, Bloomington and Indianapolis: Indiana University Press.
Lodge, T.(1985). *Black Politics in South Africa Since 1945*, Johannesburg: Ravan.
Mandela, N. (1994). *Long Walk to Freedom: The Autobiography of Nelson Mandela*, Boston and New York: Little Brown and Company.
Mangena, M. (1989). *On Your Own: Evolution of Black Consciousness in South Africa/ Azania*, Johannesburg: Skotaville.
Marx, A.W. (1992). *Lessons of Struggle: South African Internal Opposition 1960–1990*, New York.
Mkhwanazi, T. (1987). 'My Years on the Island', *Weekly Mail*, 14–20 August, August 21 to August 27, August 28 to September 3, and September 4 to September 10.
Pieterse, J.N. (ed. (1992). *Emancipations, Modern and Postmodern*, London: Sage Publications.
Schadeberg, J. (1994). *Voices from Robben Island*, Randburg, South Africa: Ravan Press.
Waldmeir, P. (1997). *Anatomy of a Miracle*, Middlesex: Penguin.
Wilkinson, B. and E. Waugh (1995). 'Behind a Wife's Happy Face, the Code to the Future of South Africa', *The Sunday Independent*, 2 June.

Section Two:
Ascribed ethnic identities

The contributions by Dlamini, McEachern, Martin, Vally and Grobbelaar address the role played by ethnicity in South African political relations and the formation of the identities of crucial segments of the South African population. These chapters leave one with the impression that although much has been achieved during the past decade regarding the development of a common South African political identity, a long road still needs to be travelled before that project can come to fulfilment. We now address the chapters individually.

Chapter 6:
The construction, meaning and negotiation of ethnic identities in KwaZulu Natal
– S. Nombuso Dlamini

Dlamini analyses the question of changing identities in the Zulu community in KwaZulu-Natal, stating that Zulu identity is centred around four criteria of identification: birthplace, descent, language and history. To these can be added *hlonipha* (to respect) and *ukukhunza* (to worship), which are customarily associated with Zulu people. Part of the point of departure of the chapter is furthermore that Zulu cultural practices have come to be associated with rural areas, poverty and backwardness, creating a rural-urban and modern-backward dichotomy. Moreover, ethnicity is interpreted as a boundary phenomenon constructed within specific and competing discursive sites and with competing and conflicting practices. One such site is the political arena.
The social identity bestowed on different racial groups by the National Party, which captured power in 1948, was not acceptable to many Zulu people. The National Party government's philosophy of apartheid was premised on the belief that racial, linguistic and cultural differences should be fundamental organising principles in society. Different types of people should be kept separate. Apartheid divided South Africa

into ten black 'nations' and three non-black 'nations', forming a legal structure dividing people on racial grounds. The identity the state gave to Zulu people was different to that embodied in Inkatha, the organisation started in the 1920s as a cultural organisation taking care of Zulu interests that seemed to be depreciated by industrialisation and other socioeconomic changes of the early twentieth century. The creation of KwaZulu-Natal added another dimension to the state-defined 'Zulu' identity. It meant that being a black Zulu speaker and resident of KwaZulu-Natal was not enough for people to qualify as 'Zulus' in the region. Allegiance to KwaZulu and Inkatha also came to imply involvement in Inkatha political activities.

Further complicating Zulu identity was the fact that the ANC had yet a different political vision. This was the vision of a non-racial, non-ethnic and democratic South Africa in which politicised ethnic nationalism was viewed as dangerous. To the ANC Zulu ethnicity became constructed as an imagined concept: a creation of Zulu politics. How to deal with a politicised ethnicity in the face of an imagined non-racial community without the binding forces of language and ethnicity became a pressing issue for the ANC.

Dlamini states that Zulu cultural practices became valuable resources for politicians to use in pursuing their goals. Cultural practices previously shared and understood could be re-examined questioned and given new meaning. One such practice was that of *ukuhlonipha*. This refers generally to respect, mainly to verbal situations in which respectful relations are supplanted by confrontational and argumentative ones. In Zulu households children are usually brought up with a strong emphasis on *ukuhlonipha abadala* (respect for adults) and non-confrontational dealings with adults, where 'adult' means anyone older than oneself. Situations where a younger person argues with an older one are interpreted as *ukungahloniphi* (disrespect) no matter how correct the younger one is.

Inkatha privileged the view of older people over those of the young. This contradicted the teaching and practice of the United Democratic Front (UDF) in the 1980s and later those of the ANC, who focused on acts of defiance against the apartheid state and its structures, including KwaZulu. Against this background the younger generation had to find their own identity. Consequently, there arose among the youth the *tsatsatsa,* a name which sounded 'cool' but was their own invention and distinguished them from the *amasinyora*, which was associated with snakelike behaviour and another group, the *amampansula*. Both the last-mentioned names were also invented and referred to youths.

The *tsatsatsa* culture is still emerging, having started in the early nineties and having increasingly integrated the governing ANC philosophy, while that of the *mampansula* dates from the 1970s, the time of Steve Biko, in which a revitalisation of black history and culture was seen as a way of dealing with changes in society. Dlamini comes to the conclusion that the *tsatsatsa* still use Zulu language, history, birthplace and descent to identify themselves as Zulu, but that their character and everyday pracices constitute a challenge to everyday meanings of Zulu identity. The practices of youths in the Zulu community indicate that their identities are complex, in spite of official attempts to place people into neat categories. Their identities are complex because they are constructed from everyday, changing and often contradictory practices, in spite of Zulu people often being viewed as a homogeneous group by the state and other cultures.

Moreover, youth cultures were not viewed by the state or Inkatha as part of the culture that made up the Zulu nation. In this sense, despite being a strong force defining the character of post-apartheid South Africa, youths in general occupied a marginal position within the state. However, issues of diversity in a nation-state can no longer be ignored in liberation struggles. Liberation movements can no longer refer to diverse groups as disruptive, random and subversive. It remains to be seen when liberation movements will begin to deal positively with them.

The chapter by Dlamini gives a rare glimpse of the theory behind the dynamics of much of the political conflict in KwaZulu Natal between the ANC and Zulu-based politico-cultural movements and organisations and the role Zulu identities of differing natures play in it. It also enlightens those having an interest of whatever nature in the generational conflict in identifiable ethnic groups.

These dynamics should also serve as a reminder of the importance of taking into consideration the sometimes widely differing identities and needs of people who are often all considered to be part of a single South African nation. The dynamics referred to also highlight the wide gulf in peoples' capacity, sometimes limited by the cultural connections forming their identity, to meet the stringent demands of present patterns of undifferentiated globalisation especially in Africa.

Zulu identity has political consequences as different parties, interest groups and individuals attempt to mobilise support by invoking certain aspects of Zulu identity. However, both urbanisation and the ANC require new political attitudes and positions that may cause internal conflict. Dlamini argues that Zulu youth identifying with the ANC may well have to reliquish their capacity to be identified as Zulus should they decide to reject Inkatha. The youth have come to terms with the limitations placed on them by the politicisation of their ethnicity. They shift between identifying themselves as Zulu and claiming to be descendents of groups other than the Zulus. Accordingly, Dlamini depicts the Zulu youth as being depoliticised.

Questions may be raised about Dlamini's description of the youth as depoliticised, the description of the Black Consciousness Movement and the benefits of representing organisations as polar opposites. Dlamini says that the *mampansula* believe the challenge of change in society can be resolved by a return to pre-capitalist and pre-colonial social orders. The author further contends that black history and black culture can help in this respect. However, does the concept of black consciousness and with it black culture not actually create a theoretical account of how black people came to be dominated and also why internal colonisation takes place? The depictions of the youth as *mampansula* and *tsatsatsa,* in spite of being represented as almost polar opposites, are in the end both views that the youth are depoliticised. Political parties use the youths' cultural practices to recruit them. It is as if the youth themselves are not seen to contribute much to the political debate between the ANC and Inkatha. They are interpreted to be merely a passive medium for translating political changes.

Smoking dagga (marijuana), weight-lifting and modelling, whether they take place in interracial groups or not, appear to be inappropriate examples of political behaviour. Their resistance as Dlamini sees it, takes place in the context of leisure, fashion, upward mobility and carelessness toward elders. This may not be a true reflection of the role played by the youth in the political upheavals that have taken place in KwaZulu-Natal in the ideological struggle between ANC and Inkatha affiliates.

The 'everyday activities' in the Dlamini analysis accordingly appear to have come to represent more than what they are. What appears to be missing in Dlamini's contribution is an analysis of whether these everyday activities actually also explicitly relate to their choices regarding power and the distribution of rights. In view of this, it may be that representing the Zulu youth as belonging to polar opposites does not do much to illuminate analyses of the identity of Zulu youth.

Chapter 7:
Mapping the memories: politics, place and identity
in the District Six Museum, Cape Town
– Charmaine McEachern

McEachern claims that the label 'the new South Africa' is the dominant form of the overall identity assigned by a variety of people to both the obvious and massive political changes undergone in post-apartheid South Africa country and the hopes for cultural and social change accompanying those changes. District Six was the sixth district of Cape Town, the oldest city in South Africa and often called the 'Mother City'. Although the Group Areas Act dated from 1950, District Six was not proclaimed 'white' until 1966. Over the next fifteen years the District was physically destroyed, street by street, to make way for white residents. Between 55 000 and 65 000 people were moved from District Six, usually to be relocated on the Cape Flats, often separated from their closest kin and friends.

District Six was an inner-city area which from the nineteenth century had housed people from the working and artisan classes, many of whom had worked in the city and nearby docks. In 1948 (the year the National Party, the 'apartheid regime', assumed government) Cape Town was the most integrated city in South Africa and had a long liberal tradition and a high coloured (people of mixed race) population. The tradition in the Cape for working class areas was that they were characteristically integrated.

McEachern's study focuses on the District Six Museum, established in 1994. The study is a case study of one of the places of engagement between the past, present and future which characterise contemporary South Africa. The museum is housed in the Buitenkant Methodist Churchon the edge of the central business district of the old District Six. In the centre of the church, covering much of the floor space, is a huge map of the District which is decorated with poems on the life of the District and linocuts by the artist Lionel Davis, himself a District Sixer and a political activist who had been jailed on Robben Island. Davis helped put together the exhibition with the map at its centre.

In the most famous chapter in his book *The Practice of Everyday Life*, de Certeau argues that walking in the city can operate as resistance to official, authoritative constructions of the city. In this manner space is transformed into place. This is exactly what District Sixers walking over the map do. The map allows the walkers to bring District Six into being again as physical space. Rather than engaging the *creators* of this space, the map allows them to engage with its *destroyers,* states McEachern. In this way the museum appears to touch a raw nerve in a South Africa in which coloured people today often express the feeling that during the apartheid era they were 'too black', while now, under the African National Congress government, they are 'too white'.

McEachern contends that the map also works through and enables the play of *synecdoche* and *asyndeton* and enables the movement between them. These are primary expressive forms operating to provide the walk through city with its texture and form – in effect, its reality. For each District Sixer, District Six starts from the epicentre of *their* home, *their* street, *their* place. The memories on the map and the stories the people tell are not just stories of some past, perfect place. Rather they are stories of a people transformed, turned into someone else from the critical perspective of who they feel they have become. The past recounted from the present is then a strategy for the construction of identity. These narratives accordingly become tales of morality as much as they are history. So the negative *urban* features many note, such as poverty, overcrowding and poor facilities are exactly those things which seem to have generated the forms of sociality, the social relationships which people today represent as *community*.

Then in memory, it is the sociality which dominates rather than the structural conditions which produced it. The big question of who people feel they became under apartheid is the crux of both the narratives of memory and the critical engagement with apartheid the map encourages. The map walkers demonstrate that for them both identity and history are space. This is very much as one would expect, given that space was central to apartheid, its ideology and its transformations of South Africa in terms of this ideology and the interests it served. Living in District Six gave coloured people an identity located in two things: the inner city and Cape Town itself, the Mother City. With the loss of District Six, these cosmopolitan people lost a significant element of their identity as South Africans. They lost their right to determine their own identity and were forced into racialised suburbia. From now on they lived in the diaspora, the Cape Flats, as the poet Adam Small said.

Within many coloured people's deep need for respectability, apartheid's residential control was shaming and diminishing. Apartheid's Group Areas Act attacked them at the very site of respectability: their residence, their home. Stories of the past are always discourses of identity. Operating as one location in which South Africans at present can make their own meanings and their own accommodations to state rhetorics about country and nation, the District Six Museum suggests that the 'new South Africa' is constituted out of a variety of identities, a variety of engagements with the past, a variety of pasts, is part of McEachern's conclusion. In the politics of memory generated by the map South Africans who were ex-residents of District Six are first asserting the social constitution of this area that apartheid managed to define in asocial terms. Second they criticise through recollection and comparison the forms of collectivity and security that apartheid policies and administrators thought desirable for many 'non-white' people. Third, the retrieval of a more desirable past provides a way into a new identity for them in post-apartheid South Africa as they take back urban citizenship, their identity as Capetonians.

In this deeply perceptive contribution McEachern captures many of the ironies and tribulations that beset the coloured people, who are profoundly a part of South Africa's social fabric. These people have made many lasting contributions to the cultural and economic life of the country, but appear to be in grave danger of becoming South Africa's permanently forgotten people. The chapter should help prevent this from happening.

Chapter 8:
What's in the name "Coloured"?
– Denis-Constant Martin

Martin asks in his chapter whether there is anything in the name 'coloured' in a South African context. The category of people called 'coloured' can only be approached as a group of individuals who were classified as such in the course of South Africa's history. Attributed physical, religious, social or linguistic features masquerading as markers of differentiation bind them to – rather than distinguish them from – the South African population as a whole. All shades of skin colour and many phenotypical features combining Asian, African and European traits are found among them. Many consider Afrikaans as their first language and some are English-speakers, although the majority are bi-lingual. They are either Christian or Muslim. Although many live in poverty, a middle class and intellectuals are to be found among the coloured population.

When the question of whether coloured people have an own 'culture' is asked, some analysts have claimed that the question is symptomatic of how the apartheid state and ideology effected separation between the people of South Africa. Others contend that coloured people have indeed created their own, unique culture. The first-mentioned analysts state that no 'coloured culture' without a 'South African culture' is conceivable. Culture as a symbolic structure of signification and comprehension exists for coloured people exist only in so far as they are fully South African. Consequently, discussions of coloured identities are inseparable from discussions of South African identities as a whole. Slaves (brought to South Africa from 1658) formed the core of the original 'coloured' people in the Cape. Afrikaans, the first parameter of identity for ultra-conservative Afrikaners, is in fact the product of a communication system established between 'masters' and 'slaves' in the Cape.

Accordingly, looking at a 'coloured culture' no longer entails separating it from South African culture as a whole. Like a continuum, coloured culture traverses all strata of South African society.

There is in the coloured community a class differentiation enforced by an elite's recognition of the value of 'respectability' that has been expressed in that elite's efforts to differentiate themselves from 'coons'. The working classes have sought solace in cultural manifestations, particularly new year celebrations, their humanness denied by white people and their cultural legitimacy by the coloured intelligentsia. The traditional New Years' celebration in Cape Town, The Coon Carnival, a colourful event and an institution since 1907, continues even at present.

It has been a training ground for many of South Africa's most outstanding artists: Abdullah Ibrahim (Dollar Brand), Basil 'Manenberg' Coetzee, Jonathan Butler and Robbie Jansen are musicians who bear testimony to the importance of the Mother City to the development of South African jazz and pop music. They also influenced musicians who came to Cape Town from other regions and different social backgrounds: Dudu Pukwana, Winston Mankulu, Simon Goldberg and Chris McGregor. The *moppies,* the *Nederlands Liedjes* (Dutch songs) and songs imported from the Americas were adapted by Taliep Peterson to the language of the musical that is very popular in South Africa.

Carnival songs and tunes sung by 'Malay' choirs have deeply influenced all kinds of South African music: jazz, pop and musical comedy. The Eoan group, a school of ballet, singing and music, has made a significant contribution to South African culture. The Afrikaans writing of Adam Small, a vehement critic of the apartheid system, forms an inseparable part of Cape Town. Some of South Africa's greatest writers born in the North or East, Peter Abrahams, Don Matera, Achmat Dangor, Bessie Head, are all coloured people. Others like Richard Rive and Alex la Guma have used the popular Cape Town dialect and social realities of District Six to introduce a new form of expression into English. The work of Zoë Wicomb (in both English and Afrikaans), like that of the others referred to, talks of the experiences of coloured people in the Western Cape. They all have a universal outreach.

Coloured 'structures of signification and comprehension' can be said to exist only in so far as they are fully South African. By the same token, South African 'structures of signification and comprehension' exist only in so far as they are *mestiza,* that is, mixed, which evidently implies coloured. Neither could exist without the connections that bind them. This demonstrates that in the end South African culture is nothing but *mestiza.* Coloured people were once the most despised people in South Africa. Even if some of those who have been labelled 'coloured' during the apartheid era do not want to be associated with the festivals and music of the Cape Town working class, these manifestations of a unique culture nevertheless proclaim the humanness that is a South Africanness that implies belonging to the universal community of human beings.

Herein lies the value of this contribution: it shows the way to building a true South African identity in which the humanity of all South Africans is recognised and acted upon. Martin also points the way for the new South Africa in general where he speaks of the dilemma of the new South Africa: how to define and recognise communities without perpetuating apartheid categories, attitudes and behaviours; how to support communal cultures in a way that will 'bring communities together' instead of setting them apart or even pitting them against one another. The African National Congress government, he says, should play a role in bringing them together. The coloured people have no exclusively coloured political organisation to further their interests.

Taken together, the studies by McEachern and Martin in a sense capture both the hope and the tragedy of a South Africa searching for its true identity in a nutshell. In so doing, they point the way to a better future for South Africans based on an emerging, imperfect, but solid identity. The coloured people of South Africa are sometimes rightly described as its 'living conscience'. They are an ongoing example, warts and all, of what South Africa could have been without apartheid. The social relations built up in the Mother City and District Six in particular between coloured people and others from greatly different backgrounds can be and should be a model of how people can live together in spite of social and deeper identity differences.

Martin's view stems from the argument that politicised identity has been confused with real identity. Moreover the question remains of 'whether they (coloured people) should occupy this category that was created by apartheid'. This deterministic perspective makes no allowances for agency. The kind of agency that is referred to is the very agency that would make it very interesting to discover how the so – called 'coloureds' navigated through not being part of the black community and never quite being seen as equals in the white community. That is to say, what did they do with their 'middle group' status other than upliftment and patrol of the working classes. The term 'coloured' is not helpful because it masks poverty and becomes a barrier to necessary coalition work.

The discussion of the debate regarding whether poorer coloured people are inclined towards escapism or daily suffering is very insightful. This is the crucial indicator that what is being argued about is an identity. This much contestation and dissent does not occur for no reason. Rather there is dissent when people have things in common.

Where Martin argues in effect that coloured identity equals apartheid, the question arises whether in the new nation there should not be any politicised ethnic identity at all. This suggests that the best way forward may be for all identifiable cultural identities to resist politicisation and accompanying accusations of complicity and violence. A problem would of course arise if the coloured cultural group wants to see itself as *mestiza* (creolised) and other groups of people created by apartheid did not. Determining who claims what role for coloured people in South Africa may be necessary to demonstrate the point made regarding 'false ethnic identity'. Such are some of the questions raised by the depth of understanding demonstrated in this remarkable contribution.

Chapter 9:
Diversity in the imagined *Umma*:
the example of Indian Muslims in South Africa
– Rehana Ebrahim-Vally

Vally investigates how the Indian Muslim people of South Africa retain their Muslim identity while their collective memory of India fades and their expression of their Muslim identity changes. Muslims all over the world are members of a single community, the *umma*. Muslims are found for instance in diverse locations such as China, India, America, Indonesia and Iran. As Muslims they are part of the mythical *umma*, a community governed by the the word of Allah, in which all people are equal but subservient to Allah. Yet, as Chinese, Bosnian or Indian Muslims, they demonstrate the significance of fusing the Islamic doctrine with local practices to give their belief a structure and their life a purpose.

The *umma* transcends boundaries, frontiers, nationalities, citizenship, linguistic differences and all other forms of cultural, political, economic and social differences. To Muslims, the *umma* is the sacred community of Allah. Although Muslims are united in this mythical holy community, their worldly differences regarding who they are and where they come from cannot be ignored. Consequently, Vally argues that there is not one Islam, but many Islams. This is also the case in South Africa: from its rudimentary beginnings in South Africa, there were multiple Muslim communities. This reality cannot be understood apart from the different social contexts within which Muslims express their religion. Islam is in its origin an Arab religion, making every non-Arab Muslim a convert. Arabia in the memory of Muslims becomes *the* space chosen by Allah.

The 'Indian' Muslims of South Africa have come to use religion as their fundamental identity parameter to negotiate their space in South Africa. The earliest evidence of Muslims in what is now South Africa were the Mardyckers from Amboya who arrived in the Cape in 1658, being either slaves or political prisoners and becoming known as the 'Cape Malays'. The second wave of Muslim immigrants came from India, starting in 1860. They were indentured labourers. From 1871 onwards, a further wave including traders from Gujarat came to South Africa, having paid their own fares and becoming known as the 'Passenger' or 'Free' Indians.

In South Africa, Gujarati acquired a status different from that in India. In India it is used as a language of communication, while in South Africa it came to be viewed as the language of Hindus. Islam, the religion of South African Muslims of Indian origin, is closely linked to their recollection of India. It also involves purging elements of Hinduism. The 'passenger' Indians brought an entire societal structure to South Africa. It was impossible for them to transpose those structures as they were to South Africa. They were expected to select the parameters of adapting to South Africa and lessen hostility towards them. The imperialistic demands of Islam have impacted on them. They use Islam as their fundamental identity parameter to invent a semblance of communal coherence in the eyes of non-Muslims, but the community is divided on which Islam to follow.

The issue of whose Islam to follow exerts pressure on some Muslims of Indian origin to follow an orthodox Islam by consciously eradicating Indian influences in Islam, while others steadfastly cling to the Islam of their ancestors in India. Although they submit their will to Allah, they practice an Islam that is neither attached to India nor removed from it. Despite internal pressures dividing 'Indian' Muslims the issue that now preoccupies them is negotiating a Muslim space in post-apartheid South Africa.

The fear of 'losing control' over members and being submerged by the Other are among the reasons that motivate them to become visible Moslems, states Vally. In so doing, Vally is in effect claiming that the 'looseness' of Muslim religious expression in South Africa may have been its own saviour by preserving a vibrant, dynamic form of Muslim religious expression well-equipped to fight for its own space in present-day South Africa. This more visible fight for its own space may prove to be essential for its survival in South Africa.

Chapter 10:
Afrikaner nationalism: The end of a dream?
– Janis Grobbelaar

Grobbelaar emphasises four major principles: the conflation of the South African state with Afrikaner nationalism, the conflict over how to define ethnicity/race/nationalism and ethnonationalism, the need for better theory on the relationship between identity and democracy and the present-day implications of a history of Afrikaner nationalism. The state in South Africa was defined by the institutionalisation of Afrikaner nationalism. Whatever the goals reflected in the political order, its core political culture was that of Afrikaner nationalism. Although Afrikaner nationalism and the South African state are inextricably bound, the former can stand on its own.

This provocative study leaves numerous issues unresolved: Afrikaners were a power group, not an ethnic group, because they utilised other groups to protect themselves. Their power was based not on familial or community ties, but on the coercion/incentives they offered non-whites and working-class Afrikaners. The dream of solidarity sharing was a grab for power and did not have anything to do with historical, linguistic, geographic or demographic coherence. Another concern is this study's reliance on Claude Ake's view that many groups in society try to dominate by proposing their own plans for social order and political authority. Undergirding Ake is a notion that the state is ultimately explained by its negotiation of plural interests. It functions as the neutral arbiter between elites and competing interests. The state then becomes the seat of a national fiction of unity generating more loyalty than local fictions of unity/alliance. This construction of the state however gives no account of the human rights of minorities. Moreover, it is problematic because the state is not the only institution in society proposing political orders.

There is obviously nothing to the artificial bond between the South African state and Afrikaner nationalism. Afrikaner nationalism persists, as does the South African state notwithstanding no longer endorsing Afrikaner nationalism. Much has been made of the Afrikaner national identity, especially in apartheid South Africa and even further in the past. Grobbelaar claims that in the decades preceding Afrikaner nationalism's victory in the (all-white) polls in 1948 the '*volk*' (nation) was, as now, wracked by internal battles. Thus, in spite of the institutionalisation of Afrikaner nationalism's core narrative of unity, its monolithic status in the eyes of 'outsiders' should be weighed carefully. Grobbelaar accordingly finds Afrikaner nationalism only 'partially coherent'.

Afrikaner nationalism is for Grobbelaar not so much the outgrowth of seventeenth century occupation of South Africa by merchants, but a more recent phenomenon originating in the last quarter of the nineteenth century. Until the 1870s Afrikaans and South Africa had no meaning politically or spiritually. That situation was changed by the discovery of South Africa's enormous mineral wealth, which brought with it fundamental sociopolitical and economic changes. In this time strong anti-British and anti-capitalist sentiments were mediated by struggles over the ownership of forces of production, giving rise to the birth of Afrikaner nationalism and ideology.

Thus Grobbelaar sees ethnicity, race, nationalism and ethnonationalism as fairly seamless stitches in the same fabric of identity construction. While positing the work of Benedict Anderson and the social constructionist explanation of ethnicity as the more universal and justice-infused theory on this subject, Grobbelaar is compelled to deal with the possibility that Afrikaner nationalism is a reactionary response to British colonial identity. Whether it is socially constructed or not, the most representative democratic order may attempt to give a voice to Afrikaner ethnic identifications rather than to 'undo' them. With that in mind, Grobbelaar invokes Ake's discussion of ethnic identity. For Ake, ethnic identity is both essential to African reality and is also not the natural base for societal conflict, thus challenging a massive body of behaviourist research in political science that suggests that ethnic conflict is the basis for natural, inevitable political conflict. Presuming that ethnicity is a problem, this body of research sees it as the opposite of cross-cutting cleavages generated by civil society.

Democratisation theorists accordingly look to means to erase its effects on the polity. Rather than interpreting ethnicity as a burden and threat to democracy, Ake emphasises its ability to create increasingly representative democracies. Ethnicity can enhance the civil society of a state. Race and even ethnonationalism can move the democratic project forward. Grobbelaar insists throughout that identity must be accounted for in democratic theory. Consequently, she is sceptical of Adam and Moodley's suggestion that non-racialism should be inserted as the national ideology of the South African state. Rather, Grobbelaar offers Degenaar's warning that a uniform multiculture will not be elastic enough to accommodate ethnic identity. Federalism would be a more salient political architecture for South Africa as it has the capacity to give an account of identity.

Grobbelaar's discussion of Afrikaner nationalism argues for a cultural rather than a political solution. The claim that the mere presence of ethnicity provides greater checks on the centralising tendencies of any government is as strange as its converse, namely that the mere presence of ethnicity prevents a government from representing the entire populace. The claim that ethnicity can make a government more representative does not tally with the fact that the apartheid South African regime effectively prohibited participation for the majority of ethnic groups. That same state banned that part of civil society endorsing the slightest representation for black people. Accordingly the relationship between identity and democracy is not so easily explained. Furthermore, does it matter that that ethnicity was used so successfully to justify the categorisation of natives as incomplete pseudo-citizens?

Lastly, since Afrikaner nationalism is so well represented in the network of organisations in South Africa: religious formations, civil society entities, school boards, paramilitary organisations, farmers cooperatives, policy studies/think tanks, the Volkstaat Council and cultural-political organisations, it should have been able to address other issues besides reasserting cultural identity and demanding the return of old privilege and unfair advantages. The reasons for using these organisations in such counterproductive ways by referring to social categories that are virtually outmoded are not clear.

Afrikaner nationalism has been writ large in the political history of the South African state. This history leaves little room for new directions in policy other than some kind of *Volkstaat* (nation state) or federalism. Whether one agrees with Grobbelaar or not on the necessity of creating space in the South African state for ethnic identity (if one accepts Afrikaner nationalism as 'ethnic identity') the very history of South Africa has to be considered in any recommendations on the future of that society.

As for Grobbelaar's conclusions, she contends that today, Afrikaner nationalism is not a thing of the past, as many would have it. Afrikaner nationalism is alive 100 years after having started, although it is ailing. Afrikaner nationalists reject both non-racialism and equity. Grobbelaar argues, perhaps controversially, that the growing international respectability and legitimacy attributed to issues of ethnicity, ethnonationalism and diversity together are playing a vital role in attempts to address Afrikaner nationalist identity. Afrikaner nationalist elites dominating the movement are at present generally committed to 'trading' and negotiating. Accordingly, the questions of 'soft' territorial boundaries are on the constitutional agenda in South Africa for the foreseeable future.

The foregoing forms the backdrop for Grobbelaar's prediction that if threats and instability grow, support for the vision of Afrikaner nationalism will grow and the last will not have been heard of this once powerful voice. This prediction relates the chapter to broader issues such as global capitalism, the possibility of capitalist imperialism and economic instability in Africa that appear to be inevitable results of, among others, the demands of globalisation in its present form.

CHAPTER SIX

The construction, meaning and negotiation of ethnic identities in KwaZulu-Natal

S. Nombuso Dlamini

Introduction and background

In attempting to examine how ethnic identities are constructed, negotiated and maintained in any given context, it is important to define satisfactorily what is meant by ethnicity as a conceptual tool for the dismantling and understanding of societies. Ethnicity has provided ways of talking about a group of people without being precise about the criteria used to identify that group. For all its vagueness, in this paper, ethnicity refers to the way individuals identify themselves, or are identified by others, collectively, and act according to those identities. What remains unclear in social science studies is the nature of the material that holds these identities together; that is, what constitutes the ties that underlie ethnic groups, and how these ties work to include and exclude people from group membership. This paper is an examination of the ties that underscore Zulu identity in KwaZulu-Natal, as well as ways in which these ties are used to legitimise certain practices located in the social and political context of a changing South Africa.

I begin by examining, in general, the development of Zulu identity and the different ties of identification generally used to define Zulus. I examine the manner in which Zulu identity intersects with formal politics, encompassing the actions of political parties and other interest groups in competition for access to power in a post-apartheid state, and interpersonal politics, that is, the negotiation of relations of power and solidarity between individuals in interaction. The last part of the chapter presents a case study of youth experiences in the townships that surround the city of Durban in KwaZulu-Natal. The purpose of this case study is twofold.

The first is to demonstrate how people's sense of identity shifts despite legitimised group ties, and that the complexity of identity construction is a result of the juxtaposition of criteria used to define individuals and groups. In this way, I demonstrate sources and consequences of the processes and practices that violate normalised ways of constructing and negotiating ethnic identities. The second purpose is to illustrate that, while the doctrines of political organisations do have great impact on people's lives, who people experience themselves to be cannot be dictated from above.

Issues discussed in the second part of this paper are substantiated by data collected in 1993 on youth groups from different townships in Durban. The data was collected over a period of eight months with a variety of participants who can be arranged into compressed circles by degree of acquaintance. From these townships, I developed about ten key close relationships with people who made up the first circle and whom I refer to as key participants. The second circle was made up of twenty or more people with whom I had regular relations. The data in this paper was drawn from the first circle of participants. The data varied from formal and recorded interviews and discussions, to brief comments people made regarding what was going on in the region at that time.

Specifically, I was interested in the way people spoke about the political conflict that engulfed KwaZulu-Natal during this period and especially how they situated themselves in the conflict. In this regard, I was interested in statements that indexed or displayed the identity of either speaker or others she/he knew. In addition to statements of identity, I observed everyday practices of the key informants, and of other people close to them. In these observations, I looked specifically at behaviour, particularly practices of language use and how these positioned people within the categories Zulu, Inkatha, or ANC whose meanings are explained in the following section. I also looked at social/cultural practices, and again the manner these positioned people within the three categories of Zulu, Inkatha and ANC.

In most of these observations, I asked people who were involved in these practices to clarify why they were involved in them and how such practices positioned them in the then ongoing struggle. In addition, I observed public political activities, specifically those of the ANC, which helped to inform me of the contradictions between what people said they did and their actual practices.

There is a vast amount of literature that analyses Zulu history, particularly the history of Shaka and the Zulu kingdom (see for example, Marks and Atmore, 1980; Marks and Rathbone, 1982; and Guy, 1979, 1980). Recently, some research and ideas have even led to a revision of the *Mfecane* story, and thus also of the relative 'greatness' of Shaka (see, for example, Cobbing 1993).

These resources are important for a conceptualisation of some of the historical issues addressed in this paper. Given space limitations, however, I have decided to focus more on the contemporary situation than the historical background to the events discussed here.

In cases where Zulu history is discussed, I have relied upon my own knowledge of this history which I learnt in a variety of ways and from a variety of sources while growing up in Zulu society. Similarly, discussions about Zulu social and cultural practices, as well as practices of political parties stem from my own experiences and observation before, during and after data collection. The discussion in this paper is designed to stand as an illustration, as opposed to a model, of cultural resistance and group identification in changing political societies.

I am limited here to a comparison within a few townships in South Africa. While broader generalisations require broader bases of comparison, I hope that the framework I provide might be useful for future undertakings on youth, culture, and identity construction in South Africa and elsewhere.

1   Ethnicity and the politics of identity in KwaZulu Natal

I see ethnicity in KwaZulu-Natal as a boundary phenomenon constructed within specific and competing discursive sites and with competing and conflicting practices. One site where the ethnic boundary is constructed is within the political arena, where, as Bell (1975) has noted, ethnicity is now a central factor in the consolidation of groups for strategic purposes. Since ethnic groups are both expressive and instrumental, the ethnicity in KwaZulu-Natal has to be understood as one used to consolidate people in relation to certain political affiliations, at the same time allowing such consolidation to be expressed not just in political terms but in lifestyles and in everyday social practices. The latter are the second site where the ethnic boundary gets constructed. Therefore, the significance of ethnicity in this region, and that of the boundary that safeguards it, is both historic and contemporary, with the latter flowing from the kinds of political and social changes that are taking place. As a result, ethnicity has come to be the focus of group identity, mobilisation and action.

The nature of the ethnic boundary in KwaZulu-Natal has always been constituted of a multiply of markers including history, language and culture and birthplace. But, like all other boundaries and the ethnic markers that they safeguard, this boundary has two sides to it, and the way it is defined on the one side may be different from the way it is defined on the other. Each group selects a differentiating feature. Moreover, even within the boundary, competing notions of how that boundary might be understood and what it means exist. For instance, the history of the political consolidation of the Zulu kingdom under Shaka is one that is full of complexities and ambiguities that individuals who want to use history as a differentiating feature have to deal with. First, within the Zulu group, there are groups that were actually conquered by the Zulu under Shaka and were then consolidated into the Zulu Kingdom.

Currently, the Zulu people are presented by the state, the Zulu monarchy, and some African nationalist leaders as a unified group, which, in itself, suppresses or ignores the presentation of the history of other groups in KwaZulu-Natal (and elsewhere) who were dominated and destroyed by the Zulu warriors. What this means is that history as a differentiating marker is complex. As Barth (1969) points out, group boundaries are constructed and at the same time mystified. This paper, then, is an examination of ways in which youth dealt with the complexity of this ethnic boundary, as well as a demonstration of how ethnic identities are not static but change over time, depending on political and other consequences.

Zulu identity in KwaZulu-Natal centred around four criteria of identification: birthplace, descent, language, and history. In addition to these criteria, what I will call 'conventionalised' ways of identification, the familiar and understood ways of behaviour, existed. Conventional ways of being included the practice of *hlonipha* (literally, to respect) and of *ukukhonza* (literally, to worship) which are customarily associated with Zulu people. Operating alongside, and often in conflict with, these Zulu cultural practices were those commonly associated with western modernisation and industrialisation. The association of industrialisation with the urban sectors of the community, and with modernity and economic progress, resulted in Zulu cultural practices being associated with the rural areas, poverty and backwardness, creating a rural-urban or modern-backward dichotomy, which added complexity to an already diverse setting.

Moreover, the four criteria of identification, practices associated with industrialisation and western modernity, and the Zulu cultural practices were given meaning in and by practices in formal politics, which in turn created difficulty for individuals to engage in either set of practices without assuming or being linked to existing political organisations.

In addition, we know that the social identity bestowed on different racial groups in South Africa by the Nationalist government, which captured state power in 1948, was not acceptable to those groups. The Nationalist Party government's philosophy of apartheid was premised upon the nationalist belief that racial, linguistic, and cultural differences should be fundamental organising principles in society. According to apartheid, different types of people should be kept separate. Each 'group' should have its own national territory and infrastructure including schools, government, media, and cultural bodies. Apartheid policy divided South Africa into ten black 'nations' and three non-black nations. In short, since whites constituted a minority of South Africa's population, the most effective way to rule was to prevent the 75% black-African population from cohering into a unified group. A key means of achieving this was an active state-controlled and sponsored encouragement of African tribalism in South Africa.

Thus, the focal characteristic of apartheid was the creation of tribal political 'Bantustans', later known as homelands, each tied to a separate black 'nation' with its own language and bureaucratic structure. All this was met with resistance from black political groups, and although the structures of apartheid were implemented, their implementation was not a smooth process (for details on black resistance to apartheid, see for example, Dlamini, 1996).

In the early stages of the struggle for socio-political independence, it was possible to define the struggle as one of blacks against whites, and to ignore, to a large extent, what being black actually meant. As the struggle intensified, and as it became important to define the character of the post-apartheid state, the groups that mobilised for action were drawn from a different grid. With the whites in the background, fuelling divisions between anti-apartheid groups with the hope of prolonging the life of apartheid, the struggle focused on conflict between Zulu and Xhosa people, or between the African National Congress (ANC) and Inkatha. But who exactly was involved in this conflict, and what were the criteria used to identify them?

Simplistically, it could be said that the conflict was between ANC and Inkatha supporters, the two leading political parties in the region, and involved youths who were believed to make up the majority of ANC followers in KwaZulu-Natal, and adults, who, it was believed, constituted the majority of Inkatha membership. The ANC and Inkatha differed in the strategies they employed to fight against white domination. This difference in strategies became increasingly articulated in the last stages of apartheid and, therefore, in defining the character of a post-apartheid state. To the ANC, a post-apartheid state meant a South Africa that realised equality for all groups, a 'non-racial' democratic state. Inkatha, however, envisioned a post-apartheid state organised according to ethnic constituencies, accommodating group rights and group vetoes.

For Inkatha, a post-apartheid state organised around ethnic constituencies ensured that the Zulus maintained control over the resources that they were allocated under the apartheid state through the KwaZulu homeland. As Lowe (1991, p. 81) notes: 'big capitalists and the state even now reward Inkatha's aspirant accumulators for their pro-capitalist stance with access to capital and joint investment schemes; ethno-regionalism would also allow Inkatha's chiefs to retain their neo-traditional authoritarian powers and means of accumulation'.

To the ANC, however, such a state would be a duplication of apartheid methods of governing which would divide people into racial/ethnic groups. To mobilise in the region, therefore, the ANC had to convince the Zulus that their rights both as Zulus and as South Africans would not be eroded if it came to power. Inkatha, on the other hand, went on a mission to paint the ANC as anti-Zulu, an agent of the Xhosa bent on the genocide of the Zulu.

The conflict centred around differences between ethnic politics perpetuated by Inkatha, as opposed to a pluralistic state politics of the ANC, in the struggle against apartheid and for control over post-apartheid South Africa. It is these differences that were played out in the politics of identity in KwaZulu-Natal, influencing the ways individuals positioned themselves politically/linguistically and ethnically, and contributing to the formation of the political economic character of a post apartheid state. It was in such political conflict that, I will argue, the activities of youths can be understood as challenging normalised ways of being Inkatha, Zulu and ANC.

2   Criteria for identifying Zulu identity

2.a)   History

There is a very complex history of political consolidation under Shaka, the great Zulu leader, who orchestrated armed resistance to British colonialism in the late 1800s, and the existence of the Zulu kingdom with its successful and continued resistance to colonial domination. As a result of this history, the name and the house of Shaka and the term 'Zulu kingdom' were historical concepts that individual Africans, as well as African politicians, continued to draw on as a way of constructing their own identity and of defining and legitimising their sociopolitical and economic struggles. However, within the use of this historic resource, complexities and ambiguities emerged that individuals had to negotiate.

Initially, the ANC was formed in 1912 as a political organisation looking after the interests of all black South Africans, while Inkatha originated in the 1920s as a cultural movement taking care of Zulu cultural interests that seemed to be depreciated by industrialisation and other socioeconomic changes of the early twentieth century. Although there was no direct nexus between these two organisations, both used the symbols of the Zulu monarchy and its history in legitimising their aims. These organisations also drew on the same membership, and had the same effect of fictionalising KwaZulu-Natal within Zulu nationalist and class-based movements. Later, beginning in the 1950s, the same symbols and histories used to construct the KwaZulu nation gave form to a new relation between the ANC and Inkatha, and were utilised by these organisations in the struggle against apartheid.

From the mid-1960s onwards African nationalist leaders focussed on gaining state recognition for the Zulu monarchy and territorial, political and cultural rights for the Zulu people. These nationalist leaders included Chief Buthelezi, whose leadership of the then Zulu Cultural Movement, Inkatha, was problematically recognised by both the South African state and liberatory organisations such as the ANC. It was to such nationalist leaders that the idea of the KwaZulu homeland appeared attractive and worth embracing. To pursue and legitimise the existence of KwaZulu and their participation in it, it became important for these leaders to present the Zulu people as a homogeneous and well-defined linguistic and cultural group.

To some extent, these politicians viewed KwaZulu as a strategy for the establishment of democratic political institutions to address the sociopolitical and economic needs of the population in the region, which could not be done within the larger South African structures. But KwaZulu was to respond only to the political and economic needs of the population, not to cultural reconstruction. To these politicians, a specific Zulu identity, centring around the Zulu monarchy and its history, was already in place. The presentation of Zulu history by these African politicians was, in itself, full of contradiction. The first contradiction had to do with the presentation of the Zulu people as a unified group, which ignored or suppressed the presentation of the history of other sub-groups in KwaZulu-Natal (and elsewhere) that were dominated and destroyed by the Zulu warriors. A second contradiction related to the issue of leadership. Were the Zulu king and the Zulu royal house the legitimate representatives of the Zulu people, or were politicians and their organisations – some of whom were closely related to Zulu royalty – the legitimate leaders?

The invention of KwaZulu added complexity in the use of this history by political organisations. First, it resulted in the claim by the KwaZulu authority that they were the legitimate 'owners' of this history. This, in turn, meant that only those political parties such as Inkatha, which supported and were simultaneously supported by KwaZulu, had the legitimate right to use this history. A second complexity arose with regard to individuals who saw themselves as inheritors of this history but did not belong to the KwaZulu supported political organisations, nor to any other political organisation for that matter. Did this mean that these individuals were no longer of Zulu heritage? Since this history was also used to distinguish Zulus from non-Zulus, to which historical group did such individuals belong?

2.b)   Language

In addition to history, language was also highly idealised and controversial in KwaZulu-Natal. Linguistic practices played a crucial role in the social and political organisation of the region, as well as in strategies for the restructuring of a post-apartheid South Africa. To begin with, Zulu is the native language of almost all black people in this region; that is, it is the language spoken in their homes and the first learned during childhood. In this sense therefore, KwaZulu-Natal has relative linguistic (and cultural) homogeneity. Owing to historical factors, particularly the history of the consolidation of Southern Africa under Shaka, Zulu is also a language of the broader Southern African region, though it is associated paradoxically with a history of bravery and resistance as well as a history of brutality. It is not surprising, therefore, that most people who migrate to KwaZulu-Natal often come with a certain knowledge of the Zulu language and culture; however, they are viewed by local Zulus as 'not real Zulu', partly because of the way they speak the language and partly because of from where they have migrated. The association of Zulu language with a history of bravery was highly controversial in the late 1980s and the beginning of the 1990s. This controversy was due to the fact that Inkatha had claimed ownership of Zulu symbolic resources, including language, which then made it difficult for other organisations to use the symbols in pursuing their aims. The use of Zulu language (and history), therefore, in particular situations, was conflated with Inkatha politics, resulting in those who used Zulu in particular public spaces being labelled Inkatha members.

Such an interpretation in the use of Zulu was legitimate if applied to areas where the Zulu language was not dominant, but instead operated alongside and in competition with other languages. These were areas such as the Transvaal province and other homelands. In KwaZulu-Natal, however, the conflict that existed set Zulu speakers against Zulu speakers, and yet each side attempted to discredit the other by projecting malevolent pictures of another linguistic group onto its Zulu brothers. Zulus aligned with the ANC were called agents of the Xhosas, and Zulus aligned with Inkatha were seen as agents of apartheid. Taken together with other cultural materials, language accent became important. Those who spoke Zulu with a slang dialect known as 'Tsotsitaal' or 'Johannesburg Zulu' were suspected of being supporters of the ANC, whereas those who spoke Zulu with a 'deep' or 'rural' Zulu accent were marked as Inkatha. In different provinces like the Transvaal, people simply reverted to other languages besides Zulu to avoid being labelled Inkatha. For ANC oriented events, English, as we will see, had long been the language of politics. The use of English then became an ANC idiom, carried across the country even where speakers were linguistically homogeneous. Behind this action was the ANC desire to stay away from ethnic terms; that is from referring to groups of people as Zulus, Xhosas, Tswanas and so on, but rather referring to all groups as South Africans.

Another interpretation of the use of the Zulu language comes from its association with illiteracy and ignorance. This interpretation was historic, and a typical example of how British colonisation and a British education system impacted on language use. With colonialism, African languages were downgraded, and the language of the colonising country, English, became the language of commerce, education and an instrument with which to measure knowledge. In South Africa, English and Afrikaans were the two official languages. Each of these languages, however, occupied different positions in black communities. In KwaZulu-Natal, as in all other black areas, English was the language of schooling, and from the point of view of the ANC and its affiliates, of politics. Afrikaans, on the other hand, was viewed as the language of oppression, of the Nationalist Party government with its most resented structures of apartheid. In this paper, by contrast, I argue that the dominant perceptions about the use of these languages were not always in tune with individual practices, nor with what operated in groups in the townships. For example, the dominant (ANC) notion that black students hated the use and study of Afrikaans was in contradiction with the practices of the dominant group of ANC students in this study. These students studied and used Afrikaans because it provided them with alternative places of employment.

More importantly, these students saw Afrikaans as a potential language with which to fight international linguistic domination, and argued that other countries would be more inclined to learn Afrikaans than an African language such as Zulu for communicating with South Africa, since these countries considered Afrikaans a white language, and, therefore, a language of power. Moreover, they argued that since Afrikaans is 'indigenous' to South Africa, 'we would be the only ones to tell the world what is wrong or correct Afrikaans, whilst with English, the British are the ones who set the standard'. It is worth noting that this interesting and new viewpoint was not well received by those people still interested in the ANC's version of students' attitude towards Afrikaans. During the data collection period, I was invited by the linguistic department of the University of Natal, Durban campus, to speak about my research and the kinds of data I was getting from the townships. When I spoke about this viewpoint, some white professors expressed disbelief, and demanded to know the names of the schools these students attended, because, as they stated, they themselves had been conducting research in township schools for a number of years, but had never received such responses. It is perhaps my own position as an 'insider' that is to be credited for the nature of data this paper presents. But it is most likely that the sociopolitical changes that were taking place in these townships and in South Africa as a whole were, to borrow from Gal (1988), mirrored in the views that people had about language and also in patterns of language use. To what degree these views were 'realistic', as some of these professors rightly pointed out, is beyond the scope of this paper.

The politics of language and identity, therefore, can be understood to have centred around the different and often contradictory positioning or valuing of languages. First, Zulu was positioned as:

- a 'neutral' local language
- representing ethnic, Inkatha politics and
- indicating ignorance and illiteracy.

Second, English was positioned as:

- colonial
- 'neutral' and
- a language of politics and education.

Third, Afrikaans was positioned as:

- apartheid and
- an instrument for accessing economic resources.

The multiple linguistic practices of individuals were hallmarks of the formation of their identities within this highly linguistically politicised region. The use of language then resulted in emergent, rather than conventional, associations with political organisations, and therefore, individuals redefined their lives through language use.

As I will demonstrate in this paper, individuals were not ready to give up their ethnic identities, irrespective of whether or not they were ANC supporters. I argue that ANC Zulu youths were proud of their Zulu heritage, despite its association with Inkatha politics, and that their use of the Zulu language was in many ways in contrast to the ANC political agenda of a non-racial post-apartheid state. This paper, therefore, is an assertion of their linguistic, ethnic/cultural Zulu autonomy, and is critical of the practices by political organisations aimed at creating political and economic unity out of linguistic, ethnic/racial disparity. The practices of the youth in this paper demonstrate that Zulus in the ANC did not want to move away from their Zulu cultural/ethnic identity, and that language and other cultural material were used not to escape the label Zulu, but rather to affirm it.

2.c)   Birthplace and descent

In its essence, this criterion requires one to have been born and raised in KwaZulu-Natal, or to have parents who were born there and had maintained ties with the region in quite undefined ways. Descent refers to the manner in which individuals trace their ancestry to the region, even if they were not born in KwaZulu-Natal. For instance, it was possible for individuals to use oral history and get information that linked their ancestry to the region of KwaZulu-Natal, and if they desired, to re-establish ties and eventually settle with their tribes through the chiefs. People were, and are, able to trace their Zulu ancestry because the tribes of Zulu-speakers are mostly known by the family or clan names (*izibongo*) of their chiefs. A few exceptions may occur – for example, *amaNgwane* – which embrace the whole tribe.

Tribal names consisting of *izibongo* do not necessarily reflect the actual composition of the tribes (just as the name Zulu did not and still does not reflect the actual composition of those people identified as Zulu). For example, while a tribe might be known as *abakwaMpanza* (Mpanza's people or Mpanza's descendants) there may be twenty or fifty different clan names (*izibongo*) represented within that tribe. What this actually means is that it was Mpanza who at one stage consolidated that tribe and his descendants, and who came to inherit the leadership role. Mpanza, however, would be referred to as the 'father' of these people and be used as proof of the profundity of these people's (Zulu) identity. This was basically the method used to categorise people. Furthermore, the process of *ukukhonza*, 'passing', allowed for people coming from other parts of (southern) Africa to take up Zulu identity through among other things laying claim to the clan name. Integrating into the clan did not result in the loss of one's *isibongo*, which largely reflected the person's place of origin and, often, time of integration. In pre-colonial society, the process of being integrated into Zulu society and keeping your *isibongo* ('*si*' = singular; '*zi*' = plural) did not present a problem, as long as one participated in the cultural practices of that clan and subsequently of the Zulu kingdom. This process of clan-tribal-kingdom association was maintained by colonial powers, and even though its purposes and structures were significantly changed it continues to date.

In addition to the knowledge of one's ancestry, generally, Zulu children are brought up with information about their descent, and the roles their ancestors played in the Zulu wars of conquest and struggle against British colonialism. Thus, phrases like *uwuZulu Zu, uZulu woqobo* (you are Zulu Zu or you are a real Zulu), are commonly used in KwaZulu-Natal to define those Zulu of 'historic' origin from those who migrated into the area, especially after 1879. Thus, those who can trace their ancestors to the period of the Zulu kingdom acquire some high status (Zulu Zu) and, indeed, long descent lines are used not only to demonstrate the profundity of one's Zulu identity but also to disqualify others from claiming full Zulu identity.

Using the aforementioned criteria of identification (history, language, and birthplace/descent), the state, Inkatha and the ANC were able to construct and formalise certain practices as Zulu, and by so doing, define the Zulu people.

3   State definition

At the beginning of the twentieth century, alternative patterns of government, labour and economic distribution, and land occupation were established and were to be given extreme expression under apartheid. Apartheid brought about massive population removals, racial separation, political exclusion, labour exploitation and concomitant repression of the vast majority of the country's people. Under apartheid, a legal definition of Zulu was constructed. The South African Nationalist Party government instituted a legal structure that divided people along racial lines, and allocated these state-defined groups resources depending on the race to which they belonged. Official segregation under apartheid also included geopolitical areas, allocated along racial and linguistic lines.

KwaZulu was one such geopolitical structure within the apartheid state, created as a home for those people defined by the Nationalist Party government linguistically and racially/ethnically as Zulu and therefore as making up a Zulu 'nation'. The legal definition of Zulu at this time referred to those black people who inhabited the region of KwaZulu-Natal and whose first language was Zulu.

4   Inkatha definition

The creation of KwaZulu, however, added another dimension to this state-defined 'Zulu' identity. It meant that being a black Zulu speaker and resident of KwaZulu-Natal was not enough for people to qualify as 'Zulus' in the region. On top of these defining criteria, people had to show allegiance to the KwaZulu 'state' and to Inkatha for them to be identified as Zulus. Showing allegiance to KwaZulu and Inkatha involved, *inter alia*, participating in Inkatha political activities, as well as in Inkatha based/ organised cultural events such as the celebration of Zulu ethnic symbols, including Shaka Day. This added criterion of identification was an important one because it became a prerequisite for individuals who wanted to access those economic resources controlled by KwaZulu homeland authority. The focus of Inkatha-defined Zulu identity was on a politicised ethnic nationalism.

5 ANC definition

Operating alongside this Inkatha defined and controlled 'Zulu' identity was the ANC version of a 'non-racial/ethnic democratic' South Africa. Within this version, politicised ethnic nationalism was viewed as dangerous, a threat to the imagined non-racial South Africa. To the ANC, therefore, Zulu ethnicity became constructed as an imagined concept: a creation of Inkatha politics. Yet the position that Zulu ethnicity was imagined did not mean that it was not socially real. During this time, ethnicity involved visible local communities based on signals of dialect, kinship, status, religion and magical practices, and the more powerful forces of intimacy produced by fear of poverty and rural isolation. Also, economically, three and a half decades of 'separate development' had created ethnically-based networks of patronage and resource distribution, of coercion and control that were not to disappear with the arrival of democracy. A more pressing issue for the ANC, then, was how to deal with the issue of a politicised ethnicity in the face of an imagined non-racial community, without the binding forces of ethnicity and language.

6 Conventionalised Zulu practices, urban cultures and formal politics

Like the Zulu history and its symbols, Zulu cultural practices became valuable resources for politicians to use in pursuing their goals. Cultural practices that had previously been shared and understood were re-examined, questioned and given new meaning. One such practice was *ukuhlonipha*. In general, *ukuhlonipha* refers to any practice of respect, be it performative or linguistic. Most often, *ukuhlonipha* applies to situations where verbal practices may shift from being respectful to confrontational and argumentative or to practices where a young person has to let a person older than herself know that she is wrong. Usually, in Zulu households, children are brought up with a strong emphasis on *ukuhlonipha abadala* (respect for adults) and on non-confrontational ways of disagreeing with adults.

It is, first, important to note that in Zulu there is no distinction between the concept of 'elderliness', such as in 'an elder sister' (one year older than me), and that of 'adulthood', meaning a mature individual. Both are referred to as *badala* (adults). Thus, in Zulu, a six year old is an adult to a five-year-old, and therefore an element of respect is always expected from the five-year-old, even in cases where the six-year-old is wrong. If a conversation develops into an argument, it is expected that where two people of different ages are involved, the younger person will back off and the older person's statement will be the last. Being the last to speak does not necessarily mean that the older person is right, but is simply interpreted as *hlonipha*. In fact, what normally happens is that the younger person would remove herself from the scene, as a way of demonstrating her disagreement. Situations where the younger person argues with the adult are interpreted as disrespect (*ukungahloniphi*), no matter how correct the younger person might be.

Political organisations were at the forefront in defining that which was Zulu culture, how it had to be practised and by whom. For example, questions were asked with regard to how and to whom the conventional Zulu practice of *ukuhlonipha* applied, and, more importantly, what happened to those who refused to embrace this practice. Interpretations and applications of this practice varied in formal politics as well as in interpersonal politics. With regard to formal politics, Inkatha was at the forefront in the practices that legitimised and conventionalised the redefinition of *ukuhlonipha*. To Inkatha, *ukuhlonipha* was a culture that had to be observed by youths with regard to elderly people as well as people in positions of power. The structure of Inkatha was such that people in positions of power were mainly chiefs and their electives. These were the people viewed by Inkatha as deserving of *hlonipha*, and whose views, according to *hlonipha*, could not be openly challenged by any subordinates, whether they were subordinate in terms of age or status. Also, as stated earlier, Inkatha had always maintained a negotiation approach in dealing with the apartheid government, and viewed the leadership of the organisation as the mouthpiece for such negotiations.

This leadership was also above challenges, and those who openly questioned it were reminded of this Zulu practice. Besides Inkatha's stance on respect for authority, in general, Inkatha, as in *ukuhlonipha*, privileged the views of elderly people over those of the young, such that very often the people who were in its top leadership came from anywhere but the youth brigade. In a nutshell, to Inkatha, the practice of *hlonipha* applied to youths first, who were subordinates mainly because of age, and then to those who did not have any status within its structures. Those people were to follow and not question what Inkatha planned, such as celebrating Shaka Day at designated Inkatha spaces. Those who questioned the structuring of Shaka Day celebrations around Inkatha's activities (mainly because they had other ideas about how and where to celebrate) were often told that they were not Zulu because they had questioned authority. They did not have *hlonipha*. Inkatha's interpretation of *ukuhlonipha* was in contradiction to the teachings and the practices of the United Democratic Front (UDF), and later the ANC. There is a particular history here: UDF strategies of the 1980s focussed on acts of defiance against the apartheid state and its structures, including KwaZulu.

It is also important to remember that because of the strategies of defiance and ungovernability, the UDF was able to nurture the militant interests of the youth. For example, the UDF promoted situations whereby youths were actively involved in destroying government property, stopping people who insisted on going to work during UDF/Congress of South African Trade Unions (COSATU) workers' strikes, and many others. In instances where youths stopped workers from going to work, many of the people stopped were in fact adults, who, because of their age, deserved *inhlonipho*. Those youths who forced adults out of their cars and back to their homes were often told by these adults '*anisahloniphi*' (you no longer respect [adults]).

The UDF's strategies of defiance were interpreted by Inkatha to mean that those youths who were in defiance against Inkatha were not only challenging its practices, but Zulu culture itself, which meant that these youths were no longer Zulu in practice. The result of these differences in political practices was that those who did *hlonipha* were associated with Inkatha, and those who did not *hlonipha*, but instead challenged and questioned authority and adults in general, were associated with the UDF. Consequently, since Zulu culture primarily took meaning in Inkatha practices, those who embraced them were labelled Zulu and therefore Inkatha, and those who did not were thought of as UDF/ANC and not Zulu.

Alongside Zulu cultural practices existed practices that were associated with urbanisation and industrialisation, practices that took form as a result of new economic and social conditions. What was important though was not necessarily just any everyday practices, but the ways in which urban practices were evaluated against Zulu cultural practices, and were simultaneously associated with political organisations. For example, *ukungahloniphi*, to disrespect, was basically viewed as an urban practice, not necessarily because this didn't happen in the rural areas, but mainly because disrespectful practices were nourished during the UDF era, whose main base was the townships. The UDF strategies of challenging authority developed into a discourse where youths questioned and verbally confronted not just authority figures such as teachers and politicians but also ordinary adults in the streets. The latter actions were in opposition to the Zulu practice of *ukuhlonipha*.

I have already pointed out that, to Inkatha, youths who engaged in the UDF strategies of defiance against the apartheid state and its structures, and who actively destroyed government property and forced adults out of their cars in attempts to prevent them from going to work during strikes, were thought to be disrespectful. Other general practices of disrespect included the use of language, and the manner in which these uses were connected to the practices of political organisations. For example, the use of Tsotsitaal and not Zulu was considered disrespectful. Tsotsitaal was associated with the urban areas mainly because it is an urban invention, used only by those who align themselves with the urban centres. It is often claimed that in practice Tsotsitaal is a language that is usually used to mark off those considered to be urban from those considered to be rural. The associations of Tsotsitaal are nevertheless wider than this simplistic description since they are tied up with age, gender, network, and in-group language practices. That is, Tsotsitaal is mainly used by young men who see themselves as belonging to the same social group. It is uncommon for Tsotsitaal to be used in a conversation with adults, this is considered to be a rude practice. Basically, the use of Tsotsitaal in the presence of adults is considered to mean that the speakers view themselves as more urban and therefore better than the (rural) non-Tsotsitaal speaker.

During this era, however, the use of Tsotsitaal also came to be associated with non-Zulu speakers. In other words, the use of Tsotsitaal was taken to mean that the speakers did not know Zulu, were not Zulus, and therefore were most likely not to be Inkatha but ANC.

Given this complex interconnection between the 'official' policies and histories that underlined who the Zulu people were and continue to be, how were these boundaries that signified and defined social identities managed, transcended or negotiated? In the following section I use youth groups to illustrate the ambiguous and complex nature of Zulu identity.

7   Youth, identity and politics

7.a)   Tsatsatsa

The name *tsatsatsa* was invented by the youths because the name sounded 'cool', and different from any other group names they were aware of, including *amasinyora* or *amampansula*, which were also invented names, but ones that used the Zulu inflectional affixes. For example, the Zulu affix 'nyo' (as in *amasinyora*) is mainly used to construct names that have associations with snake-like-behaviour. Therefore the name *sinyora* illuminates the nature of the practices of this group. The name *tsatsatsa*, on the other hand, does not indicate any semantic relation nor any grammatical information about the group itself. In fact, I was told that, for a long time, *tsatsatsa* had to explain this term to those who heard it but failed to determine or guess its meaning on the basis of any of the languages they knew.

In this paper, I use *tsatsatsa* to indicate a single group culture, and use *matsatsatsa* to refer to the individuals who made up the group. '*Matsatsatsa*' is actually the term that group members use to refer to themselves. Others referred to them as well by this term. I suspect that the use of 'ma' to prefix *tsatsatsa* was borrowed from the Zulu way of referring to groups of people. For example, in Zulu, you do not talk about the Zulus, Swazis or Vendas to indicate plurality of the people who make up these groups, but rather talk of *amaZulu, amaSwazi* and *amaVenda* respectively. But it is common to find in the written form an '*s*', similar to English, used to indicate plurality. Also, the use of '*ma*' to indicate the 'groupness' of people seems to suggest an absence of a singular state of being. I say this because '*ma*' as a plural prefix is used only with uncountable nouns such as *amanzi*, water, *amasi*, yoghurt, *amafinyila*, mucus, etc (*a* = the). Thus, it is possible that they used '*ma*'-*tsatsatsa* simply following the Zulu way of referring to a group of people.

Tsatsatsa are comprised of groups of boys and girls whose lives were affected by the UDF/Inkatha conflict which had erupted into violence by 1985. Many of these individuals had lost their families and friends during this era, and were living with relatives. The members of the *tsatsatsa* group who participated in this study, at one stage had been involved with the UDF and some had been at the forefront in organising UDF activities. At the time of the study, however, these *tsatsatsa* participants were now members or supporters of the ANC, mainly because the UDF had disbanded. It does appear, however, that before the UDF disbanded, some *tsatsatsa* participants had left the UDF mainly because they did not agree with some of its vigilante practices. The unbanning of the ANC in 1990 rescued those individuals who were already critical of some of the UDF practices but had no other political parties with whom to associate themselves. (I am not sure whether I could say that the formation of *tsatsatsa* served the political 'vacuum' that individuals experienced after leaving the UDF, but before joining the ANC, since it was still in exile).

During the UDF era, most *tsatsatsa* participants had changed schools during their secondary education, and some had even dropped out of school for a number of years but later decided to go back. All *tsatsatsa* participants had a strong commitment to finishing high school and to going into post-secondary education. Therefore, coming from broken families, participation in party politics, and a strong commitment towards education are but three of the features that characterised *matsatsatsa*.

7.b)   Tsatsatsa: general social and political practices

Generally speaking, *tsatsatsa* social practices are most often compared with and indeed understood in relation to the social practices of *mampansula*. (Like with the *tsatsatsa* and *matsatsatsa*, I use *mpansula* to refer to the group culture, and *mampansula* to refer to the members who formed the group.) *Mpansula* is a long established culture that dates back to the 1970s, while *tsatsatsa* culture is still emerging, dating to the beginning of the 1990s. In fact, it is safe to state that at the time of the study, to be *mpansula* was somehow outdated and was considered by *matsatsatsa* to be old-fashioned. *Mpansula* presented a version of what it meant to be a black youth in the 1970s, but this version has been challenged by other groups such as *tsatsatsa*, and no longer enjoys the status it had in the 1970s. The distinguishing characteristics between *mampansula* and *matsatsatsa* centre around political ideologies that govern the groups' ways of socialising and of doing (or not doing) politics. The governing philosophy of *tsatsatsa* is that of the ANC, which puts emphasis on the integration of all races and their cultures as a way of resolving or dealing with the changes in society. This philosophy influences the socio-cultural practices of *matsatsatsa* which include, for example, physical appearance, ways of spending free time, and so on. *Matsatsatsa* are said to listen to what is known as cool music such as jazz and some pop, keep their hair short, and engage in what are considered by many people in the townships as unusual recreational activities such as modelling and weight lifting. Such practices indicate a desire on the part of *tsatsatsa* to surpass racial categories which manifested themselves even in activities such as sports. Moreover, *tsatsatsa* recreational activities are marked by the presence of other races, particularly the presence of white people.

This in itself is symbolic of the ANC ideology of cultural integration and 'non-racialism'. Also, *matsatsatsa* are very careful about their physical appearance, especially the way they dress up, and ensure that it is acceptable to society. In fact, *matsatsatsa* are usually dressed in what is considered fashionable at the time, and therefore, as one *tsatsatsa* stated, are seen to adapt to modern times.

The philosophy of *mampansula,* on the other hand, is that of 'black consciousness' based on Steve Biko's teachings of the 1970s. Of these teachings, *mampansula* emphasise the revitalisation of black history and cultures as a way of dealing with changes in society. Basically, *mpansula* is premised on a belief that traditional African practices of pre-capitalism and pre-colonisation are the answer to existing social problems. Pre-colonial practices are viewed as communal in orientation; that is, there is a belief that in pre-colonial communities Africans were economically dependent on each other, and shared most of what they had. *Mampansula* argue that the revitalisation of these practices will instil in the youths a sense of pride regarding themselves and their history. Who they are is portrayed in practices such as dress and talk. *Mampansula* listen to 'Rasta' (reggae) music, for example, and grow dreadlocks because such practices are defined as black culture. There is also an element of struggle and defiance against certain kinds of state-controlled social practices found among *mpansula*. For example, the state practice to control who and how marijuana is used is not accepted by *mpansula*, who argue that pre-colonial societies owned and used 'dagga' (marijuana) and viewed it as a healing rather than as a poisonous grass.

It is common to find groups of *mpansula* youths sitting and smoking dagga, partly as an act of defiance against the state, and partly as a social habit. Another characteristic that distinguishes *mpansula* from *tsatsatsa* is social space. While it is common to find *matsatsatsa* in predominantly white social spaces forming social relations with people of different races, and to find them involved in white-oriented leisure activities such as weight lifting, *mampansula* social practices are predominantly black. That is, *mampansula* do not socialise across races and avoid those social spaces where whites dominate.

In a nutshell, the differences between *mpansula* and *tsatsatsa* are black space vis-à-vis pluralism; ways of retreating from dominant (white-defined) society, vis-à-vis ways of entering mainstream society. It is important to note further that the dichotomy between these two groups is not necessarily the past versus the present, but rather two different stances towards the present. For instance, in many cases when I asked if, by saying that *matsatsatsa* adapt to modern times this meant that *mampansula* do not, the response I received from *tsatsatsa* was that they do, but not in any significant way. It is correct to conclude then that the differences between the two are that, on the one hand, *mampansula* (re)present one version of a non-rural, 'hip', sophisticated black person, which gets expressed in politics through the activities of the PAC (Pan African Congress) and the BCM (Black Consciousness Movement); while *matsatsatsa*, on the other hand, (re)present an alternative world view of what it means to be a black person (male or female), highly influenced by the ANC ideology of a non-racial South Africa. It is also important to note that it is common to be *mpansula* or *tsatsatsa* without necessarily belonging to the BCM or ANC. All participants involved in this study were members of the ANC.

What further distinguishes *tsatsatsa* from other groups in the townships is a strong sense of purity: a desire to stay away from all kinds of criminal activities. These criminal activities may be politically-motivated, such as forcing people to stay away from work, or economically-oriented, like stealing food. To this extent, *matsatsatsa* are sometimes referred to by their peers as *abangcwele* (the holy ones). Most *tsatsatsa* participants come from economically-deprived families. However, the majority try to assist their families by getting part-time jobs such as working as a packer in a department store or working as a car washer in a garage. These economic practices are in many ways connected to *tsatsatsa* ways of socialising. Through work, *tsatsatsa* participants are able to learn more about and sometimes participate in 'white' culture; to go, for example, to places where the young white boys, with whom they work, go. A boy named Lunga, for example, works as a packer at Pick 'n Pay, one of the largest food shops in the region. At the shop he made friends with one of the supervisors, a white boy called Nick who is almost the same age as him and also works part-time. As Lunga and Nick got to know more about each other, Lunga learnt about an athletic club that Nick belonged to. Lunga had always been interested in weight-lifting, but had never been able to do it because of the lack of sports centres in the townships. After making his interest known, Nick agreed to take Lunga to the club. (It is important to remember here that the late 1980s was also a period in which the state attempted some constitutional reforms. Among these reforms was the opening up of white-designated areas to other races.) When Lunga became a member of the club, he introduced other *tsatsatsa* members also interested in weight-lifting.

That *matsatsatsa* participate in white-defined social areas is not coincidental, as might be suggested by Lunga's case, but is in fact encouraged by *matsatsatsa*. *Matsatsatsa* encourage each other to establish friendships with their white co-workers, in order to find out other possible areas of socialisation. Sizwe, for example, plays in a jazz band to which he was introduced by a white co-worker. Thulile often helps her aunt (who is also her guardian) with some of her duties in a white-owned boutique on weekends. Thulile does not get paid by the owner of the boutique but by her aunt, since she is helping with her aunt's duties. For this reason, Thulile does not have to work every weekend: going to the boutique is dependent on the amount of housework she has. The owner of the boutique has a daughter (Zee) who works in similar conditions as Thulile: she is not an employee at the boutique and is not obliged to come to the shop every weekend. Thulile mentioned this white teenager to her *tsatsatsa* friends who immediately encouraged Thulile to establish a friendship with her (which was consequently going to result in a possible friendship with the whole group). However, Thulile was not interested in a friendship with this girl, and had in fact turned down an invitation to go to a lunch-hour music concert with her. Thulile's friends did not support her decision and reminded her of how she had benefited from their own friendships with white co-workers (Thulile had auditioned for and eventually got a role in a white-owned play which performed at the Playhouse, Durban's most popular theatre). Finally, not being able to withstand the pressure she received from her friends, Thulile became friends with Zee. Despite her perception of it as boring, Thulile has maintained her friendship with Zee so as to keep smooth her relationship with *tsatsatsa*. Thulile is highly dependent on *matsatsatsa* for support, and talks of her friends as her family. To explain this dependency, Thulile stated: *Anginamuntu phela lamhlabeni ngaphandle kwabo. Bangabantu abayaziyo impilo yami. U-anti uyasebenza futhi unezinto eziningi ezihlale zisenqondweni yakhe. Angifuni ukumhlupha.* (I do not have anybody, and these are my friends who understand my life. I can talk and be with them at any time. My aunt is always working. She has a lot of things on her mind and I don't want to worry her.)

Matsatsatsa do not participate in township events such as soccer, or watching movies in a community hall, but rather they spend their free time in the newly-opened (multiracial) amusement or recreational places such as 'The Wheel'. The Wheel is a huge casino-like amusement place with movie theatres, restaurants, shops, and games. It is by far the largest of such places located at the heart of Durban, by the beach front, and away from the townships. People of all races come here to spend time, to meet with each other and just to hang out, as most teenagers do. Such places are very attractive to *matsatsatsa*, possibly because they provide opportunity for wider/international interaction and represent the dominant society's values.

The fact that *matsatsatsa* distance themselves from social activities of the townships is in part motivated by the desire to stay clean or uncorrupted. Often, community organised events get polluted and disrupted by criminal and political thuggery. For example, some people attend local events in townships not because they are interested in soccer or a movie, but because they want to hunt down political enemies. Although soccer groups are supposed to be neutral, their existence makes it possible for people to disguise their agendas and gain popularity as soccer players. As popular soccer players it then becomes easy for these individuals to recruit for certain political organisations. Even weddings and funerals are not immune to politics. In a wedding party, for example, the host would ensure that she or he invites guests of the same political orientation as a way of avoiding confrontation.

Besides the desire to stay clean or uncorrupted by political and criminal elements, *matsatsatsa* are strongly influenced by the ANC vision of a non-racial democratic South Africa, in which South Africans of all races will be able to live together in harmony. But this 'non-racial' vision comes with the baggage of elitism; it means being able to participate in places where whites are, spaces that are therefore considered elitist. The fact that *matsatsatsa* are interested in weight-lifting, for example, speaks to the desire to improve their status, since weight-lifting, like golf and tennis, is considered a white (and by implication), elitist sport.

Matsatsatsa would rather travel a half hour distance to lift weights than jog around the township as other residents might do. This is despite the fact that jogging is considered a safe activity in the townships, especially since people do it in groups. Some people are even known for belonging to identified jogging groups. Asking one non-*tsatsatsa* participant why he thought *tsatsatsa* do not like jogging, he said *'Bacabanga ukuthi yinto yoZulu, buka bangenza ngisho eyabo i club'* (They think it's a Zulu thing [meaning 'backward']. Look, they can even start their own [*tsatsatsa*] jogging club). It is safe, therefore, to say that on the one hand *tsatsatsa* are identified as a group of individuals symbolising 'purity': models of how one can live a respectable life in a period of total chaos, of political and criminal thuggery. On the other hand, *tsatsatsa* (re)present elitism: an idea of what blacks might be if given a chance to be like whites.

8   Specific representations/statements about identity

In addition to what the *tsatsatsa* do, we can also consider specific statements about the ways that these youths view themselves. These statements illuminate the manner in which *tsatsatsa* viewed themselves in relation to Zulu identity, and also in relation to political activities in the township. To begin with, *tsatsatsa* understood themselves as Zulu, and use Zulu history to define and legitimise their practices as Zulu in the making.

For example, history as a criterion was used through the calling up of historic names as illustrated by the following example. At the time of data collection, the South African Congress of Teachers' Union (SACTU), an ANC affiliate, called for a teachers' strike to protest against salaries and general work conditions. At Umganga, the school where the *tsatsatsa* study participants attended, the first week of protest was characterised by, on the one hand, students who were in the last level of high school and were concerned about the time without teaching, and on the other hand, classes with students who saw this as sort of a holiday, a break from teacher authority. Some classes went on as usual, because some teachers did not participate in this strike, either because they were Inkatha and therefore belonged to a different teacher organisation, or because they simply did not agree with the concept of strikes. Students who were in the last grade of high school took turns teaching each other, and also negotiated, together with the principal and with those teachers who did not participate in the strike, to help them with some of the subjects.

In one of the conversations I had with *matsatsatsa* they expressed concern about the strike and the way it was going to hinder their ability to do well in the final examination. Present in this conversation were Muzi, Sizwe, Lunga, Vukani, Thulile and me. Nombuso: *Siniphethe kanjani lesiteleka?* (How is the strike affecting you?) Vukani: *Hayi mina ngithi ziqhudelene Nkombose kababa. Kade sasiteleka basibone kungathi asiphili emakhanda. Ake bazabalaze nabo bezwe ukuthi kunjani.* (I say let them fight each other. We [students] have long been struggling on our own and they [teachers] have been looking at us as though we are crazy. Let them struggle and feel how it is.) (Nkombose kababa, literally, my father's Nkombose, is a name of a bird in a Zulu legendary story about a kind family who used to share even the last of their dinner with strangers. It is said that one day the family had to go without dinner when a bird flew in and demonstrated its magical powers and produced the most delicious dish of *amasi* and *uphuthu* [a traditional dish made out of sour milk and corn flour]. The family named the bird Nkombose, and believed that the bird had been sent by the god of harvest. The story goes on to relate how, because of greed and evil deeds, the family lost this bird, and how it was later retrieved because those who had committed the evil acts repented and were therefore forgiven by the gods. Overall, the phrase *Nkombose kababa* came to symbolise life and survival. So in general this phrase is used to indicate good intent, or the power of the gods, or the relationship between good and evil.)

> Lunga: *Noma kunjalo, yithi esizofa ekugcineni. Sengithi nje kungcono kulokhu ngoba noma ngingafeyila, akungenxa yami.* (Even if that's the case, we are the ones who will eventually suffer. I sometimes console myself by thinking that even if I fail this year, at least it won't be my fault.)
> Muzi: *Mina ngisovalweni. Ngithi uma ngicabanga iMaths, kuthi mangikhale. Ngizibona kulonyaka ozayo ngiphinda iclass sengimdala kangaka.* (As for me, I am in fear. Whenever I think of maths, I feel like crying. I picture myself repeating the same class next year, old as I am.)
> Sizwe: *Awu mina ngeke ingehlule. Angihlulwa yinto engakhulumi. Ngimfunge*

uCetshwayo vuke, ngizophasa lonyaka. (Not me, I won't fail maths. I have never been defeated by anything that doesn't talk. [This is a Zulu saying which expresses the power of individuals over non-linguistic objects, or, precisely, over non-living things]. I swear in the name of Cetshwayo, I will pass this year [literal translation: Cetshwayo will rise from the dead, if I do not pass this year].)

Thulile: *Kusho ukuthi eyangonyaka odlule i-Maths yayinomlomo, yikho nje wayifeyila?* (Does this mean that last year's maths could speak and that's why you failed it?) We all laughed.

Sizwe: *Ngiyanibona nje nina nicabanga ukuthi ngiyadlala. Ngiwuzulu mina, angihlulwa lutho. Nomangingayifeila in maths, kodwa ngizophasa lonyaka.* (I see. You think I am joking. I am Zulu, nothing defeats me. Even if I fail maths, I will not fail [the entire exam).

Sizwe's highlighted statements above indicate that to swear in the name of Cetshwayo is to vow to do the right, impossible, heroic and valued thing. Yet the victory won by the Zulu under Cetshwayo in 1879 was short-lived as the British staged another battle of Ulundi in which they claimed military victory and exiled Cetshwayo. But *tsatsatsa* participants do not talk about this battle because it is of no significance to them, and after all, as they reminded me, '*leyompi eyalelandela i-Sandlwana yayekwa ngoba uZulu ethembiswa izwe, hayi ngoba ehluleka*' (the peace that followed Ulundi was only attained by promising the Zulu people that they would retain possession of their land if they laid down their arms).

Tsatsatsa also spoke about their birthplaces to define themselves as Zulu or not Zulu. For example, in classroom discussions, *tsatsatsa* participants, when directly asked if they are Zulu, unanimously used the birthplace to identify themselves as Zulu. In the other informal discussions they shifted tacitly to other criteria of identity or to a different identity. In one of our classroom discussions about the Zulu language, I asked the question: why is it that Zulu people do not learn Sotho even when they work in places such as Johannesburg where Sotho is dominant? The discussion started in English, but later developed in Zulu. Vukani was first to respond to this question (this discussion was recorded and the English language mistakes are those of the speakers):

Vukani: Zulus don't want to learn it because they think they are big.
Muzi: Not that they think, *sibakhule vele. Asifuni ukukhuluma njengamazizimbane.* (Not that they think, we are real big. We don't want to speak like *mazizimbane* [a term that implies that someone is not real human/is animal like].)
Some people in the class laugh.
Vukani: *uyabona, abantu abafananani abahambe beshaya abantu ngezagila ngo*

nithi bangamazizimbane. (You see, it's people like you who go around beating people up with knobkerries because you say they are *mazizimbane*.)

Nombuso: *Awusitshele Zethu. AmaZulu ababizelani abantu ngamazizimbane.* (Tell us Zethu, why do Zulu people call non-Zulus *amazizimbane* [I directed this question to her because she was among those who had laughed at Muzi's statement].)

Zethu: *Phedula Muzi. Wuwe loqale lendaba yamazizimbane.* (Respond Muzi. You are the one who started this whole *mazizimbane* issue.)

Muzi: *(ecabanga) Hayi angazi. Yinto nje yoZulu leyo. Mina abazali bami baqhamuka eSwazini. Angizazi ezinye izinto zoZulu.* ([Thoughtfully] I don't really know. That's just something that's for Zulus. I don't know because my parents migrated from Swaziland. So I don't know such Zulu things. [But Muzi, who is *tsatsatsa*, had earlier identified himself as Zulu because, as he said, 'I speak Zulu'].)

Nhlanhla: *Awusho Mbongi Zulu omkhulu.* (Tell us Mbongi, the [real] Zulu. [Mbongi was well known in the school because of his ability to recite the praise songs of the Zulu kings from Shaka to the present king. He became popular during the school arts week where students chose projects to present to the entire school. In this class, the students had decided to perform the Zulu drama '*ukufa kukaShaka*' [the death of Shaka] which was also part of their syllabus. Mbongi had assumed the role of Shaka's praise singer known in Zulu as *imbongi*.)

Mbongi: *Hayi nami angizazi izinto zoZulu ngoba umawami owaseMalawi. Kusho ukuthi ngiwumZulu nganxanye ngiwumMalawi.* (No, I do not know Zulu things because my mother is Malawian. This means I am partly Malawian and partly Zulu.)

In earlier discussions, some of these youths had identified themselves as Zulu because of their knowledge of the Zulu language, even though some later mentioned that at home they used a different language, usually that of the place of their parents' origin. Some were also known as Zulu because of their behaviour, such as Mbongi, in the above example. However, in discussions that were critical of Zulu social practices, these young people categorically refused to be identified as Zulu, and uttered statements like: 'my parents came from Swaziland' or, 'my father is Zulu but my mother is Malawian, so that makes me partly Zulu and partly Malawian', as indicated by the above example. In fact, at one stage of discussing symbols in politics, the discussion ended with all participants having systematically denied their Zulu heritage, a heritage that, in other contexts, is the pride of most.

Another available criterion of identification was descent, and this criterion made it possible for *tsatsatsa* to view themselves not just as Zulu, but Zulu Zu or Zulu of historic origin. For example, Lunga told us about how his great-grandfather had participated in the wars that led to the Zulu people taking over control of the land around

Bergville which borders Lesotho and South Africa in the north east. He therefore considered himself as '*Inzalo yamaqhawe*' [a product of heroes] because of his ancestors' involvement in these wars of conquest. But like all other criteria, descent also has its own complexities. An interesting case is that of the *tsatsatsa*-border study participant nicknamed 'Ndabezitha' [one of the words of praise and respect used to acknowledge loyalty to Zulu royalty].

This was a name given to him by his classmates because he had been in the habit of demanding respect for himself as royalty since his great-grand father was Sibiya, who was Shaka's chief minister. Because the events that had resulted in the nickname were actually humorous, 'Ndabezitha' didn't mind the nickname and, in fact, liked it so much that he marked all his school books Thetha NDABEZITHA Sibiya. He could easily have refuted its use if he had not liked it.

In another session, we shared ideas about how other groups might feel about the use of Zulu as a national language, especially in the light of the ongoing Zulu-Xhosa conflict which characterised the Transvaal province at that time. Some participants stated that they had felt uncomfortable using Zulu in the Transvaal because the language singled them out as Zulus and therefore Inkatha, and made them open to attack by non-Zulu speakers. 'Why is this so?' I asked.

> Lunga: *angithi uGatsha (Buthelezi) ufuna sonke sibewoZulu sithathe amawisa siyolwa nabantu bakithi ukuze sitshengise ukuthi singamaqhawe.* (It's all because of Gatsha who wants us to be Zulu. He wants us to take up knobkerries and go and fight our own brothers to show that we are brave.)
>
> Sizwe: *Uthini Ndabezitha? Uthi ungakhuluma nje nabakini ebukhosini bayiyeke lento?* (What do you say, Ndabezitha? Do you think you can approach your relative in royalty to stop this?)
>
> We all laughed.
>
> Ndabezitha responded by telling us that in actual fact he was not royalty:
>
> Ndabezitha: *empeleni ukhokho* [in reality my great-grandmother] came from Cape Town, and married Sibiya *owayeyi* [who was a] Bushman, and *wayengeke abe induna kaShaka* [could not have been Shaka's Chief minister] because we all know that the Zulu had minimum contact with the Bushmen.

What we also knew, but did not talk about, was that many of Shaka's chief ministers and advisers were commoners who had come to the fore through their exceptional military ability rather that through royal birth. It is also interesting to note in this conversation Ndabezitha's shift of identity through denying his Zulu descent, and also shifts in language use.

Because of the homogeneity of the region, language on its own did not always play an important role but was always used in conjunction with other criteria. Thus , the question remains: how was it that a distinction existed between Zulu and non-Zulus if, depending on the situation, one could either be a Zulu of high status (Zulu Zu), or not Zulu at all, as demonstrated by Ndabezitha?

Conclusion

The above examples inform us about a number of things. The first is that *tsatsatsa* used history, birthplace, language, and descent as criteria for identifying themselves as Zulu, and in fact, uttered statements to this effect. The second is that the situatedness of these statements and criteria were dependent on context, place and also involved in the conversations. In fact, from these examples, it is clear that *tsatsatsa* used Zulu history and symbols to identify themselves, as well as to legitimise some of their practices, such as determination to pass an exam. In instances where Zulu practices were called into question, *tsatsatsa* either denied being Zulu or denied being engaged in these practices. In sum, therefore, the character of these youth groups, together with their everyday practices, can be understood to challenge institutionalised meanings of Zulu identity. Despite the official political attempts to place people into neat categories, the practices of youths in this paper indicate that identities are complex since they are constructed from everyday, changing and often contradictory practices.

This paper posits questions about the uniformity of cultures and practices that constitute the ethnic boundary and the position each of these cultures, and the individuals who participate in them, occupy within broader state institutions. It is clear, for instance, that while the Zulu group was considered by the state and political organisations as a well-defined homogeneous group, the cultures of those who made up this group pointed otherwise. At the same time, it is clear that it was institutionalised cultures of the Zulu, as defined by Inkatha, that had legitimacy in the eyes of the state with respect to defining who the Zulu people actually are. It is also clear that youth cultures were not viewed as part of the features that made up the Zulu nation and that youths, in general, occupied marginal positions within the state. Yet despite this cultural marginality youth were a strong force in defining the character of post-apartheid South Africa and of who the Zulu people are. Strong participation in political activities and in socio-cultural events made it difficult for the state and political organisations to ignore ways that youth wanted to be defined.

An interesting source of research, especially for education practitioners is, to investigate the ways in which ethnic boundary shifts as demonstrated by, for example, Ndabezitha, might impinge on the education of these youth. It is clear, for example, that while these youths have knowledge of and embrace part of the history of the Zulu kingdom, there exist moments wherein they have to disassociate themselves from it. How, for instance, such moments might influence classroom participation and critical pedagogies remains to be uncovered. Similarly, given the nature of educational constraints on and concerns about youth practices, it would be interesting to examine why, in the face of the social and political upheaval (that resulted in the murder of many of the *tsatsatsa* parents and guardians) some youth remain pure while others become criminals.

The foregoing discussion impacts our understanding of collective identity and of the concept of nationalism and liberation. Looking at the construction of nations, Anderson suggests three paradoxes of nationalism:

1 The objective modernity of nations to the historian's eye vs their subjective antiquity in the eyes of nationalists.
2 The formal universality of nationality as a socio-cultural concept – in the modern world everyone can, should, will 'have' a nationality, as he or she 'has' a gender.
3 The 'political power of nationalisms vs their philosophical poverty and even incoherence.

1991, p. 5

Anderson captures the way in which the construction of nations has assumed self-evidential proportions, and has lost its historicity. National identity, national allegiance and nation have become central parts of everyday lives. This paper posits questions about the myth of the nation and how it has played a major and sometimes positive role in liberation struggles. Liberation movements, such as those addressed in this study, are very often dominated by nationalist leaders who premise their practices primarily on an unquestionable nation as the unity of liberation. Assertions of other loyalties are often considered disruptive and disloyal to the cause of liberation and unity.

Indeed, liberation struggles, especially in Africa, have been framed in terms of the nation, such that struggles that threaten the construction of a nation are seen as random or contrary, biased and disruptive. They are viewed as not involving national loyalty and as addressing a construct other than that of the nation. It is also common to find these struggles referred to as regional, that is, not nation-wide, and subversive or threatening the fundamental national spirit.

One of the issues raised in this paper remains an interesting source for research centres in terms of representation in liberation struggles. At the first level of representation, this paper has raised points for discussion about some of the conflicts that result from the use of ethnicity to frame liberation struggles. In the South African struggle, for example, it is clear that part of the conflict was a result of the failure to deal with the multiplicity of ethnicities that made up this nation state, and the ways in which each of these ethnic groups viewed it as legitimate to define themselves in order to fight apartheid. Underlying questions remain about the position each of these ethnic groups occupied within the broader South African state, and about the ways in which such positioning enhanced or limited a liberation struggle whose foundation was an unquestionable black nation. This paper demonstrates that issues of diversity within a nation state can no longer be ignored in liberation struggles. Liberation movements cannot continue to refer to these groups as random, disruptive and subversive. These groups are, in fact, the core of liberation itself. How and when liberation movements will begin to deal positively with the issue of nationalism and lack of uniformity in the face of 'imagined' liberated nations remains to be seen.

References

Anderson, B. (1983). *Imagined Communities*, London: Verso.

Barth, F. (1969). *Ethnic Groups and Boundaries*, London: George Owen and Unwin.

Dlamini, S. (1996). 'Language, Social Practices and the Politics of Identity in South Africa', doctoral thesis, Ontario Institute for Studies in Education, University of Toronto.

Gal, S. (1988). 'The Political Economy of Code Choice', in M. Heller (ed.) *Codeswitching: Anthropological and Sociolinguistic Perspectives*, Berlin: Mounton Gruyter.

Guy, J. (1979). *The Destruction of the Zulu Kingdom: The Civil War in Zululand, 1879– 1884*, London: Longman.

Guthrie, G. and S. Hall (1987). 'Introduction', in H. Trueba, G. Guthrie and K. Au (eds) *Culture and the Bilingual Classroom. Studies in Classroom Ethnography*, Rowley: Newbury House.

Lowe, C. (1991). 'Buthelezi, Inkatha and the Problem of Ethnic Nationalism in South Africa', in J. Brown (ed.) *History from South Africa: Alternative Visions and Perspective*, Philadelphia: Temple University Press.

McAll, C. (1990). *Class, Ethnicity and Social Inequality*, Montreal and Kingston: McGill-Queens University Press.

Ogbu, J. (1995). 'Cultural Problems in Minority Education: their Interpretations and Consequences - Part Two: Case Studies', *The Urban Review*, 27 (4), pp. 271–97.

Mapping the memories: politics, place and identity in the District Six Museum, Cape Town

Charmaine McEachern

Introduction

In post-apartheid South Africa, 'the new South Africa' is the most obvious way in which people in all kinds of locations and structural positions confront and seek to give some name to both the obvious and massive political changes which have occurred and the hopes for cultural and social change which have accompanied them.[1] That the label 'the new South Africa' is perhaps the dominant form of an overall identity for this national polity obscures the uncertainty and precariousness of this act of confrontation. Just what is 'new' in post-apartheid South Africa? And what does it mean to be South African in the 'new' South Africa? How can this identity achieve some kind of stability, some form of integrity? Can the past be used to establish not just the fact of 'newness', but also to think about what it is, or can be, by reference to what it is not? In the past and its struggles lies the impetus for the nation conceived as unity in diversity, the principle for knowing or interpreting the past thus being embedded in the present (Boyarin, 1994, p. x). Thus also emerges the enormous significance of memory in South Africa today.

Memory is central in social theorising and critique in contemporary South Africa today (one could compare this with the relationship between nation and memory in Israel; Young, 1993, p. 210, Huyssen, 1994). The Truth and Reconciliation Commission is probably the most obvious and visible manifestation, publicly engaging the apartheid regime in terms of its oppressive strategies and human rights violations. Here, one is mindful of Boyarin's close link between the role of memory and identity as nation-state (1994, p. ix). In South Africa this process must be contextualised through other attempts to provide reconciliation and 'truth' to mark the end of oppressive regimes and signal new beginnings. Post-war Germany (see for example Geyer, 1996; Young, 1993) and Argentina's return to democracy after military rule come immediately to mind. South Africa's own particular Truth and Reconciliation process certainly drew on other attempts to heal shattered nations, the public consultation and fact gathering process including input from South American and East European countries (see Boraine and Levy, 1995). Ultimately, some forms such as El Salvador's internationally organised commission were rejected and, as Andre du Toit put it, South Africa's Truth Commission became a 'project of the state' (1995, p. 95), a decision which suited the fact that here remembering and accounting for the past are also encompassed and circumscribed within the negotiated political settlement which put an end to the apartheid regime.

Yet, at the same time that the harrowing tales of personal suffering told to the Truth and Reconciliation Commission hearings was given public form through daily media publicity and commentary, in myriad other locations apartheid is also engaged through memory, always partial and certainly from the perspective of the present. Numerous exhibitions, seminars and conferences testify to and provide critiques of the plethora of ways in which apartheid operated as a comprehensive system of rule, reaching down into the very minutiae of social life. As an exercise of remembering, the new South Africa's act of self-construction is more than the willed action and rhetoric of a new government and state. It also exists in these many accounts, all of which, though partial and often competing (Young, 1993, p. xi), have something to say about the present, the 'new South Africa', through *their* acts of remembering the past.

These themes of remembering for the understanding of both the present and the future emerge as a central problematic in all kinds of representation generally but also in the lives of ordinary South Africans striving to come to terms with what was done to them or in their name. They demonstrate the profound ways in which all kinds of macro-processes take form and power in the lives of people at the most micro-levels (Abu-Lughod, 1993). To appreciate the significance of this situatedness of historical processes of transformation (Comaroff and Comaroff, 1992), this paper considers a case study of one of the places of engagement between past, present and future which characterise contemporary South Africa. The focus of the study is the District Six Museum in Cape Town, which was established in December 1994. The study is based on two periods of participant observation in 1996 and 1997. Observation was supplemented by and interrogated through interviews and informal talks with museum staff and visitors.

The museum is a powerful engagement with South Africa's past, partly because its remembering is located in the very heart of apartheid philosophy and social engineering, the construction of the apartheid city. Not just an historical account of the harm done through this vision to people and places, the museum also provides for the active construction and performance of memory which is at the same time a critique of apartheid itself. The paper's study of this constellation of city construction, memory and critique is facilitated using the work of Michel de Certeau (1988). The insights of his work on walking the city are particularly useful for a critical understanding of the relationship between past and present within this constellation as it is manifest in the museum. In particular de Certeau provides a way of thinking about the relationship between place, people and politics in remembering. In turn, we can open up a little more the symbolic terrain of the 'new South Africa' in these very transitional times.

From District Six to the District Six Museum

District Six was the sixth District of Cape Town, an inner city area which from the 19th century had housed people from the working and artisanal classes, many of whom worked in the city and at the nearby docks. The District extended from the harbour up into the lower reaches of the Devil's Peak and from the commercial centre of the city to the edge of the suburbs. As one would expect of such an area, District Six had been very heterogeneous for a very long time, an integrated area in which white, coloured and African working class people all lived (Bickford-Smith, 1992), though actual ownership of property was largely concentrated in the hands of white landlords (Western, 1981, p. 155). There are clear indications that such heterogeneity was seen as problematic well before apartheid. As early as 1901 African people were removed from District Six to a new township, Ndabeni, ostensibly because of the outbreak of plague (Goldin, 1987, p. 162). In the twentieth century, rapid population expansion (particularly under the influence of rural in-migration) and the general disinclination of landlords and the Cape Town City Council to maintain and improve housing and general amenities produced what all researchers identify as a grossly overcrowded and rundown area – a 'slum'.

In 1948 the National Party came to power in South Africa, having run on a platform which promised to deal with overcrowded urban areas which resulted from massive and uncontrolled migration into the cities from the country. As Mabin says, 'In some respects apartheid was a (racist) response to previous failure to develop coherent urbanisation policy' (1992, p. 19). Population control thus became a cornerstone of apartheid policy as it sought to organise and channel capitalist development in South Africa for the benefit of one sector of the population, white South Africans, through what Mamdani calls 'artificial deurbanisation' (1996, pp. 28, 9).[2] This meant that the colour segregation which was already a feature of pre-apartheid South Africa (Pechey, 1994, Mamdani, 1996) was systematised and legally enforced as race became *the* factor in the distribution of rights (Christopher, 1994, p. 1). Central to the system of enforcement of racially based rights which followed was the Population Registration Act with its classifications of racial identity and the Group Areas Act which sought comprehensively to enforce racial difference by controlling non-white populations in terms of residence. Apartheid was thus a spatial system, which as Christopher notes, worked very much at the local level. In particular, the city, the urban, was central to policy. The city was seen as white,[3] built by whites for whites, so that access to the cities by non-whites for whatever purpose, residential or employment, had to be strictly controlled through the Group Areas Act in order to maintain this correct relationship between whiteness and urbanisation. Non-whites were to live and work in the urban areas only on white terms.[4]

The consequences Marks and Trapido record: over the next 25 years nearly 4 million people were uprooted, many of them several times over, in pursuit of the policies of apartheid (1987, p. 22). In 1948, Cape Town was the most integrated city in South Africa (Christopher, 1994). The Cape's liberal tradition (Bickford-Smith, 1992, Ross, 1992, Mamdani, 1996, p. 69) and the relatively high coloured population all meant that, though economics produced segregation of a kind, namely, 'civil inequality' (Mamdani, 1996, p. 69), when it came to working class areas in particular residential patterns were characteristically integrated. It was these areas which were torn apart as proclamation after proclamation declared areas white or coloured (mostly the former) forcing all other classifications of people out.

District Six was one such area. It has been eulogised as an integrated area of workers and small traders where people of all races and religions and cultures mixed, lived together and shared the hardships of poverty and neglect.[5] There was also a significant degree of intermarriage between groups, which prompted precisely the fear of both miscegenation and the blunting of European 'colour feelings' which Goldin (1987, p. 170) argues fuelled the National Party's determination to regularise and codify the *ad hoc* and often economically derived forms of segregation which were already in place in 1948. District Six thus exemplified the articulation of ideological principle and spatial organisation which underpinned the apartheid vision of the city lodged at the very heart of its regime and its way of seeing South Africa as a whole. Under the National Party, space itself was to be racialised and transformed, in turn transforming people.

Though the Group Areas Act was legislated in 1950, District Six itself was not proclaimed white until 1966. Over the next 15 years the District was physically destroyed, bulldozed street by street, to make way for white residents. All in all between 55 000 and 65 000 people were moved from District Six, usually relocated in the townships out on the Cape Flats, often separated from closest kin and friends.

In many ways District Six and *this* history of forced removal has come to overshadow the many, many other areas of forced removal from the urban area of Cape Town, like Mowbray and Claremont. It has become the symbol of the dislocation and harm caused by the Group Areas Act. In part this must be because Zonnebloem (as the apartheid authorities renamed the area) or District Six today was never effectively redeveloped. Indeed, in terms of occupation it was the state which took it over, building houses for state employees and a Technikon, originally for whites only. Hart reports that by 1985 'Zonnebloem comprised some 3 000–4 000 people, predominantly lower-middle class Afrikaans speakers and overwhelmingly state employees' (1990, p. 133). The white residential development dreamed of by apartheid authorities never came to fruition. This visibility of the state maintained District Six as a pathological symptom of apartheid and its cities, making visible the relationship between force and dislocation. The rest is emptiness and ruin, in sharp contrast to the overcrowded, urban past. It is a wasteland, marked only by the isolated, untouched churches and mosques of District Six and traces of the old cobbled streets among the weeds and rubbish.

As a wasteland, District Six did not just stand as a 'blot on the conscience of the entire nation' (Hart, 1990, p. 134). The space could still be defended by those who waited for the inevitable demise of the apartheid system. In the late 1980s the Hands Off District Six campaign formed out of the Friends of District Six in order to protect the area from British Petroleum's (BP) intended redevelopment using the private sector (see also Western, 1981, p. 158). Although BP's development plans specified that the area was to be open to people of all races and indeed stated that ex-residents would be given preference, there was strong community opposition. Hart argues of the campaign, 'Their guiding intention is that District Six be declared 'salted earth' and left undeveloped until the demise of apartheid' (1990, p. 136). As Young observes of the death camps left by the Holocaust, such ruins cannot on their own remember, it is people's 'will to remember' which endows them with meanings and significance (1993, p. 120). Still, left undeveloped, the wasteland could operate as a space on which such meanings could be inscribed in the imagination and produced as memory. The District Six Museum has become one place where the sense of absence can be linked to the District's presence in people's lives and popular memory.

The District Six Museum is housed in the Buitenkant Methodist Church on the central business district edge of the old District Six. The exhibition covers the ground floor centre space of the church. Down one side are carrels of photographs grouped around streets and areas of District Six.[6] At the altar end, high up, hang representations of the four main religions of District Six people; Hinduism, Islam, Christianity and Judaism, religious polyphony being part of the message of heterogeneity about the district that the museum seeks to convey, despite its housing in a Christian church. Below this, dramatically, a photograph of the skyline of District Six extends across the church, standing for and helping people to envisage the whole District which once stood behind the church. At the other Buitenkant Street end is a display of street signs from the old District and press clippings and information about individuals and events in District Six (and the museum) fill the other wall.

Visitors are welcomed at the museum by officers who are themselves District Sixers (the name given to ex-residents) and who willingly talk about their experiences. This makes this museum reminiscent of the Pan Pacific Park Holocaust Museum in the United States described by Young (see also Mithlo, 1995, p. 50) in these terms:

In fact, as instructive and powerful as the photographic panels were, students and teachers agreed that the exhibition's principal resource was the survivors who led them through the museum. In their presence, the photo montages came alive.

1993, p. 304

In fact, the presence of District Sixers as visitors also contributes to this 'coming alive' in the museum. The Buitenkant Church had been a struggle church during the era of apartheid, a site in the political protest history of the Western Cape. Various trustees of the museum recalled services and meetings to protest the apartheid regime, mentioning names like those of Alan Boesak and Trevor Manuel, a government minister. They talked of marches from the church and of deliberately courted arrests. Part of the symbolic power of this particular church is that it is also directly across the road from the security forces' headquarters in the Caledon Square Police Station. Through displayed materials about the church's struggle history, the history of struggle in the Western Cape is made physically to encompass the museum's exhibition in the form of the church, providing one very powerful reading or identification, perhaps a preferred reading (Hall, 1980), for the exhibition and its visitors. This creates a space for a possible continuity being drawn between the demise of District Six, *remembering* that demise and the struggle itself, which enables the recasting of the relationship between the demise and the struggle. The museum itself emerged out of the Hands Off District Six campaign of the late 1980s.

The possibility of a museum to keep alive the memory of the District Six which the campaign was defending was discussed at the very inception of the campaign (Soudien, 1990). But the museum, when it came, took form in 1994, when apartheid had ended and democracy instated. It was established within the 'new South Africa' and bears the marks of this moment in time. This is clear from the words of a central banner which hangs from the rails of the upper floor of the church which reads:

In 1966
District Six
Was declared
A 'White' Group Area
Shortly afterward
The first bulldozers
Moved in and set about
destroying homes in which
generations of families had
lived. Intent on erasing
District Six from the map

of Cape Town the Apartheid
State attempted to Redesign
The Space of District Six,
Renaming it Zonnebloem
Today, only the scars of the
Removals remain. In this
Exhibition we do not wish to
Recreate District Six as much
As to re-possess the history of
the area as a place where people
lived, loved and struggled. It is
an attempt to take back our right
To signpost our lives with those
Things we hold dear. At one
level the exhibition is about signs of
Our past. We would like to invite you
to write your names and addresses and
Make comments in the spaces around the
Exhibits and in our visitors book. This is
important in helping us to trace our past. At
another level, the exhibition is also about
Pointers to our future. We, all of us, need to decide,
how as individuals and as people we wish to re-trace
and re-signpost the lines of our future. Such a process
Is neither easy nor straightforward. It is not predictable either.

Here we see the museum's envisaging of the possible connections between past, present
and future, the connection of apartheid South Africa to the new South Africa at a time
when memory is still palpable, 'still almost visceral', providing for it a social power and
authority which the passing of time erodes or transforms (Young, 1993, pp. 169–75).
The paper will show that the way these themes and connections are played out and
given form is very much in the hands of the visitors, many of whom experienced the
destruction. And, very much in keeping with the state rhetorics of empowerment,
representation and reconciliation, this is how the museum staff want it to be. At this
level, the museum is taking on board agendas which coincide with those of the new
South African state.

But the outcome is not at all assured in these terms. This is precisely because the
actual playing out of those processes of empowerment is through the performances
of the people. As visitors and new South Africans, the people begin to take over and
engage the rhetorics in their own terms.

This has never been the kind of museum which seeks to do all of the memory-work and serve it up to the people. Museum staff comment on how they began with a two week exhibition in 1994 but are still there because 'the people wouldn't let us close'. People came to look at the photographs and the old street signs which had been saved from the destruction of the District and retrieved to be put on exhibition here. They came to write their names and old addresses on the long calico cloths hung up for this purpose. They made the exhibition into a space of what Pratt calls 'autoethnography', representations 'in which people undertake to describe themselves in ways that engage with representations others have made of them' (1994, p. 28). For the rest of this paper I consider just one of the features of the museum as it facilitates this autoethnography.

The mapping of memory

In the centre of the church, covering much of the floor space is a huge map of the District. The map is decorated with poems to the life of the District as well as linocuts by the artist, Lionel Davis, himself a District Sixer and a political activist who had been jailed on Robben Island. Davis helped put together the exhibition with the map at its centre.[7] Visibly dominant, the map is used by the museum's education officers to talk about the history and development of the District, to explain different areas, where particular landmarks were and so on. There is some ambivalence about the map, with some trustees and others arguing that it has become reified, setting District Six in stone (or paper and plastic). Certainly in some tours, it is pointed out that the map's impression of boundedness was negated by people, events and relationships spilling out into surrounding districts (the harbour, the commercial area of central Cape Town, nearby districts like Walmer Estate and Woodstock, where some moved after 1966). Few of the District Sixers who come express the same ambivalence.

The director of the museum stresses that their first priority are District Sixers, people whose history they are showing. And for these people the map is very powerful indeed. It is one site in the exhibition where people took over and turned it into something else, something living. Not just content to sign their names and put their old addresses on the cloths, the ex-residents of District Six also wrote their names on the map. They marked in their houses, their family names, shops, bioscopes (cinemas), markets, bus stops and so on.

In so doing they wrote themselves into the map; they rendered social the map's physical representation. The map is thus implicated in the declared intentions of the museum to resist apartheid's history by providing the opportunity for people to 're-possess the history of the area as a place where people lived, loved and struggled' and to 'attempt to take back our right to signpost our lives with those things we hold dear'.

Through the map, District Sixers make visible the histories which they have carried with them but which were rendered invisible in the destruction of the area.

In his most famous chapter of *The Practice of Everyday Life*, 'Walking in the City', Michel de Certeau argues that walking in the city can operate as resistance to official, authoritative constructions of the city - a construction of it as place in which meanings slip authorised versions as walkers find new ways through, attach place to memory - turning space into place. This is exactly what District Sixers walking over the map do. The map has a peculiar efficacy in engaging with apartheid. It can be seen as a core symbol of apartheid given the centrality of urban planning to apartheid's particular version of social engineering (Smith, 1994, Western, 1981). As Christopher (1994) has demonstrated, maps are particularly suitable for analysing the transformative and de-structive impact of the apartheid regime's policies and practices. As such, the map in District Six Museum is a particularly powerful ground on which District Sixers can engage with apartheid's interventions into their lives. The map representation is a physical thing, an official text which baldly lays down the basic topographical features of the district. It is empty, devoid of life, able to be manipulated in the interests of those in authority. On the basis of such a representation and armed with the official narrative of District Six which stated that it was a slum, degenerate, crime and poverty ridden, 'a blight on the social landscape' requiring redemption (Soudien and Meltzer, 1995, p. 8), the authorities could organise the systematic destruction of District Six, street by street (see Fortune, 1996). The walkers use exactly the same representation, which on the floor of the museum also began as an 'empty' representation, but their articulation of memory and walking provide for it a totally different meaning, one which resists the apartheid regime's judgement, while at the same time criticising its acts of destruction.

People obviously use the map in different ways. Some just stand and stare, often with tears in their eyes, others are looking for specific sites, trying to remember who lived and worked where. They look for old haunts, locate the homes of friends and kin, where they went to school, the swimming baths, places of fun, places of work. Where they come in with others, usually kin, conversation is intense as they exchange memories of who lived where, maybe even disagreeing with each other about places and people. They may meet others on the map and talk about *their* District Six, trying to find connections in people and places and often finding them in shared shop keepers or school teachers and principals. They may look to see from the marks on the map who of their old neighbourhood has also been here. In the summer of 1996–97 the museum saw a lot of District Sixers visit from new homes overseas in Canada, the United States and Australia. Many of these used the map to show their children who had never seen District Six where they had lived and what it was like. Many come to the museum officers who are always interested, always encourage them to tell of their relationship to District Six, to narrate their District Six. They swap stories, remember different aspects of the same event or person's history. There is a constant movement here; between differentiated histories and memories which signify many District Sixes and the more homogenised District Six, the symbol of a history greater than the District itself. Both are present in the map walking and the narratives, so that Soudien and Meltzer are right to call these popular narratives, the assertion of 'humanity, dignity and creativity (1995, p. 10), but they also seem to be particular narratives of identity.

Obviously walking on the map in these ways is a different exercise at many levels from de Certeau's walking in the city. He speaks of 'walking rhetorics' (1988, p. 100) whereby 'pedestrian speech acts' like taking shortcuts or detours or refusing to take particular routes are appropriations of urban space, at the same time bringing this space into being – as place. Such an act of appropriation and begetting is no longer given to ex-District Six residents.

Though they do visit and attend churches and mosques in the District still, there is little left to 'walk in' in the way de Certeau speaks of. There are no houses, shops, parks, just rank weeds, the odd group of squatters with little fires and the ubiquitous lines of washing, rubbish, a huge Technikon complex and some housing on the fringes. What the ex-residents do have is the spatial representation of the district, in the form of the map. It is the map that allows the walkers to bring 'District Six' into being again as physical space; but this time it is not so much in relation to the intentions of builders, architects and urban designers as de Certeau has it. Rather than the *creators* of this urban space, the map allows them to engage with its *destroyers*. Here the map fulfils both of the roles of the modern museum which Huyssen (1994, p. 15) notes make museums *the* paradigmatic institution of modernisation; collecting that which modernisation has destroyed but also serving as a site of possible resurrections. Certainly the discourse of apartheid when it decreed the destruction of District Six was that of modernisation, progress whatever its politics, so the museum 'collects, salvages' that which apartheid as modernisation destroyed. But, as Hyssen also notes, museums like memory itself, 'construct the past in the light of the discourses of the present and in terms of present-day interest', and in the light of this we see that the walkers turn the museum into a site of resurrection in an act which directly counters apartheid meanings with *post*-apartheid, regardless of the political persuasion of the walkers themselves. The walkers' practices of appropriation and enunciation (de Certeau, 1988, p. 97) bring District Six into being as something morally greater than space – place. Rather than speaking the possibilities of the space, the map works as a mnemonic, which both allows the recall of the place but also puts the rememberer back into it, as they literally have put their names back into District Six by writing them on the map. It produces a re-identification.

The map also works through and enables the play of synecdoche and asyndeton and the movement between them, for de Certeau, primary expressive forms operating to provide the walked through city with its texture and form – its reality. The map of course does stand for the whole, but just what that whole is, is provided by the walkers (and the other exhibits of course). For each, District Six starts from the epicentre of *their* home, *their* street, *their* place. It is this that they always write in first and then move out from their own place in District Six to the whole. If synecdoche 'replaces totalities by fragments' (de Certeau, 1988, p. 101), then this too is the tropic process to construct District Six as a reality that the walkers go through. As they walk over the map, pausing here or there, passing over whole blocks or retracing their steps to stop again, they speak life and form back into the destroyed District of the map. The map is transformed from a graphic representation on two planes into the repository of experiences, relationships, life; another layer is laid down over the lines and shapes by the walking feet and the spoken memories/stories which accompany them. But the life that this represents is in fragments, a mosaic of specific parts – this shop, this bioscope, this street, places and relationships which come within the direct orbit of ex-residents, so that the collective remembered whole is constructed out of overlapping mosaics. Then there are other fragments which all used to speak the special character of the District – places like the Seven Steps and the Fish Market which everyone relates to and remembers. Proper names, like Hanover Street especially, also have this power of synecdoche to be far more than simply the name of a topographical feature. Even for non ex-resident Capetonians visiting the museum, Hanover Street seems to connote District Six as an identity, a place. De Certeau argues that 'Synecdoche makes more dense: it amplifies the detail and miniaturises the whole' (1984, p. 101). This is exactly what happens to the District Six of the walkers. Their strategies exactly make District Six more dense, which is probably why they are accused at times of sentimentality and nostalgia. These processes which operate as synecdoche make the whole district accessible while focusing its identity powerfully through significant parts to stand for that whole. And in this process the foreshortening, the breaking of continuity and selecting of parts that is asyndeton, enlarge and make the chosen parts even more significant and powerful. The power of asyndeton, even when District Six was in existence, meant that certain parts of it, like the Seven Steps, were broken up and taken by people who could then take District Six with them. This is how the Museum was able to acquire the small piece of one step which is in its display.

These are then all strategies to construct the metaphorical city out of the reimagining and re-membering of this particular use of the represented city – the map. In a sense they become central devices in ex-residents' performance of their popular narratives of District Six on the map. Through the operation of synecdoche and asyndeton on the map, events and relationships in the memory merge into places as they are identified or re-found cartographically, to be re-created in the vocalisation of those memories as parts of the narratives of the people who lived in these places in the past. Such tellings make District Six exist, not again or as it was, but within a larger encompassing narrative about identity and South Africa in the 1990s post-apartheid society; that is in metaphorical form which is politically inflected in particular ways.

A significant part of this metaphorical form of District Six is in the characterising of this place as lost community. Though in a sense we do get different District Sixes in the mosaics of the visitors, there are striking similarities in the kinds of things that people say about life in District Six, life making District Six a particular kind of place.

> 'You knew everybody in District Six; it was like one big family, we knew whites and blacks, everyone.'
> 'You were safe in District Six – girls could walk in the streets at night, the kids could play on the street.'
> 'People respected each other, you could discipline someone else's child if you saw it misbehave' (this also was often linked to being able to leave doors unlocked).
> 'Street life was important – we used to sit on the stoep and talk to people going past.'

These are just a few of the kinds of comments made over and over in some form, constituting the museum as a location for the construction of 'common meaning' (White, 1991, p. 6). What they seem to be doing is clearly drawing District Six as community. They are projecting from their remembered lives there out into the entire district, characterising it as a community. And, they are certainly constructing this as a favourable form of social organisation, which as Bozzoli (1987, p. 5) notes, using Raymond Williams' work, is always the case with the concept of 'community'. Further, her insights about this positive valorisation also seem applicable to the above kinds of comments:

> The good connotations of 'community' rest in its ability to conjure up images of supportiveness; of a place of kinship ties, of rest and rejuvenation; of cross-class cooperation.

People also used particular places and experiences to evoke a sense of community as shared place. Stories around the Fish Market abounded; first remembered as a place where you could meet everyone else and which everyone shared in common, but second, articulating value and synecdoche by recounting it as a place where the supportiveness of the District was made manifest by the Market making scraps available to the poor at the end of the day. The bioscopes also seemed to feature in many people's narratives, often being the sites that were looked for on the map. While this gave the bioscopes too a synecdochal quality, at the same time loyalty to different bioscopes also seemed to signal difference within the District.

These evocations of community are in fact often accused of nostalgia or sentimentality and certainly it is hard to see anything culturally specific in the comments above. They might be heard in a multitude of places around the world, especially where the impact of modernisation and the more recent fragmentations of postmodern society are seen as destroying meaningful collectivities, producing alienation and dislocation. In a way, the cultural specificity is offered in the kinds of explanations which follow from *criticisms* of such evocations of community. Many people have argued that such evocations ignore the negative aspects of living in the District. One of the few critical comments on the cloths accused the museum of turning District Six into a 'myth' because of this.[8] Critics point out the existence of gangs, of crime and violence; they stress the poverty, the overcrowding; they demonstrate the divisions, the prejudices and the inequalities; they question whether or not there *was* community in District Six. Dullah Omar, Minister of Justice and himself a District Sixer, has taken up this issue in a variety of contexts, one of which was a television talk programme, *Felicia*, about District Six which was recorded in the museum itself during its first week. In another place Omar puts his objection like this:

> There has been a tendency to isolate District Six from its social milieu. To regard it as a special case and to mystify its history ... There appeared to be some degree of 'racial harmony'. Families lived closer together within reach of each other. A community spirit built up over generations lived on. There was the life in Hanover Street, the fish market and the many shops and hawkers. Landmarks such as the Star cinema, the Avalon, the National and the British. But there has been a tendency to romanticize [the] life of that period. Even the gangsterism – the Globe gang, the Jesters and the Killers, etc are portrayed in a romantic light together with 'The Seven Steps' and the characters who graced District Six during its lifetime. And so history will want to record District Six and its people as having been a people who enjoyed life and who were carefree – 'until the Nats came along and destroyed it all'.
>
> Jeppie and Soudien, 1990, p. 192

This too is the kind of scepticism with which some people greet the narratives which emerge in walking the map or looking at the photographs. They will ask questions about elements of disharmony, usually crime or violence as Omar suggests, but maybe also collaboration with the apartheid state.

Bozzoli argues that one way in which community forms is in terms of opposition to something – and it seems clear that, however illusory community is, however much one can point to serious rifts, differences, evidence of non-harmony and so on, this oppositional construction is exactly what is happening. In a sense this is community *post-facto* (Western, 1981, pp. 163–201), community retrospectively ascribed to ways of living in District Six in opposition to what came after. As it is evoked at the museum (Western, 1981) this may be far less community as the form of remembered social organisation and far more a moral community brought into being as critique of apartheid or at least some of the planning consequences of apartheid, given the divided political affiliations of those dislocated.[9] Clearly people were asserting their subjectivity and experience in contrast to a time in which such assertions were devalued, even impossible, making identity itself problematic (White, 1991). And here I will ultimately argue that people are talking about their identity and forms of sociality in relation to *city* as much as they are talking about community (Bickford-Smith, 1990, p. 35).

The cosmopolitan community: a politics of memory

The memories on the map and the stories which people tell aren't just stories of some past, perfect place. Rather they are stories of a people transformed, turned into somebody else – from the critical perspective of who they feel they have become. The past recounted from the standpoint of the present is then a strategy of identity construction (White, 1991, p. 8) which here provides a way of criticising that transformation, narratives becoming morality tales as much as they are history. Regardless of how romanticised it has become, District Six seems most certainly to have been a place of generational depth; Western claims seven generations. The history which was sedimented into the District as place, in part lived in the people as the map walking reveals. Then too, most accounts suggest that people did *not* live as isolated nuclear units. Rather they all had kin, as well as friends, living close-by. This is certainly borne out by the stories and map commentaries where people will also point out where their aunties, uncles and grandparents lived, with their children or others of the family and how they could as readily and freely walk into these homes, sit down and talk or eat as in their own. This takes on very particular significance when one considers that poverty also characterised the people of District Six. Kinship links were critical in coping with this poverty at a day to day level (Pinnock, 1987, p. 426; see also Western, 1981).

Again this is embedded in the help, support, redistribution and care which features in many of the stories and it is also in part the context for the integrated nature of the District. As many observers note, integration in urban Cape Town was a feature of poor, working class areas more than any other (Goldin, 1987, Bickford-Smith, 1992). So the negative *urban* features many note, poverty, overcrowding, poor facilities and so on are exactly those things which seem to have generated the forms of sociality, the social relationships, which people today are representing as community. Then in memory, it is the sociality which dominates rather than the structural conditions which produced it. In keeping with Bozzoli, the remembered community which people then build on these social accommodations of poverty and self help is also opposition. It is community as a kind of critique – a remembered community based on stories of the sociality which is brought into being from the perspective of where they are now, in order to criticise the transformations of their lives under apartheid. Two examples help make the point. First, it is clear that, for many of the coloured population, particularly those moved early, the standard of housing into which they were moved was superior in many ways to their District Six accommodation (Western, 1981). Though small and very basic, the houses were clean, had full facilities, small plots of land and people were able to have modern conveniences. At the same time, they remained poor, and now they had to spend more money on commuting to work, as well as the often higher prices that shops and services with monopolies in the townships could charge. But, because of the way in which the Group Areas Board (often called 'the Board', see also Rive, 1989, pp. 93–104) allocated new housing, more often than not people were now living far away from kin and neighbours with whom they had built up long-term networks of support and cooperation. Now they were isolated in their poverty, made to feel it much more, and despair (Adams and Suttner, 1988; Western, 1981).

This was particularly hard on women left isolated and some women talked of walks of several miles that they made across townships to visit mothers and sisters similarly isolated. So forms of sociality changed; as they recount it, to their impoverishment.

The second example concerns the most contentious claim of the map walkers, that District Six was safe. This, as indicated, is the thing that people most often pick up. It is a question often asked of the education officers when they are conducting tours of the museum. What of violence and crime? What of the gangs? This is hardly a surprising question given the amount of media attention to this feature of the new South Africa, but it is very valid as an historical question also (Pinnock, 1987). The position that District Sixers seem to take is that, yes there were gangs, but they were mostly a problem for each other or outsiders, not the people of the District who could mostly keep out of their way. Further, they fought with knives and fists rather than today's full arsenals. Now part of the context for this must be the activities of the organisation People Against Gangsterism and Drugs (PAGAD) which has greatly heightened people's awareness of these things.[10] But, as Pinnock reports, this also seems to be the perception of gangsters themselves at the time. He quotes Stone, the leader of the Mongrels gang in Grassy Park:

> It was tough then. But you knew where you stood. You were never short of kroon (money) or people who would pull in to help you. Ja, we had our fights, but there wasn't all the killing. The families were big, you know, and you knew everybody. They would all help you when you fell in the shit.
>
> 1987, p. 427

Here gangs and community (or communal families as Pinnock argues) go together rather than being incompatible. There seem to be two kinds of things being brought out in these accounts. First the narratives seem to deny a place in District Six for the level of violence they experience today (Hanover Park was one township often used to exemplify this), for its randomness and the possibility of being murdered which meant that not for the townships but the life on the *stoep* or the streets. People stayed inside and kept their children inside almost from the moment of moving out into the Cape Flats, testimony I think to their fears of a place where they did not know the people they were living among, an alien residential experience for them (Fortune, 1996, p. 105). Their memories of street life then are not just expressions of community which was symbolically constituted on the street (Soudien and Meltzer, 1995) but also seem to be constructed with the intention of testifying to changing social patterns of violence. And this is as much directed at today's post-democratic rule as it is at apartheid, particularly where the speaker is anti-ANC. Yesterday's violence had a kind of social meaning which for them is denied in the experiences of contemporary violence and crime in the townships. Implicated in this, echoed in Stone's comments in a way too, are the changing forms of sociality which ultimately changed coloured subjectivity and identity. Life, and people, became more individualised. Instead of living in large communal families, they turned inwards, into the nuclear family, into the house, not going out, not knowing their neighbours, isolated as many walkers said, 'out on the Cape Flats'. Comments echo the words of a Mowbray coloured resident forcibly removed to the Cape Flats under the Group Areas, to whom Western spoke:

> I was really living then, now I'm not sure I am. I mean, I live for my job. That is the money I can make so we can make the home comfortable for the family and to invite people in and be proud of it. But it's very rarely we can get up a party and go out dancing or to a movie. In Mowbray there was too much to be done outside – people would participate with you – here we live too much in our houses.
>
> 1981, p. 239

This comment has the diasporic structure of feeling which Small (1986, p. 11) argues characterised District Sixers removed to the townships of the Cape Flats. These big questions of who people feel they became under apartheid, are the crux to both the narratives of memory and the critical engagement with apartheid that the map encourages.

And here the relationship between map and city is crucial. The map walkers demonstrate that, for them, both identity and history are space. This is very much as one would expect, given that space was central to apartheid, its ideology and its transformations of South Africa in terms of this ideology and the interests it served. The map on the floor symbolises the social emptiness of District Six as inner city which was necessary to make Cape Town into a quintessentially apartheid city, the city which Christopher (1994) argues was most transformed under apartheid's social engineering. And the people walking the map respond to this, criticising apartheid's policies and actions in making Cape Town an apartheid city, by repeopling, resocialising, the inner city with their stories, their presence as coloured people, however momentarily.

Living in District Six gave coloured people an identity located in two things; the inner city and Cape Town itself, the Mother City. It is the first of these that Western's informant seems to be engaging. He was living then, on the Cape Flats he's not so sure ... What people lost by being shipped out to mono-race spaces was the experience of city living itself, an experience which had become part of their very identity. They lost the heterogeneity, the openness, what Hannerz (1992, p. 173) calls the 'cultural complexity' of the city and city living, which had shaped who they were, as people. We need only to think of the short story 'Moon over District Six', by Richard Rive (1989), a writer who *did* talk about District Six as a 'slum', in which the same New Year moon shines on 'the teaser-man', the 'young buck and his girlfriend', the 'early celebrator' drinking from a paper cup reading KISS ME SWEETIE who is chastised by the 'prim, light-brown lady who lived in Walmer Estate and only spoke English at home', the 'dandy in pink socks' at the cinema, the 'housewife' out on the town, the 'Cheeky, yellow youth' playing dice, a guitar-playing 'cuuuuulid' serenader, the full cast of a fight including the white policeman armed with revolver who came to break it up and the 'street-corner Jesus-jumper' preaching to the drunks. No wonder the Cape Flats seemed so alien. They didn't necessarily like their co-residents in the District and the map walkers show that they carved out their own spaces within the whole, but these other lives, these other spaces and times (Pechey, 1994) of District Six were also part of their District Six and part of *them* as District Sixers, an identity which became all the poignant when they lost it.[11]

These people were cosmopolitans, forced into a racialised kind of suburbia, a mode of living and an identity which was not of their own choosing. And in doing so they lost a significant element of their identity as South Africans. They lost their right to determine their own identities. And they lost their place in Cape Town itself. As Small says, from now on they lived in the diaspora, the Cape Flats. There is such a strong sense of this in many of the stories visitors and officials tell, as they recount their lives in District Six as city, cosmopolitan lives. They talk about how they used to use the whole city, the harbour, Canal Gardens, the Mountain, the sea. All of these places were theirs, part of their space, who they were. As they talk, it is clear that difference was also important in the city, that structural and category differences, around religion and class for example, constituted part of the knowledge about people which they negotiated in their social relationships with them (see Hannerz, 1980, p. 149). They also talk of life around the harbour and the people from overseas who came into the District from the ships. Some speak of their 'colouredness' as a result of this as seamen and adventurers landed and established relationships with local women. Their whole 'differentness' is bound up in Cape Town the seaport, the cosmopolitan city connected to the other side of the Atlantic by sea and ship.

Cape Town is called the Mother City, the city of origin for both whites and coloured people, both of whom made it, despite apartheid's claims to the contrary when it annexed the cities for whites. The location of District Six close-by the original city centre with its monuments to colonialism, the Art Gallery, the House of Parliament, the Natural History Museum and so on elided its identity with that of Cape Town proper, while Table Mountain also drew the two into one, by encompassing them both as horizon.

As Western notes:

> By removing Coloureds from District Six, the Whites are doing more than clearing slums or underpinning their exclusive claim to central Cape Town's sacred space. *They are also destroying one of the symbols of whatever Coloured identity may exist, a space in part at least seven generations deep and one with associations with the emancipation of the slaves.*
>
> 1981, p. 150, italics in the original

In so doing the apartheid authorities transformed Cape Town as they had always intended, but at the same time they diminished it historically, since they destroyed Cape Town, the coloured city. They removed part of the sedimentation of history which *was* Cape Town. And museum people want to argue that they were an important part. One of the trustees expressed this through architecture.[12] Using also the photographs on the museum walls, he talked of how his home, an old 19th century two storey house, had been destroyed and of how an important part of Cape Town's history disappeared in this and other such demolitions. Obviously, its early establishment gave District Six a deep sedimentation of historical material culture. As coloured people were diminished then, so too was their city. This they are also saying in their stories of the lost jazz clubs, dance halls and cinemas, the lost street life, the colour, the noise, the vibrancy. They lost their cosmopolitan identity, but so in a way did Cape Town, since white society did not replace these things, these forms of sociality, these kinds of relations and practices.

This transformation of city and coloured identity has also to be seen as betrayal, something reflected in the stories of how people felt in their interactions with 'the Board' (see also Rive, 1989, Fortune, 1996, Adams and Suttner, 1988). People talk about shame in being told that they had to go, of being told where to live. In part this is shame at the interference of authority into the lives of people who deeply valued 'respectability'. Many analysts (see Western, 1981, Ross, 1992, Goldin, 1987 for example) have noted the importance of respectability in coloured culture, and it is possible that this had its roots in a mimetic response to dominant white, particularly English, culture, where in Taussig's terms (1993) mimesis is part of an appropriation of dominant culture which is all about coping with domination (see also Ross, 1992). Within a deep need for respectability, apartheid's residential control was shaming, diminishing. Several people told with enormous satisfaction how they had got together enough money to resist such control by buying a house of their own choosing. Further, the townships were places of control and surveillance, built in such a way that they could be sealed off and scrutinised in times of unrest (Christopher, 1994). The self-determination which accompanies respectability was undermined by the Group Areas Act. At the same time, the home and family seems to have been a crucial site of respectability so that the assault on respectability featured particularly in women's stories and the distinctions they made between themselves and others. Apartheid's Group Areas thus attacked coloured people at the very site of respectability — their residence, their home.

Another context of perceptions of betrayal is the privileging of the coloured population over the African population, particularly in the Western Cape, where coloureds were seen both as being more like the whites, and also useful as a buffer between whites and Africans. Afrikaans speaking in the main, coloured people were cultivated by those who in the 1950s appeared to turn on them and cast them out. Thus we find things like coloured people never having to carry passes as Africans did and in the Cape jobs were reserved for coloured people under the Coloured Employment Protection Act (Goldin, 1987, Humphries, 1992). Yet at the same time that a special relationship between white and coloured was being encoded in law, urban coloured people were decreed a threat and forcibly removed to the Cape Flats, as Africans had been before them.

Apartheid's betrayal provides a reconciliation function for the museum, which criticises apartheid at a collective and structural level through its focus on community.[13] And interestingly here, we find a final engagement with the state rhetorics of the new South Africa.

At one level the museum does provide a site in which people may express a relationship of identity between themselves and a new South Africa. They often assert that District Six already was what ideologues in the 'new dispensation' argue South Africa should strive to be today – a unity in diversity. Here they stress heterogeneity and respect for differences in culture, religion and race. For them the state rhetorics and narratives of nation are given concrete form, reality through memory and District Six somehow stands for 'the new South Africa'.

To understand walkers in the museum as playing out state rhetorics though is problematic if it implies necessary intention. For, even in the museum, but certainly outside, there is real ambivalence, are real divisions among coloured people, about the new South Africa and particularly the ANC government. Particularly in the Western

Cape, there are also very real differences of opinion about and support for the National Party and its role in the apartheid past.

Even among a group of people who share the experience of dispossession and dislocation under apartheid, people have different histories of response to the apartheid regime (James *et al.,* 1996). So it is also people with these different political histories who walk the map, constituting their pasts through similar processes.

In many ways, it is the encompassment of the walking within the museum with its overarching critique of apartheid which constitutes these acts as political acts of resistance. It is this encompassment in a post-apartheid South Africa which refigures the remembering of disruption and dispossession from within a variety of orientations towards apartheid as an act of protest. Within the overarching critical narrative suggested through the museum, apartheid is interrogated through one of its policies which was central to its entire ideological project. Yet this does not necessarily accompany or indeed constitute a full, overt or radical political critique on the part of the walkers. It certainly does not entail automatic approval of the regime today. And here again, it is the Cape Town identification which emerges as having potential in an identity politics which is characterised through such uncertainty, ambivalence and differentiation.

Imagining a South African identity for themselves *is* radical, though not necessarily thought of as such, in the context of a past in which a South African identity was denied to non-whites who were expected to develop an identity in terms of their racial category and 'South African' was reserved for whites (again coloureds were somewhat ambiguous in this regard, harder to see as a separate nation, since they had no separate space which was not also claimed by whites).

What is *also* radical in the context of apartheid's declaration of the city as white is the way in which some visitors and staff also saw themselves as Capetonian, occasionally even privileging this over South African. Here identity involved a reappropriation of the city which was taken from them. But this is only one side of such an appropriation. It can certainly be *made* radical in the context of the exclusions of the past, but if one shifts the context to the present and the building of a national identity, post-apartheid, this embracing of a Capetonian identity may also involve something different, more troubling and precarious. First, Capetonian may obscure the very real differences and conflicts among coloured people, particularly around current political allegiances. But second, and related to this, people seemed to be suggesting that, within South Africa, the content of 'South African' seemed to be uncertain and that 'Capetonian' was somehow clearer, less uncertain, easier. Given the massive obstacles in the way of delivering the 'brave new world', of overturning the inequalities of apartheid, just what is really 'new' is still problematic. And the TRC itself has contributed to this, demonstrating clearly the different worlds and realities inhabited by those today who would be South African.

It is not clear from the comments of the District Six walkers whether all South African people can yet imagine sharing history and memory to the point where they can embrace a clear new *South African* identity. This leaves something lesser (or different) available as identity. Because of the exclusions of apartheid, to embrace the identity of Capetonian *is* new, *is* engaging with present and future in a new polity, so it is also attractive, and attainable, as a position. It is radical, precisely because it is a re-appropriation, a demand for inclusion and the claiming of an identity taken away by apartheid as a fundamental principle of that regime.

Maybe here too we have 'Capetonian' synthesising the work of reconciliation which many feel is necessary *before* South Africa can become a single nation. Here, as Boyarin (1994, p. 2, see also Geyer, 1996) suggests, is a *politics* of memory in which memory actually constitutes the politics of national identity, rather than only the process of mobilising the past for political purposes, though of course this is *also* happening in South Africa today.

Conclusion

Geoffrey White (1991) notes that stories of the past are always discourses of identity. We see this in the stories which people recount prompted by the map in District Six Museum, but we also see operating White's corollary, that stories of the past actually constitute identity. This is a political process, producing a politics of memory which is fundamentally a construction of the present through an engagement with the apartheid regime. Post-apartheid is a substantial dimension of the politics of South Africa today. Operating as one location in which South Africans contemporarily can make their own meanings and their own accommodations to state rhetorics about country and nation, the District Six Museum suggests that what the 'new South Africa' is constituted out of a variety of identities, a variety of engagements with the past, a variety of pasts (Pechey, 1994). In the politics of memory enabled, generated by the map, South Africans who were ex-residents of District Six seem to be first asserting the social constitution of this area that apartheid managed to define in asocial terms, either as a problem, a desirable position for whites or simply a physical space to be managed and redeployed. Second they criticise, through recollection and comparison, the forms of collectivity and sociality which apartheid policies and administrators thought desirable for non-white people. Third, the retrieval of a more desirable past provides a way into new identity for them in post-apartheid South Africa as they take back urban citizenship, their identity as Capetonians. What is new is imagined in terms of, in engagement with, how they recollect the past.

Notes

1   This article is based on a 10 week period spent in Cape Town in the first half of
    1996 and a follow up visit in December 1996 and January 1997. I wish to thank the
    Department of Social Anthropology at the University of Cape Town for hosting
    my visit. I would especially like to thank the staff at the District Six Museum for
    their friendship, their generosity, kindness and enthusiasm. Without them this
    study could not have been done. Thanks also to the anonymous reviewer whose
    comments on an earlier version of the paper have proved invaluable in rewriting it.

2   Mamdani argues that the focus on territorial segregation in South Africa can be
    traced back to Smuts and that the way in which such policies were first and fore-
    most political, generated by what was seen as 'the native question' which was a
    question of minority control over a majority population, links South Africa under
    apartheid to colonialism in Africa generally, rather than differentiating South Africa
    from the rest of the continent.

3   Interestingly, in the case of a much earlier Cape Town, 1894, whites taking advan-
    tage of their generally greater wealth and moving into the suburbs had prompted
    some speculation that Cape Town's city could be left for coloureds, so producing
    the residential separation of white and coloured (Bickford-Smith, 1992, p. 48).

4   As many writers have stressed (see for example Smith, 1992, Lemon, 1995, Marks
    and Trapido, 1987), this enforcement was only ever imprecise, as non-white people
    resisted and evaded the controls, ultimately causing the breakdown of strict influx
    controls and residential segregation which was so central to apartheid's conception
    of the city.

5   People classified as coloured made up the largest grouping, but there were smaller
    populations of whites and Africans living in the area.

6   The museum from time to time mounts exhibitions which require the modifica-
    tion of this first layout. This initial format is important for the way in which it
    made clear the assumptions and aims of the museum creators.

7   When in January 1997 Robben Island was opened to tourists, as a one-time pris-
    oner, Lionel Davis was one of the tour guides appointed.

8   Another visitor expressed great anger at the exhibition, seeing it as romanticism
    and declaring that this was not what the struggle was for. He gave the poverty,
    overcrowding and lack of life chances for the children as factors to counter what he
    saw as an overly romantic view.

9   The similarities in the comments of Western's (1981) informants a short time after
    coloured people were moved from Mowbray seem to confirm this identification of
    critique as much as described past.

10 A Cape Town movement of mainly the Islamic coloured population, PAGAD set
    itself up to oppose the gangs and drug pushers in the townships. Its activities have

been highly visible in the media and full of controversy as gun related deaths have marked various demonstrations. Despite this, there has been approval that some action is being taken, the perception being that the police are unable to control violence and the possession of guns and drugs in the townships. In January 1997, a PAGAD demonstration which ended at the Caledon Square Police Station, outside the Museum created enormous interest and sympathy among visitors to the Museum.

11 One woman expressed this perfectly when she said that she had not really realised what was happening until the day they had to move and then she cried and cried.

12 Architecture was very topical at this time, since the Museum was mounting an exhibition of a photographic record made of District Six architecture as it was being destroyed. This exhibition actually straddled the map and was a source of some contention, since for some it undermined the power of the map. Certainly people had to crawl under the exhibited photographs to find their streets on the map.

13 Here it speaks to another dimension of apartheid not much covered by the Truth Commission with its focus on human rights violations to individuals.

References

Adams, H. and H. Suttner (1988). *William Street, District Six*, Diep River: Chameleon Press.

Bickford-Smith, V. (1992). 'A 'Special Tradition of Multi-racialism'? Segregation in Cape Town in the Late Nineteenth and Early Twentieth Centuries', in W.M. James and M. Simons (eds) *Class, Caste and Color: A Social and Economic History of the South African Western Cape,* New Brunswick (USA) and London: Transaction Publishers.

– (1990). 'The Origins and Early History of District Six to 1910', in S. Jeppie and C. Soudien (eds) *The Struggle for District Six: Past and Present,* Cape Town: Buchu Books.

Boyarin, J. (ed.) (1994). *Remapping Memory: The Politics of TimeSpace,* Minneapolis and London: University of Minnesota Press.

Bozzoli, B. (ed.) (1987). *Class, Community and Conflict: South African Perspectives,* Johannesburg: Ravan Press.

Braude, S. (n.d.). *People Were Living There: Sandra Braude Interviews Sandy Prosalendis,* Project Directory of the District Six Museum, Cape Town, distributed by District Six Museum.

Christopher, A.J. (1994). *The Atlas of Apartheid,* London and New York: Witwatersrand University Press.

Comaroff, J. and J. Comaroff (1992). *Ethnography and the Historical Imagination*, Boulder: Westview Press.

de Certeau, M. (1988). *The Practice of Everyday Life*, Berkeley: University of California Press.

Fortune, L. (1996). *The House in Tyne Street: Childhood Memories of District Six*, Cape Town: Kwela books.

Geyer, M. (1996). 'The Politics of Memory in Contemporary Germany', in J. Copjec (ed.) *Radical Evil*, London: Verso.

Goldin, I. (1987). 'The Reconstitution of Coloured Identity in the Western Cape', in S. Marks and S. Trapido (eds), *The Politics of Race, Class and Nationalism in Twentieth Century South Africa*, London: Longman.

Hannerz, U. (1992). *Cultural Complexity: Studies in the Social Organization of Meaning*, New York: Columbia University Press.

– (1980). *Exploring the City: Inquiries Toward an Urban Anthropology*, New York: Columbia University Press.

Hart, D.M. (1990). ' 'Political Manipulation of Urban Space' The Razing of District Six, Cape Town', in S. Jeppie and C. Soudien (eds) *The Struggle for District Six: Past and Present*, Cape Town: Buchu Books.

Humphries, R. (1992). 'Administrative Politics and the Coloured Labour Preference Policy during the 1960s', in W.M. James and M. Simons (eds) *Class, Caste and Color*.

Isaacson, M. (1996). 'Sharpen those Pencils, Roll up those Sleeves – the Stuggle may be Over but the Book is not Closed', *Sunday Independent*, 26 May.

James, W., D. Caliguire and K. Cullinan (1996). *Now That We are Free: Coloured Communities in a Democratic South Africa*, Cape Town: Institute for Democracy in South Africa.

James, W.G. and M. Simons (eds). (1992). *Class, Caste and Color: A Social and Economic History of the South African Western Cape*, New Brunswick (USA) and London: Transaction Publishers.

Jeppie, S. and C. Soudien (eds). (1990). *The Struggle for District Six: Past and Present*, Cape Town: Buchu Books.

Lemon, A.(ed.). (1995). *The Geography of Change in South Africa*, Chichester: John Wiley and Sons.

Mabin, A. (1994). 'Dispossession, Exploitation and Struggle: An Historical Overview of South African Urbanization', in D. Smith (ed.) *The Apartheid City and Beyond*.

Marks, S. and S. Trapido (eds). (1987). *The Politics of Race, Class and Nationalism in Twentieth Century South Africa*, London: Longman.

Mithlo, N.M. (1995). 'History is Dangerous', *Museum Anthropology*, 19 (2), pp. 50–7.

Pechey, G. (1994). 'Post-apartheid Narratives', in F. Barker, P. Hulme and M. Iversen (eds). *Colonial Discourse/ Postcolonial Theory*, Manchester and New York: Manchester University Press.

Pinnock, D. (1987). 'Stone's Boys and the Making of a Cape Flats Mafia', in B. Bozzoli (ed.) *Class, Community and Conflict: South African Perspectives*. Johannesburg: Ravan Press.

Prosalendis, S. (1995). 'Foreword', in South African National Gallery, *District Six: Image and Representation*, Cape Town: South African National Gallery and the District Six Museum.

Rive, R. (1989). *Advance, Retreat. Selected Short Stories*, Cape Town: David Philip.

– (1986). *'Buckingham Palace', District Six*. Cape Town: David Philip.

Ross, R. (1992). 'Structure and Culture in Pre-industrial Cape Town: A Survey of Knowledge and Ignorance', in W.M. James and M. Simons (eds) *Class, Caste and Color*.

Rossouw, R. (1996). '"District Six' under Threat Again', *Mail & Guardian*, 25 April.

Small, A. (1986). *District Six*, Linden: Fontein Publishing.

Smith, D.M. (ed.) *The Apartheid City and Beyond: Urbanization and Social Change in South Africa*, London and New York: Routledge and Witwatersrand University Press.

Soudien, C. (1990). 'District Six: From Protest to Protest', in S. Jeppie and C. Soudien (eds) *The Struggle for District Six: Past and Present*, Cape Town: Buchu Books.

Soudien, C. and L. Meltzer (1995). 'Representation and Struggle', in South African National Gallery and the District Six Museum, *District Six: Image and Representation*, Cape Town: South African National Gallery.

Taussig, M. (1993). *Mimesis and Alterity: A Particular History of the Senses*, New York: Routledge.

Western, J. (1981). *Outcast Cape Town*, London: George Allen and Unwin.

White, G.M. (1991). *Identity Through History: Living Stories in a Solomon Islands Society*, Cambridge: Cambridge University Press.

Young, J. (1993). *The Texture of Memory: Holocaust Memorials and Meaning*, New Haven and London: Yale University Press.

CHAPTER EIGHT

What's in the name 'Coloured'?

Denis-Constant Martin

The South African usage of the terms 'coloured',[1] 'culture', or the combination 'coloured' and 'culture' are not value free. Questions and debates surrounding the validity of these terms and expressions illustrate the extent to which apartheid classification policies as defined in the Population Registration Act of 1950 have impacted upon all aspects of social life and been interiorised by South Africans.

If, even today, after 1990 and 1994, a section of the South African population continues to be called coloured, if many people still use that word to talk about themselves, it is because systematic and recurring practices of designation and separation have cemented a distinctive community from heterogenous elements. It is also because the men and women who have been, so to speak, 'locked in' the same group for over three centuries had to invent a way of living together, which eventually contributed to consolidating their difference from the other South Africans. It is finally because many of these men and women thought that this style of community living was the foundation of their social universe and adopted, even though reluctantly sometimes, the appellation 'coloured' which had been originally imposed on them by others.

Hence the group called coloured can only be approached as one composed of individuals who were classified as such in the course of South Africa's history.[2] It is impossible to operate a distinction between coloureds and other South Africans. Attributed physical, social, religious or linguistic features masquerading as markers of differentiation bind them to, rather than distinguish them from, the South African population as a whole: as a matter of fact, we find all shades of skin colour, ranging from very fair to very dark amongst them, as well as various types of phenotypical features combining Asian, African and European traits. Though many live in extremely poor conditions, we find a middle class and intellectuals amongst them. They are either Christians or Muslims. Many consider Afrikaans as their first language, while the majority is bilingual, and in some families only English is used. These factors amplify the bonds they have in common with the rest of the South African population, and cannot subsequently be considered as markers of distinction. However, the sole criterion for distinguishing coloureds from the other South Africans is the result of the Group Areas Act of 1950: as a consequence of apartheid, a majority still live in particular neighbourhoods – the former specifically demarcated 'coloured townships' – although since 1990 some of those who can afford it tend to move to other areas. A further distinction would have to be made between urban dwellers and those living on farms in close contact with their white employers, and at times in contact with workers belonging to different categories.

What's in the name 'Coloured'?

In other words, a group of human beings was defined and nominated by governmental decree.[3] Members of this designated group invented specific life-styles which gave form, content and substance to otherwise scattered pockets of people. Invented life-styles and traditions helped bond the group into a community allowing outsiders to this invented community to identify it as a singularly different entity within the mosaic of South African populations. The combination of partly representing the designs of a racist state and partly being the product of a self-invented singularity renders the issue of a 'coloured culture' problematic. Especially from within the coloured community.[4]

The very idea of a coloured culture is, to some, symptomatic of how the apartheid state used it to effectuate a separation between South Africans. They reject the term coloured on the ground that it has been used as a means to mask the squalid living conditions of the oppressed in South Africa, and to prevent the victims of apartheid from finding a common cause against the oppressor. It therefore follows that these critiques condemn and proscribe all forms of tools and mechanisms which are likely to undermine the unity of the wretched of South Africa. Thus, the only demarcating line acceptable to these critiques is one that demonstrates the effects of segregationist policies: the dominating whites and the oppressed 'blacks'. 'Blacks' in this instance becomes the homogenous category depicting the suffering and the exclusion of a set of human beings denied the right to design and influence their own destiny.

To others, coloureds did create a unique culture whose manifestations are obvious, a culture they have the right to claim and be proud of. This point of view can be expressed with a variety of nuances. Some wish that a coloured identity should be asserted and defended by political groups and institutions, the dream of an autonomous coloured state – a 'kleurlingstan' – being sometimes, although exceptionally, mentioned. Others stress the contribution of coloureds to South African culture as a whole and therefore insist that they are fully South African.

This discussion takes place mainly among the 'elite'. A great number of coloureds – probably a majority of them workers, traders, artisans, the unemployed – continue to live in areas where they were once forced to dwell, and live there in a way they consider their own. Occasions of fun and happiness, whether involving families and friends (like weddings or picnics) or voluntary organisations (such as concerts and competitions of choirs, brass bands or new year clubs) are not so many and therefore have great sentimental value.

Coloureds were oppressed by the apartheid regime; they were considered with scorn by the dominant group and, to a certain extent, they interiorised that stigma. Under the Group Areas Act, in the 1960s and 1970s, they have been removed from areas where families had been living for a long time. Lots of memories have a bitter taste. Today, life is hard. Disadvantaged groups in the coloured community are still threatened by social scourges like unemployment, alcoholism, drug addiction and gangsterism. This makes it all the more important to strengthen communities.[5] To many, festivals and celebrations are a great help in this respect and the idea of a culture does not mean more than living on and keeping traditions alive, but activities showing the reality of this culture are essential: it is not so much talked about, elaborated upon, as enacted.

From slaves to Coloureds

The diversity of these viewpoints is indicative of the existence of social, ideological and political differences within the coloured community. These differences developed over the last three centuries. Slaves formed the original core of the coloured population of South Africa. The first slaves were brought to the Cape in 1658, and in 1834, the moment of emancipation, slaves numbered 36 274. They originated from many varied regions: the East Indies (the actual Indonesia and Malaysia), India, Madagascar, East Africa and West Africa.[6] The majority of the slaves worked in the Cape colony, either on farms or vineyards and were in close contact with the white farmers.[7] Of the remaining, approximately one third worked in towns as domestic servants, craftsmen and salesmen.

Almost as long as slavery lasted, those born outside South Africa outnumbered the 'Creoles'. Frequent sales in the Cape colony led to a scattering of the slave population. Dispersion and the difficulty to maintain contact between slaves hampered the formation of slave family groupings, and subsequently that of a slave community. This practically obliterated the possibility of slaves rebelling as a group. Left with individual strategies to escape slavery, individuals fleeing their masters sought refuge among the Khoi-San or Bantu speaking peoples. Where possible, they bought their freedom, and later that of their relatives or beloved ones.[8]

Thus by 1838, the population of the Cape colony was made up of white colonists, Khoi-San aborigines and a group of heterogenous people whose sole common feature was that they were of mixed parentage: descendants of European pioneers and Khoi-San women; of settlers and slaves; former 'free blacks' – i.e. political prisoners deported from the East Indies, and emancipated slaves – former slaves; and all those individuals who could be considered as neither white nor indigenous Africans. Initially this heterogenous population mostly lived in rural areas. This changed with the emancipation laws, which allowed them to migrate towards the cities, especially Cape Town, making it a real melting pot.

In Cape Town, people of different origins and diverse life experiences rubbed shoulders and lived in close neighbourliness in the same areas. This led to the inventing of a common lifestyle which helped to interpret the world through a new but common prism. This way of adapting to an urban life-style allowed them to play a major role in this 'Tavern of the Seas', as the port-city was sometimes dubbed. As domestic servants, artisans, workers and hawkers, fisherfolk and stevedores, they came into contact with all those who set foot in South Africa. Thus with white commoners, Jews, Portuguese, Greeks, West Indians, Americans and others who only passed through – especially sailors who left them with lasting impressions of a world bursting with experience through languages, stories and songs.

The brushing together of different peoples in the Cape colony was accompanied by the crystallising of differences between them. Among the political exiles at the Cape were Muslim Saints who laid the foundations of a South African Islam which gained many followers among the slaves. Later, Christians too began to show an interest in the slave population and their descendants.[9] The Christians' concern for the spiritual well-being of the slaves led to a large number of them becoming Catholics, Calvinists, Anglicans, or followers of other Protestant churches.

Among the 'free blacks' an elite group developed, which illustrates the burgeoning differentiation that was to be seen in the Cape. This elite differentiated itself from the rest in economic and intellectual terms. Due to family networks and an education provided by the Christian and Muslim schools, these 'free blacks' were able to encourage and sustain entrepreneurship among the traders and craftsmen. As a result, certain parts of the city became associated with particular groups: the area around the mosques of the Bo-Kaap, at the foot of Signal Hill, was occupied by middle and working-class Muslims, known as 'Malays'. The Malays distinguished themselves from the other groups by claiming relations (real or mythical) with the political exiles from the East. In the area between Table Mountain and the port, which later was to become District Six, lived families of Muslim and Christian dock workers, industrial labourers (mainly from the textile industry) together with hawkers and pedlars. Lastly, the well-to-do settled in various neighbourhoods, from Walmer Estate, just above District Six, to the Southern suburbs.

Facing white power

Despite being subjected to discriminatory measures and being objects of social ostracism, coloureds at the end of the 19th and opening of the 20th centuries enjoyed a measure of civil rights that were denied to the other blacks. They could vote, be elected into political office, form political organisations which inevitably were led by economic and intellectual elites. The *modus operandi* of these political organisations was to demand an improvement of living conditions. The Stone[10] and the African People's Organisation under the leadership of Dr Abdurahman were both activist and legalist movements; they were examples of how political activity within the coloured community was centred around the idea of upliftment. The elite members of these political organisations were aware that the majority of coloureds were eking out a living in degrading moral and material conditions. Thus, uplifting their standard of living through the medium of education was also a means of acquiring points in the desire to be recognised as civilised: points on the civilisation scale determined according to the canons of white South African society.

The few whites, like I.D. du Plessis,[11] who later took an interest in the culture of the coloured and Malay peoples in the Cape, played a major role in reinforcing the idea that white culture epitomised the principles of civilisation. To this end they worked relentlessly to prove that coloureds were different from the Africans. This alleged difference allowed I.D. du Plessis to attach coloureds to the Afrikaner population, and thus to the whites, but in a subordinate position.[12] They were considered subordinate because the majority of coloureds still had to comply with the so-called established norms of civilisation tipping in the favour of whites.[13] As part of this strategy of 'divide and rule' internal distinctions within the coloured community were sharpened, and 'Malay' culture was given precedence over coloured culture.

For a long time the coloured elite struggled to be recognised by the white rulers. Thus, even when they placed themselves in opposition to the dominant white power base, they sought to prove their level of civilisation by demonstrating to what extent they had succeeded in assimilating those very same codes and values that the whites used as markers of differentiation. In contrast, their attitude towards the coloured working class was ambiguous: they wanted to distance themselves from the ordinary people in order to demonstrate their ability to enter into a dialogue with the white rulers; but, at the same time, they claimed that their mission was to 'uplift' the community and that they had a right to speak on behalf of all coloureds.

Political attitudes got polarised after the National Party came into power in 1948 and, even more, after it passed laws eventually depriving the coloured people of all their civil rights in 1956. At first, some considered there was no other alternative than collaboration with the rulers and participation in the system while others (notably followers of the Non European Unity Movement) adopted a systematic boycott strategy (see Lewis, 1987). Later, with more and more people being affected by the Group Areas Act and other apartheid laws in the Cape region, struggles against apartheid became more intense and reached a climax in the mid-1980s with the students' revolt; many coloureds then joined or supported organisations linked to the United Democratic Front.

Among coloureds, visions of South Africa, and of their place in the country, were therefore very complex. There was a general ambivalence towards white domination. A process of class differentiation had generated differences in attitudes and political strategies, and a political rift between collaborationists and anti-apartheid activists had developed. Those factors were entangled, producing paradoxical side-effects such as the will of a militant intellectual elite[14] to distance themselves from the working class culture because they saw it as expressing a bad image of coloureds – reinforcing the stereotype shared by many whites that all coloureds were 'Coons', that is, individuals behaving in a degrading fashion and therefore reinforcing white prejudices – when the very criteria they used to assess this working class culture were those of white bourgeois conformism. Thus they were disowning underprivileged members of their community in the name of values forged by those whose rule they were fighting. Yet, the working classes found in their cultural manifestations, and in particular in the new year festivals, solace from the ordinary oppression they had to endure and claimed in their own way, in symbolic expressions and sometimes not without hesitations caused by the interiorisation of the inferiority stigma, a humanness they were denied by the whites and a cultural legitimacy they were refused by the coloured intelligentsia.

It is against this contrasted backdrop that indecisions as to whether to accept and support a coloured identitarian discourse or not, to recognise or reject the existence of a coloured culture must be understood.[15] Before 1948, the idea of a coloured culture, largely identified with the working class, seemed acceptable, even if with some condescension, insofar as it was construed by the elite as a set of manifestations revealing not just the destitution of the coloured people, but also their inventiveness, their communal solidarity and their ability to uplift themselves. It should be remembered that Dr Abdurahman, leader of the African People's Organisation from 1905 to 1940, a medical doctor trained in Great Britain and the most important coloured politician of the first half of the twentieth century, was a patron of the reorganised Coon carnivals in the 1920s.

After 1948, once 'coloured' had become transformed into a rigid legal category,[16] these same manifestations, which had indeed been manipulated by the white authorities in charge of 'coloured affairs', became perceived by the anti-apartheid activists as a spectacle given to the 'masters' and displaying the servility of people accepting the stereotype of the 'jolly and happy Coon', staying away from the struggle, while collaborators pretended to continue representing the community in spite of the humiliations that were showered upon them year after year. 'Coloured culture' therefore could only appear, from an anti-racist point of view, as a concept reinforcing the ideological system of apartheid, although the manifestations that gave it life were not at all understood in that manner by those who organised them and participated in them. Recently, since the abolition of the hated apartheid laws, these popular manifestations once again rouse the interest of members of the coloured intelligentsia (academics, teachers, professionals) who cannot be suspected of harbouring any sympathy for the former rulers.

The resilience of what is eventually construed as 'culture' (whatever meaning is given to that word), the reservoir of creativity that it undeniably constitutes, and the hopes as well as anxieties entertained about the 'new South Africa', probably explain these symptoms of a change of attitude. This also indicates that, in the 1990s, more people may feel like emphasising a coloured identity, whatever content they put into it. In this post-apartheid situation, coloured identity and coloured culture are becoming political stakes, as both national and local elections have demonstrated. The National Party, the African National Congress, and other political or non-political organisations now proclaim they recognise coloured culture and coloured identity, and that they are their best advocates.[17] What is interesting is that, for the time being, no exclusively coloured organisation of some standing has emerged in politics, even Western Cape politics, exclusively to defend 'coloured interests'.

Cross fertilisation and invention

One of the reasons for this situation may have to do with the extremely diverse nature of the manifestations embodying coloured culture, in the broadest sense. Spending New Year's Eve and the morning of New Year's Day in the streets of the Bo-Kaap, watching the Malay Choirs then the Coons march and sing; analysing musical repertoires, body languages, costumes and make-up, etc. is enough to convince anyone of the conclusion that it can only be defined as a culture of the heterogeneous. Some musical repertoires and certain festivals are indisputably particular to coloured people or, to be more precise, to a majority of those who live in the Western Cape Province. Slaves were already judged 'gifted' for music and rich whites hired them for their balls and parties. After emancipation, these talents flowered to entertain not only the white public but coloureds themselves. And in the process of community formation, music did occupy a central place: collectively elaborated, distinct from other types of music heard in South Africa at the end of the nineteenth century, although sometimes borrowing from them, it provided a shared and unique sound environment for family gatherings, especially weddings, picnics and religious festivals. Sufi Islam did not object to music, Christian services made large use of singing. The possible sources of inspiration were many and varied: old Dutch songs, Christian hymns, African or Eastern tunes reformulated during the times of slavery and sailors' songs and shanties from all over the world. To these was added, in the middle of the 19th century, all that was circulating as 'international variety music' or 'parlour music' (see Van der Merwe, 1989), notably music used in English or American 'black face minstrel' shows.

New Year festivals provided numerous opportunities to present this culture and its unending reformulations: in South Africa it is summer, it is holiday time, it is the festive season. These are the 'big days', when one can temporarily forget the ordinary worries of the rest of the year. Two series of celebrations took shape in the Bo-Kaap and District Six at the end of the nineteenth century; they became more formally organised in the course of the twentieth century and today are still very much part of Cape Town's new year atmosphere. On New Year's Day, costumed revellers known as Coons throng the streets of Cape Town in their magnificent and brilliantly coloured costumes.[18] This represents months of intense and arduous preparations by the different troupes competing for the most coveted glory of winning the trophies. The Coons take possession of the city, even though fleetingly, they march through areas where coloured people were not allowed to live, affirming thereby that they belong to the Cape – and that the Cape belongs to them – despite prejudices and laws. Through the originality of their music, their dances and their dress, they proclaim the existence of their members as creative human beings. And by the same token, in the face of the narrow cultural parochialism of the dominant group, they paint Cape Town with the bright colours of Africa, Asia, America and Europe. In so doing they assert that they are part of the wider world.

After January 1907, the carnival became institutionalised. Troupes assembled in stadia and confronted one another in various competitions. Their right to parade in the streets was disputed on several occasions. The cradle of their culture, District Six,[19] was destroyed during the decade 1970–80, but ultimately, nothing could stop the Coons from celebrating their New Year carnival. In the small hours of New Year's Day, before the Coons reveal their magnificent costumes to the public, choirs invade the streets of the Bo-Kaap, the old 'Malay Quarter' of Cape Town. Going from house to house and street to street, they sing lively songs with humorous lyrics which at times are a deriding comment on current social problems. Known as 'moppies', these songs are accompanied by string instruments and the emblematic drum, the ghoema. Moppies sung to the beat of ghoemas form part of the repertoire of the Coons as well. But the old *Nederlands Liedjes*, sentimental songs sung by a soloist with melismatic ornamentations, characteristic of Far Eastern music, are the forte of the Malay Choirs.

The soloist sings in front of a group whose response to his sentimental lamenting is based on simple Western tonal chords. Also known as the 'Nagtroepe' (night troupes) when appearing on New Year's Day, they hold their own competitions in late January, or in February, and sometimes even in March, where the best Malay Choirs are chosen.

The coloureds in South African culture

Muslims and Christians alike join the Coons. Malay Choirs have a predominantly Muslim membership.[20] It is not unusual to belong to both a carnival club and a choir, and some choir 'coaches' are also musical directors of a Coon troupe. There is no rift between them; they represent two essential facets of Cape Town's coloured culture, or, more precisely, of the Cape peninsula working class subcultures. To the coloured intellectual elites and the bourgeoisie the Coons, choirs, carnivals and competitions were obstacles in the process of political conscientisation. To them this sub-culture was a form of escapism. A degrading exercise where participants were seen as impersonating clowns and making spectacles of themselves for the pleasure and amusement of their white masters.

This criticism was more specifically directed at the Coons. It should be pointed out that this elite, in considering especially the Coon carnival as an overt manifestation of culture as defined by the apartheid system, was in essence denying disadvantaged members of the coloured community the opportunity to make light of their daily sufferings. What they perceived as an acceptance of the classification imposed by the apartheid system was for the more disadvantaged members of the community an opportunity to rejoice, to have fun. A break in their ordinary life which helped them to bear scorn and poverty, which contributed to bind segments of the community together and gave them strength to endure trials and tribulations. An occasion when they could demonstrate their creativity.[21]

As a matter of fact, if 'coloured culture' cannot be reduced to these festivals, it would be futile to deny that an important part of coloured people's contribution to South African culture derives from them, that is, from what was invented to make New Year's entertainments more exciting, to beat other teams in the competitions. Here probably lies the very basis of the controversy about 'coloured culture'. It is not possible to conceive of such a culture if the expressions that are the more particular to it (like festivals and music) are separated from other phenomena which tie this 'culture' to a global South African culture to which people formerly classified as coloured have also contributed a great deal.

It can even be argued that 'it is impossible to apprehend a 'coloured culture' which is not South African, or a 'South African culture' which is not mixed and therefore has not been fertilised by creations originating in the various communities forming the South African population. The Afrikaans language is the first and most profound example of this: Afrikaans which, in the opinion of the ultra conservative Afrikaners, is the first perimeter of their 'identity', is in reality the product of a communication system established between the slaves and their masters at the Cape. Eating habits, the style of furniture, like the language of communication, are but examples of a protracted process of cultural cross-fertilisation between the different populations at the

Cape. But, for the sake of brevity, let us look more closely at music as a an example of cultural interaction.[22] New year celebrations in Cape Town were the training ground for many of South Africa's outstanding artists: Abdullah Ibrahim (Dollar Brand), Basil 'Manentierg' Coetzee, Jonathan Butler, Robbie Jansen are musicians who bear testimony to the importance of the Mother-City in the development of South African jazz and pop music. They also influence musicians who came to Cape Town from other regions and from different social backgrounds: Dudu Pukwana, Winston Mankuku, Simon Goldberg and Chris McGregor. The *moppies*, the *Nederlands Liedjes*, and songs imported from the Americas were adapted by Talie Petersen to the language of the musical that is very popular in South Africa. At the same time, the coloured elite of Cape Town joined or supported the Eoan Group, a school of ballet, singing and music. In this way they aspired to break into the Western culture of arts which was dominated by the whites, and prove that they could represent it skilfully. The Eoan Group, originally founded by whites for coloureds in the 1930s, produced remarkable results. It produced the first South African troupe to stage Italian operas sung in Italian.[23]

Despite the difference of interest, bridges were built between the plebeian festivals and the academy of classical music: Joseph Manca, a longtime director of the Eoan Group, was also an adjudicator for carnival competitions. Moreover, some of the most famous South African opera singers, like Joseph Gabriels, started their careers as stars of the Coons.

A similar situation developed in the field of literature. The writings of Adam Small, the coloured poet in Afrikaans, form an inseparable part of Cape Town. A vehement critic of the apartheid system, he uses Cape Town and the experiences and sufferings of the coloured and Malay people to portray the inhumanity of the regime. Some of South Africa's great writers born in the North or in the East, like Peter Abrahams, Don Matera, Achmat Dangor or Bessie Head, are coloureds. Others, like Alex La Guma and Richard Rive, have used the popular Cape Town dialect and social realities of District Six to introduce a new form of expression into English. However Richard Rive, who superbly captured the generation gap and the lack of understanding between the coloured proletariat and the elite, made a clear political statement by refusing the epithet 'coloured' and called his (1981) autobiography *Writing Black*.

Messages, exchanges, connections ...

All things considered, the divergent opinions expressed about 'coloured culture' are perhaps only a further illustration of the ambiguity of the term 'culture' itself, and of the way it is used in South Africa. If culture implies 'civilisation' within a hierarchical paradigm wherein 'civilised' and 'uncivilised' coexist, then the content of a 'coloured culture' is a stake in the confrontation between those who deny its existence and consider it to be just the barbarous mode of expression of an 'uncivilised' people, and those who demand that the persons who have created it be recognised as 'civilised' and respected as such.

Both these views function on the basis of mutual exclusivity. It is therefore not surprising that they were bandied about in South Africa, moulded and formed by a discourse rooted in a philosophy of separation and classification. However, adopting a different view of culture and concurring with the anthropologists' view – culture as a largely symbolic structure of signification and comprehension – ties in with the philosophical idea of culture being a web of connections.[24] An idea that has its origins in the philosophy of aesthetics, and which allows us clearly and unambiguously to situate the coloureds of South Africa.[25] Like a continuum, coloured culture can traverse all strata of society. It ranges from the more specific, for instance the popular festivals in Cape Town, to the general which embodies elements of structure, meaning and understanding shared by *all* South Africans, and which is part of human universal creativity.

In this perspective, looking at 'coloured culture' no longer entails separating it. In fact, such a view entirely breaks with the stereotypes of 'colouredness'. For, if it is to make any sense, it demands that relations and interactions be emphasised. Approaching coloured culture then implies considering a series of practices carried out in settings that can be historically, geographically and socially located and takes into consideration their links to other practices carried out in other settings. In so doing one realises that locating certain practices is impossible without establishing their links with practices elsewhere. It also requires examining cross-fertilisation processes that result from the relationships existing between those two sets of practices. They influence and can be influenced; they are necessarily hybridised.

To illustrate, let's look at the linguistic domain, which, as in the case of Afrikaans spoken by coloured of the Cape, undoubtedly contains a dialect, or even dialects. The social and cultural specificities revealed by the studies of Gerald L. Stone (1991) and Achmat Davids (1991) are relevant and meaningful because they represent an aspect in the use of Afrikaans in the South African context where the different facets of Afrikaans also englobe a standard form of Afrikaans as taught at schools, Afrikaans used by rural Afrikaners, Afrikaans spoken by bilingual speakers whose first language is English, and Afrikaans heard on television and radio. The same applies to culinary habits: the distinctions made between Malay cuisine, Indian specialities and South African recipes in fact reveal the extent to which all of these different forms of cuisine are related. The boboties, koeksisters, curries and biryanis, and of course the ubiquitous samoosa are examples of dishes that are appropriated by more than just a single community.

Similarly in music, there are evident traces of interaction between the music of coloured people and that of white rural dwellers, the *boeremusik*. Carnival songs and tunes sung by Malay Choirs have deeply influenced all kinds of South African music: jazz, pop and musical comedy (see David Coplan, 1985 and Veit Erlmann, 1991). The writings of Adam Small, Richard Rive, Alex La Guma and Zoë Wicomb (in both English and Afrikaans) talk of the experiences of the coloureds of the Western Cape. But, just like the short stories of Achmat Dangor and the novels of Bessie Head, they clearly have a universal outreach. These examples illustrate conclusively that those individuals classified as coloured – and as such expected to draw on a particular 'coloured culture' – have contributed in creating a South Africanness that transcends the racial and ethnic boundaries imposed by the apartheid state. In other words, coloured 'structures of signification and comprehension' can be said to exist only insofar as they are fully South African. By the same token, South African 'structures of signification and comprehension' exist only insofar as they are *mestiza*, that is mixed, which evidently implies coloured. Neither of them could exist without the connections that bind them. This demonstrates that, finally, South African culture is nothing but *mestiza*.

Even if some of those who have been labelled coloured during apartheid do not want to associate themselves with the festivals and the music of the Cape Town working class, these manifestations of a unique culture nevertheless proclaim the humanness (that is a South Africanness which implies belonging to the universal community of human beings) of those who were the most despised people in South Africa.[26] This ambiguity is well captured in the way some coloureds readily describe themselves as 'in-betweeners'. Sandwiched between the majority of the blacks and whites who have or who wielded power, they consider their present position in South Africa noninfluential. This form of political fatalism was fed by National Party propaganda, which instilled in many the fear of Africans. To this we can add the trials and tribulations that characterised the experiences of coloureds in the Cape. The expulsions from District Six, some well-to-do suburbs and other areas in the southern suburbs form part of a painful experience and is still vivid in the memory of many (see Shamil Jeppie and Craig Soudien, 1990).

All along, this feeling of helplessness has been counterbalanced by efforts to build a community, despite the contempt, the segregation and the repression. When members of the community describe it, it often sounds like the dream of an ideal world where all human beings would be united, helpful, lively, gifted and witty, and tolerant of differences, religious in particular; a community in which there would be no dearth of parties and festivals enlivened by music and dance. It is an idyllic vision that is evoked when one discusses the New Year celebrations with supporters of the Coons and the choirs. District Six is usually presented as the proof that this vision can be real; and nostalgic stories tell of the time when even gangsters were kind-hearted.[27] The 'culture' that gets its best exposure during the New Year celebrations had a dual function: to express this dream and, in a more concrete fashion, to build up relationships within the community and strengthen feelings of belonging. But at the same time, it allowed the community to avoid being trapped in the ghetto the government wanted to impose upon them by maintaining cultural ties linking the Cape with Europe, the East and the Americas. Thus, not only did it answer coloureds' desire to keep in touch with the wider world, it also provided a frame of reference to all those who were designated as coloured by the segregationist regime and contributed to the organisation of various concepts of 'colouredness', even when they were developed in opposition to this culture. Finally, it served as one of the most fertile grounds in which grew and blossomed talents which are evidence of the contribution of members of the coloured community to South African and universal arts.[28]

'They have a culture to be proud of ...'

The debate is not yet over. On the contrary, it has been recently revived. This is because the position that coloureds are going to occupy in the future South African society is not clear, and because they fear the unknown; and because the question of whether they should occupy one particular position just because of their belonging to one of the former apartheid categories is still an object of discussion.[29] Frequently invoked in this discussion is the creation in the new political dispensation of a province where coloured people are a majority (the Western Cape Province), the fact that in this province a great number of coloured voters, in particular in the working class, supported the National Party and allowed a former Minister for Law and Order, Hernus Kriel, to become regional Premier. If it is clear that there was a 'coloured' vote in the 1994 election and that it accounts for the results, the motivations behind this vote are complex (see Martin, 1994). Current anxieties raised by the debate on 'affirmative action'; disappointments at what some see as a lack of interest for coloureds on the part of the ANC government, compounded by the National Party leadership in the provincial government, tend to increase the feeling that in the new South Africa there is none to take care of 'coloured interests'. In front of recurrent social problems such as unemployment and lack of good educational facilities, drug addiction and gangsterism generating violence, the temptation is great to retire within the community, to put forward ideas of auto-organisation and support self-defence groups, to adhere to a fundamentalist conception of Islam or Christianity.

When one considers the question of a 'coloured identity' in today's South Africa, what emerges is a situation full of ambiguities and contradictions: people who were formerly opposed to the very idea of a 'coloured culture' are now rediscovering it and presenting it as a contribution to South African culture as a whole;[30] people who claimed they would never vote for a 'kaffir', a 'terrorist who spent a long time in prison' (interview), felt honoured when President Nelson Mandela opened the 1996 carnival, wearing a Coon uniform while delivering his inaugural speech; people who until recently professed religious tolerance but whose daily life is affected by a level of violence that neither the provincial nor the national governments seem able to curb are now supporting PAGAD (People Against Gangsterism and Drugs), an organisation that accommodates fundamentalist Muslim views (although non-Muslims also participate). PAGAD advocates violent retaliation against drug dealers; they march and demonstrate to impress the authorities and the public, and frighten targeted gangsters; some members carry arms in public. Although PAGAD claims to have no hidden political agenda, their strong grassroots base in coloured townships could allow them to develop into an instrument of political mobilisation.

Finally, the ANC is confronted with an acute crisis in the Western Cape, because of its incapacity to be, at the same time, the main force in the national government, the party defending the interests of 'the people' as a whole – that is the majority of South Africans – and the political home for Western Cape coloureds. In his address to the 1996 Provincial Conference, Rev. Chris Nissen, a former ANC Western Cape leader, expressed very precisely the challenge the party is confronted with.

> It is important to give due recognition to the coloured people of this province. Gone are the days when we talk about so-called coloureds. They are not superior to anyone or inferior, they have a culture to be proud of.
>
> *Weekly Mail & Guardian*, 1996

The ANC needs to recognise this and give them its full support. The ANC must play a role in bringing communities together. Chris Nissen nowhere elaborates on the 'culture to be proud of'. He seems to admit that people who have lived 'through the coloured experience' (as some now say) or who 'have been forged from the coloured cauldron' (Vincent Kolbe, personal communication) probably share a set of common traits or values, implicitly derived from that experience. Just as people having lived through other experiences are likely to share other traits and values. His speech, and in particular the two last sentences, shows that discussing coloured identity is once again inseparable from discussing the nation as a whole.

It highlights the dilemma of the new South Africa in general: how to define and recognise communities without perpetuating apartheid categories, attitudes and behaviours; how to support communal cultures in a way that will 'bring communities together' instead of setting them apart or even pitting them against one another.

Notes

– A French version of this article was published by *Les Temps Modernes* (no. 585, November-December 1995: 613–29). I wish to thank Mr Vincent Kolbe, of the

District Six Museum, Cape Town, for his commentaries on a previous English version of this paper, and Dr Rehana Ebrahim-Vally, of the University of the Witwatersrand, Johannesburg, for her suggestions and corrections which helped clarify some issues raised in this paper, and also made it easier to read.

1   In this paper, I follow a usage common both in speech and in print and, for the sake of simplicity, use the word 'coloured' without inverted commas; this of course does not mean, as this chapter will show, any adhesion to or support for ideologies and behaviours separating human beings in terms of 'race' or culture.

2   The apartheid state classified 3 378 000 people or 8.38% of the population as coloured. 1 119 000 or 56.8% of the coloured group live in the Western Cape Province where they constitute 52% of the total population (*Race Relations Survey 1993/4*).

3   This does not deny the existence of affinities which can push individuals to gather involuntary organisations or to try and live close to one another; what is meant here is that individuals or families were not allowed to reject the categories imposed upon them and to refuse the policies applied to them; those who opposed them did so at a great risk. However, when possible, a small number chose another strategy and decided to 'try for white'; this required total rejection of the community of origin. For a more detailed account, see Watson (1970).

4   Part of the data used in this article was collected during field research trips in Cape Town in 1993 and 1994. Funded by the Centre d'Etudes et de Recherches Internationales (CERI, Paris) and the Institut Français de Rrecherche en Afrique (IFRA, Nairobi), with support from the University of Western Cape, the research was conducted on New Year festivities in Cape Town. The viewpoints on the coloured community and coloured culture (which forms the object of this article) were drawn from non-directive interviews recorded in the course of this research.

5   One of the recurring themes in interviews of leaders of carnival clubs or choirs is that they aim at 'keeping the youth off the streets' where they run the risk of becoming 'bad elements'.

6   It is estimated that 36.40% of the total of the slave population in South Africa came from India; 31.47% from the East Indies; 26.65% from Africa (of which more than half were brought from Madagascar). For more information see Da Costa and Achmat Davids (1994) p. 2, Worden (1994) and Shell (1994).

7   Direct contact between slaves and white masters was facilitated by the size of the farms. Most of the farms being small meant that slaves on these farms numbered between 5 and 20.

8   As in other British colonies, emancipation was followed by a four-year period of 'apprenticeship'. Hence, slaves were granted total freedom in 1838 only.

9   The Dutch East India Company prohibited the sale of baptised slaves. As a result, their value considerably diminished, thus discouraging missionary activities.

10   Open air meetings took place from May 1901 near a large boulder 'at the top of

Clifton Street [District Six], Sunday morning, weather permitting, at 10 o'clock'. See Lewis (1987).

11 I.I. du Plessis, an Afrikaner poet, made extensive use of coloured culture and dialect of the Afrikaans language in his poetry. His attitude and approach towards coloureds and Malays in the Cape made him, especially within the Afrikaner community, a patron (he was instrumental in the creation of the Cape Malay Choir Board) and 'expert' of coloured and Malay communities (this led to him being appointed as a Secretary of Coloured Affairs after 1948).

12 'Dr I.I. Du Plessis, Secretary for Coloured Affairs, told the discussion group on race relations of the University of Stellenbosch last night that he hoped the time would come when that section of the coloured intelligentsia who withheld cooperation from the Department of Coloured Affairs because its work was done on a basis of separation would realise that this work did not push the coloured man away, but clasped him, as a Westerner, even more strongly to the West' (*Cape Times,* 1960).

13 Jan Smuts, Prime Minister of the Pretoria government from 1919 to 1924, and from 1939 to 1948, repeatedly emphasised the 'traditional special position of the Cape coloured people as an appendage to the whites', quoted in Lewis (1897), p. 210.

14 Those, for instance, who wrote in *The Torch,* a weekly newspaper based in Cape Town, or read it.

15 In one of the group interviews conducted in the Cape in 1994, one of the interviewees, speaking about the Coons who march in the streets and enter into competitions at the beginning of each year, said: 'there came a time especially during the apartheid years when ... it was seen as a coloured culture ... now I would like to be part of that but if that makes me a stereotype then I say no ...'

16 On the evolution and transformations of the meaning of 'coloured' in South Africa, see Rehana Ebrahim-Vally (1995), especially pp. 28–41.

17 It is clearly not the case of Mervyn Ross' KWB, a tentative 'coloured party' which has failed to attract a following.

18 These colourful costumes were originally inspired by the stage-costumes of the American black-face minstrels. Hence the name 'Coons', a term which in nineteenth-century show business vocabulary was synonymous to 'black face minstrel'. The racist connotation that the word 'Coon' acquired in the Southern states of the USA – where it was used in a derogatory way to refer to African Americans – is a possible reason why it is considered offensive. Though most of the members and the leaders of the carnival troupes do not really object to it, it is sometimes replaced with 'Minstrels'. Originally, in the United States, black face minstrels were white comedians who blackened their faces to resemble black rural slaves. They danced and sang in a comical way which was supposed to depict the comportment of the slaves but which in fact ridiculed them. E.P. Christy led the troupe of American

minstrels who first visited the Cape in the 1860s. They made a powerful impact resulting in local groups adopting their style of entertainment. Thus Coon minstrelsy became an indispensable ingredient of any show staged in Cape Town. Minstrelsy had indelibly marked coloured culture and more so since American and European sailors enjoyed entertaining locals with similar songs and antics in the inns and bars of the 'Tavern of the Seas'. The influence of minstrelsy on the first carnival clubs of Cape Town was reinforced by the long sojourn in South Africa, and in particular in Cape Town, of African-American minstrels, Orpheus McAdools Virginia Jubilee Singers. For more detailed accounts see Toll (1974) and Veit Erlmann (1991).

19 This area situated close to the heart of the city was mainly populated by coloured workers, but among its inhabitants were also members of the coloured elites, Jewish shopkeepers, poor whites and even Africans and West-Indians. It harboured an active social life whose memory acquired the proportions of a myth after its inhabitants were driven away, following the enactment of the Group Areas Act, and re-settled in soulless areas away from the city. See Shamil Jeppie (1990) and Shamil Jeppie and Craig Soudien (eds) (1990).

20 But there are a few examples of Malay choirs consisting exclusively of Christians. This is the case in Wellington, a small town north-east of Cape Town.

21 Space does not allow me to present here a third aspect of those festivals: the Christmas Choirs, Christian brass bands who play at Christmas and on many other occasions during the year and also organise their own competitions in January and February.

22 Music provides ample evidence of multiple cross-fertilisation processes: when one listens to the variety of musics produced today in South Africa, it is clear that so-called 'white' music contains elements of 'black' music, and vice-versa. See: David Coplan (1985) and Veit Erlmann (1991).

23 'Rigoletto' by Verdi, performed at the City Hall in Cape Town in October 1960, directed by Joseph Manca.

24 'The cultural space where a particular group lives, works, reasons or talks (communicates) is the space of isomorphies. The sum total of constant relations and elements of each of these spaces recognised as being separate. The group does not inhabit its history, or its religion, or its myths, or its science, or its technology, or its family structure, it nests in the bridges that allow these islands to communicate. Culture, its culture, is not a qualified space or spaces, it is exactly the isomorphic space between these designated spaces' (Michel Serres, 1975, pp. 102–3).

25 For a more detailed discussion of this concept of culture, see Bennetta Jules-Rosette and Denis-Constant Martin (1987).

26 Even though they occupied an intermediate economic and political position in a South African society characterised by segregation and apartheid, the coloured

people were always the object of utter contempt because they were said by the ruling group to have no history or culture they could claim their own: they were not considered as being part of European 'civilisation' (they were said to be just 'an appendage to the whites') nor could they benefit from ties with a culture, even 'primitive, or 'backward', attached to a particular land, like Africans and Indians. They were 'bastards' or, in words attributed to the wife of former South African President F.W. De Klerk, 'leftovers' (*The Sunday Tribune,* 1989). If poor, they were despised even more.

27 I have collected several such stories in the interviews I conducted in Cape Town and this vision of District Six has been given literary life in Richard Rive (1986).

28 For a more detailed analysis of the history and social signification of Cape Town New Year's festivals, see Denis-Constant Martin (1997).

29 'Coloured consciousness and identity, rather than being self aware, empowering and confident, are constructed fearfully, out of threat and opposition, and defined in negative relation to the other, not through a positive perception of the self [...] Coloureds are not so much racist as they fear non-racialism. The big unknowns for coloureds are non-racialism, freedom and equality. This is what confounds those, including coloured,activists who have fought all their lives for these values; that at the moment of victory, when the promised land is to be constructed, the wilderness is preferred' (Ebrahim Rasool, 1996).

30 The discussion on language is fascinating in this respect; some coloureds whose mother tongue is Afrikaans and who decided not to speak that language any longer because it was perceived as the language of the ruling group are now using it again and considering the possibility of registering their children in schools where it is the medium of teaching (interviews).

References

African Communist, 1993.

'Coloured People Belong to the West', *Cape Times*, 26 August 1960.

Coplan, D. (1985). *Township Tonight! South Africa's Black City Music and Theatre,* London: Longman.

Da Costa, Y. and A. Davids (1994). *Pages from Cape Muslim History,* Pietermaritzburg: Shuter and Shooter.

Davids, A. (1991). 'The Afrikaans of the Cape Muslims from 1815 to 1915', MA dissertation, University of Natal, Durban.

Ebrahim-Vally, R. (1995). *La stratification interne de la communauté dite indienne d'Afrique du Sud,* Paris: Université Paris I — Pantheon Sorbonne.

Erlmann, V. (1991). 'A Feeling of Prejudice: Orpheus M. McAdoo and the Virginia

Jubilee Singers in South Africa, 1890–1891', in *African Stars, Studies in Black South African Performance,* Chicago: University of Chicago Press.

Jeppie, S. (1990). 'Aspects of Popular Culture and Class Session in Inner Cape Town circa 1939–1959', MA dissertation, University of Cape Town.

Jeppie, S. and C. Soudien (eds) (1990). *The Struggle for District Six, Past and Present,* Cape Town: Buchu Books.

Jules-Rosette, B. and D.-C. Martin (1987). *Cultures populaires, identités et politictue,* Paris: Centre d'Etudes et de recherches internationales.

Lewis, G. (1987). *Between the Wire and the Wall, A History of South African 'Coloured' Politics,* Cape Town: David Philip.

Martin, D.-C. (1994). 'Pourquoi les Métis ont voté De Klerk', *Libération,* 5 July.

– (1997). ' 'The Famous Invincible Darkies', Cape Town's Coon Carnival, Aesthetic Transformations, Collective Representations, and Social Meanings', presented at *Confluences,* a conference held at the Faculty of Music and Dance, University of Cape Town, 16–19 July.

Rasool, E. (1996). 'Unveiling the Heart of Fear' in W. James, D. Caliquire, K. Cullinan (eds), *Now That We Are Free, Coloured Communities in a Democratic South Africa,* Cape Town: IDASA.

Rive, R. (1964). *Emergency,* Cape Town: David Philip.

– (1981). *Writing Black,* Cape Town: David Philip.

– (1986). *Buckingham Palace, District Six,* Cape Town: David Philip.

– (1990). *Emergency Continued,* Cape Town: David Philip.

Serres, M. (1975). *Esthotiques sur Carpaccio,* Paris: Hermann.

Shell, R. C.-H. (1994). *Children of Bondage, A Social History of the Slave Society at the Cape of Good Hope, 1652–1838,* Johannesburg: Witwatersrand University Press.

South African Institute of Race Relations (1994) *Race Relations Survey 1993/4,* Johannesburg.

Stone, G.L. (1991). 'An Ethnographic and Socio-Semantic Analysis of Lexis Among Working Class Afrikaans-Speaking Coloured Adolescent and Young Adult Males in the Cape Peninsula, 1963–1990', MA dissertation, University of Cape Town.

Toll, R.C. (1974). *Blacking Up, The Minstrel Show in Nineteenth Century America,* London: Oxford University Press.

Watson, G. (1970). *Passing for White, A Study of Racial Assimilation in a South African School,* London. Tavistock.

Weekly Mail & Guardian, 4 October 1996, p. 9.

'What Marike De Klerk Once had to Say About Other Race Groups', *Sunday Tribune,* 2 February 1989.

Worden, N. (1994). *The Chains that Bind Us: A History of Slavery in the Cape,* Cape Town: University of Cape Town, Department of Adult Education and Extra-Mural Studies.

CHAPTER NINE

Diversity in the imagined *Umma*: the example of Indian Muslims in South Africa

Rehana Ebr.-Vally

Muslims all over the world are members of a single community, the *umma*. Within the all-encompassing community, ethnic or linguistic differences are used to illustrate the spread of Islam in the world. Muslims can be found in such diverse locations as China, India, America, Indonesia and Iran. As Muslims, they are part of the mythical *umma*[1], a community governed by the word of Allah in which all people are equal but subservient to Allah. Yet, as Chinese, Bosnian or Indian Muslims, they demonstrate the significance of fusing the Islamic doctrine with local practices to give their belief a structure and their life a purpose. They cannot discount or ignore and can only with difficulty reject or eliminate their internalised 'non-Islamic' past. This cultural baggage of their past and their present is a necessity that allows them to make sense of their reality, of the present and of their being as Muslims in countries outside the holy land.

The *umma* for Muslims transcends boundaries, frontiers, nationalities, citizenship, linguistic differences and all other forms of cultural, political, economic or social differences. To Muslims, the *umma* is the community of Allah. It is sacred. Though Muslims are united in this mythical holy community, their worldly differences regarding who they are and where they come from cannot be ignored. Nor can they conceal their origins. In its practised form, we could argue that there is not one Islam, but many Islams. How do Muslims who firmly believe in their divinely ordained membership of the mythical Islamic community of the *umma* reconcile and live this apparent paradox?

This chapter, in regarding the *umma* as a myth, uses the example of South African Muslims of Indian origin to show that beyond the official orthodox discourse and the portrayed image of homogeneity and unity there are various Islams. Defining the South African Muslim as a convert, we will briefly outline the historical origins of Islam in South Africa and show how from its rudimentary beginnings there were different Muslim communities to be found. There are multiple Muslim communities in South Africa and in order to understand this reality, it is important to consider the different social contexts within which Muslims practise and live their religion. This influences the way in which Islam is modified to respond to different societal demands. How are the differences that make up the different communities to be understood? What do these differences consist of? What functions do they perform? How do they contribute to the essence of being a Muslim? Lastly, we will conclude with the idea that Muslim converts in reconstructing their social memory through the bias of Islam as their most significant identity parameter actually acquire the capacity to renegotiate their Muslim/Islamic space - however imaginary - in order to reinvent themselves according to the societal challenges and needs they perceive.

The impact and influence of imperialistic Islam

Islam in its origin is an Arab religion, making every Muslim who is not an Arab, a convert. Even Islamic countries like Pakistan, Iran, Indonesia or Iraq are countries of converts to Islam. The uniformity of Islam functions because it imposes very strict codes on how to be a Muslim. It makes imperialistic demands. As the last of the revealed reli-gions, Muslims consider it as the seal of monotheism. As a revealed religion it succeeds in imposing its imperialistic demands on Muslims. In accepting the universe, the world and everything it contains and represents as the creation of Allah, Muslims are inclined to accept a hierarchy of values (secular or not) as divinely ordained. Allah, in choosing to reveal His Word to Mohamed and make him the last of the prophets, has influenced Muslim penchant towards Islamic Arabia. Arabia in their memory becomes *the* space chosen by Allah. And the Prophet becomes the role model par excellence. Wearing a beard, a *kurta* or a *jillaba* for men, wearing a *burkha,* a scarf, or covering the entire body in a loose fitting tunic with only the eyes visible, for women, eating off the floor and from a communal plate or using a *miswak* to brush their teeth (a tooth-stick made from the bark of a special tree teased into bristle) are examples of some Muslims literally emulating the epoch of the Prophet. Today, Muslims can be seen sporting jeans, wearing a fez, wearing a beard and the message on the printed T-shirt worn is 'Live like Mohamed (P.B.U.H. [2] - peace be upon him) and die like Hussain.'

The convert, in accepting the Islamic world-view, accepts altering, even discrediting, his or her history, culture and language in short narrative. The convert makes a conscious decision of turning away from everything that is his or hers and supplanting it with the memory of Arab Islam. In this way, the holy lands of Islam: Mecca, Medina, (often the whole of Arabia is regarded as sacred by many Muslims) Jerusalem (known to Muslims as Al-Quds) and so forth, become the locations of memory instead of the country of which he or she is a citizen. The sacred language of the convert is Arabic and though he or she may not communicate in Arabic, the convert's language is regarded as inferior to Arabic. In rejecting their own story, converts become, whether they like it or not, a part of the Arab story. They then develop fantasies about who and what they are. The imperialistic demands of Islam, which require Muslims to place Islam before all else (because life on earth is ephemeral), creates neuroses. The space outside Islamic geographic space acquires a lesser importance – yet has to suffice. Thus, Muslims outside Islamic Arabia are constantly negotiating their space and their being. For the mythical space of belonging created by Islam, the *umma*, does not correspond to, nor offer, responses to the societal demands and challenges exerted in the non-Islamic space in which they live.

The example of 'Indian' Muslims of South Africa

To understand how South African Muslims use religion as an identity parameter to create subgroups (to effect cohesion or division), requires us to trace the history of practices, rituals and beliefs of Muslims in South Africa. These practices, rituals and beliefs which act as mutual signs of recognition allow individuals to situate themselves within the larger community of Muslims. Such signs which help determine an individual's membership to a subgroup are not recognisable to all. They form the expertise of an initiate. Only an 'initiate' – a person familiar with the mode of functioning of signs and other parameters of mutual recognition – can correctly assign the signs and other markers to particular subgroups. These signs which can be equated to accents in spoken language, act as markers to an initiate which allow her or him to interpret them in a specific manner - assigning them to a particular people and regarding them as functioning within a specific space or location. South Africans generally (or those initiated into the use of South African English) are capable of placing the English spoken by an individual into a geographical space. From the accent of an individual, the informed ear is capable of locating the speaker as originating from a specific region in South Africa, for example, the Cape or Gauteng. Similarly, an initiate, Muslim or not, interprets the signs manipulated or sometimes displayed by Muslim individuals as markers of identification and mutual recognition to indicate their membership of the different subgroups which constitute the Islamic community of South Africa. How and why did the different subgroups emerge? What are the signs that act as markers of distinction between them? What are the signs-symbols that individuals use to mutually identify each other as members of a subgroup, the Us or the Other?

It is possible to study the emergence of Islam in South Africa by concentrating on its institutionalised form – building the first mosques, the arrival of the first *Imams*, building the first *madrasah* (Koranic school – which does not correspond to or include a subgroup's perception of Islam). For though a study of Islam in its institutionalised form reveals the duplication of institutions that serve sections of a community, this falls short of explaining why a duplication of institutions prevails. In other words, while the duplication of institutions within the Muslim community corresponds to using the same infrastructure to propagate adherence to the basic tenets of Islam, it obscures the reasons that explain the present status quo. Moreover, the institutionalised form/s as well as the individual perception/s are both closely related and responses to the political and social conditions experienced in the country and/or, internationally.

Using Islam as an all-embracing category under which to group or define all Muslims is not incorrect. They *are* Muslim but it precludes an understanding of how religion, in this instance Islam, is used to invent different subgroups which represent the reality of the functioning of Islam in South Africa. Therefore, to avoid reductionism it is imperative to analyse the Muslim community of South Africa in terms of its subgroups. In this respect, we will concentrate on selected parameters to illustrate mutations of beliefs and practices that subgroups use to consolidate and propagate *their* Islam. These beliefs and practices are meaningful to members of a subgroup as well as to the larger Islamic community. For, in such instances, the beliefs and practices act as markers of mutual recognition that determine the cohesion of the subgroup as well as informing their quotidian acts. In doing this, we will understand how 'Indian' Muslims as converts use religion as their fundamental identity parameter to negotiate *their* space in South Africa. The 'new' space negotiated through the prism of Islam can become either inclusive or exclusive. If the 'new' space is open and located within the ambit of South Africanness, it is inclusive but if defined within the boundaries of Islam emulating the *umma*, it is exclusive – meaning that only Muslims can be members. How Muslims in South Africa perceive and negotiate their space in this country also explains the relationship that they have with the Other in South Africa as well as the State.

The first wave of Muslim immigrants

In terms of the Population Registration Act of 1950, apartheid South Africa was divided into four population groups (Africans, Coloureds, Indians and Whites). The Muslim population was concentrated amongst Coloureds and Indians. An immediate problem arising from this classification could be the inclusion of Muslim within the Coloured population group. For, by definition, the term Coloured - as denoting hybrid and 'impure' - was used in opposition to White and by extension, European and 'pure'. Thus, the official census of the Cape of 1875 and 1891 made no distinction between *Kaffir* and *Coloured* (Goldin, 1987).

In this way, the first Muslims to arrive at the Cape originating from the Malaysian archipelago and practising a different religion to Christianity, were grouped under the umbrella term Coloured. In other words the 'Others' were immediately distinguishable from the European by different phenotypical criteria and/or, by adhering to belief systems or religions different from Christianity. This form of classification is significant in understanding the divisions and existence of subgroups within the Muslim community of South Africa. For the fact that Muslims came to South Africa in two or, we argue, three [3] distinct waves of immigration is still relevant in operating a macro distinction within the Muslim community: the Malays/Coloureds and the Muslims of Indian origin.

The earliest evidence of Muslims in what is now South Africa, were the Mardyckers from Amboya who arrived in the Cape in 1658 (Tayob, 1995, pp. 39-40). The establishment of the Cape by the Dutch East India Company as a halfway route to India, influenced the Dutch to use the Cape as a political prison as well as a slave 'colony'. In the century and a half that followed the arrival of Jan van Riebeeck at the Cape in 1652, the Dutch as well as other European traders brought slaves to the Cape. Some of these slaves came from parts of Indonesia and many hailed from parts of India. From India, they came from the Bengal, Coromandel and Malabar coasts where Islam was already well established.[4] These Muslims brought to the Cape from either parts of India or parts of Indonesia can be regarded as the first settlement of Muslims in what is now South Africa.

These first Muslims at the Cape of either Indonesian or Indian origin preserved their Muslim faith by forming the larger category of 'Cape-Malays'. In this way, the original ethnic identity of these first Muslims was 'sacrificed' or supplanted by a shared religion. Within the realm of a shared religion, slaves and political prisoners of Muslim conviction could create a space of expression and translation for their collective difficult, even torturous, conditions of living at the Cape.

Amongst the political prisoners exiled to the Cape from the Indonesian islands by the Dutch were leaders and scholars of Islam in their countries of origin. Shaikh Yusuf who was brought to the Cape in 1694 is regarded as the first great exile among Malay-speaking religious leaders. The Rajah of Tamborah, another exile imprisoned at the Castle in Cape Town in 1697, or Abdullah Kadi Abdus Salaam (d.1807) who was brought to the Cape in 1780 and held captive on Robben Island, are examples of notables who possessed the necessary skills and abilities to provide leadership to the ordinary Muslim slaves at the Cape. Thus, a visible Muslim community under the spiritual guidance of these scholars began to exist at the Cape. This was evident in the establishment of the basic Islamic institutions in the form of mosques and madrasahs (religious schools/seminaries). Such institutions served the purpose of formalising the teaching of Islam to ordinary Muslims as well as providing a form of education to slave and Free Black children.

This institutionalisation of Islam at the Cape during the century and a half that followed the arrival of Jan van Riebeeck in 1652, was not uniform. The different leaders – *imams* – of the various mosques that provided guidance to the ordinary

Muslim often differed in their reading of Islam. Conflicts regarding the correct Islamic practices often were the root of religious dispute between the different *imams* (Tayob 1995: 46-48). Such disputes concerned details of practice rather than the accepted Islamic doctrine that codified their belief system.

Tayob's example of such disputed detail is self explanatory. He argues that the opening of the Suez Canal did much to create links between the Muslims in the Cape, Mecca and the Middle East. When in the Cape, the Muslim community was unable to decide on the performance of the Friday prayer and a solution was sought by sending a delegation to Mecca. Though this emphasised and exemplified the political tussle that existed between the different *imams, shaykhs,* they did not disagree on the core doctrine that constitutes the basic tenets of Islam. To overcome this unjustifiable state of affairs, the Moslem Judicial Council (MJC) was formed in 1945. In South Africa, the MJC is the umbrella body which mediates among the variety of practices of Muslims without adhering to a specific school of Islamic thought.

The second wave of Muslim immigrants

The second wave of Muslim immigrants into South Africa came from India. They came in two distinct waves, in different proportions and much later than the Cape Muslims. Their migratory patterns of entering the country reflected the two major trends that characterise Indian migration into South Africa.

The first Indians – as 'British Indians' – arrived on the 'SS Truro' and walked ashore into the British Colony of Natal on 16 November 1860. They were the first group of indentured labourers (342 men, women and children) who sailed from the port of Madras in India. The 'SS Truro' was followed by the 'Belvedere' with 351 people on board. It set sail for Natal from the port of Calcutta and arrived a few days after the 'SS Truro'. These men, women and children formed the core of indentured labourers to enter the British Colony of Natal.

The indentured labourers came to work on the sugar plantations of Natal after a tripartite agreement was reached between the Colony of Natal and the governments of Britain and India. These indentured workers responded to a recruitment campaign of colonists in Natal who were looking for cheap and efficient labour. In this regard, they followed the example of the island of Mauritius which had successfully recruited cheap labour from India. Between 1860 and 1911, 384 ships with 152 184 passengers docked in Durban.

These ships sailed to Durban from either Madras or Calcutta. By 1911, according to Bhana and Brain (1990, p. 36), a total of 149 791 Indians had settled in South Africa. Two thirds of this total population were either Tamil or Telegu speaking Hindus, with other religious denominations making up the remaining third.

Using the ships' lists to determine the religious affiliation of indentured workers, Bhana (1991) concludes that 8.5% of the indentured workers who responded to the recruitment campaign between 1860 and 1902 were Muslim: 3% came from Madras and the remaining 5.5% from Calcutta [5]. The Muslims who embarked at Madras were recruited in Malabar, Mysore and Hyderabad while others were recruited in northern India and embarked at Calcutta.

The indentured Muslims or *Hyderabadees*

Though the Muslims formed a minority group among the indentured workers, they are generally referred to as *Hyderabadees*. This generic term used to refer to the first Indian Muslims is an example of a horizontal internal stratification which characterises the South African Indians. Here, it should be noted that it is difficult to choose a tense to discuss South African Indians. Over the years, they have discarded as well as adopted 'new' parameters or mutated selected parameters of their identity. Thus, a parameter which was considered of paramount importance as early as ten years ago, could have either 'disappeared', or mutated, or exist as doubly reinforced. Therefore, while some sub-communities may have rejected a parameter, another would refuse to even consider any possible change. Hence, the use of either the present or the past tense in referring to certain aspects or practices among South African Muslims, even Indians, is problematic.

Naming and referring to the Muslims of indentured origin as *Hyderabadees* reflects a need that Indians experience/d to categorise themselves into 'knowable' and manageable groups. For, these Muslims did not automatically hail from Hyderabad. We can only infer the reasons why the generic term of *Hyderabadee* was used. Maybe it was a practice among indentured workers to refer to the Muslims as *Hyderabadees*. Or, the Muslim indentured workers coming from the port of Madras originated from the present Andra Pradesh and from the administrative districts of Hyderabad. Nevertheless, the *Hyderabadees* can be regarded as the first community of Indian Muslims to settle in present day South Africa.

As a significant minority, they too had to adjust to the loneliness and isolation and overcome problems of communication that characterised indenture. Moreover, the possibility of only a Muslim or two being allocated to an estate made it difficult to even form a religious sub-group. On the other hand, where several Muslims were allocated to the same employer, the possibility of forming a tightly-knit Muslim cell was stronger.

The absence of professional priesthood in Islam means that every Muslim needed to be capable of performing the basic requirements of Islam. Thus, every Muslim is expected to have a reading knowledge of the Koran and be able to perform the ritual prayers in Arabic. The ability to perform the obligatory ritual prayers five times a day, demands memorising the prayer verses in Arabic. The ability of Muslims to recite and perform Islamic rituals in Arabic is incidentally regarded by them as creating the unity and oneness of Islam.

Therefore, despite the hardships experienced as indentured workers or problems of communication between Muslims speaking different Indian languages, it was possible to observe some of the rituals of Muslimhood. Provided a few Muslims were allocated to the same estate, they could perform their prayers together. It should nonetheless be noted that men rather that women perform prayers in congregation. In the case of women, prayers are as a general rule performed individually and in the confines of their home. Religion as a communal affair in such instances was able to cement links between Muslims on estates and maybe even between Muslims from different estates. Brain (1988, p. 216) rightfully suggests that religious life for married Muslims was much easier. She then suggests that the proselytising nature of the faith anxious to find converts to Islam, as well as the individual obligation to have a sound knowledge of the faith and give a good example, were reasons for Muslims to remain Muslim.

This raises the question as to the number of Muslim women there were among the indentured labourers. Using a caste breakdown of migrant labourers from Calcutta and Madras, Swan (1985, pp. 281-282) presents the following statistics. Between 1860 and 1910, a total of 2 323 migrant labourers from Madras landed in the Colony of Natal. Among them were 751 women. From Calcutta, a total of 1 384 indentured labourers – i.e. 455 women and 929 males – arrived at the port of Natal from 1860 to 1906. A detail that is of specific interest to us is the way Muslims as well as Christians are grouped as part of the caste category.

Altogether 145 Muslims arrived from Calcutta and among them were 74 women, while 72 Muslims arrived from Madras of which only 17 were females. After the indenture period was completed, Muslims, like their Hindu counterparts, usually left their employers. The majority moved into towns engaging in some form of commercial activity and many settled around Durban (Brain: 1988, p. 217).

The third wave of Muslim immigrants

The first wave of Indian immigrants was followed by a second distinct wave from 1871[6] and predominantly from the State of Gujarat in India. Among them were Indian traders from established cities in India wanting to expand their commercial operations in this country. The majority, however, were people who came from rural backgrounds and who were forced to leave India because of British land policies having destroyed Gujarati trade. Since they paid their own fare to South Africa, they were known as 'Passenger' Indians, or 'Free Indians' because of not having had any contractual obligations.

In this country, the 'passenger' Indians were distinguished from their indentured counterparts by the following features: 1) they paid for their voyage to South Africa; 2) they were not recruited and therefore not subjected to any contractual obligation. Having come as British subjects and not as indentured workers, they were in many ways protected from the humiliation, isolation and loneliness of working on estates. Moreover, they enjoyed privileges denied to indentured workers.

Unlike their indentured counterparts, the 'passenger' Indians were not confined to enter the colony of Natal or present-day South Africa uniquely through the port of Durban. They came through the South African ports of Durban, East London, Cape Town as well as through Delagoa Bay in the present Mozambique – which was a Portuguese colony – and via the island of Mauritius. Having entered South Africa through different ports and as subjects of the British Crown (even if this status was questioned), no colonial records exist for them. Consequently, their exact number as well as their origins in India had to be determined. This was further complicated by the fact that after 1897 many entered the country clandestinely.

The problem of their origins in India was solved partly by the fact that they, more than their indentured counterparts, kept a lively correspondence with family remaining in India. Using this as a starting point, Bhana was able to do cross reference checks using the 1936-1937 and the 1938-1940 editions of South African Indian Who's Who and Commercial Directory and the 1960 edition of Who's Who together with 631 interviews conducted between 1986 and 1990 to determine the different regions from which 'passenger' Indians originated. The 631 people (some as children and others as very young adults) he interviewed came to South Africa between 1896 and 1900. In this way, he was able to map their places of origin and concluded that the majority of them came from regions in the State of Gujarat.

A small but significant number came from the presidency of Bombay. They were the Konkani. After 1890, Khojas arrived in South Africa. The Khoja are disciples of the Aga Khan and a sect in Shi'a Islam. Of the 'passenger' Indians, almost 80% were Muslim.

How is one to understand the predominance of Muslims among the 'passenger' Indians? What are the reasons – if any – why the percentages between Hindu (indentured) and Muslim ('passenger') should be inverted? Why did a majority of Muslims respond to the invitation to come to this country to serve the singular needs of the indentured workers?

If, as some historians rightfully argue, the implementation of British land policies in Gujarat as well as the long periods of drought were reasons for all Gujaratis to emigrate, why did Hindus not respond as enthusiastically as Muslims?

Reasons for migration

In the absence of concrete reasons as to why Muslims rather than Hindus responded to invitations to come to this country and serve the peculiar needs of the indentured workers, we offer some explanations. Abubaker Jhavery, from the village of Porbandar (Gujarat, India), was already a well established merchant serving the needs of indentured workers on the island of Mauritius. In 1863, three years after the first indentured workers arrived in Natal, Abubaker Jhavery saw the potential of establishing commercial networks in Natal. As such, he became the first Indian merchant to set foot in Natal. We do not know how many indentured workers were to be found in Natal in 1863, but in 1866 the Indian population in Natal numbered 6 445 people [7]. The indentured workers on the sugar plantations received the basic food products from the farmer. This was in accordance with the tripartite agreement. Thus the indentured workers were given rice, lentils, dried fish and clarified butter (ghee). All other needs and requirements related to cuisine and religious rituals as well as items of clothing had to be procured by the indentured workers themselves. Therefore, Indian merchants supplied an Indian clientele made up of indentured workers [8]. The successful commercial ventures of Abubaker Jhavery in South Africa are a plausible reason for Muslim merchants from Gujarat and Bombay, particularly Mehmons from the villages of Kathiawar and Kutch and Sunni Vohras from Surat to have followed his example.

Social structure of 'passenger' Indians in South Africa [9]

The 'passenger' Indians further differed from their indentured counterparts by the way they formed and organised sub-communities. Unlike indentured workers who were forced to compromise on religious and social values, the 'passenger' could use these to form the different sub-communities that closely resembled the Gujarati social structures they knew. This was also facilitated by the fact that 'passenger' Indians came to this country with either their families or were later joined by family members once basic social and economic conditions allowed this. There are examples of individuals on a reconnaissance trip having decided to remain and who were more often than not joined by their families. Not only did 'passenger' Indians ensure that families were reunited but they also encouraged friends and members of their village entourage to join them in South Africa.

An inherent purpose of such reunion exercises was to allow 'passenger' Indians to recreate much of the social and religious structures with which they were familiar. In this way, people from the same village and/or surrounding villages in India began to establish systems of networks. The village of origin among the 'passenger' Indians was of paramount importance in that it served as a reliable, even infallible, criterion to determine the status of a family and so a person. In some cities and towns where they settled, they did much to reinvent the village community of India. People from the same village and its immediate environs formed a *kutum* (in the absence of an exact translation in English, it is translated as a clan) within which mutual support (financial and, or, other) was defined, and marriages were arranged. In this way village links were maintained and/or reinforced.

Marrying within the *Kutum* or creating an own space

We could argue that marriages are generally contracted between individuals of the same religious denomination. In the case of the majority of 'passenger' Indians in South Africa (until fairly recently), marriages contracted between only Muslims, only Hindus or only Christians displayed and recalled the village structures of origin. Thus, marriages were arranged as a reunion of families originating from the same village and its environs. In practice, this translated as Mehmons and Surtees for example marrying within their own communities. This meant that as a rule Mehmons and Surtees did not intermarry. These tight restrictions that operated in the arranging of marriages were bound to disappear in view of the law forbidding Indians from bringing wives from India and the reality that the 'passenger' Indians in South Africa constituted too small a number to continue such practices of exclusiveness in providing marriage partners from traditionally sanctioned circles.

This problem was overcome by using the vernacular language as a criterion to combine the different localities of origin in India into a larger group. Thus, subgroups using the vernacular languages as markers of differentiation were formed. In this way, the strict restrictions of villages of origin in India made way for 'new' subgroups to be formed. Using the Mehmon community as an example, this changed from Ranavav Mehmons, Bhanvad Mehmons, Porbandar Mehmons, Jamnagar Mehmons and Ratnagiri Mehmons to MEHMONS. Where before marriages were arranged to reflect village origin in India, they were now being arranged to reflect the linguistic community.

Language as a marker of stratification

In a cursory manner, we have noticed the following:

- the first Muslims in South Africa were either slaves or political prisoners known as the 'Cape-Malays'.
- Indian immigrants came to South Africa in two waves: the indentured la-

bourers followed by the 'passenger' Indians.

- these Indian immigrants in South Africa followed distinct patterns of settlement reflecting their status as indentured or not. They did not mix.
- differentiation was practised within both the Indian communities. The result was that they formed various sub-communities which reproduced and were modified versions of many of the social stratification structures that they had internalised in India.

Whilst retaining the idea of stratification, Indians in South Africa, for political reasons beyond their control, introduced systems of differentiation that differ from those found in India. These changes were also responses to the social and political conditions experienced in this country. Since the South African government banned bringing wives to South Africa it also prevented families from being reunited. To circumvent this, links and networks had to be broadened. The *kutum* had to be enlarged, to cancel or rewrite the rule of mutual exclusion. The opening of the *kutum* was nonetheless subjected to strict rules. It did not follow a haphazard pattern where, for example, all Indians regardless of being of indentured origin or of 'passenger' origin would form a single homogenous group. The distinction introduced was based on language. In the first instance, this differentiation allowed the Indians to recognise who were/are of indentured origin and who of 'passenger' Indian origin.

Indentured Muslims

Since the majority of the indentured stock came from South India, they spoke either Tamil or Telegu and the Muslims amongst them were either Tamil- or Urdu-speaking. We have seen that despite the hardships experienced as indentured labourers, Islam permitted especially the men to perform their prayers in congregation and in Arabic.

This allowed them to override any linguistic differences during times of prayer. However, an interesting phenomenon of language change occurred among the indentured labourers. In the absence of concrete data, we can infer that Tamil-speaking Muslims – a numeric minority – stopped using Tamil and adopted Urdu as their vernacular. In this way, there could be no doubt that they were/are Muslim for Tamil was/is clearly regarded as a language spoken by Hindus.

'Passenger' Muslims

The majority of 'passenger' Indians came from the state of Gujarat. There were also small numbers who came from the Presidency of Bombay and other parts of India.

They did not form a single community but chose to replicate the stratified social structures that they knew in India. Thus, when it became impossible to increase the number of Indians in this country through inviting wives and other persons from India to join them, they formed linguistic groups. The following groups among the Muslims illustrate how they created links that went beyond localities of origin in India.

Muslims of Gujarat

Muslims originating from Gujarat consisted of different linguistic groups. Among them we find speakers of Gujarati, Urdu, Mehmon and Konkani.[10] Within each of these linguistic groups, members were (and some still are) able to recognise the different localities of origin in India. On arriving in this country, the majority Muslims from Gujarat spoke Gujarati. Since Gujarati is spoken by both Hindus and Muslims, speakers are able to recognise the religion of a person through the lexicon that is used. Further, they were also able to recognise from which villages in Gujarat a speaker's ancestors came.

In South Africa, Gujarati acquired a status distinct from that in India. Whilst in India where it is used as a language of communication, here it is viewed as the language of Hindus. This is probably so because the Hindu Gujaratis make an effort to be literate in it. They send their children during the afternoons or on Saturdays to learn the basics of Gujarati. At these Gujarati schools, children are inter alia taught Indian history, some Indian politics and arithmetic through the medium of Gujarati. They learn the national anthem of India as well as folk songs and some dance. In this way, it acquires a religious status for Muslims for their *madrasahs* perform a similar function in that children are taught the basics of Islam. First it was in Urdu and now in English and in both languages, the child learnt/learns of Islam and its geographic spaces and not India. How do we explain this shift? Why do most Gujarati-speaking Muslims continue to use the language and consider it as belonging to Hindus? Whilst this phenomenon is recent in South Africa, it is closely tied to the teaching of Islam in South Africa.

The 'passenger' Indians of Gujarat came to South Africa and used Gujarati as a language of communication. No religious distinction was made between the speakers. In fact, one could argue that in the State of Gujarat they received their basic education in Gujarati. Because of this, many corresponded (and still do) with relatives in India in Gujarati. In South Africa, the Hindu Gujarati-speaking 'passenger' Indians started Gujarati schools where children received a basic education in Gujarati. They were taught to read and write the language. In addition, they were also taught arithmetic, Indian history, Indian geography and religion.

Many Muslim parents sent their daughters to these schools with the understanding that they would concentrate on only the learning of the language. Daughters were sent for a number of reasons. First, literacy in Gujarati increased the prospects of arranging a 'good' marriage. Not only did it prove their proficiency in the language but they could either continue the correspondence with the family in India or begin correspondence with the in-law's family in India. Second, daughters could attend Gujarati school for the onset of menses automatically prevented them from continuing their religious education at the *madrasah* (Koranic school). Third, in most instances, the onset of menses meant that daughters were removed from the western school and were kept at home and 'prepared' for marriage.

The reasons Muslim parents sent their daughters to Gujarati school can be ascertained by expanations offered by Muslim women who attended Gujarati schools in Johannesburg and Durban until the 1950s. These explanations were a way of informing me of their 'good' marriage. If Gujarati as language allowed Muslims to maintain links with their village in India, why and how did it acquire the status of a Hindu language? If, as a vernacular it allows Gujarati-speaking Muslims to maintain a distinction between them and the Urdu- or Konkani-speaking Muslims, why do they continue to use it to name their sub-community and still consider it as a privilege marker of the Hindus?

The madrasahs

The *madrasahs* in South Africa, like everywhere else in the world, taught the uniqueness of Islam. Children were taught to respect and to adhere to the basic tenets and to recite all prayers in Arabic, the language of the Koran. Since their arrival and until South African Muslims of Indian origin were able to form their own teaching corps for the *madrasahs*, 'passenger' Indians brought teachers from India.

These teachers having qualified in India spoke Gujarati, Urdu and very little or no English. Their knowledge of Arabic was limited to performing prayers and reading the Koran. Children attended – and still do – *madrasah* every afternoon after school and were/are taught to read the Arabic text of the Koran. Access to the meaning of the Koran was found in commentaries and translations written in Urdu. This exclusive availability of commentaries and explanations of Islam meant that each child at a *madrasah* had to learn Urdu. Urdu became for the early 'passenger' Indian Muslim the only gateway to understanding their religion. It was the vector of Islam. In reality, however, most Muslims learnt to read Urdu as they were taught to read the Koran in Arabic, understanding very little. In small towns with a small Muslim community, the *madrasah* was run by the person considered to be the most apt in teaching Islam – normally a person who had memorised the Koran, the *hafez'ul Koran* or a woman recognised for her piety and knowledge of Islam to teach the girls.

This changed when commentaries, translations and interpretations became available in English which were also translated into Afrikaans. The Koran is still read in Arabic but it is no longer necessary to learn Urdu. Further, at that point in time (the late sixties), children were more fluent in English or Afrikaans rather than in an Indian vernacular, unlike their Gujarati counterparts who used their vernacular amongst themselves and in most instances. They began to ask for lessons in English or Afrikaans. They did not object to learning to read Arabic for it was the language in which Allah had revealed the Koran to the Prophet Mohamed.

A factor that influenced Muslims to regard Gujarati as the language of the Hindu is the script in which it is written. Gujarati is of Sanskritic origin and written in the Sanskritic script. It is taught at Gujarati schools run by Hindus like *The Surat Hindu Association* and Sanskrit is the holy language of the Hindus. This amalgam in the minds of the second and later generation Muslim had the effect of giving literacy in Gujarati a religious dimension.

These changes of perception towards Gujarati as a language were linked closely to the image of India in the memory of the Muslim 'passenger' Indian descendants. Since Gujarati schools were operated uniquely by Gujarati Hindu associations and *madrasahs* by the Muslims, later generations came to regard them as either Muslim or Hindu institutions. Moreover, the 1948 partition of India into India and Pakistan further exacerbated this idea. (Young Muslims watching a cricket match between Pakistan and India are more likely to root for Pakistan because they are Muslim. Their parents and more their grandparents support the Indian team because India is where their ancestors originate from).

The fading of India in the memory of 'Indian' Muslims

In the 1960s the majority of the South African Muslims of Indian origin were of the third generation. Memories of the village of origin and so of India began to fade. This, in large measure, can be attributed to their experiences in South Africa: Indians in this country were regarded with contempt by Blacks and especially the Whites where proficiency in English and/or Afrikaans improved levels of adaptation. The time spent at primary school as well as adapting to the demands of commercial enterprises in South Africa were factors that pushed the vernacular into the family sphere. Their survival in South Africa did not depend on how well they spoke their vernacular languages but on how proficient they were in the official languages of this country. Thus, the quasi-disappearance of the vernacular languages impacted not only on the image and memory they retained of India but also the form Islam would take.

Islam, the religion of South African Muslims of Indian origin, is linked closely to their recollection of India. The fading of India in their memory is also the purging of 'hinduness', or Indianness, in their practice of Islam. As such, Islam as an identity marker allows us to recognise and understand how they have modified their identity to conduct a distance between them and India and in so doing implant themselves more firmly in South Africa. To understand how Muslims of Indian origin in South Africa formulated their proximity to different forms of Islam as practised in Muslim countries requires us to consider some aspects of the Islam of their ancestors in South Africa. In doing this, we would have an idea of the shifts operated to make their Islam less Indian and therefore of a more orthodox form.

From the onset, it should be noted that whilst some Muslims agree on purging Islam of all traces of Hindu influences, there is no real consensus as to which Islam should replace it. At the same time, there are also other Muslims who regard what they call *Baap-Dada ka Islam* (the Islam of the founding Father) as relevant and valid.

The Islam of the 'passenger' Indians

The 'passenger' Indians brought an entire societal structure to South Africa. In the impossibility of transposing these structures *tel quel*, they were expected to change, or select parameters to accelerate the process of adapting and more importantly lessen feelings of hostility that they experienced through encounters with other South Africans. What societal structures did they retain? Which aspects were modified? These are questions that will help to elucidate areas in their identity that once mattered but which today have become mythical recollections of a distant past sometimes best forgotten.

Though Islam as an equalising and egalitarian religion rejects the caste system, forms of social stratification resembling the caste system were to be found among the 'passenger' Muslims. The most striking example was the arranging of marriages that in many ways recalled kinship ties based on caste in India. Muslims vehemently deny the presence of any form of social stratification informing their world view, but examples of marriages arranged within the *biradari* (fraternity), the *kutum* [11] (joint household), the *jat* or *jati* as well as specific marital rituals practised by well defined groups in South Africa show how converts to Islam in India transformed and Islamified erstwhile Hindu practices. These are in fact examples of what some Muslims in South Africa challenge as Hindu practices and therefore see them as unorthodox and even impure.

Marriage to many Indians and therefore also to South Africans of Indian origin, is a family affair. It is seen as the union of two families rather than of two individuals. During the initial period, marriages were arranged between *gamwallahs* (village relations). Later, for reasons mentioned earlier, the village group was extended to include all speakers of the same language. This today is being reorganised to include all persons of the same faith.

Stratification among the Muslims

Originating from India, the question that can be asked is how and to what extent these converts to Islam succeeded in eliminating forms of stratification that are considered to be hallmarks of the Indian caste system? Whether their ancestors were regarded as *ajlaf* or *ashraf,* the fact that they lived in India, where they internalised forms of social stratification, needs to be addressed. The term *Ajlaf* is an Arabic-Persian term, the plural of *Julf,* carries the meanings vile, base or non-noble. It is the opposite of *Ashraf,* also an Arabic-Persian term, the plural of *Sharif* meaning noble.

The terms of *Ajlaf* and *Ashraf* were used to distinguish between locally converted Muslims in India - the *Ajlafs* - and the descendants of Afghan, Arab, Persian and Turkish immigrants. The *Ashraf* form the superior stratum of Muslim society in India.

'Indian' Muslim marriages

Marriage is one of the most significant rites for Muslims. It represents a milestone in Islam[12], for it is a contractual engagement to found a family and sustain Muslim society [13] and is an important social event. It is almost always an extremely colourful affair celebrated with splendour. It represents the union of two families and by extension consolidates the clan.

In informal conversations with young adolescent women dressed in the latest fashion the following arguments in finding future partners emerged:

  – they all agreed that they would only marry Muslim;
  – some would only marry within their specific cultural and linguistic group, explaining that a Gujarati should marry a Gujarati and a Mehmon should marry a Mehmon and so on;
  – to the question 'Why?', they offered the explanation that they wanted good marriages and good families.

Marriage, normally an ostentatious celebration, is an occasion to invite as many friends and all the family. The number of guests can vary from two hundred to two thousand. Inviting only the *kutum* and their immediate relations can mean a few hundred guests. For, according to customary practices at least one person from each family should be invited. In the event of a single person being invited, care is taken that that person has the status to represent his/her family.

Almost always such an invitation would be extended to the head of the family. Distinction is made between close family and distant family.

The *Nikah*

The *nikah* is the ceremonial service where the man and the woman become husband and wife. It is almost always performed at the mosque. Women who are excluded from the mosque and from the ceremony are represented by *wakils*. A *wakil* is the legal representative of the bride. The *wakils* are normally the bride's uncles, maternal and paternal and three in number, who bear testimony to her consent to marry. The ceremony takes place in two parts. 1) The chief *wakil* and two witnesses first go to the bride's home where she is asked if she consents to the marriage. Once she has replied 'yes', it indicates that the chief *wakil* can report her answer to the 'official' ceremony at the mosque. The ceremony at the mosque is performed at a fixed time, often a few hours after the bride has accepted. During the ceremony, the *wakil* informs the *mullah* (the priest) of the bride's consent and after obtaining the consent of the groom, the marriage is declared as valid. It is recorded in the register kept by the *jamaat* (the mosque committee). This is the only procedure prescribed by Islam. Anything beyond it is optional.

For Muslims of Indian origin, the *nikah* is preceded as well as followed by a series of events. Many of these events resemble North Indian marriage rites. Some of them are: 1) the exchanging of presents *peramri* a few days before the *nikah* to mark the process of the union of the two families and 2) the exchange of *koonchas* (literally trays in Urdu and Gujarati) which are presents to the bride and groom from the opposite family. The bride – rather her family – presents gifts elaborately decorated and wrapped to the groom and vice versa. It is possible that this form of exchanging of gifts originated from the dowry system as practised among the Hindus.

The *peramri*

The *peramri* is hosted by the bride's family. The groom's family, his parents, brothers, sisters, cousins and uncles and aunts, maternal and paternal, visit the bride's home carrying gifts. These gifts are for the bride's parents, grandparents, brothers, sisters and other family members regarded as important. Presents are chosen to represent the rank of the receiver. Gold jewellery for example would be presented to the bride's mother, a wrist watch to her father, shirts to the brothers and fabric or costume jewellery and other objects to the sisters and aunts. In India, men were given shawls which in South Africa have been replaced by shirts.

The object of this visit is to break the ice between the two families. They would tease each other and sometimes behave in a manner not normally associated with good upbringing.

More gifts

Gift ceremonies are rituals that Indians use to evaluate their places in their *kutum*. Neglecting to give a gift to the bride and her parents can lead to the severing of ties between families. The *moharoo* among Gujarati-speaking Muslims and Hindus is named *mosala* among Urdu-speaking Muslims and *mamero* among the Mehmon. *Moharoo, mosala* or *mamero* precedes the wedding by a few days. This is when the bride's father's *kutum* and her mother's *kutum* visit the bride's home bringing gifts for the bride and her parents. The mother and the bride-to-be receive gold jewellery and the father the proverbial shirt or a sum of money. In this instance, members of the *kutum* required to offer gifts are the parents and their sons and daughters. In other words, the bride-to-be will receive gifts from her maternal and paternal grandparents, uncles and aunts. Her parents will receive gifts from their respective parents, brothers and sisters as well as from their in-laws.

The *mehndi*

Mehndi is henna. A few days preceding the wedding, the bride's hands and feet will be decorated in *mehndi*. A party is organised where the groom's representatives, his sisters and sisters-in-law, come to the bride's home to draw intricate *mehndi* designs on her hands and feet. In addition, the bride receives a *punjabi* dress with matching pants and *dhuputta* (a long scarf in chiffon or silk) and a *chandi* (silver) set (a necklace, a pair of earrings, a ring and a bracelet). Tradition requires seven people from the groom's entourage to put the *mehndi* on the bride's hands and feet. More often than not they make their dot while the intricate designs are drawn by an expert. Today, the *mehndi* among Muslims in South Africa has been transformed to include the western kitchen-tea party. The bride-to-be invites her friends, all female, to celebrate her fast-approaching marriage. Though not a rule, friends offer gifts.

The gift ceremonies as well as the henna party are examples of rituals preceding the *nikah* still being observed by many Muslims of 'passenger' Indian origin. However, there are Muslims who have rejected these rituals as being Hindu and therefore not to be practised. It is difficult to determine which segments have rejected completely these practices for some erstwhile proponents of Hindu-cleansing of Islam are today accepting the re-introduction of some of these practices. Their daughters it seems have reintroduced the *mehndi* albeit under a new name: the girl's party.

The red *audni*

The red *audni* is a red stole in chiffon or silk with gold embroidery. It is only worn by the Mehmon bride. She wears it during her *nikah* ceremony. On the wedding day, the bride is the first to enter the banquet hall accompanied by a brother or male cousin. Once the Mehmon bride is seated, members of the husband's entourage place a red stole on her head. She wears it for a brief few minutes after which it is removed. This custom among the Muslims is strictly limited to the Mehmon community. Few Mehmons today know the symbolism of wearing the red *audni*. I should nonetheless point out that some Mehmon women I talked to and who were knowledgeable and forthcoming about other issues seemed to evade this issue through a 'I don't know' or a 'I don't remember'.

A lady informant and not a Mehmon, explained it in the following way. Hindu women wear red saris on their wedding day, she began. The Mehmons, she continued, are ex-Gujarati Hindus and therefore, according to this informant, it is not surprising that the Mehmon bride wears something red. My remark that she could be an *Ashraf,* was met with silence. Red in Hindu symbolism is the colour of marriage and it also keeps evil spirits away. Therefore the Hindu bride in wearing a red sari or a red something and the Mehmon bride in wearing the red stole are both keeping evil spirits out. These are rituals once shared by Hindus and Muslims of 'passenger' Indian origin that have almost 'disappeared' because of being Hindu.

The *pithi*

This is a rite of purification of the bride practised by Gujarati-Hindus was in South Africa and was until recently a part of the marriage rituals among a segment of the Gujarati-speaking Muslims. The *pithi* is a paste made with turmeric and sweet smelling oils. A few days before and until the wedding, the bride-to-be assisted by other women rubs this paste all over her body. The night before the wedding, the bride does not wash this paste off. She does so on the morning of the wedding. This is to enhance the glow the turmeric paste gives to the skin. A religious ritual among the Hindu, it was adopted by Muslims for cosmetic purposes.

The *garba* or *rasra*

Gujarati Hindus call it the *garba* and Gujarati Muslim Mehmons the *rasra*. *Garba* or *rasra* takes place either a few days or the day before the wedding. It is a traditional dance with only women as participants. The Mehmon were the only segment among the Gujarati

Muslims to assiduously host a *rasra*. Women participating in a *rasra* form a circle, singing traditional songs and dance to the beat of a drum, the *dholak,* played by a woman in the centre of the circle. Sometimes, in addition to the drum *patelis,* aluminium pots from the kitchen were used to play the beat. The *rasra* was an opportunity for women to be among themselves and without a care throw all caution to the wind. The *rasra* has in a manner of speaking disappeared from the repertoire of wedding festivities among the Mehmon. My informant (in her early sixties) who was a sought after *rasra* player in the 1960s regrets this and blames the youth for having lost their zest. In many small towns, the *rasra* was attended by Gujarati Hindu women as well. It was an occasion of abandon for these women.

Disputed marriage models: social or religious

'Indian' Muslim marriages celebrated in pomp and splendour have come under much scrutiny and are strongly criticised by the orthodox segment of the 'Indian' Muslim community. They disagree with the customs that precede the *nikah* ceremony and think about them as Indian and by extension as Hindu. These orthodox Muslims wish to replace the pompous wedding celebrations with a more austere model. They believe that Muslim marriages should follow the Islamic example to the letter. In their opinion the *nikah,* which is the only obligatory rite, should be a solemn and discreet affair and definitely should not be preceded by what they consider to be pretentious ceremonies that are vestiges of Hindu influences.

Marriage to 'Indians' of South Africa is *the* important event at both a religious and social level. This is evidenced by how 'Indian' Muslims in celebrating a marriage as the union of two families and the perpetuation of the *kutum,* also regard it as fulfilling their Islamic duty. At a social level Muslims, like their Hindu or Indian Christian counterparts, who use religion and/or language to locate themselves within *their* group and as part of the 'Indian' community in South Africa, are prepared to walk many extra miles to ensure that ceremonial obligations are performed in pomp and splendour.

Coming from India, the 'Indian' Muslims of South Africa brought with them societal structures that helped them to maintain a sense of communal life in this country. Unable to transpose these structures *tel quel,* they transformed them to suit societal conditions in South Africa. The example of marriage demonstrates how some rituals have changed or been made to 'disappear' because they have become controversial and/or their force in maintaining community links has waned. This waxing and waning or 'writing out' of rituals practised by 'Indian' Muslims of South Africa can be understood through their desire of purging Islam of residues of a Hindu past. This creates a negotiating space where 'old' or 'new' rituals are rejected, adopted or modified in terms of the Islamic orthodoxy they possess. This negotiating space expected to introduce uniformity in Islam actually highlights the ambiguity that characterises 'Indian' Islam in South Africa. It shows the extent to which religion is used to identify (in their case) proximity or distance with India.

This highlights areas of contradiction that stem from being a converted Muslim. Marriage as the most important rite in the life of the Indian individual should be the rite that demonstrates the unifying power of Islam that some Muslims are striving to introduce. Nonetheless, our example of marriage among the 'Indian' Muslims of South Africa shows the tensions and disagreements that exist. They form sub-communities within the larger community of followers of Islam. These tensions arise from different interpretations of Islam. The segments who believe in respecting the Islam of their ancestors are in their own way challenging Islamic orthodoxy. This is further noticed in the domain of prayer.

Praying and prayers

A Muslim is one who accepts the oneness of Allah and the status of Mohamed as His messenger. This forms the *Kalimah Tayabah* which is the first tenet of Islam. It is recited during prayer, sometimes chanted on prayer beads and today, it is brandished on rear windscreens of cars, on front doors of homes and even on commercial outlets as part of the billboard. Where the commercial outlet is an eating place, the signs of *halaal* (permitted meat), written in both Roman and Arabic script, used to be the only signs indicating a Muslim establishment. Today, the *halaal* signs are often matched with *Kalimah Tayabah* and the *Kalimah Tayabah* is often paired with 786 [14] (numerology for 'in the name of Allah'). As stickers on cars or part of a billboard on shops and displayed on front doors of homes (some homes have their doors carved to read the *Kalimah Tayabah)*, they act as signs of brandishing their Muslimness and as markers of mutual recognition for Muslims. It is as individuals that Muslims use the stickers cited above on their cars or apply for personalised car registration plates to include the 'holy' numbers of 786.

Logically, the area of interest becomes: how do individual Muslims pray? The performance of prayer is prescribed. Muslims have a fixed number of prayers per day that are compulsory. This is the *salaat* (Arabic for prayer, which is also called the *namaaz*). Prayers are performed five times a day. The first before sunrise *(fajr)* and the last an hour or two after sunset *(esha)*. In between there are the midday*(zohr)* (never performed at 12 noon on the dot – always after), the late afternoon prayer *(asr)* performed at around 16h30 and the sunset prayer *(maghreb),* to be performed before darkness sets in. These five prayers are compulsory for Muslims and are prayed in Arabic. Men are advised to perform them in mosques in congregation and should a man perform even a single prayer alone (outside the mosque), in his home for example, Islam has a special name for him: *Munfarid.* It is believed that the prayer of men performed in congregation and in a mosque carries more reward than a prayer performed individually.

This does not extend to women. Women in some countries have the choice of performing their prayers in a mosque, but they pray in sections specifically provided for them. It could be a curtain separating the women from the men or a specially built room where they can hear the voice of the *imaam* through a speaker and thus, pray in unison with the men without being seen or without looking. For, Islam does not advocate the mixing of the sexes. The separation of the sexes which is assiduously followed in South Africa means that the majority of women always pray at home. [15]

In a mixed congregation, prayers are led by men. Never a woman. If there is one male in a gathering of women, the male shall lead the prayer. Given the dominance of the male in the domain of prayer, women exercise an advantage in areas that are considered inferior to formal prayer. These prayers are considered as additional and not obligatory for women perform them in addition to those prescribed by Islam. These prayers are often a means to deal with the uncertainties of life on a personal level. In order to illustrate this, we will now consider a number of these different kinds of prayer.

The *nazr*

From Urdu, the term *nazr* signifies an offering. This offering is made to avert the evil eye to which an individual has fallen prey. It is performed to expel an evil spell. When a person suffers a series of problems like constant headaches, or repeatedly hurting the same limb or the same side of the body, or recurring financial problems, it is believed that the person has become the victim of an evil spell cast to destroy her/him. To expel the evil spell, a *nazr* is performed. The *nazr* is performed by women. In a family or *kutum,* a woman, often elderly and accepted as having the 'gift', performs the ritual of exorcising the evil eye. From the many examples that exist, we have chosen one that demonstrates the syncretism involved.

We have chosen the following examples because they illustrate the exchange operated in transforming rituals and customs and carrying them over to their 'new' world.

Nazr can be performed in many different ways. The ingredients used can differ from using spices from the kitchen to grass broom bristles as well as sacrificing an animal or using a live animal. The example we have chosen requires the use of a live animal. The victim of a *nazr* spell is expected to provide a fowl, preferably black. The woman officiant performing the exorcising ritual takes the fowl (normally a hen) and ties its wings together. Holding it by its tied wings, she places herself in front of the victim and the exorcising ritual is begun. The officiant starts by holding the fowl at the victim's feet. She starts from the right circling the fowl seven times around the victim:

from feet to head ending with the feet. During this time she recites the *Durud Sharif,* a verse from the Koran. Thereafter, she (often the task is relegated to a younger member of the family or even the domestic servant) walks away from the victim always in a forward direction and will not look back for fear of the spell ricocheting on the victim. She or the appointed person walks with the fowl in hand until the nearest crossroads. There she places herself in the centre of the crossing and releases the fowl. The fowl, it is believed, will now carry the spell away from the victim through the direction it chooses to go. The officiant or her appointee should return from the crossroads without looking back to see which direction the fowl has taken. In doing this, the victim feels assured of the curse having 'disappeared' with the bird.

The Indian Muslims, as we have illustrated above, have internalised many Hindu practices that date from their conversion to Islam in India. These practises show how Muslim converts in India have expressed their need to retain certain – in their opinion – practices necessary to make them their own. By operating a fusion between a previously (internalised) Hindu practise and Islam and by adding a verse from the Koran, it facilitated appropriating the ritual. A ritual thus Islamified, did lead to Hindus either transforming some rituals or eliminating them from their repertoire.

Mithi nazr

Mithi nazr in Urdu means sweet curse. It is not meant to wilfully harm a person but can influence their performance negatively. It too needs a form of exorcising and the officiant is a woman. This curse is not intentional and on the contrary expresses a good intention and even if the 'culprit' is known, it will not affect the relationship. This curse is best understood as arising from receiving compliments for tasks well done. If Mrs. X is always praised for her best samoosas, for example, and should the samoosas that she makes begin to flop after an occasion she remembers, she will attribute this failure to a *mithi nazr.* To counteract this sweet curse and recover her samoosa-making talents, she will offer a *sadaqa.* The *sadaqa* is translated as dole – the giving of charity [16] and consists of seven items of varying quantities found in the kitchen. It includes packets of salt, sugar, rice and flour, some eggs, a tin of fish (in the inland areas where fresh fish was a scarce commodity, the Indian Muslims, we believe, substituted the canned variety for the fresh one), and a bottle of oil. These offerings are given to the caretaker of the mosque, known as the *Bangi.* [17] In South Africa, the *Bangi* is a special reference to Zanzibari Muslims.

Mithi nazr can also affect babies. From birth, babies wear black cotton threads around their wrists and sometimes loosely around their necks. In some families, a tiny penknife is pinned onto the infant's bib. In affluent families, the black thread-bracelet has become a bracelet of onyx and gold beads. These bracelets are often given to the baby by an aunt. It is believed that the bracelets and penknife would in some way protect the baby from *nazr*.

Despite the baby wearing amulets to ward off even the well-intentioned compliments, it is believed such praises can negatively affect her/him. This is deduced when the baby cries a lot, or is restless, or has lost his/her appetite. In this case, either a *sadaqa* is offered or the *nazr* is averted by a burning ritual. The burning ritual comes after the *sadaqa*. The burning ritual consists of putting dry red chillies, some grass broom bristles and salt in a paper bag. This bag is circled around the infant followed by a chant. The bag is then burnt. In this way, the 'sweet curse' the baby was inflicted with is burnt as well.

Imploring the favours of Allah

'Indian' Muslims use different methods to implore the favours of Allah. Among them and of interest to us, are those that exceed the boundaries of Islam. Many of these practices are performed by individuals.

The *mannat*

Mannat among Indian Muslims and *badda* among Hindu Gujaratis is what an individual performs when confronted with problems or challenges of life: for example, an important exam needs to be passed, a job interview is scheduled, a marriage proposal is made, financial problems are experienced, debtors are insisting on being paid. To face these challenges and problems, the 'Indian' Muslims who adhere to their *Baap Dada ka Islam* will implore the help of Allah by making a *mannat*. The *mannat* is a pact which they make with Allah. Women perform the *mannat,* in the name of men who experience problems.

For men do not make *mannat*. Some may publicly scorn it and secretly expect their mothers, wives or sisters to make vows on their behalf. The designated woman makes the vows in the name of the individual in the family or *kutum* who is experiencing a problem or facing a challenge. Thus, women will perform the *mannat* for men. We will consider two among them.

1 The *Nurnama*

The *Nurnama* is of interest to us because it is an example of how a text written in 17th century India has acquired a status comparable to the Koran. Before touching the text, an ablution is performed and the head is covered to 'pray' it.

The *Nurnama* – the Book of Light – was written by a Pir Mashaik, a *nizari* missionary saint in Gujarat, India, in 1688. Pir Mashaik was disillusioned by the Islam his followers practised. To educate them in the way of Islam, he believed that they needed guidance which would allow them to eliminate the Hindu practices which they regarded as Islamic. To this end, he wrote thirteen treatises of which the *Nurnama* is the first one. To reach a maximum number of Muslim converts, he wrote in Gujarati, Hindi and Urdu.

The *Nurnama* is written in verse form and is meant to be read aloud and thus transmitted orally. It narrates aspects of the life of the prophet Mohamed as well as some other prophets of Islam and some biographic details. According to S.C. Misra (1964, pp. 63-64), Pir Mashaik intended the *Nurnama* for the *nizaris* thus, for the *Khojas,* a Shi'ite sect of Islam.

In Gujarat, some Sunni Muslims adopted the *Nurnama* and transformed it into a sacred text, because it recounts aspects in the life of Prophet Mohamed. The Sunni Muslims in South Africa use and read it under the same conditions as they would the Koran. However, this text is not used in the same way as the Koran. It is used by Sunni Muslims for specific reasons. When an individual – as we have indicated above – implores the help of Allah to overcome an obstacle, a pact will be concluded. Using verses from the Koran, the pact will read, 'O Allah please help me in overcoming this obstacle' and to this a verse, normally the Durud Sharif from the Koran,will be added to authenticate the *mannat*. The *mannat* also contains elements of understanding and accepting Allah's choice in not helping. In concrete terms, if a child fails an exam despite having made a pact of reading a certain number, say, forty *Nurnamas* for Allah, the failure will be explained as 'it is Allah's will' or 'it is my *taqdeer*' (fate) and 'Allah's ways are difficult to understand'.

2 The *Dargah* : the tomb of the Muslim saint

In some cases, a vow is made to send monies to a *dargah*. The *dargah* is the tomb of a Muslim saint. While many send money to *dargahs* in India, South Africa too boasts the presence of *dargahs*. In Durban, two *dargahs* are to be found. Shaykh Ahmad, a Sufi saint, is purported to have come to Natal as an indentured labourer. After an early release from indenture, he hawked fruit and vegetable in the Durban mosque market until his death in 1886. Majzoob Badsha Peer, as he is popularly known, exuded some prodigious charisma and power and so became regarded as a saint by some locals. The 'Indian' Muslims and others who believe in the power of Badsha Peer make vows and even visit his tomb. Second, Shah Ghulam Muhammad Soofie Siddiqui, popularly known as Soofie Saheb, is the second sufi who was sent to South Africa. He arrived in

Durban in 1895 and according to popular Durban legend, he discovered the grave of Badsha Peer. He established the celebration of the anniversary (*urs*), of the death of Badsha Peer. The *urs* is celebrated each year and many in Durban believe that Soofie Saheb encouraged the development of 'folk practices as symbols to distinguish poor Indian Muslims from Hindus' (Tayob 1995, pp. 71–72). To introduce lines of demarcation as well as permit Indian Muslims to continue certain practices, he introduced the *ta'ziyyah*, the commemoration of the martyrdom of the Prophet Mohamad's grandson. A Shi'a ritual performance, it finds a place among the Sunni Muslims of South Africa.

These two saints are revered among certain segments of 'Indian' Muslims in South Africa. They visit the *dargahs* where upon entering they donate some money by depositing it in an urn meant for this purpose. If they are unable to visit the saintly tombs, they send their monies and other gifts with a relation or friend or via the post office. The saints according to my informant – a woman – act as *wakil* (intermediaries) between the mortal being and Allah. The favours of the saints are implored in different ways. We will briefly consider some of them:

- the *Glaf* or shroud – the tomb of the saint is covered with a green shroud. Individuals can make a vow where they undertake to cover the tomb with a new *glaf*. Two conditions have to be met: the fabric as mentioned before has to be green and the metreage has to be an odd figure 7, 9 or 11 metres in length.
- the *Kafni* or a Special Tunic – the *kafni* is a special tunic that is either made at home as part of the vow, or it is borrowed from the *dargah*. A vow involving wearing the *kafni* is normally made by the sick. In the majority of instances, according to my informant, it is made by mothers with 'sick' children. The mother takes the child to the *dargah* where she drapes the *kafni* around the child and then presents the infant to the saint.
- the *Tola* or weight – this again involves the sick. A child for example will be taken to the *dargah* and be weighed. The equivalent of his weight in sugar will be donated to the poor who come to the *dargah*.

Strict procedures regulate all visits to the saintly tombs. They are reciting the *Durud Sharif,* followed by the *fateha (*which is the offering of prayers to the saints) and the *Surah Yasin,* commonly regarded as the 'heart' of the Koran. The performance of these rituals in imploring the favours of a saint to act as a *wakil* between the officiant and God is still widely practised in this country.

Some Mehmon women, when imploring the help of Allah, vow to stop eating a particular fruit or a favourite food for a specified time or until the calamity has passed. Or they take a vow never to touch that fruit or food again.

Though these practices are criticised by orthodox Muslims as vestiges of a Hindu and heathen past, they nonetheless allow us to understand how segments among Muslims united in the mythical community of the *umma* exist. As a final example, we will consider some of the controversial rituals performed at funerals.

Death in an 'Indian' Muslim family

According to orthodox Islam, the dead are to be buried as quickly as possible. Some in this country believe that the body should not lie in state for longer than fourteen hours. Further, Islam does not prescribe a period of mourning – meaning that, in South Africa, the issue of death in a Muslim family will determine which Islam they follow. Of interest to us is the funeral procedures observed by followers and believers of *Baap Dada ka Islam*.

These rites come into practice after the men escorted the body to the cemetery where they buried it according to orthodox Islamic rites.

These rites strongly resemble Hindu rites and explain the migratory stages of the soul. According to Hinduism, the soul upon leaving the body is errant and mortals on earth can through prayers guide the soul in finding its destined path. The Hindus, to help the soul find its way, perform ceremonies on the third and sixteenth day after the funeral.

On the third day, Indian Muslims upholding their ancestral traditions organise a meal in the name of the deceased. This ceremony is called the *ziyarat*. It is believed that the soul of the deceased because it is searching, is 'visiting' the family. The prayers that are offered at this meal are to help the soul find its way.

This meal is followed by reading the Koran for a period of forty days. This reading is held every Thursday at the house of the deceased. Women from the neighbourhood congregate at the '*mayet*' (funeral) house and share the reading. For such occasions, the Koran is printed in thirty volumes, each volume representing a chapter. Thus, each woman, on entering the room where the prayers are held, takes a chapter off the pile, finds a place on the floor and prays. After forty days have elapsed, a meal is organised where family and all the women who participated in the reading sessions of the Koran are invited. This meal represents the closure of the official mourning period. For these Muslims, unlike their orthodox counterparts, Islam prescribes a period of mourning.

Upholding these funeral rites and practices is closely linked to their perception of Islam. It would by analogy be possible to argue that the Muslims who observe such practices in a way subscribe to the cult of the ancestor, which can be translated as z*Baap Dada*. Orthodox Islam, totally rejects these practices for reasons previously outlined.

Conclusion

The imperialistic demands of Islam have, to a large extent, impacted on how 'Indian' Muslims in South Africa perceive themselves. They use Islam as their fundamental identity parameter to invent a semblance of communal coherence in the eyes of non-Muslims, yet the community is divided on which Islam to follow. The issue of whose Islam is valid results in a kind of internal pressure where some segments insist on following an orthodox Islam, by consciously eradicating Indian influences in Islam and others steadfastly uphold the Islam of their ancestors. Though they submit their will to Allah, they practice an Islam that is either attached to India or removed from it. Despite the internal tensions that divide the 'Indian' Muslim community on the question of Islamic practices, the issue that now preoccupies them is negotiating a Muslim space in post-apartheid South Africa. The fear of 'losing' control over members and being submerged by the Other are reasons that motivate them to become visible Muslims.

Notes

1   In its origin, the invention of the *umma* was a political strategy used by Mohamed to unite the Meccan and Medininian Arabs who were hostile towards each other. The *umma* invented after 622 AD also marks year one in the Muslim calendar. It is known as the Hegira or the year of emigration.

2   Muslims do not take the Prophet's name in vain. To distinguish him from ordinary mortals, 'Peace Be Upon Him' is added. This is probably to save him from any form of profanation he can suffer from Muslim mortals.

3   It is not wrong to regard Muslims in South Africa as having arrived in two waves. This explains their arrival as the Cape Muslims having entered the country first, followed by the second wave, the Indians. However, since the Indian Muslims operated a distinction between the Free Muslims and those of indentured stock influences us to argue that like Indians in South Africa who are accepted as having arrived in two distinct ways, the Muslims among them should be regarded as following the same pattern. Furthermore, the initial subgroups that operated among the Indian immigrants in South Africa considered the status of 'free' or 'indentured' as paramount in establishing rules of interaction. Thus, Muslims of indentured stock were considered a group apart by their Free counterparts.

4   It is an accepted fact that Islam has been present in India for eleven centuries, ever since the first century of Hegira, – the century that effectively formed Islam – Arab traders not only traded spices but also converted some Indians to Islam. The first Hegira corresponds to 7th and 8th centuries of the Christian era.

5   The low number of Muslims among the indentured labourers is partly explained
    by the fact that the farmers in the Colony of Natal considered Madrassi Muslim
    labourers as not good enough. See S. Bhana and JB Brain, 1990; *Setting Down Roots:
    Indian Migrants to Natal, 1860–1902;* Witwatersrand University Press, Johannes-
    burg.

6   According to some historians like J.B. Brain the first "passenger" Indians arrived in
    1875.

7   Bhana (1991, p. 3).

8   Natal was one of the many British Colonies to have used indentured Indian la-
    bour. Where indentured workers were to be found, Indian merchants followed.
    This invariably constituted a consecutive second migratory wave. Examples of
    colonies: East Africa, Guyana, Fiji and British West Indies.

9   For more detail on social and kinship structures among the 'passenger' Indians in
    South Africa see Ebr.-Vally (1995).

10 Many Konkanis in South Africa also originate from the Bombay Presidency but, are
    popularly regarded as part of the Gujaratis.

11 The *kutum* is a restricted kinship group tracing descent through a male head. His
    kutum consists of people with whom he can trace consanguinity through a paternal
    grandfather. The *kutum* forms the body of essential members who are obliged to
    attend all formal and informal functions, ranging from birthday parties to wed-
    dings and prayers. It is also a support group where members mutually assist each
    other in times of need and are for example, consulted before a marriage is arranged.
    The *kutum* is the conscience of a family. A member's status in the *kutum* is deter-
    mined by age and sex. The young are subordinate to the old and women to men.

12 Very often invitation cards to a Muslim wedding include a saying of the Prophet
    where marriage is regarded as completing half one's faith.

13 Orthodox Muslims reason that children are a gift of God and are therefore against
    any form of birth control measures. On the other hand there are Muslims who
    believe in small families and do not regard this as making them 'less' Muslim.

14 The use of the 786 as indicating "In the name of Allah" is a controversial issue.
    There are some Muslim organisations in South Africa that contest the use of such
    numerology. However this falls outside the limits of this paper. See 'Have culture,
    will travel', *Culture in the New South Africa: After Apartheid Volume Two.*

15 Recently a few mosques led by progressive Imaams (Muslim religious leaders), are
    making space for women available. However, this right to be able to pray in mosques
    is still in its formative stages and is frowned upon by both men and women.

16 See glossary in *Lessons in Islam,* a translation of *Ta'limul Islam* (Complete) p. 7.
    Originally written in Urdu by Al-Lama Mufti Muham-mad Kifayatul-lah, (1872–
    1952) from 1912 the Grand Mufti of India. Translated into English by Sabihud-
    din Ahmad Ansari, this text formed/forms part of the core texts in teaching Islam

to children. Published in India by Kutub Khana Azizia, in New Delhi, it bears no date of publication, making knowledge of its first publication pure speculation. Yet, its importance in informing 'Indian' Muslims and especially children about performance of rituals and customs in Islam is monumental. According to some of my informants 'every Muslim home should have one.' Written in a question and answer form, it acts as a ready reference and as an introductory text to Islam. To paraphrase the translator, the *Lessons in Islam* is a sort of catechism on Islam (p. 1).

17 'Indian' Muslims, we would argue, choose to give their 'sadaqa' to the Bangi because he fulfils two roles: 1) as the caretaker of the mosque the alms are sure to go to a Muslim and 2) as the caretaker one is assured that the 'sadaqa' is given to a needy person as prescribed.

References

Ahmad, I. (1984). 'The Islamic Tradition in India', *Islam and the Modern Age*, 12 (1), pp. 44–62.

– (ed) (1973). *Caste and Social Stratification Among the Muslims*, New Delhi: Manohar Book Services.

Argyle, W.J. (1982). 'Muslims in South Africa: Origins, Development and Present Economic Status', *Journal: Institute of Muslim Minority Affairs*. 3 (2), pp. 222–255.

– (1986). 'Migration of Indian Muslims to East and South Africa: Some Preliminary Comparisons' in Gaborieau, M. (1982). *Islam and Society in South Asia*, Paris: Collection Purusartha, Collections de l'EHESS.

Arkin, A.J., K.P. Magyar and Pillay G.J. (1989). *The Indian South Africans: A Contemporary Profile*, Pinetown, South Africa: Owen Burgess Publishers.

Bhana, S. and J.B. Brain (1990). *Setting Down Roots: Indian Migrants in South Africa 1860–1911*, Johannesburg: Witwatersrand Univ. Press.

Bhana, S. (1991). *Indentured Immigrants to Natal 1860–1902. A Study based on Ships' Lists*. New Delhi: Promilla and Co Publishers.

– (ed) (1991). *Essays on Indentured Indians In Natal*. London: Peepal Tree Press.

Chetty, D. (1992). ' "Indianness", Identity and Interpretations: Stories from the Natal cane Fields', paper presented at the conference: *Ethnicity, Society and Conflict in Natal*, Univ. of Natal Pietermaritzburg, pp. 14–16 September.

Dangor, S. (1992) 'The Muslims of South Africa: Problems and Concerns of a Minority Community', *Journal: Institute of Muslim Minority Affairs*, London: 13 (2), pp. 375–381.

Digby, S. (1986). 'The Sufi Shaikh as a Source of Authority in Mediaeval India', in Gaborieau, M. (1986) *op. cit.*, pp. 57–89.

Ebr.-Vally, R. (2001). *Kala Pani: Caste and colour in South Africa*, Cape Town: Kwela Books.

Esack, F. (1988). 'Three Islamic Strands in the South African Struggle for Justice', *Third World Quarterly*, 10 (2), pp. 473–498.

Etienne, B. (1987). *L'Islamisme Radical.* Paris: Hachette. Coll. Biblio-essais.

Gaborieau, M. (1994). 'Le Culte des Saints Musulmans en tant que Rituel: Controverses Juridiques', *Archives des Sciences Sociales des Religions*, 85, pp. 85–98.

Hussain, M. (1988). 'Caste among non-Hindu Indians: An exploratory study of Assamese Muslims', *The Eastern Anthropologist*, 41 (4), pp. 273–285.

Kuper, H. (1960). *Indian People in Natal,* Pietermaritzburg: Univ. of Natal Press.

Meer, F. (1969). *Portrait of South African Indians*, Durban: Avon House.

Swan, M. (1985). *Gandhi. The South African Experience*, Johannesburg: Ravan Press.

Tayob, A. (1995). *Islamic Resurgence in South Africa. The Muslim Youth Movement*, Cape Town: University of Cape Town Press.

CHAPTER TEN

Afrikaner nationalism: the end of a dream?

Janis Grobbelaar

The South African state is in transformation. Legally defined and officially entrenched Apartheid is no longer formally operative. The country, as we all know, held its first ever democratic election during April 1994 and a government of national unity is in place. Four and a half decades of official Afrikaner nationalist rule over South Africa has ended. What of Afrikaner nationalism? Any endeavour to examine sociologically the future of Afrikaner nationalism needs not only to consider its historical genesis and contemporary nature substantively but also to look broadly at some of the attempts to deal with comparable phenomena conceptually.

Many of us, myself included, would prefer to argue for a sociological conceptual approach which does not in principle or by way of departure problematise diversity or view race, ethnic or nationalist representations as inherently or generically conflict generating. The so-called *social constructionist* views on nations, nationalism, ethnonationalism, race and ethnicity as articulated by a range of theories (including Marxism and pluralism), provide persuasive arguments that such phenomena are essentially ideological products and/or inventions. Ethnic groups and *volke* are according to these approaches ultimately 'imagined communities', as Benedict Anderson (1983) would have it. Their significance is devised and/or developed at specific historical conjunctures in 'a far from innocent political discourse' (see for example Anderson, 1983; Hobsbawn, 1990; Vail, 1989; Sharp, 1988 and Lever, 1995). In the wake of the recently officially deceased Apartheid experience, where race and ethnicity were idealised and reified, and race and ethnic gerrymandering reached unprecedented levels, the allure of analyses which suggest that they are ideological and obfuscatory creations, which can be undone, is overwhelming. All the more so – because of the deep primordialist claims made by the ferocious advocates of Afrikaner nationalism!

Ethnicity, race and ethnonationalism as influential and even determining variables are 'evident' in countries and regions all over the world. The Nigerian social scientist Claude Ake suggests that ethnicity is a 'a most significant element of the African reality' and further that we do violence to the African reality by failing to explore the possibilities of ethnicity, by failing to follow its contours and its rhythm, for that would be part of starting with the way we are instead of discarding it for what we might be. (1993, p. 5) He goes on to suggest that ethnicity fills (can fill) the public sphere or civil society in Africa and as such provide(s) 'checks' to the centralising tendencies of the post-colonial state. Given the argument that the vitality and depth of democracy is joined inextricably to the existence of civil society, Ake (1993) is in fact suggesting that, in the drive for more accountable and representative forms of governance in Africa, ethnicity is not inevitably a problem. It can act as a 'space creating' phenomenon encapsulating the key notion of relatively autonomous domestic entities as the basis for healthy democracies.

In Central and Eastern Europe it is clear that Lenin's so-called *national question* was not efficaciously 'resolved' during the socialist era. In the former Soviet Union and Yugoslavia, for example, bitter ethnonationalist and ethnic conflicts rage and one is forced to confront the question as to whether ethnicity and/or race can be disassociated from an autonomous or a relatively autonomous polity and territoriality (i.e. from a position that theoretically draws on primordialist theory). Furthermore, in Western Europe and North America one needs to address the apparent failure of the modern western state to deal with the ethnonationalist growth of separatist movements in the wake of the development of capitalism. In this regard, the Quebec and Basque separatist movements come to mind. Because nationalisms persist and sustain themselves, we need (again) to ask what they are and how they can come to be accommodated. Are they mere social constructions?

As I have tried to indicate in this brief exposition, sociologists and social scientists in general find it very difficult to present a clear analytic or explanatory account of these complex phenomena. It is not at all obvious or clearly self evident what it is that we are discussing when we, as social scientists, speak of nationalism, race or of ethnic movements. Whilst the literature on the subject matter is extensive it tends also to be descriptive and circular. The many theoretical and conceptual debates often raise more questions than they provide answers. In my view then we have not developed adequate social scientific accounts of race, ethnicity, ethnonationalism and/or nationalism.

Having thus attempted briefly to draw attention to the conceptual problems in the field, let me attempt to shed some light on the question of Afrikaner nationalist dreams of self-determination or *selfbeskikking*, and their relevance to the problems of identity and democracy in a South Africa in transformation in 1995.

In their latest work, the respected South Africanist authors Heribert Adam and Kogila Moodley have both jointly and severally (1993a, 1993b and 1994) been exploring the issues of nationalism and its various forms *vis à vis* non-racialism, as competing ideologies of the post apartheid state. They suggest further that 'democratic transformation in South Africa rests partially on the skillful management of racial and ethnic perceptions' and that non-racialism is the core ideology of the new state (Adam, 1994, p. 15). In other words, South Africa needs a non-racial integrative identity for the new state.

According to the eminent South African political philosopher Johan Degenaar (1995), no attempt should be made to build a South African nation nor can one in fact be built. Degenaar moreover argues that the imposition of a uniform culture or identity in a multi-cultural context would not only almost inevitably lead to ethnic and/or nationalist conflict, it would also fatally flaw any attempt at nation building in South Africa. In his view, endeavours at nation building will inevitably stimulate ethnonationalisms such as Afrikaner and Zulu nationalism, and hence any nation building project is doomed (1995, p. 9). He posits the view that regionality, diversity and ethnicity should be accommodated in a federally structured and constituted state of sorts. He notes:

> If we discussed this notion of a 'national' identity and accept the idea of democracy instead, it is possible to find a different focus for our loyalty. In a multicultural society loyalty is focussed around a constitution that has been collectively arrived at. At the same time the citizens of the country may feel a loyalty towards a specific culture, language and religion without making nationalistic demands in that regard.
>
> 1995, p. 9, translation

Adam and Moodley (1993; 1994) as well as Degenaar (1995) probe the questions of diversity, of identity, of social movements, of groups and group related ideologies and phenomena of a South Africa in transformation. The latter are viewed by the authors as extremely significant variables in coming to understand the South African polity and the potential it holds for a democratic future. Questions of trade-offs, of tradables, of accommodation and of the politics of negotiation accordingly remain at the centre of the quest for a democratic South Africa.

If we accept that questions of ethnicity, race and ethnonationalism have consequences in South Africa – that is, notwithstanding their controversial, somewhat intangible, and perhaps even shifting boundaries – there are at least four ideal general policy options that could be considered on the part of decision makers. In this regard it may be argued that the prospects of the Afrikaner nationalist dream can (moreover) be usefully located within the ambit of these ideal typical policy options.

In a first option it would be necessary to ensure that hypothetical policy guaranteed equal opportunity, outcome and impact for all groups in South Africa. That, in the face of very serious and even debilitating historical circumstances, all ethnic and/or racial groups be afforded not only the scope to gain access to the system but also the benefit of a range of appropriate and congruous strategies that will ensure equitable and affirming outcomes and impacts for all groups. If such a policy (or vision of equity) were to be decided upon, it would have to be sensitive to the feelings of wrongfulness which would undoubtedly be experienced by, for example, the previous ruling and privileged Afrikaner nationalist elite. We have only to take note of recent unemployment statistics released by the Central Statistical Services – 40% of 'black' South Africans are unemployed against only 6% of 'white' South Africans – to see that opportunity geared towards equity in outcome and impact would drastically effect group employment ratios in South Africa. When jobs are lost (or there is a perception that they will be), it is possible that people would not only fall back into the organic or laager-like comfort of group mobilising identities like Afrikaner nationalism, but also that the loss of self-esteem and dignity experienced would contribute towards radically undermining a vision and strategy of equity across the board.

Second, a policy to negate the broad sociological significance of group diversity – such as one of non-racialism – could be followed. In an ideal typical situation, and in the event of it being carried to its logical conclusion, the socio-political significance of group membership in terms of this policy will need to be actively demythologised and debunked. We should ask whether very much would change in the material life conditions of ordinary South Africans if this approach became formal government policy. Clearly not.

Third, a policy facilitating some or other form of cultural or ethnic political autonomy could be followed. Here diversity would be built into policy and a range of tradables would need to be negotiated. For example, the state would need to take on a more decentralised or even federal form and, ideally, ethnic needs would be met at a 'secondary level'.

Finally, secession or radical partition remains for some an ideal policy option. If this strategy were to be seriously considered it would have to stand against the weight of South African history where geographical partition has been used to deny people not only their dignity and humanity, but, more importantly, reasonable life chances, via a process of systematic and brutal structured exploitation. I will return to these four policy options. Afrikaner nationalism is not a social movement, an ethnonationalist force or coherent ideology reaching out from the mid-seventeenth century merchant capitalist occupation of the Cape of Good Hope, as the great majority of Afrikaner nationalist historians (including those of the present post apartheid era) would have us believe. It is not evidenced, for example, in Adam Tas's historic rebellion against Van der Stel, the events in the Eastern Cape that have come to be known as the Slagtersnek rebellion or even, for that matter, The Great Trek, and the much idealised Battle of Blood River. These incidents, together with many others, have been carefully selected and incorporated into the inevitable and necessary 'myth making' process that is inherent in the construction of appropriate histories for any social movement – particularly a nationalist one.

Contrary to the above notion, the genesis of Afrikaner nationalism in Southern Africa is rooted in the events that took place during the last quarter of the nineteenth century. This point is well made by, inter alia, the Afrikaans historian Floors van Jaarsveld (1961). He sketches the context immediately preceding the inception of Afrikaner nationalism as follows:

> We can best begin by describing the condition of the Afrikaans-speaking population shortly before the 70s and 80s of the last century. At that time terms such as South Africa or Afrikaans people had no spiritual or political meaning for them; since they lacked unity and national consciousness, such terms could not denote a 'fatherland' or a 'nation'. In short, they had not yet become 'nationally' minded. Over a distance of nearly 1 500 miles, stretching from the Cape to the Zoutpansberg, there were isolated groups and there was only limited intellectual exchange.
>
> F.A. van Jaarsveld, 1964, p. 33

What happened to change this state of affairs? South Africa's enormous mineral wealth was 'discovered'. These events heralded an era of fundamental socio-political and economic change in the region. In their wake came urbanisation, emergent industrialisation, and later commercial agriculture.

Strong anti-British imperialist and capitalist sentiments developed in the struggles that took place over the ownership of the forces of production. Together, these events and the dynamics they unleashed formed the crucible from which the Afrikaner nationalist ideology and social movement initially sprung (see, e.g., Van Jaarsveld, 1964; Du Toit, 1975; 1983a and b). Afrikaner nationalism has been a principal, if shifting product of South African history for the past 100 years, and not for 300 years as most would have it or want it.

Afrikaner nationalism, the strategies and organisational infrastructures forged to give it momentum, the rewards and patronage with which it has endowed its adherents and the mobilising and modernising tendencies it has engendered lead to the creation of the formal apartheid state. In 1948, the latter led to the further embourgeoisment of the majority of white South Africans – especially those of Afrikaner descent – via an extremely successful policy of racial and ethnic patronage in the civil service and in a series of white Afrikaner dominated parastatals that were established. (White Afrikaner males were the special recipients of these very rewarding affirmative action strategies.)

In the decades preceding Afrikaner nationalism's victory at the polls in 1948 the *volk* was, as now, wracked and torn by internal battles (see e.g. Roberts and Trollip, 1946 and Furlong, 1987). Hence the routine cry for unity – *unity is strength* – or in the words of one of its most prominent ideologues, the much revered Vader Kestell:

> We have after all to be united as a nation. With us it is not a matter of blood being thicker than water. It should not be like this. We need to feel that our fellow Afrikaners are our own flesh and blood. My nation is in great peril. The biggest peril facing my nation is its division.
>
> 1941, p. 46, translation

Given Afrikaner nationalism's partial coherence over time, and the institutionalisation of in its core narrative – its monolithic status in the eyes of 'outsiders' should be carefully weighed. Particularly when evaluating the actions and role of the apartheid state over time. The short review that follows is 'punctuated' by the formation of the Conservative Party of South Africa under the leadership of the breakaway National Party cabinet minister Andries Treurnicht in 1982. It denotes the start of an era of reinvigorated and resuscitated Afrikaner nationalist activity, which itself is perhaps best understood in terms of watersheds and historical parallels. It can be divided into three periods – 1982 to 1992 (Neo-Verwoerdian); 1992 to 1994 (a period of innovation) and 1994 to the present (a period of 'renewed' constitutional participation and of ethnic/ racial 'trading').

So-called monumental Afrikaner nationalism constructed under the tutelage of the National Party from 1948 via the instruments of its apartheid state apparatus formally split into two major groups in 1982: the 'new' National Party, and the so-called white right wing. As I have argued elsewhere (1991), the latter became, and is, the torchbearer of a reconstituted Afrikaner nationalism. Accordingly the white right wing should be understood to embody and symbolise not only the historical guardianship of the Afrikaner nationalist dream but also its contemporary striving for self-determination, and hence a threat to the present state.

It may be suggested further that given its present, quite fragile organisational and strategic hegemony, it is also a threat to government at a less constituted level. We need only to recall and consider the 1993 political assassination of Chris Hani, the South African Communist Party chief!

For a period of approximately ten years the Conservative Party of South Africa (CP) stood at the centre of a resuscitated Afrikaner nationalist movement – that is, up until and including the 1992 white-only referendum. Its formation, as has been suggested, was the culmination of wide ranging dissonance on both the levels of ideology and praxis within the ranks of the governing white Afrikaner elite – in the face of the wider South African socio-political and economic crisis. Until approximately 1992, the party's policy was dominated by a neo-Verwoerdian notion of political praxis. It believed throughout this period that it could win power through the ballot (i.e. in the old dispensation) and fully implement its 1913/1936 Land Act political option of *Partition*. (This lack of understanding of the political realities of South Africa still bedevils what is left of this party.)

The CP mobilised, as had the NP earlier, via a broader network of white Afrikaner organisational complexes and formations. This cultural, racial and nationalist mobilisation lies at the root of the historical 'successes' of Afrikaner nationalism and at the core of the CP's attempt to win power, at both the local and national levels. This network or *volksfront* (people's front), of which the party came to be not only a constituent, but also the core element, was, and is, characterised by cross-cutting and coinciding memberships and interlocking elites. For analytic purposes it can be understood to be made up as follows: party political organisations in a participatory constitutional sense (until the April 1994 elections the CP was not only the primary representative but at times also the official opposition in Parliament – since the 1999 election, Viljoen's Freedom Front (FF) has become the representative of this strand); religious formations; policy study and/or think tank units; paramilitary organisations; other civil society entities and *kultuurpolitieke* (cultural political) organisations.

Nonetheless, up to and including the 1992 referendum result, the CP did not succeed in gaining more than 30% of the white vote at a national level, that is 3 out of 10 white voters at most cast their ballots for the CP. On the other hand, it should be remembered that these votes, in fact, represented at least 50% of white Afrikaner votes in the former Orange Free State and Transvaal provinces (i.e. excluding the wider Johannesburg metropole). Throughout this period strife and debate raged within the Afrikaner nationalist right wing, but the Conservative Party reigned.

This was not because it managed to develop new or viable policy, but because it was able to provide security on at least two important levels. In the first place, it developed, as had the National Party in a previous era, an excellent grassroots organisational infrastructure that 'held' people concretely. The party regularly organised local meetings; called on its constituents methodically to collect membership fees; mobilised to win control over school boards, farmer's cooperatives and so on and encouraged membership of the wider *volksfront* organisations. In the second place the CP's apartheid rhetoric and its effective organisation on the ground also 'spoke' to those who were beginning to feel lost and alienated as the Botha regime, the primary Afrikaans churches, and the international community suggested a message of change – apartheid was unacceptable! If South Africa were to survive it needed to adapt – it needed to reform. (The Botha regime, needless to say, had begun a tentative reformist and technocratic path towards survival from the early 1980s onwards.)

Furthermore, the success of the mass democratic movement and the African National Congress in their resistance and liberation campaigns throughout the 1980s continued to chip away at Afrikaner nationalist ruling class confidence. Of vital importance, and as a consequence of the above, the South African economy continued its backward slide. In these circumstances the right wing, with the CP at its centre, under the leadership of an ex-Dutch Reform Church dominee, also an ex-president of the Afrikaner-*Broederbond*, promised a 'way back'. It provided for psychological security, for a familiar group consciousness and the conviction that the dream of white Afrikaner self-determination was, notwithstanding, defensible and viable. It promised the return to a *gemeinschaft* ethos that had once been the hallmark of Afrikaner nationalism – away from growing alienation.

Despite evidence of tensions *vis à vis* the need for pragmatic and viable new policy amongst its adherents, the CP could not act forcefully or seriously on this matter. F.W. de Klerk's announcement on *Rooi Vrydag* (Red Friday) (2 February 1990) seemed to lull it further into a state of false consciousness and, objectively speaking, policy impotence. It entered the 1992 referendum without a 'new' strategy and it achieved disastrous results – only 3 out of 10 whites voted NO. Participation in the referendum proved ultimately to be not only the strategic blunder which 'lost' the party its central role in the Afrikaner nationalist movement but also the battle for political power within the parameters of the 'old' South African constitutional script.

These 1992 events heralded a new discourse in the battle of and between Afrikaner nationalists. The pressure to act, as well as to reconstruct policy against the backdrop of the fast moving South African political scenario ushered in two significant events. First, the 'generals' under the leadership of Constand Viljoen entered the arena. They brought with them not only technocratic and strategically 'advanced' but also innovative approaches to the vexing questions of policy formulation, negotiation and military resistance. They were, after all, products of the *total onslaught* era and experts in counter revolutionary strategy and warfare. (The CP was refusing to negotiate at Kempton Park. The ANC did not represent a *volk* and hence the process itself undermined the party's reason for being.) As a result of their initiatives first COSAG (The Concerned South African Group) and then the Freedom Alliance was formed (1993). These alliances brought conservative black groups, including the Inkatha Freedom Party (IFP), together with Afrikaner nationalists in an attempt to create a bulwark against the ANC and NP defined negotiation strategies. Moreover, the umbrella rightwing alliance, the Afrikaner *Volksfront* (AVU), was formed with the goal of uniting and mobilising the rightwing in the more emphatic pursuance of the goals of Afrikaner self determination through engagement and negotiation.

Second, the CP's fragile unity was shattered in 1992 when it lost seven Members of Parliament to Andries Beyers's newly formed *Afrikanervolksunie*. The latter was intent upon entering the Kempton Park negotiation arena in the wake of the referendum defeat in an attempt to 'save' something for Afrikaner nationalists. In practice, Viljoen and his generals with their technocratic visions and skills began to 'take over' the Afrikaner nationalist movement. They kept their options open on the issues of direct negotiation with the ANC, on participation in the then forthcoming April 1994 elections and on a territorially smaller *volkstaat* for Afrikaner nationalists. The death of Andries Treurnicht in 1993 proved to be the final blow to the now posturing Conservative Party. Viljoen and his people became not only 'movers and shakers' but

Viljoen more personally embodied Afrikaner nationalism's hope *'if all else failed'*. (Afrikaner nationalists have throughout the period under discussion, that is, from 1982 onward, believed, that if 'all else failed' they could rule South Africa via their military strength – or at least make it impossible for anyone else to do so!) Viljoen kept all options open – he registered a political party, The Freedom Front (on 4 March 1994), for possible participation in the April 1994 election. He also went ahead in attempting to consolidate a paramilitary commando system (the Boere Krisisaksie). Then the so-called Bophuthatswana debacle took place in March of 1994. As a result Viljoen would forcefully commit himself to a radically different constitutional route – a hitherto unthinkable thought for the majority of the believers in *'die erwe van ons vad're* (Afrikaner nationalists)' – that of constitutional participation. In pursuit of a consitutional route (given the clear collapse of a military option as reflected in the Bophuthatswana military defeat of the white Afrikaner forces), and just before the April 1994 elections, Viljoen and the FF negotiated, in exchange for participation, an amendment to the Interim Constitution. Article 34 of Schedule 4 (i.e. the enshrined Constitutional Principles of 1994) made constitutional provision for a notion of the right to self-determination by any community sharing a common cultural and language heritage, whether in a territorial entity within the Republic or in any other recognised way. The relevant article goes on to enshrine the above if there is *substantial proven support*. Furthermore Chapter 11A of the Interim Constitution made provision for the establishment of a *Volkstaat* Council. The Council, according to the Constitution, shall serve as a constitutional mechanism to enable the proponents of the idea of a *Volkstaat* constitutionally to pursue the establishment of such a *volkstaat*.

Viljoen and the FF are now actively part and parcel of legitimate constitutional activity in South Africa. They had nine seats in the national parliament and fourteen in the nine provincial parliaments in 1995. Viljoen himself has stature beyond the formal and quite limited numerical constituency he represents – both nationally and internationally. He is presently committed to the path of constitutional engagement. In other words the dream of achieving a 'new' Afrikaner nationalist *volkstaat* and hence self determination appears, at present, to be not only indistinguishably constitutionalised and endorsed via government participation as well as in the activities of the *Volkstaatraad*, but also through the strategies of elite accommodation. In the words of a *Volkstaatraad* member (June 1995) 'Afrikaners are a competitive and skilled minority – their accommodation would clearly be of benefit to the government of national unity' (personal interview). Nevertheless and clearly the primordialist roots of Afrikaner nationalism are, as always, evident.

What was the state of the dreamed-of *volkstaat* in 1995? According to the *First Interim Report of the Volkstaat Council* (May 1995) it was: 'A state, the inhabitants of which belong primarily to a specific *volk* – people' (1995, p. 7). In 1941 during an earlier era of Afrikaner nationalist mobilisation, Nico Diedericks (later to become a long serving South African minister of finance and State President under the National Party government), said of the *volkstaat* for which the NP was then striving:

> It will stop being the neutral, colourless state it is today that can be used by any government majority of the day to the detriment of the core of the Afrikaner volk and to the advantage of foreign powers and elements. It will become the servant of a genuine, well-established volks community. It will have to positively pursue volks values. It will be the mightiest of weapons in securing the freedom of this volk.
>
> 1941, pp. 128–29, translation

The *Volk* State Council (remember that this Council is part of the state apparatus in terms of the 1994 Constitution) defines self-determination as *political sovereignty*. It enables a *volk* to determine its own destiny and to give expression to its need for freedom from suppression and discrimination, for pursuing the development of its human and natural resources and for deciding on the form and nature of its government (1995). It has nothing to do with racially exclusive categories, in other words.

The report itself is the product of compromise between two broad groups of Afrikaner nationalists who serve on the Council and whose *volkstaat* strategies differ from one another quite significantly. On the other hand, they share a pledge to pursue constitutional participation and negotiation. (In a June 1995 interview a council member went so far as to suggest that the notion of the *volkstaat* and the survival of Afrikaner nationalist dream had in some ways been promoted by the ANC's 'coming to power').

A second report (June 1995), also dealing with the question of the future of Afrikaner ethnonationalism and self determination, was released by the so-called extra-parliamentary Afrikaner nationalists. (Those who are members of what is left of the once powerful Afrikaner *Volksfront*). This group is essentially made up of the now fragmenting CP. Its report was completed under the auspices of the *Volksrepubliek-werkkomitee* (the National Republic Work Committee), a sub committee of the AVF. *Patriot*, weekly official newspaper mouthpiece of the CP, comments on the two reports in the following terms: The differences are dealt with in a single remark. One report, that of the *Volkstaatraad*, was in the first place submitted to President Mandela and is a report that is intended to be discussed in the communistic council chambers of this country.

However, the report of the *Volks* Republic Work Committee has been submitted by its chairman, Dr Willie Snyman, to Dr Hartzenberg for presentation to the Boer *volk*! The VRWC report is a report from the *volk* to the *volk* in aid of the *volk*. (*Patriot*, leader article, 9 June 1995, p. 6) With these words the CP again underlined the fact that it was unable to come to terms with the material and tangible reality of the government of national unity. It was unable to break the confines of a now empty ruling class posturing. This severely limits its proficiency to be practical. Its territorial claims are considerably greater than those of the *Volkstaatraad* and under the leadership of Hartzenberg it has lost its significance. In short, by its own volition, it largely has excluded itself from the present debate on Afrikaner nationalism's future. In summary, there are three main 'poles' in this debate: the Freedom Front 'linked' members of the *Volkstaatraad*; the *Afrikanervryheidstigting* or Boshoff-Orania 'linked' members of the *Volkstaatraad*, and those that cluster around the now almost defunct AVF and the dying CP.

Before attempting, in conclusion, to situate the Afrikaner nationalist dream, some commentary on those white Afrikaners who make up the majority of the white Afrikaans speaking population in South Africa is appropriate. It would, I believe, be fair to say that the majority of these people voted for the National Party in 1994 (see e.g. Reynolds, 1994). The NP rejects, it says, ethno-nationalism and has embraced non-racialism together with 'political federalism' as its core ideology and policy. What does this mean?

Some 22 years ago, on the occasion of his inaugural presentation at the University of SA (*Die Profiel Van 'n Afrikaner*), Connie Alant put forward a four category typology of white Afrikaners. Contemporary white Afrikaner members of the National Party could best be placed in his C category – that of '*die Kompromis* (compromise minded) Afrikaner'. Alant says of this category of Afrikaners:

> It is obvious, however, that this type of Afrikaner acts in a 'dual' manner in the sense that the Compromising Afrikaner on the one hand supports traditional values, but on the other hand desires to make 'the necessary adjustments' under the pressure of circumstances.
>
> 1978, p. 7, translation

This, then, and notwithstanding the NP's formal policy, is the natural constituency of the Freedom Front. What would prompt white Afrikaners to join the latter? According to 'insiders': growing lawlessness, that is, conditions of deteriorating law and order; (further) economic decline; attacks on the symbols of the white Afrikaner culture such as the present 'attack on the Afrikaans language'; threatening the *eiesoortigheid* (particularity) of Afrikaner schools and places of learning; nationalisation of land; taxation of agricultural land; the negation of the *volk* and a programme of radical affirmative action.

I am suggesting that the thrust of Afrikaner nationalist self determination strivings are at present coalesced around the state sponsored *Volkstaatraad* and the Freedom Front. That they, as well as the government of national unity, are in 1995 endeavouring, via constitutionalised means and a strategy of elite accommodation, to normalise ethnicity and ethnonationalism. At the same time they want to *trade* ethnicity and ethnonationalist capacity with the other. This boils down to attempts to launder ethnicity and to deracialise it in the cauldron of South Africa's future and in the light of white Afrikaners' apartheid crime against humanity.

The *Volkstaatraad* report itself presents us with two strategic options. In the first place, the notion of a *constituent state* is placed on the table. One which is eventually to become politically sovereign but is nevertheless part of a wider federated South African state and its economy. Attached to it will be two further units – areas of limited self determination called *autonomous units* and *civic councils* via which cultural self-determination can be established for small pockets of Afrikaner nationalists throughout wider South Africa. This approach is clearly envisaged to be one of flexibility and of progressiveness on the part of its proponents.

It rests on twin pillars, one of trade-off and one of technocracy. It is, in other words, largely an elite driven enterprise. What does it see itself as offering? Its supporters argue a competitive, skilled and potentially motivated core of people who will commit themselves to a peaceful and prosperous South Africa and who are able and will be willing to contribute to the RDP. If their Afrikaner nationalist sentiments are not accommodated, they will, they argue, be 'lost to South Africa' – they will take what they can without regard, and/or they will leave South Africa and/or they will plan insurrection. In short, they offer an argument that they could quite easily become a real liability instead of a potential asset. Inversely, Afrikaner nationalists could, 'if all else fails', look to the IFP and Zulu nationalism. In so doing they would greatly exacerbate the problems of democratising South Africa by generating ethnonationalist conflict instead of, in their terms, broadening democracy for all in South Africa by being accommodated constitutionally in group terms.

This approach draws on the laws of rationality, of science, and is 'biddable' in the eyes of its upholders. It departs, and this is very significant, from the notion of territorial self-determination in territories (and it argues that such areas exist) within which the Afrikaner will be in a position to capture the majority vote through the democratic process (*Volkstaatraad*, 1995(a), p. 8). On the other hand, there is an anomaly evident in the report. It 'adds on' the *Afrikanervryheidstigting* (Afrikaner freedom option) or the Boshoff option and herein lies the obvious split within the Council.

The *Afrikanervryheidstigting* argues for a *Declaration of Intent* to be included in the final constitution. Its visionaries believe that a *volkstaat* for Afrikaner nationalists will only be viable when a 'substantial' group of people want it, and are willing to move to, occupy, and build in a territory which is at present underpopulated and undeveloped. Its arguments rest on the 'will of the citizenry' rather than that of the elites. It believes that it will not be possible to engineer a *volkstaat* from above. The latter vision does not rest on the precondition of existing majority territorial occupation. It suggests an Afrikaner *volkstaat*, in an underpopulated area of South Africa to be enabled by a constitutionalised *Declaration of Intent* to be taken up in the new Constitution – if sufficient Afrikaners should desire it. It deals with the question of race by arguing that a *volk* needs to do its own 'work' – that is, the application of the principles of *selfversorging* (self-direction) and *eiewerksaamheid* (autonomy). This essentially excludes people of colour acquiring residence.

In conclusion, and simply in relation to the four ideal typical policy options spelt out towards the beginning of this address, it can be concluded that Afrikaner nationalists reject both a policy of non-racialism as well as that of equity. They are concerned with the relative or federal political autonomy option and, 'if all else fails' with that of radical militarised secession. Please allow me to share a few largely speculative impressions. In my view Afrikaner nationalism is alive approximately 100 years since its birth. The era of Afrikaner nationalist activity in South Africa is not quite the vestige of the past that most of us would want to believe it to be. It is, however, most certainly ailing. It is also clear that the growing international respectability and legitimacy attributed to issues of ethnicity, ethnonationalism and diversity together with the culture of dialogue and negotiation in South Africa, are playing a vital role in attempts to address Afrikaner nationalist identity. Afrikaner nationalist elites dominating the movement are at present and in general committed to 'trading' and negotiating. The questions of soft territorial boundaries and relative cultural autonomy are on the constitutional menu in South Africa for the foreseeable future.

To suggest that Afrikaner nationalism is a completely empty and spent force would be to misunderstand the modern history of South Africa. On the other hand, to argue in the light of the available evidence, as was illustrated throughout this paper, that it would be easy for present day Afrikaner nationalist forces to act as a cohesive unit would be equally untrue. Finally, if threat and insecurity in general were to become the dominating culture in South Africa, it is more than likely that support for the vision of the believers in *die erwe van ons vadre* would grow significantly amongst white South Africans and we will not have heard the last of this once powerful force.

References

Adam, H. (1994). 'Ethnic versus Civic Nationalism: South Africa's Non-Racialism in Comparative Perspective', *South African Sociological Review*, 7 (1).

Adam, H. and K. Moodley (1993a). 'Comparing South Africa: Nonracialism versus Ethnonationalist Revival', *Third World Quarterly*, 14 (2).

– (1993b). *The Negotiated Revolution: Society and Politics in Post-Apartheid South Africa*, Johannesburg: Jonathan Ball.

Ake, C. (1993). 'What is the Problem of Ethnicity in Africa?', *Transformation*, 22.

Anderson, B. (1983). *Imagined Communities: Reflections on the Origin and Spread of Nationalism*, London: Verso.

Baynham, S. (1995). 'Prospects for Peace and Stability in Africa', *African Security Review*, 4 (1).

Bekker, S. and J. Grobbelaar (1987). 'The White Right Wing Movement in South Africa: Before and After the May 1987 Election', in D.J. Van Vuuren, L. Schlemmer, H.C. Marais, and J. Latakgomo (eds) *South African Election 1987*, Pinetown: Owen Burgess.

Bekker, S. and J. Grobbelaar (1989a). 'Durban. Has the Conservative Party Bandwagon Slowed Down?', *Indicator S.A.* 6 (1/2), Center for Social and Development Studies, University of Natal.

– (1989b). 'Durban. The Conservative Party: Conviction at the Crossroads', *Indicator S.A.*, 6 (3), Centre for Social and Development Studies, University of Natal.

Conservative Party of South Africa (1982). *Programme of Principles and Policy*.

Degenaar, J. (1995). 'Suid-Afrika kan nie nasie bou nie. *Insig*, Mei, Kaapstad.

Die Afrikaner (1986–94). Official weekly newspaper of the Herstigte Nasionale Party.

Du Toit, A. (1975). 'Ideological Change, Afrikaner Nationalism and Pragmatic Racial Domination in South Africa', in L. Thompson and J. Butler (eds) *Perspectives on South Africa*, Berkeley: University of California Press.

– (1983a). 'No Chosen People. The Myth of the Calivinist Origins of Afrikaner Nationalism and Racial Ideology', *American Historical Review*, 88.

Du Toit, A. and H. Giliomee (1983b). *Afrikaner Political Thought: Analysis and Documents. 1 (1780-1850)*, Cape Town: David Philip.

Friedman, S. and D. Atkinson (eds) (1994). *South African Review 7 the Small Miracle*, Johannesburg: Ravan Press.

Furlong, P.J. (1987). *National Socialism, the National Party and the Radical Right in South Africa, 1934–1948*, U.M.J. Dissertation Information Service, Ann Arbor, PhD, University of California.

Grobbelaar, J. (1989). 'Parliament in the Promised Land — the CP and the Ultra-Right', Durban: *Indicator South Africa*, 6 (4), Centre for Social and Development Studies, University of Natal.

– (1991). 'Ultra-Rightwing Afrikaners: a Sociological Analysis', D Litt et Phil, University of South Africa.

– (1992). '*Bittereinders*: Dilemmas and Dynamics on the Far Right', in G. Moss and I. Obery (eds) *South African Review*, 6 – from 'Red Friday to Codesa', Johannesburg. Ravan Press.

Grobbelaar, J., S. Bekker, and R. Evans (1989). 'Durban, *Vir Volk en Vaderland*. An *Indicator South Africa* Issue Focus', Centre for Social and Development Studies, University of Natal.

Hobsbawm (1990). *Nations and Nationalism since 1780*, Cambridge: Cambridge University Press.

Jalali, R. and S.M. Lipset (1992/1993). 'Racial and Ethic Conflicts: a Global Perspective, *Political Science Quarterly*, 107 (4).

Kestell, J. (1941). *My Nasie in Nood*, 'Tweede Trek', reeks no 3, Bloemfontein: Nasionale Pers.

Lever, J. (1995). 'Conceptualising Diversity – A Sociological Perspective?' unpublished paper.

Malan, D.F. (1959). *Afrikaner volkseenheid en my ervarings op die pad daarheen*. Kaapstad: Nasionale Boekhandel.

Patriot (1986–95). Official weekly newspaper of the Conservative Party of South Africa.

Reynolds, A. (ed.) (1994). *Election 1994 South Africa*, Cape Town: David Philip.

Roberts, M. and A. Trollip (1946). *The South African Opposition 1939/45*, London: Longmans, Green.

Sharp, J. (1988). 'Ethnic Group and Nation. The Apartheid Vision in South Africa', E. Boonzaier and J. Sharp (eds) *South African Keywords*, Cape Town: David Philip.

Smith, A.D. (1983). *State and Nation in the Third World*, Brighton: Wheatsheaf Books.

Treurnicht, A.P. (1975). *Credo van 'n Afrikaner*, Tafelberg: Kaapstad.

Vail, L. (ed.) (1989). *The Creation of Tribalism in Southern Africa*, Berkeley: University of California Press.

Van Jaarsveld, F.A. (1961). *The Awakening of Afrikaner Nationalism 1868–1981*, Cape Town.

Van Rooyen, J. (1994). *Hard Right*, London: I.B. Tauris Publishers.

Van Onselen, C. (1982). 'The Main Reef Road into the Working Class (Proletarianisation, Unemployment and Class Consciousness amongst Johannesburg's Afrikaner Poor, 1890–1914)'. *Studies in the Social and Economic History of the Witwatersrand 1886–1914, 2: New Miners*, Johannesburg: Ravan Press.

Volkstaatraad (1995). *First Interim Report of the Volkstaat Council*, May.

– (1995). *Getuienis gelewer voor die Volkstaatraad*, Deel 1, 2 en 3, Mei.

Wilson, M. and L. Thompson (eds) (1971). *The Oxford History of South Africa, 2, 1870–1966*, London: Oxford University Press.

Section Three:
Reconciliation in South Africa

The last two chapters are both attempts at providing useful guidelines for healing the cataclysmic chasm in racialised relations brought about by colonialism and apartheid in South Africa. By pointing towards what has been done in order to heal these, at least at a political level through the Truth and Reconciliation Commission and providing theoretical points of departure for the way forward, these chapters provide a unique understanding of contemporary South Africa and the problems it faces. Together, they convey the message that the problems facing a unified identity for the new nation of South Africa are not insurmountable.

Chapter 11:
The Truth and Reconciliation Commission in South Africa:
tentative implications drawn from public perceptions and
contemporary debates
- Ian Liebenberg and Abebe Zegeye

In Chapter 11, Liebenberg and Zegeye touch upon the process of truth and reconciliation in South Africa after apartheid, its ascendancy and future. Arguing that reconciliation is "not merely a question of identity and letting bygones be bygones", the authors claim that acknowledgement and disclosure of the truth are essential if future human rights violations are to be avoided. A collective conscience as a reminder of pain is an implicit recognition that people would have likes things to be different. By reminding oneself of past horrors, one would sustain or revive the hope for a better future. Significantly in terms of the aims of this book, such a reminder also reflects the notion that 'total amnesia' is tantamount to a 'total loss of identity'.

By the nature of it, the TRC in South Africa represents political compromise. Some South Africans were justifiably of the view that there had to be a judicial process to deal

with human rights violations under apartheid, while others disagreed. The final institution of the commission therefore was a compromise between general amnesty for
human rights violators, thus 'drawing a line through the past' and a judicial process to
punish these offenders. South Africans remain deeply divided over the value of the
TRC as a tool of reconciliation.

More may have to be done to realise the ideals of the TRC in South Africa.
Liebenberg and Zegeye suggest re-training programmes for people in security and
intelligence structures concerning the function of security institutions within a working
democracy and a state in which justice is done in terms of the law and Bill of Rights.
Those in security institutions should better understand that military institutions in
democracies are subject to the constitution and the control of elected politicians. Security
personnel should also gain a better appreciation of a social order with a strong human
rights focus. At the same time, the public/community/civil society should be encouraged to interact with political electees in such a manner that the elected officials serve
the citizenry. Emphasis should be placed should be placed on the institutionalisation
and cultivation of South Africa's own culture of human rights.

One suggestion as to how this can be accomplished is the cultivation of a common
memory of the past between people of different social identity backgrounds. This
could take the form of a regular conference of historians, a historians debate along the
lines of the German *Historikerstreit*. Such a historians' dialogue (in which social theorists
and practitioners and civil society participate) should ideally include a debate on the
morality of coming to terms with a collective past and the necessity that the dominance
of sheer power should never be repeated.

A 'new' history ought to be written through critical reflection and within the
ambit of critical theory, including deconstructive, radical, anarchistic, structuralist and
post-structuralist/post-modernist questioning and discourse in the widest sense of
the word. In all this, the TRC report has the potential to serve as a launching platform
for far-reaching human rights reforms and also as the basis for deepening democratic
processes. South Africa through its TRC process may indeed according to Liebenberg
and Zegeye be on the threshold of restorative justice rather than retribution.

Chapter 12:
Conclusion:
depoliticising ethnicity in South Africa
- Abebe Zegeye

In this chapter, Zegeye claims that identities and identity formation in contemporary
South Africa have the potential to inform the social and political analyst's understanding of diversity and democracy. The politicised nature of communities and individuals

in South Africa under apartheid has set the stage for democracy and thus a choice in terms of the kind of society communities wanted for themselves. Zegeye points out that the majority of the population (Africans) was not to be satisfied merely by autonomy for their group. Rather, they insist that the economic (and other) inequalities of the past be remedied for everybody that was disadvantaged by apartheid.

In answering the question of whether a democratic society can treat all its members as equals and also recognise their specific cultural identities, Zegeye states that the answer is 'yes' if culture is defined as Alexander suggested as the common core of humanity and practices that all human beings engage in. When culture includes the tangible beliefs and philosophies that are reflected in the ways people recreate their humanity, culture can play a decisive role in democracy. The South African constitution seeks to foster a single community while respecting the existence and worth of cultural communities. The resolution of the language question offered by the constitution, the incorporation of traditional leaders and customary law are the outgrowths of respect for culture. The art of complex mapping can be applied in order to understand the role of culture in consolidating the South African democratic polity. Thereafter the lessons learned from this mapping of identity in South Africa can be used to enrich democratic theory elsewhere.

The prospect of creating a common democratic culture or consolidating working democracy is realisable in heterogeneous communities according to the analysis by Zegeye. In this respect however, one would do well to recall at this point Alexander's warning (referred to in the introductory chapter to this volume) that a South African nation cannot be 'fabricated' by what Said calls 'the process of identity enforcement'. Alexander is however also at pains to make the point that South Africa faces the real problem that if it does not promote national unity - in other words arrive at a core of common values, practices and national projects, it may fall apart into warring ethnic groups, each with its own more or less separatist agenda. Recent history in Europe, Asia and Africa illustrates the point.

Zegeye utilises the metaphor of mapping to show that the cultural, linguistic, racial, religious and ethnic groups in the new South Africa indeed know how to sustain a heterogeneous society without resorting to the rigid measures of the previous minority regime. They provide evidence for the fact that heterogeneity does not preclude harmony, sympathy for others or commiseration, which are prerequisites for sustaining a community life. In fact the assumption that communities are automatically uniform has repeatedly been the Achilles heel of authoritarian schemes. Zegeye concedes that societies attempting to consolidate democracy usually politicise some social category so that people can become either citizens or non-citizens. However, he disagrees that stable democracies use this overarching category in ways that exclude other cross-cutting and overlapping identities that residents may claim and use. Consequently, the metaphor of mapping lends credence to Zegeye's assertion that South African society can avail itself of knowledge of how to achieve equity despite its multi-racial, multi-class and multi-lingual composition.

In the Zegeye analysis, the apartheid system cemented a division of labour and citizenship on a racial and ethnic basis, which resulted in the development of ontological commitments to racialised and ethnic identities. The current government aims at de-emphasising the apartheid-constructed divisions through its policy of non-racialism and the construction of a national identity. This should not be done in a manner that subordinates the immediate interests of sub-groups to a given, undifferentiated national interest. Its point of departure should be that people are what they are by virtue of how they actually live, produce and reproduce themselves; how they actually shape and reshape their everyday world. The theoretical and practical issue is whether there is sufficient commonality in South Africans' sufferings and hopes, the modes and sources of their oppressions and expressions and in the creation of a social order to eliminate destructive divisions and forge a concrete unity in diversity. When all is said and done, this involves commitment to the ideal of maintaining own integrities without encroaching on the integrity and well-being of others.

The Truth and Reconciliation Commission in South Africa: tentative implications drawn from public perceptions and contemporary debates

Ian Liebenberg and Abebe Zegeye

In the second half of the 20th century, various options have been pursued by democratising societies to deal with a past of collective and sustained violence. This chapter investigates the rationale behind the current process of truth and reconciliation in South Africa, its ascendancy and its potential impact. Particular attention is paid to the background to the current process, the inception of the Truth and Reconciliation Commission (TRC) and its possible results and consequences for South Africans. Furthermore, a number of imponderables are discussed.

These include the commission's potential to start a debate on how the history of a recent violent past should be written, how it should be reflected upon and how it could be interpreted. In this regard, a few thoughts are offered on what implications a South African version of the German *Historikerstreit* would have for contemporary historiography.

No more than provisional comments can be offered as yet, since the process and debate have not drawn to a close and not enough South African civil society institutions and research institutes have yet involved themselves in studies like this on a continuous basis. Our hope is that these comments will contribute to a better understanding of the truth and reconciliation process in South Africa and elsewhere.

Truth Commissions in context

It is useful to refer to Priscilla Hayner's definition of a truth commission to establish a solid context: 'Truth commissions, as I will call them generically, are bodies set up to investigate a past history of violations of human rights in a particular country'. The violations 'can include violations by the military or other government forces or by armed opposition forces' (Hayner, 1994, p. 600). The executive or legislative branch of a (new) government, the UN or non-governmental organisations (NGOs) can sponsor such commissions. Zalaquett lists three conditions which must be met in dealing with a legacy of human rights violations.[1] These are:

- the complete truth must be established in an officially sanctioned manner, rendering an authoritative version of events
- the policy of human rights must represent the will of the people and victims must be heard
- the policy or actions taken by the commission or the state must not violate international law relating to human rights

The Truth and Reconciliation Commission's work in South Africa is aimed at enabling South Africans to come to terms with their past. The then Minister of Justice stated in an interview in 1994 that, 'Reconciliation is not simply a question of identity and letting bygones be bygones. If the wounds of the past are to be healed, if a multiplicity of legal actions are to be refrained from, if future human rights violations are to be avoided, disclosure of the truth and its acknowledgement are essential'. This is closely akin to the South African theologian Joap Durnad's assertion that a collective conscience as a reminder of pain is an implicit recognition that one would have liked things to be different. By reminding oneself of past horrors, one will sustain or revive the hope for a better future. It also reflects the notion that 'total amnesia' will lead to a 'total loss of identity'.

The struggle against apartheid exacted a high toll both among those who fought against apartheid and among those who fought for the maintenance of the apartheid state. In the process, a great number of people, many of them civilians, were killed or scarred immeasurably. As examples, one may mention the Church Street bomb attack on the Air Force headquarters, the destruction of the Cassinga refugee camp in a military operation in Angola and the Sharpeville, Soweto, Boipathong and Bisho massacres. Moreover, many thousands of people throughout the country, among them in District Six in Cape Town, were forcibly removed from their homes and 'relocated' elsewhere, thereby attacking their identities at the very place where they were most vulnerable. This cannot but have altered their identities and affected their personhood for long into the future, sometimes indeed forever.

In the end more than 16 000 people, many of them manipulated by third force and/or covert operators, died in inter- 'ethnic' fighting. 'Struggles within the struggle', as the Zimbabwean political scientist, Masipula Sithole (1979) called them, also claimed their victims from the ranks of the African National Congress and Pan-Africanist Congress. We should not forget that whilst there was a common enemy, namely the apartheid regime, South Africans remained deeply divided amongst themselves about the strategic choices to be made in the heat of the struggle. Internal and strategic divisions haunted South Africans from early on. Pixley ka Isaka Seme warned against this from as early as 1906. These divisions have led to violence between the UDF and Inkatha, the ANC and the PAC, ANC and AZAPO and within the organisations themselves. Especially the PAC was the hardest hit. (Further information can be obtained from evidence supplied by Stephen Ellis and Tsepo Sechaba [1992].)

The Truth and Reconciliation Commission (TRC) was brought into being in South Africa against a backdrop of continuous power struggle, the abuse of power and dehumanisation that followed after the institutionalisation of the apartheid ideology in 1948 by the National Party. Since the 1970s and especially after the Soweto rebellion (1976) repression increased.

The Total Onslaught ideology came into being underpinned by heavy security measures. After 1983 sham reform and extreme repression became a dual strategy for maintaining minority rule, resulting in mass detentions (with concomitant torture in detention – especially in the Eastern Cape Province), covert operations against activists and militants (inclusive of murder and assassinations) and cross-border raids against ANC guerrillas and sympathisers.

South Africa's first democratically elected parliament instituted the TRC in accordance with Act 34 of 1995, also known as the Promotion of National Unity and Reconciliation Act. Its task was to investigate 'gross human rights violations' which occurred between 1963 and 1993. Three committees; one for amnesty applications, one for human rights violations and the other for restitution/reparation fulfilled their functions for victims. One of these committees is still in session, namely the committee tasked with hearing evidence and providing amnesty after due consideration of the submissions of applicants. The TRC was given two years to complete its work: to investigate all human rights violations, to make it public and to draw up a report. Adding to the difficulty, of its task, the commission had to perform its task publicly. This approach differed from the one followed by other similar commissions elsewhere and created new problems (logistically, administratively and socio-psychologically) for the TRC.

South Africans did not conceptually invent the truth and reconciliation commission. In terms of the broad definition of commissions instituted to unearth the truth about violent past histories close to 20 commissions have been embarked upon while countries like the Surinam and Namibia are reportedly considering instituting similar processes.

Truth commissions similar to South Africa's gained prominence in Latin America after states like Argentina, Bolivia, Uruguay and Chile appointed such commissions to investigate gross human rights violations. Of these, the Chilean commission received the most attention internationally, and is seen by some as the most successful (Bronkhorst 1995, pp. 70–72 and Fraser and Weissbrodt 1992, p. 622).

Such commissions are increasingly seen as a way to expose human rights violations and to enforce corrective measures regarding the long-term protection of human rights.

However in more recent times the international debate seems to have moved towards deploying international tribunals, one has to add.

Some case studies

President Alfonsin, first democratically elected Argentinean head of state, appointed the Sabato Commission to investigate the disappearance and death of 9 000 people. During the extremely authoritarian rule of a military junta Argentina experienced wide-ranging violations of human rights between 1976 and 1983). In the war against leftist 'subversion' or guerra suica (dirty war), which was euphemistically called national re-organisation, many people fell victim to violent anti-revolutionary action by the Argentinean junta. The Sabato Commission was instituted after a democratically elected government came to power. It published its report, entitled *Nunca Mas* (Never Again), in 1986. The commission reported on the death of 8 961 people and implicated 1 300 of the military, in these murders. Preliminary court proceedings were held, but were called off due to pressure from right wing and military pressure groups.

Priscilla Hayner is positive about the Argentinean commission:

> Notwithstanding criticism, the truth commission of Argentina was the first to receive widespread international attention and some look toward Argentina as an example for other countries searching for truth and justice in times of difficult political transitions.
>
> Hayner 1994

The legal experts Fraser and Weissbrodt are of a similar opinion (1992, p. 622).

The most successful commission in the eyes of some human rights practitioners though, was that of Chile (Bronkhorst, 1995; Hayner, 1994). Lead by Rettig, the commission investigated human rights violations that occurred between 1973 and 1990. The new democratically elected government of Patricio Aylwin decided to form the commission. It had to investigate nearly two decades of dehumanisingly authoritarian rule by Gen. Augusto Pinochet and his military followers. The aim was to investigate human rights violations as well as to put forward proposals for national reconciliation. The *Comission National para la Veridad y Reconciliation* (or Rettig Commission) had to uncover the truth about years of military repression, strive for national reconciliation and let justice be done 'insofar as is possible'.

For Zalaquett, a commission member, they had to try to uncover the truth about the past (truth phase), and justice had to be done 'insofar as is possible' regarding both the offenders and the victims alike (justice phase). This was not an easy task to perform.

A committee representative of the population and politically neutral insofar as possible was appointed, on which human rights and legal experts from different political backgrounds served. Within nine months they investigated 3 400 gross human rights violations, the greater part of which were disappearances and 164 of which were political assassinations or executions without due process. The committee drew up a report of 1 350 pages not only detailing the violations, but also making recommendations as to how they can be prevented in future. Attention was also given to issues like restitution and setting up and guaranteeing an independent judiciary.

The commission received much international attention and praise. 'Chile, much more than Argentina and Uruguay, had managed to settle some accounts of the past in a way which actually contributed to national reconciliation' (Du Toit 1994, p. 66).

South Africa and the TRC

The TRC in South Africa was thus not created de novo, but rather followed in the footsteps of states like Argentina, Chad, Chile, Bolivia and Uruguay which had travelled down this road with a lesser or greater degree of success. By the nature of such things the TRC is a political compromise. Some South Africans feel – and justifiably so – that there had to be a judicial process to deal with human rights violations.

However the commission as it was eventually instituted was a compromise between a general amnesty for human rights violators, thus 'drawing a line through the past' as the legal expert Kollapen (1993: 5) argues Zimbabwe did and a judicial process to punish these offenders (Liebenberg 1992, pp. 14–15).

Needless to mention, South Africans appear to be deeply divided about the Commission, its work and potential effect. In this regard the Human Sciences Research Council (HSRC) found in an Omnibus survey (1995, released 23 October 1996) that while the majority of South Africans in the sample favoured general amnesty, certain segments of the population harboured doubts about the success potential of the TRC as a tool of reconciliation. Later research by Gibson and Gouws seems to support the same broad findings.

Some of the dynamics of this division are that while many people agree that an officially sanctioned process should deal with past abuses of human rights, acknowledgement and national reconciliation, there are widely differing interpretations and expectations of the working of the TRC. When the TRC was established, the act declared that there was a need for understanding, but not vengeance; a need for reparation but not retaliation and a need for commonality but not victimisation. Afterwards, the ANC called for disclosure of all human rights abuses by all parties involved. The ANC (among others) have also argued that apartheid crimes and human rights abuses are qualitatively different from abuses committed during the struggle for liberation.

Clearly possible tension exists here. There were those, especially those in the right wing, who argued that a detailed disclosure of the truth (especially if coupled with retribution) would only lead to further polarisation in an already divided South African society. The result could be a right-wing reaction to what may be perceived as a witch hunt (especially if the TRC fails to deal adequately with human rights abuses by the liberation organisations). This could undermine the legitimacy of the newly-established democracy and hence could undermine political stability. It could also undermine the eventual consolidation of democracy.

Some people were of the opinion that without a focus on retribution, the process will be meaningless. Some of the families and relatives of the victims have shown signs of getting impatient. Many believed that 'horse trading' and compromises might eventually render the commission ineffective. Others, including the Biko, Lubowski and Mxenge families, have challenged the very notion of a TRC. They would have preferred a judicial process, notably criminal and civil court cases, to deal with perpetrators of (apartheid) violence and human rights abuses. To reconcile these views is a daunting task if not virtually impossible.

To these problems, one can add the possibility of both security personnel and combatants closing ranks, protecting colleagues and destroying evidence, for example files. As in Argentina, ex-military and other security personnel in the previous regime can pressurise the new government to stop or water down the process of disclosure or to put into effect amnesty without full acknowledgement of the truth about past abuses. This factor was compounded by the fact that evidence was probably destroyed on a large scale before the election of 1994 and the coming to power of the new government, which resulted in the TRC not having access to all the documents and information needed for its deliberations.

The TRC, which started its work in April 1996, had a rather difficult task to perform, given the time frame (two years) and especially since the South African society is complex and still relatively deeply divided. There were observers who rightly argued that strong claims from civil society that justice should be done were inevitable during and in the aftermath of the process. The calls by the Azanian People's Organisation (Azapo) and the PAC 'that justice must be seen to be done' still has much appeal. In reports to the commission and TRC proceedings things came to light of which many South Africans (especially Afrikaners) knew little; others had suspicions about, but for various reasons never voiced them; while yet others would like to deny that such things ever happened. But there are those who painfully experienced this violence.

To be confronted with the naked truth about a history of violence and the abuse of power is no simple experience and there is no easy way to relate these abuses to moral codes for future conduct given South Africa's collective past experience and historical recollection. Neither is it easy to make sense of these things in a lasting way without driving the general public into the arms of embitterment and alienation. To top it all, publicising the truth has to be reconciled with the consolidation of democracy, democratic transparency and existing (imposed) social identities (See Zegeye, Liebenberg & Houston, 2000).

South Africans must come to terms with the loss of life suffered at Sharpeville, Langa, Boipatong, Cassinga, Pabalello, Mamelodi, Quattro and others. In the same manner as the Chileans and Germans had to choose never to repeat such violations of humanity, so must the TRC try to give shape to the 'never again' principle in South Africans' communal lives.

Not only meditation and reflection on South Africa's violent history, but real concrete steps are needed. Steps to inculcate a human rights culture of the highest standards are needed. Such a culture, which has as its basis the Bill of Rights (Chapter 2 of the Constitution) which the Constituent Assembly adopted in 1996, must succeed in comprehensively restoring humanity in our society (The Constitution of South Africa, Act 108 of 1996). Apart from the role constitutional mechanisms and national/social consensus could play, there are further steps that can be taken to prevent human rights violations in future. Some such mechanisms have consequently been put into practice: an independent judiciary, enabling the Constitutional Court to function within its constitutional mandate, full-time ombudsman functions to monitor and investigate possible human right violations by security forces, proper supervision by multi-party parliamentary committees and a civilian controlled Defence Secretariat to oversee the functioning of the military and military/national intelligence services.

More may have to be done. We submit the following for possible consideration: as was the case in Argentina and Chile, re-training programmes should be created for people in security and intelligence structures concerning the function of security institutions within a working democracy, a state in which justice is done in terms of the law and the Bill of Rights. It is of great importance that those in security institutions not only have a better grasp of the fact that military institutions in democracies are subject to the constitution and the control of elected politicians, but also gain a better appreciation of a social order with a strong human rights focus. At the same time the public/community/civil society must be encouraged to interact with political electees in such a manner that the elected officials serve the citizenry. To put it briefly: in terms of democratic oversight, politicians should be interpreted as overseers of the military and civil society.

Therefore emphasis should be placed on the institutionalisation and cultivation of our own culture of human rights. South African society's dedication to a culture of common humanity, tolerance, accommodation and coexistence should be more comprehensive. Apart from this the need for tolerance of various (evolving) social identities, their protection and growth will have to be managed.

The TRC may have helped in this, but South Africans themselves and their political leadership, whatever their political affiliation, will have to consciously cultivate the social attitudes of tolerance, acceptance of various historical 'memories' and human dignity. It would also be significant if following South Africa's truth and reconciliation process (assuming that it is a process rather than a once-off ritual), leadership should be informed by community leaders as to how to deal with the accommodation of those of various identity backgrounds (i.e. victims, those belonging to the oppressing and oppressed classes). In reality such a commission and the protagonists of such an approach should provide a reminder, without alienating or labelling/negatively stereotyping people, that spurs South Africans to a more meditative discourse on their history and legacy.

This is no small task and will require political wisdom and a constant awareness of the dignity of 'the other'. Nelson Mandela in many respects has set an example in this regard. It remains to be seen whether his example will be followed by governments and heads of state succeeding him.

Aside from restitution, one suggestion as to how one should deal with the past – the TRC seems to lag behind in this because of a lack of resources – seems to be to cultivate a common memory of the past through dialogue between different social identity background categories. One suggestion comes from a philosopher: a conference of historians, much like the one German historians and political philosophers participate in regularly, could be held at regular intervals to reflect on the violence of apartheid and the struggle against it as well as its social impact. Such a conference could play a potentially important role in the re-evaluation of South Africa's recent past. It follows then that a South African version of a Historikerstreit, or historians debate could well evolve. The existence of different (clashing) historical interpretations held by various groups and categories of people in a divided society, does not equal a *Historikerstreit* as such. A *Historikerstreit* implies dealing with the past in normative terms, not merely re-writing history for power purposes.

The argument made by Tom Lodge in 1994 that the (co-) existence of different historical paradigms informing our past and present equals a moral debate may assist in reconciliation. But perhaps it could go further. An inclusive Historians Dialogue (in which social theorists and practitioners as well as civil society participate) should ideally include the morality of 'coming to terms with a collective past' and 'never to repeat' the dominance of sheer power.

Is a South African 'Historians' Debate' inevitable?

Is it morally necessary and/or perhaps socially inevitable that the TRC and the truth and reconciliation process will give rise to our own version of a historians' debate? As the people in the Soviet Union and Nazi Germany need a process of historical reflection following an intensely painful past, South Africa needs to remember and re-think its past of power struggle and the dehumanising effect it had on South African society. In remembering South African history, it should be considered that new social identities are emerging in the post-apartheid era primarily as a result of the abolition of apartheid laws and the gradual instantiation of a democratic ethos of rule by all the citizens of South Africa. This is happening through increased social mobility, migration, access to jobs, access to training and education and the reform of the South African police service and South African military. That this instantiation process is taking place more slowly than expected can probably be ascribed inter alia to a lack of public money, dissatisfaction in some quarters over the manner in which social mobility has been increasing, differential access to jobs, a high rate of unemployment, dissatisfaction with the pace at which inequality in South Africa is declining and a high crime rate.

The theoretical approach in the present chapter takes the factors referred to in the previous paragraph into account. It builds on work in the field of social identities which argues that identities are multiplicative, shaped by power relations and institutions designed to maintain those power relations, capable of being shifted when power relations shift, are linked to South Africa's history of rigidly defining cultural practice as the totality of group identity formation and that individuals and groups are actively choosing how to express their social identities at the same time as institutions are attempting to shape and construct their existence and options.

Should the process involving the TRC contribute to reflections on the past and imprint on our collective memory the principle of 'never again', it would have been of value. Should it furthermore facilitate greater understanding and thereby national remorse and the acceptance of communality aimed at reconciliation and healing, it would be a turning point of historical significance for post - apartheid South Africa and a significant moment of truth. A re-evaluation of history would provide South Africans with a way to collectively heal the wounds of apartheid and to make peace with a past so terrible the country cannot afford to repeat it.

Philosophers, sociologists and ordinary citizens and to a lesser extent historians and political scientists, will probably spearhead the South African debate. In Germany it was Margaret Mitscherlich and Jürgen Habermas who, from a theological and philosophical angle, put forward progressive and reflective (critical-theoretical) arguments, while historians like Nolte were reluctant to let go of the apologist's point of view of German nationalism.

Harrison Wright (1977) points out that a lively liberal-radical debate or "controversy" about South African historiography has been conducted these past years. Compare the historiography by Kotze, Walshe (1987), Lacour Gayet (1977) and Davenport (1977) to that of Eddie Roux (1964), Mokgheti Motlhabi (1985) Palmberg (1983) and Pampallis (1991) or Meli (1988). It goes without saying that the debate on the historiography of post-apartheid South Africa will be influenced by the historical moments that the reflective social scientist is investigating, as well as the debate on past events. When debates on morality, social recollection, power struggles, control over 'the real history' and notions such as commonality enter the debate historiography will not only be confronted with different paradigms but also the morality underlying it and the socio-ethical imperatives underpinning it.

A history of naked power-struggle and violence in South Africa (not to mention regional spill-overs) is being documented by the TRC and needs to be elucidated and interpreted. Naturally there were historians and philosophers and perhaps a political scientist who realised how fragile (misleading and/or inappropriate) the term 'object-ivity' was and who touched upon the issue (see Lodge 1983; Roux 1964; Davenport, 1977 and Odendaal 1984 in this regard). Most political scientists and historians, espe-cially those at Afrikaans or liberal universities and research institutions such as the HSRC however, favoured nationalist historiography for many years and avoided the question with the argument that 'objectivity' presupposes academics to be outside the political arena. And by opting for that choice, also left philosophical-historical questions such as morality and social ethics largely unattended with the exception of people like Andre du Toit, Johan Degenaar, Duvenage and Motlhabi and some other progressive intellectuals.

In this, the community history and history studies fraternity in its entirety was not involved in the debate during the course of the TRC process. Neither was the nature of historiography, its manipulation and issues such as participatory historiography sufficiently enough examined. It becomes ever more important to do so in view of the current disclosures. A 'new' history ought to be written through critical reflection.

These tasks can now be taken up afresh in a historical account by South Africans themselves within the disciplines of historiography, philosophy, political science, so-ciology, theology, victimology and gender-related studies. New areas of inter-discipli-nary economic and political historiography and civil-military relations are pertinent here. But will South Africans stand up to the challenge?

These challenges are daunting. This is one of the reasons why the South African TRC process is more far-reaching than that of any other TRC. The South African process has also attracted more international attention and brought about new per-spectives on a collective history of violence. In all this, the TRC report has the potential to serve as a launching platform for far-reaching human rights reforms and also as the basis of deepening democratic processes when read and acted upon in conjunction with constitutional imperatives and the Bill of Rights (Chapter 2 of the South African Constitution Act No. 108 of 1996). South Africa through its TRC process may just be set for restorative justice rather than retribution.

A new approach will be to the greater benefit of (South) Africans – and even Pan-Africa – and is much needed and might even benefit the much talked about African Renaissance the outcomes of which might be positive but are as yet undetermined.

And it would also benefit South Africans as people involved in reconstruction to analyse critically their own historical reconstruction because in hyperbolic terms: 'At the rise of all new civilisations, the elements of barbarism are co-born.'

Notes

1   See Liebenberg I. and Zegeye, A. 'Pathway to democracy? The case of the South African Truth and Reconciliation Process'. *Social Identities* 4(3), p. 547. This article can also be consulted by readers needing an earlier analysis of the Truth and Reconciliation process.

References

Asmal, K., Asmal L & Roberts, R.S. (1996). *Reconciliation Through Truth:* A *Reckoning of Apartheid's Criminal Governance*, Cape Town: David Philip Publishers & Mayibuye Books.

Bronkhorst, D. (1995). *Truth and Reconciliation: Obstacles and Opportunities for Human Rights*, Amsterdam: Amnesty International Dutch Section.

Dix, R.H. (1994). 'Military Coups and Military in Latin America', *Armed Forces and Society* 20 (3), pp. 439–456.

Du Toit, A. (1994). 'Laying the past to rest', *Indicator SA*, 11 (4), pp. 63–69.

Hayner, P. (1994). 'Fifteen Truth Commissions –1974 to 1994: A Comparative Study', *Human Rights Quarterly*, 16, pp. 597–655.

Liebenberg, I. & Zegeye, A. (1998). 'Pathway to Democracy? The Case of the South African Truth and Reconciliation Process', *Social Identities*, 4 (3), pp. 541–558.

Liebenberg, I. (1996). 'The truth and Reconciliation Commission in South Africa: Context, future and some imponderables', *South African Public Law*, 11, pp. 123–159.

Liebenberg, I. (1997). 'Die Waarheids- en Versoeningskommissie (WVK) in Suid-Afrika en die implikasies daarvan vir 'n Suid-Afrikaanse Historikerstreit en eietydse geskiedskrywing', *Journal for Contemporary History*, 22 (1), pp. 98–114.

Weissbrodtt, D. & Fraser, P.W. (1992). 'Book Review: Report on the Rettig Commission/Chilean National Commission on Truth and Reconciliation', *Human Rights Quarterly*, 14, pp. 601–622.

Zegeye, A, Liebenberg, I & Houston, G. (2000). *Resisting ethnicity from above: Social identities and democracy in South Africa*. Pretoria: HSRC Publishers.

CHAPTER TWELVE

Conclusion:
depoliticising ethnicity in South Africa

Abebe Zegeye

Simply put, South African history is a divided history. Clashes over scarce resources, ideology and static interpretations of (ethnic) groups all contributed to this. The centralist imposition of identities caused further conflict. However, in resistance, shared identities developed. Through resistance against apartheid South Africans shared not only values but also daily life strategies and tactics within the social movements they partook in (they shared in a mutual economy before that – even if only partially). These factors impact on the future.

The newly enfranchised – rights, access and privilege

The position of those enfranchised since 1994 is problematic. For a deepening of democratic precepts to occur in South Africa, the newly enfrancised must be protected by new laws and policies. Administrators at all levels of government will have to be responsive to their interests. The newly enfranchised will have to ensure that their organisations become lobbying instruments with as much clout as other groups. Their ability to constantly develop social capital and to plug into the existing networks in civil society as well as create new ones will have to be ensured. While the newly enfranchised have much to gain by supporting their government, they also have much to lose. They will have to prove that their recognition as full members of society will promote democracy. More importantly, in joining institutions in formal politics, the newly enfranchised may have to loosen their former ties and focus on social and political mass movements.

Thus, during democratic consolidation they face particular disadvantages. They will have to reconstitute constituencies and establish organisations based on different principles. However, to conclude that the newly enfranchised will threaten democracy smacks of the same sort of justifications used to deny them the franchise.

We concede that differences may prevent a society from sustaining democracy because such differences may be used to justify non-conciliation, non-reparation, or the outright punishment of members in the society. In this chapter, we contest the insistence in the debate on democratic consolidation that the newly enfranchised are more likely to use their political identities as a basis for oppressing their fellow citizens than others. Rather, we argue that a consolidated democracy would be characterised by the absence of fear about difference.

This does not mean that differences can be resolved by pretending that they do not exist, nor that we promote the liberal view of equality wherein personal habits and customs are confined to the private sphere. We suggest that the hysteria surrounding what the newly enfranchised may do with identity, culture or civil society should be diffused. And perhaps the most effective way to reveal the baselessness of this fear of difference is to reveal how societies cope with difference. Perhaps we can begin with the indigenous understanding that the landscape of democracy in South Africa is already known – and can be mapped.

Identification with sub-groups is not at all dysfunctional, since people can – and do – have multiple identities. In fact, if people are not forced to rank their identities they can bring more of themselves and more crosscutting cleavages into democracy (Spivak and Lorde, 1992). This was amply illustrated in a South African context in the contributions by McEachern and Martin, who found a cosmopolitan and more tolerant racial identity among the mainly coloured people living in District Six during the years before statutory apartheid, before the sharp bite of apartheid brought them to an abrupt end by relocating the inhabitants to other areas.

If democratic political systems cannot accommodate identification with sub-groups then something else will be necessary to guarantee participation in electoral and constitutional politics for excluded groups. However, forcing people to rank their identities resembles the hegemony created by apartheid. The people who fought against apartheid achieved their identity by varied entry points. They mobilised distinctly as socialists, democrats, women's rights activists, artists, traditional leaders, cultural nationalists, anarchists, farmers or rural dwellers and so on.

And yet the overarching anti-apartheid ideology did not eradicate their local identities. In fact, they were able to see their local identities as resources that could enhance the anti-apartheid movement.

A politics of erasure underlies some of the debate on the dysfunctional nature of ethnicity. Moreover, a level of confusion has crept into the debate on democratic consolidation. The fear that ethnicity will rip societies apart is not based on the historical reality that nation-sized communities are ethnically, linguistically or religiously heterogeneous. The debate on democratic consolidation by means of the denial of ethnicity is in fact based on the authoritarian and not the democratic approach to identity. A democratic political system consists, then, of any variety of measures which ensure, first, that citizens with their various identities participate fully in the political system in their country and second, that the government acts in accordance with the preferences of its citizens.

The process of democratic consolidation in South Africa

A number of issues relating to political identity became prominent during the negotiations for a democratic South Africa.[1] The first was the ruling National Party's constitutional proposals which emphasised group rights and protection for minorities; the second was the issue of federalism and regional autonomy for KwaZulu-Natal and the third was the right-wing demand for a *Volkstaat* or homeland for the Afrikaner volk.

During the late 1980s and early 1990s the NP shifted away from its emphasis on statutory group rights. This was clearly stated in 1991 by the new NP leader, FW de Klerk: 'We commit ourselves to the creation of a free and democratic political system ... in which ... the rights of all individuals and minorities defined on a non-racial basis shall be adequately protected in the constitution and in a constitutionally guaranteed and justifiable bill of rights' (cited in Kotze, 1994, p. 61).

However, the NP's Charter of Fundamental Rights (1993) set out to protect certain rights of apartheid-defined groups. In particular, it stipulated that every state-aided educational institution (as well as the parent community of every state or state-aided school) should have the right to determine the medium of instruction (the NP often interpreted this to be Afrikaans) and the religious and general character (mostly interpreted by the NP to be Christian and white) of such an educational institution or school. The Charter also called for the protection of the right to free association, which, in the absence of the application of a non-discrimination clause, would enable walls of privilege to be built around nearly all social institutions (Asmal, 1993).

The NP's proposals in its *Constitutional Rule in a Participatory Democracy* (1991) as well as its submissions to the Convention for a Democratic South Africa (CODESA) at the end of 1991 called for a system of power-sharing that would guarantee minority participation in government. The NP argued that 'the political party is the most effective means of furthering the interests' of groups and therefore proposed a form of 'participatory democracy' at national and regional levels in which 'a number of parties effectively participate and in which power-sharing therefore takes place, as contrasted to the Westminster model in which one party exclusively enjoys power'. Such a system was necessary because it 'takes into account the diversity of South African society and the reality of the existence of a multiplicity of socio-economic and cultural interest groups' (cited in Asmal, 1993, p. 56). For the NP government, minority participation was to be ensured through the participation of minority political parties in both the executive and the legislative organs of the state.

Executive authority was to rest in a presidency constituted on a multi-party basis with the leaders of the three to five leading parties sharing the chairmanship of the presidency on a rotational basis. All decisions of the presidency were to be taken by consensus, effectively providing a veto on all executive functions. The leading political parties were to be allocated an equal number of seats in a second house with the same powers as a first house. The principles of 'participatory democracy' and power sharing for the leading political parties and 'effective measures for minority protection' were also to be extended to the regions (Asmal, 1993, pp. 56–57).

KwaZulu Natal was the first provincial government to draft a provincial constitution. Underlying this eagerness was the Inkatha Freedom Party's (IFP's) quest for a federal system with strong regional powers. The IFP identified a strong central government in a unitary system as an obstacle to democratisation because, they argued, it would inevitably lead to authoritarianism. A federal constitution which conferred on the regions their own legislative, administrative, judicial and executive powers within a broad unifying framework would be 'intrinsically' more democratic.

As the IFP power base was in the province of KwaZulu Natal, it was important for the IFP to strengthen provincial autonomy. However, the IFP notion was declined in the Multiparty Negotiating Party (MPNP) which drew up the interim Constitution in late 1993 (*Journal for Contemporary History*, 1996, p. 43).[2] After 1994, the Western Cape followed suit in writing a provincial constitution.

The IFP only agreed to participate in South Africa's first election after the ANC and the NP signed the Agreement for Reconciliation and Peace on 19 April 1994. The ANC and NP consented to international mediation on provincial powers, the role of traditional leaders and the constitutional role of the Zulu king. The IFP argued that these issues were not dealt with adequately in the interim Constitution. Above all else, the IFP was concerned with constitutional issues relating to the powers of the provinces (Smith, 1995). Since then the IFP has consistently pointed out that the new Constitution, adopted in 1996, does not deal adequately with these issues. Part of this relates to – apart from identity issues – the fact that the IFP adhered to an obsolete notion of federalism at the time.

The Afrikaner right wing, organised into the Afrikaner Volksfront (AVF) under the leadership of General Constand Viljoen, demanded that freedom for the Afrikaner be accommodated through the formation of a volkstaat. The AVF consisted of 21 right-wing parties and organisations, including the Afrikaner Weerstandsbeweging (AWB) and the Conservative Party (CP). The AVF rejected a unitary state and said that Afrikaners wanted a volkstaat, which would be part of a future confederation of states. It aimed to unite all Afrikaners behind this ideal and to embark on a three-phase programme to achieve the *Volkstaat*: political pressure; popular resistance, including mass action, boycotts and strikes and as a last resort, secession from South Africa by an Afrikaner state. This ethno-nationalist ideal was temporarily accommodated in the negotiation process by amendments to the Interim Constitution which made constitutional provision for the right to self-determination by any community sharing a common cultural and language heritage. It also provided for the establishment of a Volkstaat Council to enable the proponents of the idea to pursue its establishment. These issues reflected a concern for minority group rights, a resurgence of ethnic separateness and the manifestation of cultural exclusivity.[3]

The results of the first democratic election in April 1994 were another demonstration of the salience of group identity in South African politics. The election results reflected a racial census although considerable cross-racial voting took place with all major parties drawing support from every race group. The NP was supported by 65% of the coloured and Indian voters nationally, with 60–70% of coloured voters in the Western Cape voting for the party (Reynolds, 1994).

Apartheid-indoctrinated fears of African domination and distrust of African administrative competence, loss of relative status in the racial hierarchy and competition for jobs and housing were in large part responsible for this support (Finnegan, 1994; Adam, 1994).

The IFP was supported by more than half of the voters of KwaZulu-Natal in the provincial election, with almost 85% of the IFP's national total coming from this region. The Freedom Front received just over 2% of the national total. A huge proportion of the support gained by the ANC came from the African community and predominantly from speakers of Xhosa, Sotho, Venda, Ndebele, Tswana and Tsonga, although one-third of its supporters were Zulu speaking (Reynolds, 1994).

After its victory, the ANC adopted the approach followed by most post-colonial governments, namely emphasising nation building in non-ethnic and non-racial terms. The ANC after the election victory was overtly non-racial in terms of its core ideology, seeking to decrease the barriers between different identities, language groups and cultures. The ideology of non-racialism rejects an ethnic nation in favour of a civic nation, based on equal individual rights, regardless of origin and equal recognition of all cultural traditions in the public sphere.

The ANC's *Constitutional Guidelines for a Democratic South Africa* (1989) advocated a unitary, democratic and non-racial state in which sovereignty was to be exercised through a central legislature, executive, judiciary and administration. Provision was made, however, for delegation of the powers of the central authority to subordinate administrative units (Welsh, 1989). The guidelines posited the need for a national identity in the following terms:

> It shall be state policy to promote the growth of a single national identity and loyalty binding on all South Africans. At the same time, the state shall recognise the linguistic and cultural diversity of the people and provide material for free linguistic and cultural development.

The ANC identified a bill of rights as the means of guaranteeing the fundamental rights of all citizens. The legal right of parties to exist was based on a prohibition of the advocacy or practice of racism, Fascism, Nazism or the incitement of ethnic or regional exclusiveness or hatred (Welsh, 1989). The ANC's major policy document, *Ready to Govern*, presented in 1992, provided further references to the nature of the constitutional order. The ANC rejected the association of political power with race or ethnicity as well as the protection of group rights or the representation of racial interests through political parties. It was argued that this approach would promote racial conflict rather than harmony and was not in the ultimate interest of minorities. Asmal (1993) pointed out that minority protection became necessary when the minority was in a position of subordination to a majority, which would clearly not be the case in a democratic South Africa.

Basic citizenship rights and constitutionalism were thus presented as an antidote to authoritarian ethnic and racial group rights. The nation was to be constituted on the basis of a 'community of equal, rights-bearing citizens, united in patriotic attachment to a shared set of political practices and values' (Ignatieff, 1993, pp. 3–4, cited in Wilson, 1996, p. 2).

The ANC's Revised Draft Bill of Rights (1992), which stated that language, cultural and religious rights should be protected in a new constitution, was in line with the internationally recognised method of protecting minority rights contained in Article 27 of the International Convention on Civil and Political Rights. This convention provides that, 'in those states in which ethnic, religious or linguistic minorities exist, persons belonging to such minorities shall not be denied the right, in community with the other members of their group, to enjoy their own culture, to profess and practice their own religion, or to use their own language' (cited in Asmal, 1993, p. 56).[4] However, as Asmal pointed out, there was a difference in emphasis as to the extent to which the equality principle, especially that prohibiting discrimination on the grounds of race, should apply to exercising these rights. Differently stated, the right to associate should not allow persons the right to exclude others from participation in activities associated with, for example, schooling, sports, hospitals.

One way of exploring minority rights vis-à-vis equality in the new South Africa is to examine the ANC's conception of culture and its place in the new South Africa. The ANC's Reconstruction and Development Programme (RDP) pointed to the depoliticisation of ethnicity by affirming cultural unity at the national level and cultural diversity at the personal but not the community level (Venter, 1996). Furthermore, culture is conceived of as art and not as lifestyle-of-an-ethnic-group and as such must be incorporated into the national culture. Thus, ethnic association and exclusion, particularly in inter alia schools and sports, are counteracted by the demand for non-discrimination, which underpins the ideology of non-racialism as espoused by the ANC until 1997. These seemingly paradoxical notions may well imply some social tensions – but more about this later.

The new South African Constitution made provision for the establishment of a Commission for the Promotion and Protection of the Rights of Cultural, Religious and Linguistic Communities (Chapter 9, sections 185 and 186). The primary objectives of this commission were to promote respect for the rights of these communities; to foster and develop peace, friendship, humanity, tolerance and national unity among cultural, religious and linguistic communities on the basis of equality, non-discrimination and free association and to recommend the establishment or recognition of a cultural or other council(s) for a community or communities in South Africa. The commission was potentially empowered to monitor, investigate, research, educate, lobby, advise and report on issues concerning the rights of cultural, religious and linguistic communities (Dlamini, 1998).

The four-year negotiation process in South Africa culminated in the acceptance of a consensus-based Government of National Unity (a cabinet staffed on a proportional basis by members of the majority party and the two leading opposition parties, the NP and IFP). Proportional representation ensured the participation of smaller parties in the legislature, while the Government of National Unity (GNU) was extended to the provinces whose executive committees were also staffed on a proportional basis. Minority participation in government was also guaranteed by the so-called 'sunset clause', which guaranteed the jobs of civil servants and members of the security forces (both comprising largely white Afrikaner males, but including civil servants of the former homeland and tricameral administrations) for five years. Nine African languages were added to the list of official languages (in the previous era Afrikaans and English were the only official languages) thus demonstrating a commitment to equal recognition of the rights of the different language communities.

The negotiating parties also agreed to entrench the powers of the regions in a new constitution, and that a special majority would be required for any change in the powers, structure and competence of regional government. At the centre of the debate around the nature and functions of the provinces was the question of federalism.

Support for federalism in South Africa at the time came largely from the Democratic Party and the IFP, while the NP called for regionalism with strong federal elements. The ANC's regional policy of 1993, on the other hand, opposed the formation of political groupings on racial, ethnic or linguistic bases. The ANC aimed to discourage 'political mobilisation on the basis of race, ethnicity or language and to prevent state power at any level from being used for purposes of ethnic domination, intolerance and forced removals of population' (cited in Venter, 1996, p. 13).

De Haas (1993) outlined three preconditions for the establishment of a federal system. First, a federal constitution should be predicated upon specific communal identities or building blocks; second, communal identities should operate within a definable geographic base; and third, either the said geographical base is economically viable, or the central political organ is willing to subsidise the federal constituents through fiscal transfers. However, the conglomerations of sub-groups sharing the same living space in South Africa made it virtually impossible to demarcate ethnically homogeneous or economically viable units (Hislope, 1998, p. 83).

In July 1997 the ANC released a discussion document entitled *National Formation and Nation Building*, which dealt with the national question and the nature of the nation. The document re-affirmed the ANC's non-racial stance and commitment to deracialising South African society. However, the ANC emphasised that 'the liberation of black people in general and Africans in particular' should be the main content of the national democratic revolution. The document acknowledged the reality of diversity and the persistence of cultural, religious and other identities in South Africa (Filatova, 1997). Over the years the ANC repeatedly reaffirmed its commitment to the Charterist ideal of the South African nation as a union built on cultural diversity and equality while seeking to promote the growth of a single national identity (Filatova, 1997, p. 49).[5]

Another ANC discussion policy document, *Building the Foundation for a Better Life*, mentioned an 'African nation' and 'the affirmation of our Africanness as a nation' but also stresses 'equality among the racial, ethnic, language, cultural and religious communities' within 'a united nation', 'multiple identities' in 'the melting pot of broad South Africanism' and the importance of 'an over-arching identity of being South African' (cited in Filatova, 1997, p. 55). The central thrust of ANC policy was to encourage the development of a national identity based on unity-in-diversity.

Two contrasting ways in which the ANC government responded to the apartheid-constructed group identities are noted here. On the one hand, it retained certain apartheid identities as a means of addressing imbalances of the past, for instance through affirmative action and black empowerment. On the other hand, overarching identities, which cut across race and ethnicity, were encouraged in a variety of ways. For example, group identification across racial and ethnic boundaries was promoted in labour, business, sport, youth, rural and womens affairs and the affairs of the disabled, in order to make group identification as inclusive as possible and participation in institutions and processes, including consultative bodies, parliamentary public hearings, and consultative conferences and workshops, as representative as possible.

However, as Grobbelaar points out in this volume, there are dangers in both strategies. Strategies that aim at equitable and affirming outcomes for all groups could reinforce racial identification in certain ways and could be used to solicit group support for political parties. First, addressing racial imbalances implies a drastic reduction of white and in particular Afrikaner access to the socio-political system, wealth and opportunities.

The danger then exists that 'people will not only fall back into the organic or laager-like comfort of group-mobilising identities like Afrikaner nationalism, but also that the loss of self-esteem and dignity experienced would contribute radically towards undermining a vision and strategy of equity across the board'. Second, affirming strategies could reinforce racial identities within the black population if they are seen to apply only (or largely) to the African segment of this group. For instance, coloured people may experience relative deprivation vis-à-vis the African population because the black majority government is seen to adopt policies that reaffirm the former 'second class' status that coloured people held under apartheid. Indeed, such a perception recently led to the formation of 'coloured' political and cultural movements in the Western Cape and Gauteng. Within the Indian communities the same problem surfaced.

Group identity as a driving force in South African politics can be seen in the efforts of some coloured people to use the term 'coloured' as a symbol of collective identity against other groups, in particular white people and Africans (Maré, 1995). The appeal to this sense of identity lies in their perception of marginalisation, which, it could be argued, has continued into the democratic South Africa. Affirmative action has also brought claims of new forms of racial discrimination from white people as well as Indian people and coloured people – although these complaints must be scrutinised since in most parts of the country 'black' empowerment is understood by many policy implementers as 'non-European' empowerment. The new non-racial democracy has been criticised for undermining the contingent 'benefits' of the tricameral parliament (in terms of jobs, houses and education) during the 1980s (Maré, 1995, p. 7). It is perhaps here that the role of civil society could nurture a culture of democracy, human rights and (communal) tolerance. Attempts to include stakeholders take many forms. The new government embarked on various strategies to attempt inclusion.

The National Economic Development and Labour Council (Nedlac), a statutory consultative body, for example, was formed in 1995 to consider all matters relating to economic and social issues before they are placed before parliament or implemented. Nedlac includes representatives of organised labour and business, as well as women's organisations, rural dwellers, young people and the disabled.

These constituencies are organised on a non-racial basis and participate in Nedlac as units in their respective categories. This national institution has contributed to a growth in the organisation and co-operation of these categories across racial and ethnic barriers. This is one area in which the democratic government is moving towards establishing overarching identities – for workers, youth, women, rural dwellers, disabled people and businessmen – which are not based on racial or ethnic identities.

The South African case has the potential to inform our understanding of diversity and democracy. The politicised nature of communities and individuals in this country under apartheid has set the stage for democracy and thus a choice in terms of the kind of society communities wanted for themselves. The majority was not to be satisfied with simple autonomy for their group. Rather, they insisted that the economic inequalities of the past be remedied for everybody that was disadvantaged by apartheid.

Conclusion

'Can a democratic society treat all its members as equals and also recognise their specific cultural identities?' (Taylor, 1992). The answer is yes if culture is defined as the 'common core of humanity' and 'practices that all human beings engage in' (Alexander, 1989). When culture includes the tangible beliefs and philosophies that are reflected in how we recreate our humanity, culture can play a decisive role in democracy. The South African Constitution seeks to foster a single political community while respecting the existence and worth of cultural communities. The resolution of the language question offered by the Constitution, the incorporation of traditional leaders and customary law are the outgrowths of respect for culture. We suggest that the art of 'complex mapping' be applied in order to understand the role of culture in consolidating the South African democratic polity. Thereafter the lessons learned from this 'mapping' of identity in South Africa can be used to enrich democratic theory elsewhere.

The 'prospect of creating a common democratic culture, or consolidating working democracy' (Liebenberg and Duvenage, 1996) is realisable in heterogeneous communities. In South Africa, the very existence of multi-racial, multi-lingual, multi-cultural and multi-class communities reveals the major flaw in theories of democracy that presume that homogeneity of society or community is a prerequisite for a working democracy. Some democratic theorists further presuppose that diverse communities make social identity less of a contest and more of an amicable necessity. While not following exactly the same route as the multi-culturalists, we assert that heterogeneity is not necessarily a threat to political order. We utilise the metaphor of mapping to illustrate that the cultural, linguistic, racial, religious and ethnic groups in the new South Africa indeed know how to sustain a heterogeneous community without resorting to the rigid measures of the previous minority regime. They provide evidence for the fact that heterogeneity does not preclude harmony, sympathy for others or commiseration, which are the bases for sustaining a community.

In fact, the assumption that communities are automatically uniform has repeatedly proven to be the Achilles heel of authoritarian schemes. We concede that societies attempting to consolidate democracy usually politicise some social category so that people can become citizens or non-citizens. However, we disagree that stable democracies use this overarching category in ways that exclude other crosscutting and overlapping identities that residents may claim or create. Hence the metaphor of mapping gives credence to our assertion that the South African society can avail itself of knowledge of how to achieve equity despite its multiracial, multi-class and multi-lingual composition.

Civil society is no new concept in the analysis of democratic systems (Gorus, 1996). Camerer (1992; 1997) sees civil society as 'an inherently pluralistic realm, distinct from, yet interacting with the state and consisting of numerous associations organised around specific issues and seeking to form links with other interest groups without seeking to become an alternative to the institutionalised state'. Using the social capital generated through association and organisation around policy concerns and interests, civil society sustains negotiations and bargaining with the state.

However, lately, civil society is claimed to be the invention of theorists who favour multi-party democracy. As a matter of course, these theorists accept that civil society should be distinct from the state and if possible exercise its activities peacefully. The debate on civil society and its role today in South Africa can contribute to establishing rules about who governs and under what conditions – and may turn out to develop differently from manifestations of civil society elsewhere.

Bekker argues that 'in civil society South Africans are free to choose from a menu of identities ... at many levels' (1996, p. 32). To put this into practice may be more problematic given South Africa's historic legacy. We argue here that civil society need not be strictly a liberal or 'one-community' construct. It embodies both the potential and reality of a flux of identities within the broader community of self-chosen citizens.

Civil society (or the civil community) is the arena in which democratic attitudes, including tolerance, have to be developed. Civil society can be fostered by government but it is, in turn, part of its cultural basis (Maxted, 1999). The following are some questions to help evaluate the role of civil society in an emerging democracy: How does civil society contribute to good governance, accountability and sound opposition politics amid balanced reconstruction? How can civil society maintain such a role during the growth of the state? What lasting role can it have and under what conditions? Can (or should) it counteract tendencies towards one-party dominance? What should its role be – strengthening government or opposing it, strengthening the state or weakening it, strengthening elite pacts and/or political parties or weakening them? These are important questions in any democracy and more so in emerging democracies.

We are concerned with how interpretations of and allegiance to the concept of identity will influence civil societies because these determine the nature of checks on the state. Identity creates the requisite social capital to mobilise interest groups. We want to know how identity and identity issues (as reflected by civil society) impact on local government, regional/provincial government, national government, intergovernmental relations/management, civil-military relations, foreign affairs and international economic integration/globalisation (or resistance to it), democratic opposition and one-party dominance. Civil society organisations participate in debates at each level of government. Such organisations provide critical security against the over-extension of governmental powers (Foley and Edwards, 1996).

The very fact that group identities are associated with volatile social issues and concerns about redistribution should not be seen as an automatic threat to the consolidation of democracy. As new players are brought into government, parastatals, education and the public service in South Africa today, the right to freedom of speech and assembly allows civil society to actively investigate and change government policy. For example, the 1999 ISCOR case against affirmative action policies, the replacement of the RDP by the Growth, Employment and Redistribution (GEAR) programme and nation-wide criticism of the unemployment crisis and the prevalence of anti-crime strategies indicate that civil society is rather effective at challenging government. Moreover, these challenges did not come from homogeneous groups of people but from conglomerates of citizens 'agglutinated' by their common concerns.

Within the new democracy, heterogeneity and unity have to be negotiated and reconciled more or less continually. South Africans furthermore have to reflect to what extent they want cultural, religious, ethnic, linguistic and racial identities to shape the reconstruction of national, community and individual identity (Singh, 1997). Identity is furthermore complicated by the fact that the new government has embarked on reconciliation and nation-building simultaneously, as noted by Liebenberg and Zegeye in their earlier chapter. The apartheid system cemented a division of labour and citizenship on a racial and ethnic basis, which resulted in the development of ontological commitments to racialised and ethnic identities. The current government aims at de-emphasising the apartheid-constructed divisions through its policy of non-racialism and the construction of a national identity. This should not be done in a way that subordinates the immediate interests of sub-groups to a given national undifferentiated interest. It should begin from the point of departure that people are what they are by virtue of how they actually live, produce and reproduce themselves; how they actually shape and reshape their everyday world. The theoretical and practical issue is whether there is sufficient commonality in our sufferings and our hopes, in the modes and sources of our oppressions and expressions and in the creation of a social order to eliminate destructive divisions and forge a concrete unity in diversity.

The continuous excursion through a 'rainbow' of differences involves more than a concern on the part of people to tell their own stories and in so doing reaffirm themselves, as was done in many of the contributions to this volume. It involves a thorough consideration of why their histories and culture – the modalities of being in the life-world – are meaningful and important; why they have an integrity worth preserving while subjecting it to progressive refinement brought about by the continuing need to live together with others of different identities. It involves commitment to the ideal of maintaining our own integrity without encroaching upon the integrity and well-being of others.

Notes

1   For background on the negotiations, see Rantete (1998), Sisk (1995, pp. 88ff, 166ff, 249ff), and Tjonneland (1990).

2 Note that the IFP's notion to write a 'provincial' constitution started earlier, namely 1986/87/88 with the 'Indaba'-experiment.
3 The 'Far Right' later split into many minor groups, with the AVF becoming the Freedom Front (Vryheidsfront).
4 This idea found itself eventually espoused in the South African Constitution (Act No. 108 of 1996), Chapter 9, sections 185 and 186 on the Protection and Promotion of the Rights of Cultural, Religious and Linguistic communities.
5 The national democratic revolution and the Reconstruction and Development Programme (RDP) was jettisoned in favour of 'state-building' and GEAR.

References

Adam, H. (1994). 'Ethnic versus Civic Nationalism: South Africa's Non-racialism in Comparative Perspective', *South African Sociological Review*, 2 (2).

Alexander, Neville (1989). *Language Policy and National Unity in South Africa/Azania*, Cape Town: Buchu Books.

Asmal, K. (1993). 'Neighbourhood Laager: The Devolution of White Power', *Indicator SA*, 10 (3), Winter.

Bekker, S. (1996). 'Conflict, Ethnicity and Democratisation in Contemporary South Africa', in S. Bekker and D. Carlton (eds), *Racism, Xenophobia and Ethnic Conflict*, Durban: Indicator Press.

Camerer, L. (1992). 'Civil Society and Democracy: The South African Debate', paper delivered at the Bi-annual South African Political Science Association Colloquium, October, Broederstroom, South Africa.

Camerer, L. (1997). 'Party Politics, Grassroots Politics and Civil Society', *Orientation*, December, pp. 21-35.

De Haas, M. (1993). 'Ethnic Mobilisation: KwaZulu's Politics of Secession', *Indicator SA*, 10 (3), Winter.

Dlamini, C. (1998). 'The Protection of Individual Rights and Minority Rights', in B. de Villiers, F. Delmartino and A. Alan (eds), *Institutional Development in Divided Societies*, Pretoria: Human Sciences Research Council.

Filatova, I. (1997). 'The Rainbow Against the African Sky or African Hegemony in a Multi-cultural Context?', *Transformation*, 34.

Finnegan, W. (1994). 'The Election Mandela Lost', *New York Review of Books*, 20 October.

Foley, M.W. and Edwards, B. (1996). The Paradox of Civil Society, *Journal of Democracy*, 7 (3), pp. 38-52.

Gorus, J.F.J. (1996). 'Grijpt Afrika zijn Kans? De Rol van Societe Civile in Transitieprocessen in Centraal Afrika', *Noord-Zuid Cahier*, 21 (1), Maart, pp. 27-38.

Hislope, R. (1998). 'The Generosity Moment: Ethnic Politics, Democratic Consolidation and the State in Yugoslavia (Croatia), South Africa and Czechoslovakia', *Democratization*, 5 (1), Spring.

Ignatieff, M. (1993). *Blood and Belonging*, London: Vintage.

Kotze, H. (1994). 'Federalism in South Africa: An Overview', in H. Kotze (ed.), *The Political Economy of Federalism in South Africa: Policy Opportunities and Constraints of the Interim Constitution*, University of Stellenbosch and Konrad Adenauer Stiftung, Johannesburg.

Liebenberg, I. and Duvenage, P. (1996). 'Can the Deep Political Divisions of South African Society be Healed? A Philosophical and Political Perspective', *Politeia*, 15 (1), pp. 48-61.

Mare, G. (1995). 'Ethnicity, Regionalism and Conflict in a Democratic South Africa', *South African Journal of International Affairs*, 3 (1), Summer.

Maxted, J. (1999). 'Globalisation, Spatial Restructuring and Social Exclusion in South Africa', paper presented to Dept. of Sociology, University of South Africa, Pretoria, October 1999.

Reynolds, A. (ed.) (1994). *Elections 94 South Africa*, London: James Curry.

Singh, M. (1997). 'Identity in the Making', *Suid-Afrikaanse Tydskrif vir Wysbegeerte*, 16 (3).

Smith, P. (1995). 'Playing with Fire: Inkatha's Fight for Federalism', *Indicator SA* , 12 (2), Autumn.

Spivak, G.C. and Lorde, A. (1992). 'French Feminism Revisited', in J. Butler and L. Scott (eds), *Feminists Theorise the Political*, New York: Routledge.

Taylor, R. (1992). 'South Africa: A Consociational Path to Peace?', *Transformation*, 17.

Venter, D. (1996). 'It May be Art, But is it Culture? The ANC's Conceptions of Culture and Orientation Towards Ethnicity in the 1994 RDP Booklet', *Politikon*, 23 (1), June.

Welsh, D. (1989). 'The Governing of Divided Societies: A South African Perspective', *Africanus*, 19 (1).

Wilson, R.A. (1996). 'The Sizwe Will Not Go Away: The Truth and Reconciliation Commission' – Human Rights and Nation-building in South Africa', *African Affairs*, 55 (2).

Index